MW01526045

All inquiries, suggestions and comments should be addressed to the Worldwide Distributor:

RUSH Publications and Educational Consultancy, LLC

1251 N Miller Rd, Scottsdale

AZ 85257

United States

e–mail	: rusen.meylani@asu.edu; meylani@superonline.com
phone	: +1 480 884 1597; +1 480 308 0210
Author	: Ruşen MEYLANİ

Cover design by   : Pınar ERKORKMAZ; **e–mail:** mail@pinare.com

All graphics and text based on TI 83 - 84 have been used with the permission granted by Texas Instruments.

From: Bassuk, Larry <l-bassuk@ti.com>
Sent: Thursday, February 27, 2002 16:23 PM
To: Meylani, Rusen <meylani@superonline.com>; Foster, Herbert <h-foster@ti.com>; Vidori, Erdel <e-vidori@ti.com>
RE: USAGE OF TI 83+ FACILITIES IN MY SAT II MATH BOOKS
Rusen Meylani,
Again we thank you for your interest in the calculators made by Texas Instruments.
Texas Instruments is pleased to grant you permission to copy graphical representations of our calculators and to copy graphics and text that describes the use of our calculators for use in the two books you mention in your e-mail below.
We ask that you provide the following credit for each representation of our calculators and the same credit, in a way that does not interrupt the flow of the book, for the copied graphics and text:
Courtesy Texas Instruments
Regards,
Larry Bassuk
Copyright Counsel
972-917-5458

-----Original Message-----
From: Bassuk, Larry
Sent: Thursday, February 21, 2002 9:14 AM
To: 'Rusen Meylani'; Foster, Herbert
Subject: RE: USAGE OF TI 83+ FACILITIES IN MY SAT II MATH BOOKS
We thank you for your interest in TI calculators.
I am copying this message to Herb Foster, Marketing Communications Manager for our calculator group. With Herb's agreement, Texas Instruments grants you permission to copy the materials you describe below for the limited purposes you describe below.
Regards,
Larry Bassuk
Copyright Counsel
972-917-5458

-----Original Message-----
From: Rusen Meylani [mailto:meylani@superonline.com]
Sent: Wednesday, February 20, 2002 5:57 PM
To: copyrightcounsel@list.ti.com - Copyright Legal Counsel
Subject: USAGE OF TI 83+ FACILITIES IN MY SAT II MATH BOOKS
Dear Sir,
I am an educational consultant in Istanbul Turkey and I am working with Turkish students who would like to go to the USA for college education. I am writing SAT II Mathematics books where I make use of TI 83+ facilities, screen shots, etc. heavily. Will you please indicate the copyright issues that I will need while publishing my book?
Thanks very much in advance. I am looking forward to hearing from you soon.
Rusen Meylani.

From: Pam Bentley [mailto:pbentley@enc.org]
Sent: Wednesday, August 04, 2004 6:21 PM
To: rushco@superonline.com
Subject: SAT II Math with TI

Good morning.

I am writing from the **Eisenhower National Clearinghouse**. **ENC** is funded by the **US Department of Education** as a place **to bring quality math and science products** together **under one roof**. We let our teacher audience know about these products through our website, www.enc.org.

Our Mathematics Content Specialist saw your book **SAT II Math with TI** on your website and would like to **add it to our collection**. Would you consider sending a review copy to me at the address below?

Once here, ENC staff will build a descriptive record and export that record to our site. Teachers can then search the site and all orders are referred back to the publisher/distributor.

I invite you to browse our site and let me know if I can answer any questions. Teachers have come to rely on ENC for product information. During our last bi-monthly period over 30,000 simple searches were recorded from our curriculum resources pages.

Thanks very much.

Pam Bentley

Acquisitions Specialist
ENC
1929 Kenny Road
Columbus, OH 43210-1079
614-688-3265
pbentley@enc.org
www.enc.org

ACKNOWLEDGMENTS

I would like to thank the students from USA, Turkey and all other countries for their helpful comments and suggestions; I have made sure that in this edition we have observed them all.

I would like to thank TEXAS INSTRUMENTS for providing scientists and mathematicians such powerful hand - held computers, the TI family of graphing calculators. With these wonderful machines, teachers of mathematics can go beyond horizons without the need to reinvent the wheel all the time. I would also like to thank TEXAS INSTRUMENTS for providing me with a limited copyright to use the graphs that have been produced by the TI 83 / 84 Family of graphing calculators throughout this book.

I would like to thank Eisenhower National Clearinghouse (formerly funded by the US Department of Education) for adding this very book in their catalogue in order to let the math educators know about it.

I would like to thank Erdel VIDORI of TEXAS INSTRUMENTS for his suggestions on the organization and title of this book as well as his invaluable efforts in establishing the link between myself and TEXAS INSTRUMENTS.

I would like to thank Zeynel Abidin ERDEM, the chairman of the Turkish - American Businessmen Association (TABA) for his valuable support and contributions on our projects.

I would like to thank Emel UYSAL and Seda EREN for their valuable contributions.

I would like to thank Pınar ERKORKMAZ for her excellent work on the cover design.

I would like to thank Yorgo İSTEFANOPULOS, Ayşın ERTÜZÜN, Aytül ERÇİL, Bayram SEVGEN, Zeki ÖZDEMİR, and Nuran TUNCALI for whatever I know of analytical thinking.

I would like to thank my mother and my father for being who I am. Therefore I dedicate this book to them.

PREFACE

What Sat Math Subject Tests are All About

Mathematics Level 1 and Mathematics Level 2 are the two subject tests that the College Board offers. Both tests require at least a scientific, preferably a graphing, calculator. Each test is one hour long. These subject tests were formerly known as the Math Level IC and Math Level IIC subject tests.

Mathematics Level 1 Subject Test

Structure

A Mathematics Level 1 test is made of 50 multiple choice questions from the following topics:
- Algebra and algebraic functions
- Geometry (plane Euclidean, coordinate and three-dimensional)
- Elementary statistics and probability, data interpretation, counting problems, including measures of mean, median and mode (central tendency.)
- Miscellaneous questions of logic, elementary number theory, arithmetic and geometric sequences.

Calculators in the Test

Approximately 60 percent of the questions in the test should be solved without the use of the calculator. For the remaining 40 percent, the calculator will be useful if not necessary.

Mathematics Level 2 Subject Test

Structure

A Mathematics Level 2 test also is made of 50 multiple choice questions. The topics included are as follows:
- Algebra
- Geometry (coordinate geometry and three-dimensional geometry)
- Trigonometry
- Functions
- Statistics, probability, permutations, and combinations
- Miscellaneous questions of logic and proof, elementary number theory, limits and sequences

Calculators in the Test

In Math Level 2, 40 percent of the questions should be solved the without the use of the calculator. In the remaining 60 percent, the calculator will be useful if not necessary.

Which calculator is allowed and which is not:

The simplest reference to this question is this: No device with a QWERTY keyboard is allowed. Besides that any hand held organizers, mini or pocket computers, laptops, pen input devices or writing pads, devices making sounds (such as "talking" computers) and devices requiring electricity from an outlet will not be allowed. It would be the wisest to stick with TI 84 or TI 89. Both of these calculators are easy to use and are the choices of millions of students around the world who take SAT exams and also university students in their math courses. It is very important to be familiar with the calculator that you're going to use in the test. You will lose valuable time if you try to figure it out during the test time.

IMPORTANT: Always take the exam with fresh batteries. Bring fresh batteries and a backup calculator to the test center. You may not share calculators. You certainly will not be provided with a backup calculator or batteries. No one can or will assist you in the case of a calculator malfunction. In such case, you have the option of notifying the supervisor to cancel your scores for that test. Therefore, always be prepared for the worst case scenario (Don't forget Murphy's Rules.)

Number of questions per topics covered

The following chart shows the approximate number of questions per topic for both tests.

Topics	Approximate Number of Questions	
	Level 1	Level 2
Algebra	15	9
Plane Euclidean Geometry	10	0
Coordinate Geometry	6	6
Three-dimensional Geometry	3	4
Trigonometry	4	10
Functions	6	12
Statistics	3	3
Miscellaneous	3	6

Similarities and Differences

Some topics are covered in both tests, such as elementary algebra, three-dimensional geometry, coordinate geometry, statistics and basic trigonometry. But the tests differ greatly in the following areas.

Differences between the tests

Although some questions may be appropriate for both tests, the emphasis for Level 2 is on more advanced content. The tests differ significantly in the following areas:

Geometry

Euclidian geometry makes up the significant portion of the geometry questions in the Math Level 1 test. Though in Level 2, questions are of the topics of coordinate geometry, transformations, and three-dimensional geometry and there are no direct questions of Euclidian geometry.

Trigonometry

The trigonometry questions on Level 1 are primarily limited to right triangle trigonometry and the fundamental relationships among the trigonometric ratios. Level 2 places more emphasis on the properties and graphs of the trigonometric functions, the inverse trigonometric functions, trigonometric equations and identities, and the laws of sines and cosines. The trigonometry questions in Level 2 exam are primarily on graphs and properties of the trigonometric functions, trigonometric equations, trigonometric identities, the inverse trigonometric functions, laws of sines and cosines. On the other hand, the trigonometry in Level 1 is limited to basic trigonometric ratios and right triangle trigonometry.

Functions

Functions in Level 1 are mostly algebraic, while there are more advanced functions (exponential and logarithmic) in Level 2.

Statistics

Probability, mean median, mode counting, and data interpretation are included in both exams. In addition, Level 2 requires permutations, combinations, and standard deviation.

In all SAT Math exams, you must choose the best answer which is not necessarily the exact answer. The decision of whether or not to use a calculator on a particular question is your choice. In some questions the use of a calculator is necessary and in some it is redundant or time consuming. Generally, the angle mode in Level 1 is degree. Be sure to set your calculator in degree mode by pressing "Mode" and then selecting "Degree." However, in Level 2 you must decide when to use the "Degree" mode or the "Radian" mode. There are figures in some questions intended to provide useful information for solving the question. They are accurate unless the question states that the figure is not drawn to scale. In other words, figures are correct unless otherwise specified. All figures lie in a plane unless otherwise indicated. The figures must NOT be assumed to be three-dimensional unless they are indicated to be. The domain of any function is assumed to be set of all real numbers x for which f(x) is a real number, unless otherwise specified.

Important Notice on the Scores

In Level 1 questions the topics covered are relatively less than those covered in the Level 2 test. However, the questions in the Level 1 exam are more tricky compared to the ones in Level 2. This is why if students want to score 800 in the Level 1 test, they have to answer all the 50 questions correctly. But in the Level 2 test, 43 correct answers (the rest must be omitted) are sufficient to get the full score of 800.

Scaled Score	Raw Score in Level 1 Test	Raw Score in Level 2 Test
800	50	43
750	45	38
700	38	33
650	33	28
600	29	22
550	24	16
500	19	10
450	13	3
400	7	0
350	1	-3

How to make the most of this book

This book is designed for all college bound students who have to take either or both of the Math Level 1 and Math Level 2 subject tests. Topics are classified in accordance with their relevance to the specific test, Level 1, Level 2 or both. Please follow the guideline shown at the legend on top of the Table of Contents. Each chapter contains the key concepts that must be learnt as well as tons of fully solved examples. The model tests are up to date reflecting the trends in standardized testing in the last three years and the solutions to the model tests have been produced in a very detailed fashion.

We are sure that this book will be of great help to students worldwide creating many perfect scorers in the SAT Math subject tests.

Best of luck,

Ruşen MEYLANİ.

TABLE OF CONTENTS

LEGEND

1–2	Covered in both Level 1 and Level 2
1	Covered in Level 1 only
2	Covered in Level 2 only
O	Optional topics (likely to appear in the future)

Those who are not bound to get any rest never get tired.

Mustafa Kemal Atatürk

CHAPTER 1 – Functions

1.1 ALGEBRA AND BASICS

Interval Notation

$(a, b) = \{x \mid a < x < b\}$ $(a, b] = \{x \mid a < x \leq b\}$ $(a, \infty) = \{x \mid x > a\}$ $(-\infty, a) = \{x \mid x < a\}$

$[a, b] = \{x \mid a \leq x \leq b\}$ $[a, b) = \{x \mid a \leq x < b\}$ $[a, \infty) = \{x \mid x \geq a\}$ $(-\infty, a] = \{x \mid x \leq a\}$

Number Sets

Complex Numbers $= \{a + bi \mid a \text{ and } b \text{ are real numbers and } i = \sqrt{-1}\}$

Subsets of Real Numbers:

Natural Numbers $= \{1, 2, 3, ...\}$

Whole Numbers $= \{0, 1, 2, 3, ...\}$

Digits $= \{0, 1, 2, 3, 4, 5, 6, 7, 8, 9\}$

Integers $= \{... -3, -2, -1, 0, 1, 2, 3, ...\}$

Rational Numbers $= \left\{\dfrac{a}{b} \mid a \text{ and } b \text{ are integers with } b \neq 0\right\}$; any repeating decimal is a rational number.

Irrational Numbers $= \{x \mid x \text{ is not rational}\}$. Irrational numbers include all n'th roots that cannot be written as a fraction. All non repeating decimals as well as the numbers e and π are irrational.

Prime Numbers: $\{2, 3, 5, 7, 11, 13, 17, 19, 23, 29, 31, ...\}$ A number is called prime if it has exactly two distinct positive divisors.

Properties of the Real Numbers

For all real numbers a, b, and c:

Commutative Properties : $a + b = b + a$; $a \cdot b = b \cdot a$

Associative Properties : $(a + b) + c = a + (b + c) = a + b + c$; $(ab)c = a(bc) = abc$

Distributive Properties : $a(b + c) = ab + ac$; $(b + c)a = ba + ca$; $a(b - c) = ab - ac$; $(b - c)a = ba - ca$

Identity Elements : $a + 0 = 0 + a = a$; $1 \cdot a = a \cdot 1 = a$

Inverse Elements : $a + (-a) = (-a) + a = 0$; $a \cdot \dfrac{1}{a} = \dfrac{1}{a} \cdot a = 1$ where $a \neq 0$

Null Element : $a \cdot 0 = 0 \cdot a = 0$; $\dfrac{0}{a} = 0$ where $a \neq 0$

Important Concepts

Division by zero is not defined.   0 is even, not prime, not positive, not negative.

If $a \neq 0$: $a^0 = 1$; 0^0 is undefined.   1 is odd, not prime and positive.

Fractions

$$a : b : c = d : e : f \Rightarrow \frac{a}{d} = \frac{b}{e} = \frac{c}{f}$$

$$\frac{a}{b} + \frac{c}{d} = \frac{ad + bc}{bd} \; ; \; \frac{a}{b} \cdot \frac{c}{d} = \frac{ac}{bd} \; ; \; \frac{\frac{a}{b}}{\frac{c}{d}} = \frac{a}{b} : \frac{c}{d} = \frac{a}{b} \cdot \frac{d}{c} \; ; \; \frac{-a}{b} = \frac{a}{-b} = -\frac{a}{b}$$

Inequalities

If $u < v$ and $c > 0$, then $uc < vc$.   If $0 < u < v$ or $u < v < 0$ then $\dfrac{1}{u} > \dfrac{1}{v}$.   If $u < v$, then $u \pm w < v \pm w$.

If $u < v$ and $c < 0$, then $uc > vc$.   If $0 < u < 1$ then $u > u^2 > u^3 > u^4 ...$ If $u < v$ and $v < w$, then $u < w$.

Letters in the English Alphabet

The English alphabet has 26 letters:

ABCDEFGHIJKLMNOQRSTUVWXYZ are the **capital** letters.

abcdefghijklmnopqrstuvwxyz are the **small** letters.

A – a, E–e, I – i, O – o, U – u, are the **vowels** and the rest of the letters are **consonants**.

Unit Conversions

Length	Weight	Money
1 mile (mi) = 1760 yards (yd)	1 pound (lb) = 16 ounces (oz)	1 penny = 1 cent (¢)
1 yard = 3 feet (ft)	**Volume**	1 nickel = 5 cents
1 foot (ft) = 12 inches (in)	1 gallon (ga) = 4 quarts (qt)	1 dime = 10 cents
1 inch = 2.54 cm	1 quart (qt) = 2 pints (pt)	1 quarter = 25 cents
		1 dollar ($) = 100 cents

Number of Divisors and Sum of Divisors of an Integer

Example: N = 720.

a. How many distinct positive factors does N have?

b. How many distinct negative factors does N have?

c. How many distinct factors does N have?

d. How many distinct positive odd factors does N have?

e. How many distinct negative odd factors does N have?

f. How many distinct odd factors does N have?

g. How many distinct positive even factors does N have?

h. How many distinct negative even factors does N have?

i. How many distinct even factors does N have?

j. What is the sum of the distinct positive factors of N?

k. What is the sum of the distinct negative factors of N?

l. What is the sum of the distinct factors of N?

m. What is the sum of the distinct positive odd factors of N?

n. What is the sum of the distinct negative odd factors of N?

o. What is the sum of the distinct odd factors of N?

p. What is the sum of the distinct positive even factors of N?

q. What is the sum of the distinct negative even factors of N?

r. What is the sum of the distinct even factors of N?

Solution: $720 = 2^4 \cdot 3^2 \cdot 5^1$

a. Number of distinct positive factors is $(\mathbf{4} + 1)(\mathbf{2} + 1)(\mathbf{1} + 1) = 30$.

b. Number of distinct negative factors is also 30.

c. Number of distinct factors is 30 + 30 = 60.

d. Number of distinct positive odd factors is $(\mathbf{2} + 1)(\mathbf{1} + 1) = 6$.

e. Number of distinct negative odd factors is also 6.

f. Number of distinct odd factors is 6 + 6 = 12.

g. Number of distinct positive even factors is $(\mathbf{4})(\mathbf{2} + 1)(\mathbf{1} + 1) = 24$.

h. Number of distinct negative even factors is also 24.

i. Number of distinct even factors is 24 + 24 = 48.

j. Sum of the distinct positive factors is $(1+2+2^2+2^3+2^4)(1+3+3^2)(1+5) = 2418$.

k. Sum of the distinct negative factors is –2418.

l. Sum of the distinct factors is 0.

m. Sum of the distinct positive odd factors is $(1+3+3^2)(1+5) = 78$.

n. Sum of the distinct negative odd factors is –78.

o. Sum of the distinct odd factors is 0.

p. Sum of the distinct positive even factors is $(2+2^2+2^3+2^4)(1+3+3^2)(1+5) = 2340$.

q. Sum of the distinct negative even factors is –2340.

r. Sum of the distinct even factors is 0.

Rules of Divisibility

- By 2 = 2^1: Last digit must be 0 or divisible by 2.
- By 4 = 2^2: Last 2 digits must be 00 or divisible by 4.
- By 8 = 2^3: Last 3 digits must be 000 or divisible by 8.
- By 5 = 5^1: Last digit must be 0 or 5.
- By 25 = 5^2: Last 2 digits must be 00 or divisible by 25.
- By 125 = 5^3: Last 3 digits must be 000 or divisible by 125.
- By 3: The sum of the digits must be an integer multiple of 3.
- By 9: The sum of the digits must be an integer multiple of 9.
- By 11: The difference between the sum of the even digits (2nd, 4th, 6th, 8th, etc.) and the sum of the odd digits (1st, 3rd, 5th, 7th, etc.) must be an integer multiple of 11.
- By 10 = 10^1: Last digit must be 0.
- By 100 = 10^2: Last 2 digits must be 00.
- By 1000 = 10^3: Last 3 digits must be 000.
- If an integer N is divisible by A and B, then N is divisible by the LCM (least common multiple) of A and B as well. For example, if N is divisible by 6 and 10, it is also divisible by 30 which is the LCM of 6 and 10.
- If an integer N is divisible by AB given that A and B are relatively prime (meaning that their greatest common divisor is 1) then N is also divisible by A and by B. For example, if an integer is divisible by 15, it is divisible by 3 and 5.
- If an integer N is divisible by A then it is also divisible by every integer divisor of A.

Example: 234AB is divisible by 15. What is the maximum possible value of A + B?

Solution: The number is divisible by 15 therefore it must be divisible by both 5 and 3. Therefore B is either 0 or 5. The maximum value of B is 5. The number is divisible by 3 therefore the sum of the digits that is 14 + A must be a multiple of 3. A can be 1, 4 or 7. The maximum value of A + B is 7 + 5 = 12.

Absolute Values

1. $\sqrt[n]{x^n} = \begin{cases} x & \text{if n is odd} \\ |x| & \text{if n is even} \end{cases}$ $\sqrt{x^2} = |x|$ $\sqrt[3]{x^3} = x$

2. $|x| \geq 0$

3. Given that A > 0

    $|x| = A \Rightarrow x = \pm A;$ $x^2 = A^2 \Rightarrow x = \pm A;$ $|x| = |A| \Rightarrow x = \pm A$

4. $|x| < A \Rightarrow -A < x < A$

   $x^2 < A^2 \Rightarrow -A < x < A$

5. $|x| > A \Rightarrow x > A$ or $x < -A$

   $x^2 < A^2 \Rightarrow x > A$ or $x < -A$

6. $B \leq |x| < A \Rightarrow B \leq x < A$ or $-A < x \leq -B$

   $B^2 \leq x^2 \leq A^2 \Rightarrow B \leq x \leq A$ or $-A \leq x \leq -B$

7. $y = |x| = $ abs (x)

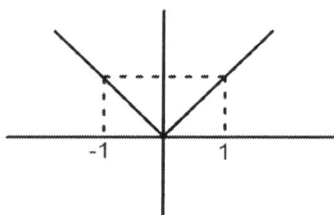

8. Graph of f(x)

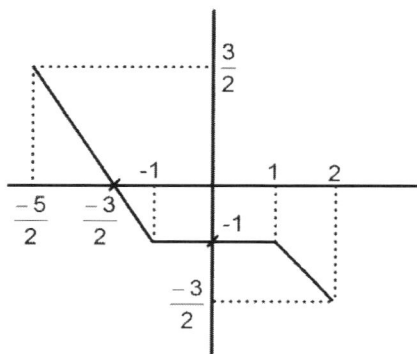

Graph of f (|x|)

Duplicate RHS (+ ve x portion of f(x))

by reflecting across the y axis.

Suppress LHS (–ve x portion of f (x))

LHS: Left Hand Side

RHS: Right Hand Side

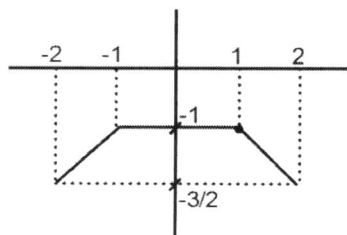

Graph of f (–|x|)

Duplicate LHS

Suppress RHS

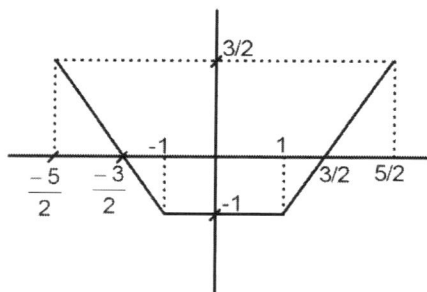

9. If $f(x) = f(|x|)$ or $f(x) = f(-|x|)$ then f (x) must be even and therefore symmetric in the y – axis.

10.

| $\|x\| + \|y\| = A$ | $\|x\| - \|y\| = A$ | $\|y\| - \|x\| = A$ |

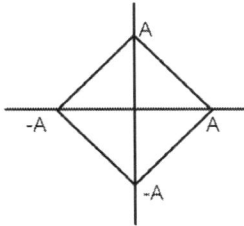 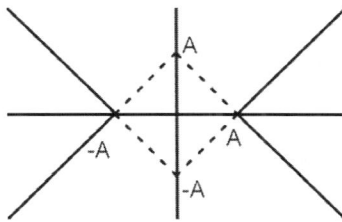 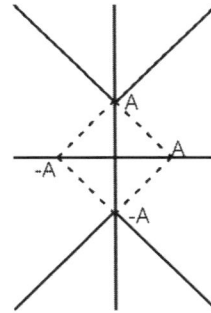

11. $|-a| = |a|$

12. $|ab| = |a| \cdot |b|$; $\left|\dfrac{a}{b}\right| = \dfrac{|a|}{|b|}$

13.   For all numbers a and b, the triangle inequality holds: $\left\| a \right| - \left| b \right\| \le \left| a + b \right| \le \left| a \right| + \left| b \right|$

14.   For all a the following inequality holds: $-\left| a \right| \le a \le \left| a \right|$

15.   Graph of $|x - a| < b$:

16.   Graph of $|x - a| \le b$:

17.   Graph of $|x - a| > b$:

18.   Graph of $|x - a| \ge b$:

19.   If $a < x < b$ then $\left| x - m \right| < r$ where $m = \dfrac{b+a}{2}$ and $r = \dfrac{b-a}{2}$

29.   If $x < a$ or $x > b$ then $\left| x - m \right| > r$ where $m = \dfrac{b+a}{2}$ and $r = \dfrac{b-a}{2}$

Example: The standards in a light bulb factory state that for a certain type of light bulb the longest diameter must be at least 2.5 inches and at most 2.8 inches. If x is the diameter of a light bulb produced in this factor then $\left| x - m \right| \le r$. Find m and r.

Solution:

m = (2.8 + 2.5) / 2 = 2.65 and r = (2.8 − 2.5) / 2 = 0.15; therefore $\left| x - 2.65 \right| \le 0.15$.

Means

A = Arithmetic mean $= \dfrac{a_1 + a_2 + a_3 + \ldots\ldots\ldots\ldots\ldots + a_n}{n}$

G = Geometric mean $= \sqrt[n]{a_1 \cdot a_2 \cdot a_3 \cdot \ldots\ldots\ldots a_n}$

H = Harmonic Mean $= \dfrac{n}{\dfrac{1}{a_1} + \dfrac{1}{a_2} + \dfrac{1}{a_3} + \ldots\ldots\ldots + \dfrac{1}{a_n}}$

In general $H \le G \le A$ and equality holds if and only if all terms are equal: $H = G = A \Leftrightarrow a_1 = a_2 = a_3 = \ldots\ldots\ldots = a_n$

1.2 MOST COMMON GRAPHING CALCULATOR TECHNIQUES

Solving Equations with TI 83 – 84

When solving a polynomial or algebraic equation in the form **f(x) = g(x),** perform the following steps:

- Write the equation in the form: **f(x) – g(x) = 0.**
- Plot the graph of **y = f(x) – g(x).**
- Find the x – intercepts using the **Calc Zero** of TI – 84 Plus. However when the graph seems to be tangent to the x – axis at a certain point, you may use the **Calc Min** or **Calc Max** facilities but you should make sure that the y – coordinate of the minimum or maximum point is zero.

Solving Inequalities with TI 83 – 84

When solving an inequality in the form **f(x) < g(x),** or **f(x) ≤ g(x),** or **f(x) > g(x),** or **f(x) ≥ g(x)** perform the following steps:

- Write the inequality in the form: **f(x) – g(x) < 0 or f(x) – g(x) ≤ 0 or f(x) – g(x) > 0 or f(x) – g(x) ≥ 0.**
- Plot the graph of **y = f(x) – g(x).**
- Find the x – intercepts using the **Calc Zero** of TI – 84 Plus. However when the graph seems to be tangent to the x – axis at a certain point, you may use the **Calc Min** or **Calc Max** facilities but you should make sure that the y – coordinate of the minimum or maximum point is zero.
- Any value like **–6.61E–10** or **7.2E–11** can be interpreted as 0 as they mean **–6.6x10^{-10}** and **7.2x10^{-11}** respectively.
- The solution of the inequality will be the set of values of x for which the graph of f(x) – g(x) lies below the x axis if the inequality is in one of the forms **f(x) – g(x) < 0** or **f(x) – g(x) ≤ 0.** The solution of the inequality will be the set of values of x for which the graph of f(x) – g(x) lies above the x axis if the inequality is in one of the forms **f(x) – g(x) > 0** or **f(x) – g(x) ≥ 0.** If ≤ or ≥ symbols are involved, then the x – intercepts are also in the solution set.
- Please note that the x – values that correspond to asymptotes are never included in the solution set.

Example: $P(x) = 2x^2 + 3x + 1$; $P(a) = 7 \Rightarrow a = ?$

Solution:

$2a^2 + 3a + 1 = 7 \Rightarrow 2a^2 + 3a - 6 = 0$

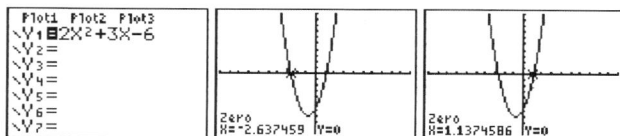

Answer: –2.637 or 1.137

Example: $f(x) = \sqrt{3x+4}$ and $g(x) = x^3$. If is given what (fog)(x) = (gof)(x), then what is x?

Solution:

$(fog)(x) = \sqrt{3x^3+4}$ and $(gof)(x) = (\sqrt{3x+4})^3 \Rightarrow \sqrt{3x^3+4} = (\sqrt{3x+4})^3 \Rightarrow \sqrt{3x^3+4} - (\sqrt{3x+4})^3 = 0$

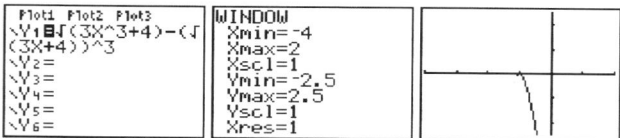

Answer: –1

Example: $| x - 3 | + | 2x + 1 | = 6 \Rightarrow x = ?$

Solution: $| x - 3 | + | 2x + 1 | - 6 = 0$

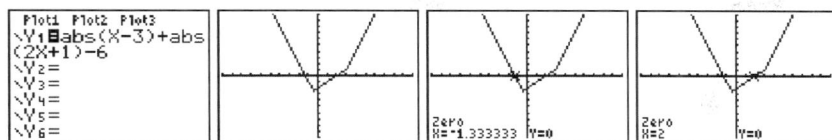

Answer: x = −1.33 or 2

Example: $2^{x+3} = 3^x \Rightarrow x = ?$

Solution: $2^{x+3} - 3^x = 0$

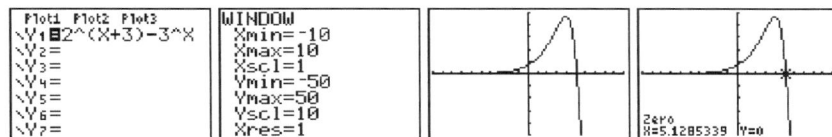

Answer: 5.129

Example: $\log_x 3 = \log_4 x \Rightarrow$ What is the sum of the roots of this equation?

Solution: $\log_x 3 - \log_4 x = 0$

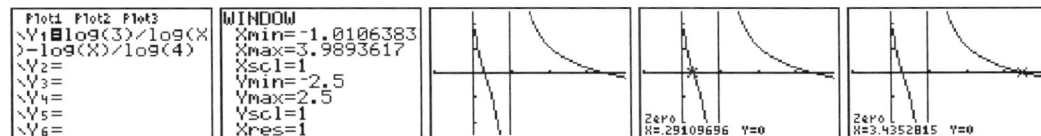

Answer: 0.291 + 3.435 = 3.726

Example: Solve for x: $\dfrac{|x-2|}{x} > 3$

Solution: $\dfrac{|x-2|}{x} - 3 > 0$

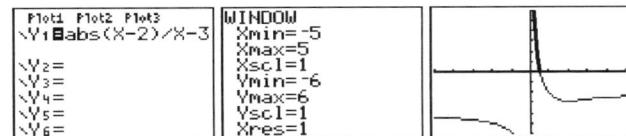

Answer: (0, 0.5)

Example: $x^2(x - 2)(x + 1) \geq 0$

Solution:

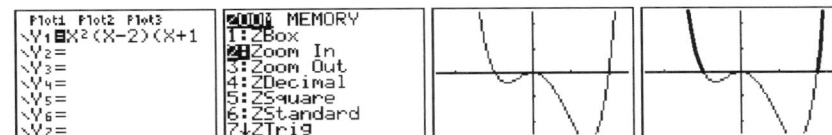

Answer: (−∞, −1] or {0} or [2, ∞)

1.3 FUNCTIONS

Definition

Cartesian product of the sets A and B denoted as A × B is the set that contains the ordered pairs (x, y) such that x is chosen from A and y is chosen from B.

For instance if A = {1, 2} and B = {a, b, c} then A × B = {(1, a), (1, b), (1, c), (2, a), (2, b), (2, c)}. Any subset of A × B is a **relation** from A to B where A is called the **domain** and B is called the **range** of the relation. For a relation to represent a function:

- Each element in the domain must have an image in range.
- No element in the domain can have more than one image in range.

Therefore every function is a relation but every relation may not be a function.

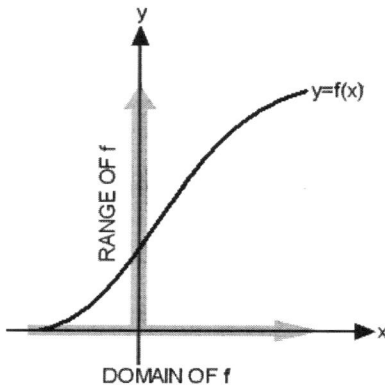

When a function is given in the form y = f(x), the set of all possible values of x constitute the domain of f(x) and the set of all possible values of y constitute the range of f(x). A function can also be defined as a mapping between the elements in the domain and the elements in the range.

Example: A relation f is given by {(1, 2), (3, 2), (4, 1)}. Find the domain and range of this relation and state whether or not it represents a function.

Solution: Domain = {1, 3, 4}; Range = {2, 1}; f represents a function.

Example: Find the domain and range of each relation and state whether or not it represents a function.

1. $\beta = \{(x, y)|x^2 = y^3; x, y \in R\}$.
2. $\beta = \{(x, y)|x^3 = y^2; x, y \in R\}$.

Solution:

1. Let $y = 1 \Rightarrow x^2 = 1 \Rightarrow x = \pm1$: Two different elements in the domain may have the same image. Therefore f represents a function.
2. Let $x = 1 \Rightarrow y^2 = 1 \Rightarrow y = \pm1$: An element in the domain may not have two different images. Therefore f does not represent a function.

Vertical Line Test

This test gives whether or not a given graph represents a function; if a vertical line cuts the graph of a function at more than one point, the graph does not represent a function and the function fails this test.

Horizontal Line Test

This test gives whether or not the inverse of a given graph represents a function; if a horizontal line cuts a graph at more than one point, the inverse does not represent a function.

Example: State which of the following functions represents a function of x.

(a)	(b)	(c)

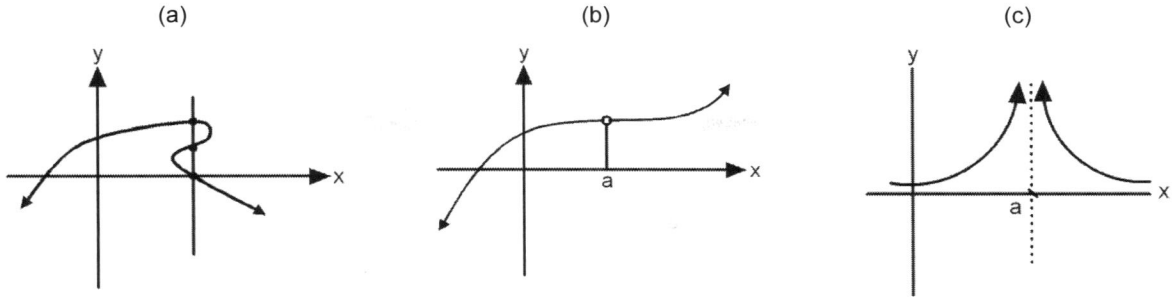

Solution:

(a) The given relation does not pass the vertical line test therefore it does not represent a function.

(b) and (c) The relation given is undefined at x = a. Therefore if the domain is R then the graph does not represent a function. However if the domain is R – {a} then the graph represents a function.

Example: Find the domain and range each time, state if the graph may correspond to a function or not.

a)

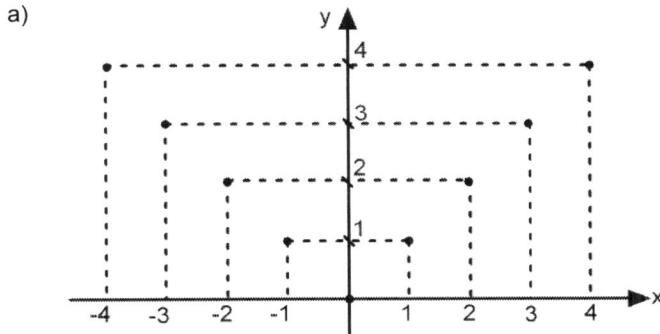

Solution:

Domain = {-4, –3, –2, –1,0, 1, 2, 3, 4}

Range = {0, 1, 2, 3, 4}

The graph may correspond to a function.

b)

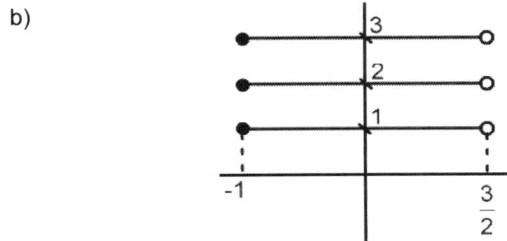

Solution:

Domain = $-1 \leq x < \dfrac{3}{2}$

Range = {1, 2, 3}

The graph does not correspond to a function.

c)

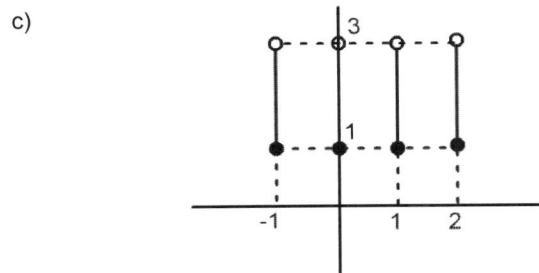

Solution:

Domain = {–1, 0, 1, 2}

Range = $1 \leq y < 3$

The graph does not correspond to a function.

d)

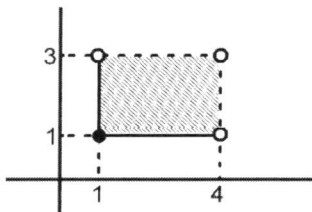

Solution:

Domain = $1 \leq x < 4$

Range = $1 \leq y < 3$

The graph does not correspond to a function.

e)

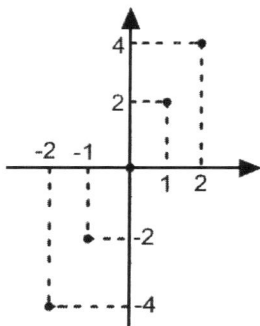

Solution:

Domain = {−2, −1, 0, 1, 2}

Range = {-4, −2, 0, 2, 4}

The graph may correspond to a function.

f)

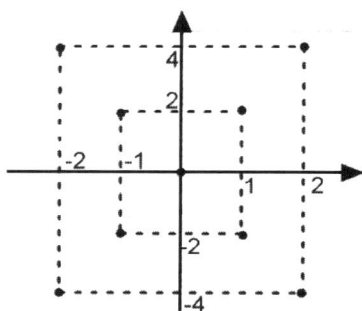

Solution:

Domain = {−2, −1, 0, 1, 2}

Range = {-4, −2, 0, 2, 4}

The graph does not correspond to a function.

Types of functions

Into function

(range is not completely covered)

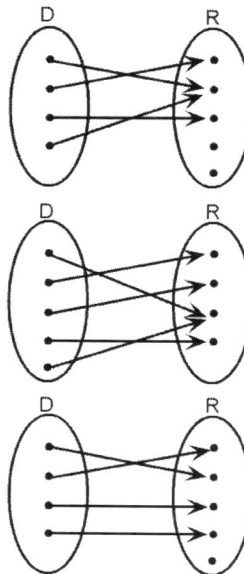

Onto function

(range is completely covered)

One to one function

(no two elements in the domain have the same image in range)

Many to one function

(some elements in the domain do have the same image in range)

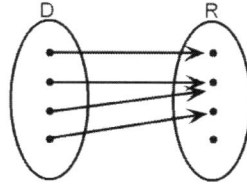

Constant function: f(x) = C

(all elements in the domain have the same image in range)

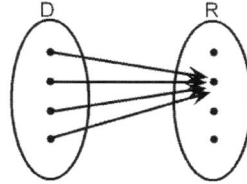

Identity function: $I(x) = x$; (every element is mapped onto itself).

When a function is **one to one and onto**, it is called **bijective** and **invertible**; that is, its inverse will also be a function; such functions pass the horizontal line test.

Multivariable Function: A multivariable function maps more than one variable to a single value. They are often written as f(x, y) or f(x, y, z) depending on what the free variables are.

Examples:

$f(x, y) = 2x^2 - y^2$, $g(x) = 5^x \Rightarrow g(f(4, 3)) = g(2 \cdot 4^2 - 3^2) = g(23) = 5^{23} = 1.2 \cdot 10^{16}$

$f(x, y) = \sqrt{3x^2 - 4y}$ and $g(x) = 3^x \Rightarrow g(f(2, 1)) = g(\sqrt{3.2^2 - 4.1}) = 3^{\sqrt{8}} = 22.4$

Polynomial Function:

$P(x) = a_n x^n + a_{n-1} x^{n-1} + a_{n-2} x^{n-2} + \ldots + a_5 x^5 + a_4 x^4 + a_3 x^3 + a_2 x^2 + a_1 x + a_0$

For P(x) to be a polynomial function a_n values must be complex numbers (in SAT II context they will all be real numbers) and n values must be nonnegative integers.

Domains of Specific Functions

Type of Function	Domain	Type of Function	Domain
$f(x) = P(x)$	All real numbers	$f(x) = \log_{P(x)} Q(x)$	$Q(x) > 0$ $P(x) > 0$ $P(x) \neq 1$
$f(x) = \dfrac{P(x)}{Q(x)}$	$Q(x) \neq 0$	$f(x) = \sqrt[3]{P(x)}$ $f(x) = \sqrt[2n+1]{P(x)}$	All real numbers
$f(x) = \sqrt{P(x)}$ $f(x) = \sqrt[2n]{P(x)}$	$P(x) \geq 0$	$f(x) = \dfrac{1}{\sqrt[3]{P(x)}}$ $f(x) = \dfrac{1}{\sqrt[2n+1]{P(x)}}$	$P(x) \neq 0$
$f(x) = \dfrac{1}{\sqrt{P(x)}}$ $f(x) = \dfrac{1}{\sqrt[2n]{P(x)}}$	$P(x) > 0$		

P(x) and Q(x) are polynomial functions

Example: Find the domain of each of the following functions:

(1) $f(x) = \dfrac{x+1}{x^2 - 4}$ (2) $f(x) = \sqrt{x-1}$ (3) $f(x) = \dfrac{1}{\sqrt{x+1}}$ (4) $f(x) = \sqrt{x^2 - 1}$

(5) $f(x) = \dfrac{1}{\sqrt[3]{x^2 - 1}}$ (6) $f(x) = \sqrt[3]{x^2 - 1}$ (7) $f(x) = \log_2(x-3)$ (8) $f(x) = \log_{(5-x)}(x-1)$

Solution:

(1) $x^2 - 4 = 0 \Rightarrow x^2 = 4 \Rightarrow x = \pm 2$; therefore domain is $R - \{-2, 2\}$.

(2) $x - 1 \geq 0 \Rightarrow$ Domain: $x \geq 1$.

(3) $x + 1 > 0 \Rightarrow$ Domain: $x > -1$.

(4) $x^2 - 1 \geq 0 \Rightarrow x^2 \geq 1$; domain is $x \geq 1$ or $x \leq -1$

(5) $x^2 - 1 = 0 \Rightarrow x^2 = 1 \Rightarrow x = \pm 1$; therefore domain is $R - \{-1, 1\}$.

(6)   Domain is R.

(7) $x - 3 > 0 \Rightarrow$ Domain: $x > 3$.

(8)   The following conditions have to be satisfied at the same time:

     (i) $x - 1 > 0$

     (ii) $5 - x > 0$

     (iii) $5 - x \neq 1 \Rightarrow$ Therefore the domain is $1 < x < 5$ and $x \neq 4$.

Operations on Functions

1. $(f \pm g)(x) = f(x) \pm g(x)$

2. $(a \cdot f \pm b \cdot g)(x) = a \cdot f(x) \pm b \cdot g(x)$

3. $(f \cdot g)(x) = f(x) \cdot g(x)$

4. $\left(\dfrac{f}{g}\right)(x) = \dfrac{f(x)}{g(x)}$

5. $(f^n)(x) = [f(x)]^n$

Example: $f(x) = 3x - 1$ and $g(x) = 2x + 5$. Compute the following:

(a) $f^2(x)$ (b) $(f + g)(x)$ (c) $(f - g)(x)$ (d) $(f \cdot g)(x)$

(e) $(\dfrac{f}{g})(x)$ (f) $(\dfrac{1}{f})(x)$ (g) $(2f - g)(x)$

Solution:

(a) $f^2(x) = (f(x))^2 = (3x - 1)^2 = 9x^2 - 6x + 1$

(b) $(f + g)(x) = f(x) + g(x) = 3x - 1 + 2x + 5 = 5x + 4$

(c) $(f - g)(x) = f(x) - g(x) = 3x - 1 - (2x + 5) = x - 6$

(d) $(f \cdot g)(x) = f(x).g(x) = (3x - 1).(2x + 5) = 6x^2 + 13x - 5$

(e) $(\dfrac{f}{g})(x) = \dfrac{f(x)}{g(x)} = \dfrac{3x - 1}{2x + 5}$

(f) $(\dfrac{1}{f})(x) = \dfrac{1}{f(x)} = \dfrac{1}{3x - 1}$

(g) $(2f - g)(x) = 2f(x) - g(x) = 2\cdot(3x - 1) - (2x + 5) = 4x - 7$

How to Find the Inverse of a Function

In order to find the inverse of $y = f(x)$ carry out the following procedure:

(i)   replace $f(x)$ with y.

(ii)   switch x and y in $y = f(x) \Rightarrow x = f(y)$.

(iii)   solve for y; express y as a function of x only.

(iv)   replace y with $f^{-1}(x)$.

Example: Find the inverse of the function f(x) = 3x − 1.

Solution:

$f(x) = 3x - 1$

$y = 3x - 1$

$x = 3y - 1$

$y = \dfrac{x+1}{3}$

$f^{-1}(x) = \dfrac{x+1}{3}$

Function Compositions and Inverses

1. (fog)(x) = f(g(x)) and (gof)(x) = g(f(x))

2. f o I = I o f = f where I(x) = x is the identity function.

3. f o f $^{-1}$ = f $^{-1}$ o f = I

4. (fog) $^{-1}$ = g $^{-1}$ o f $^{-1}$

    (gof) $^{-1}$ = f $^{-1}$ o g $^{-1}$

5. (fogoh) $^{-1}$ = h $^{-1}$ o g $^{-1}$ o f $^{-1}$

6. In general (fog)(x) ≠ (gof)(x). If (fog)(x) = (gof)(x) then one of the following cases must hold:

    - f(x) = g(x)

    - f(x) = g $^{-1}$(x) or g(x) = f $^{-1}$(x)

    - f(x) or g(x) or both are identity.

Example: Given that f(x) = 3x − 1; g(x) = 2x + 5; and I(x) = x. Compute the following:

(a) f $^{-1}$ (x)   (b) g $^{-1}$ (x)   (c) (f o f $^{-1}$)(x)   (d) (f $^{-1}$ o f)(x)   (e) (fog)(x)

(f) (gof)(x)   (g) (fog) $^{-1}$ (x)   (h) (gof) $^{-1}$ (x)   (i) (f $^{-1}$ o g $^{-1}$)(x)   (j) (g $^{-1}$ o f $^{-1}$)(x)

(k) (foI)(x)   (l) (Iof)(x)   (m) (f $^{-1}$ofog)(x)   (m) (fogog $^{-1}$)(x)

Solution:

(a) $f(x) = 3x - 1 \Rightarrow f^{-1}(x) = \dfrac{x+1}{3}$

(b) $g(x) = 2x + 5$

     $y = 2x + 5$

     $x = 2y + 5$

     $y = \dfrac{x-5}{2} \Rightarrow g^{-1}(x) = \dfrac{x-5}{2}$

(c)   (f o f $^{-1}$)(x) = $(3x - 1)o(\dfrac{x+1}{3}) = 3.\dfrac{x+1}{3} - 1 = x = I(x)$

(d)   (f $^{-1}$ o f)(x) = $(\dfrac{x+1}{3})o(3x - 1) = \dfrac{3x - 1 + 1}{3} = x = I(x)$

From parts (c) and (d) please notice that f o f $^{-1}$ = f $^{-1}$ o f = I (rule number 3).

(e)   (fog)(x) = (3x − 1)o(2x + 5) = 3.(2x + 5) − 1 = 6x + 15 − 1 = 6x + 14

(f)   (gof)(x) = (2x + 5)o(3x − 1) = 2.(3x − 1) + 5 = 6x − 2 + 5 = 6x + 3

From parts (e) and (f) please notice that fog ≠ gof (rule number 6).

(g) $(fog)(x)=6x+14$

$y=6x+14$

$x=6y+14$

$y=\dfrac{x-14}{6}$

$(fog)^{-1}(x)=\dfrac{x-14}{6}$

(h) $(gof)(x)=6x+3$

$y=6x+3$

$x=6y+3$

$y=\dfrac{x-3}{6}$

$(gof)^{-1}(x)=\dfrac{x-3}{6}$

(i) $(f^{-1} o g^{-1})(x) = (\dfrac{x+1}{3})o(\dfrac{x-5}{2}) = \dfrac{\dfrac{x-5}{2}+1}{3} = \dfrac{\dfrac{x-5+2}{2}}{3} = \dfrac{x-3}{6}$

(j) $(g^{-1} o f^{-1})(x) = (\dfrac{x-5}{2})o(\dfrac{x+1}{3}) = \dfrac{\dfrac{x+1}{3}-5}{2} = \dfrac{\dfrac{x+1-15}{3}}{2} = \dfrac{x-14}{6}$

Please notice from parts (h) – (i) and (g) – (j) that $(fog)^{-1} = g^{-1} o f^{-1}$ and $(gof)^{-1} = f^{-1} o g^{-1}$ (rule number 4).

(k) $(foI)(x) = (3x-1)o(x) = 3x-1 = f(x)$

(l) $(Iof)(x) = (x)o(3x-1) = 3x-1 = f(x)$

Please notice from parts (k) and (l) that $foI = Iof = f$ (rule number 2).

(m) $(f^{-1}ofog)(x) = \dfrac{x+1}{3}o(6x+14) = \dfrac{6x+14+1}{3} = 2x+5 = g(x)$

(n) $(fogog^{-1})(x) = (6x+14)o\dfrac{x-5}{2} = 6\cdot\dfrac{x-5}{2}+14 = 3x-1 = f(x)$

Please notice from parts (m) and (n) that $f^{-1}ofog = g$ and $fogog^{-1} = f$

Finding other function when the composition and one function are given

Case 1: $(fog)(x)$ is given, $g(x)$ is given, $f(x) = ?$ $\Rightarrow$ **Method: i.** Find $g^{-1}(x)$ **ii.** $(fog)og^{-1} = f$

Case 2: $(fog)(x)$ is given, $f(x)$ is given, $g(x) = ?$ $\Rightarrow$ **Method: i.** Find $f^{-1}(x)$ **ii.** $f^{-1}o(fog) = g$

Example: $(fog)(x) = 2x + 3$; $g(x) = 4x - 5$; $f(x) = ?$

Solution: $g(x) = 4x - 5 \Rightarrow g^{-1}(x) = \dfrac{x+5}{4} \Rightarrow f = (fog)og^{-1} = (2x+3)o(\dfrac{x+5}{4}) = 2\cdot\dfrac{x+5}{4}+3 = \dfrac{2x+22}{4} \Rightarrow f(x) = \dfrac{2x+22}{4}$

Example: $f(4x - 5) = 2x + 3 \Rightarrow f(x) = ?$

Solution: (take the inverse of the inside of f; plug in x)

$y = 4x - 5 \Rightarrow x = 4y - 5 \Rightarrow y = \dfrac{x+5}{4}$

$f(4\dfrac{x+5}{4} - 5) = f(x) = 2\cdot\dfrac{x+5}{4}+3 = \dfrac{2x+22}{4}$

(Please notice that the previous two examples are identical but they are given differently.)

Example: $(fog)(x) = 2x + 3$; $f(x) = 4x - 5$; $g(x) = ?$

Solution: f(x) = 4x − 5 $\Rightarrow f^{-1}(x) = \dfrac{x+5}{4} \Rightarrow g = f^{-1}o(fog) = (\dfrac{x+5}{4})o(2x+3) = \dfrac{2x+3+5}{4} = \dfrac{x}{2} + 2$

Example: $(fog)(x) = x$; $f(x) = 4x - 5 \Rightarrow g(x) = ?$

Solution: g(x) = f^{-1} (x) = $\dfrac{x+5}{4}$

Examples:

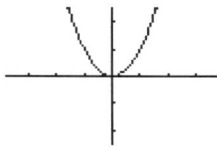 $\Rightarrow$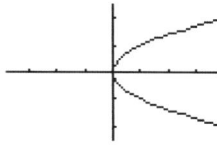

$f(x) = x^2$ $\qquad\qquad$ $f^{-1}(x) = \pm\sqrt{x}$

Inverse is not a function as it fails the vertical line test.

 $\Rightarrow$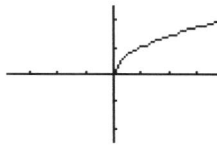

$f(x) = x^2$ and $x \geq 0$ $\qquad$ $f^{-1}(x) = +\sqrt{x}$

Inverse is a function as it passes the vertical line test.

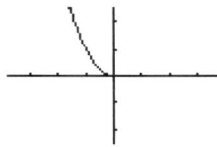 $\Rightarrow$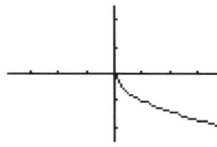

$f(x) = x^2$ and $x \leq 0$ $\qquad$ $f^{-1}(x) = -\sqrt{x}$

Inverse is a function as it passes the vertical line test.

3. $\qquad f(x) = \dfrac{ax+b}{cx+d} \Rightarrow f^{-1}(x) = \dfrac{-dx+b}{cx-a}$ (a and d change places and are multiplied by − 1)

Derivation:

$f(x) = \dfrac{ax+b}{cx+d}$

$\Rightarrow y = \dfrac{ax+b}{cx+d} \Rightarrow x = \dfrac{ay+b}{cy+d}$

$\Rightarrow x(cy+d) = ay+b$

$\Rightarrow cxy+dx = ay+b$

$\Rightarrow cxy-ay = -dx+b$

$\Rightarrow y(cx-a) = -dx+b$

$\Rightarrow y = \dfrac{-dx+b}{cx-a} \Rightarrow f^{-1}(x) = \dfrac{-dx+b}{cx-a}$

Procedure for Completing the Square

$y = ax^2 + bx + c$

i. write the x terms in the parenthesis of the leading coefficient a.

$y = ax^2 + bx + c = a(x^2 + \dfrac{b}{a}x) + c$

ii. add the square of half of the coefficient of x to the inside of the parenthesis; that is add

$(\frac{b}{2a})^2 = \frac{b^2}{4a^2}$ to the inside; and subtract $(a \cdot \frac{b^2}{4a^2}) = \frac{b^2}{4a}$ from the outside of the parenthesis.

$$y = ax^2 + bx + c = a(x^2 + \frac{b}{a}x) + c = a(x^2 + \frac{b}{a}x + \frac{b^2}{4a^2}) - \frac{b^2}{4a} + c$$

iii. the parenthesis becomes a perfect square.

$$y = ax^2 + bx + c = a(x^2 + \frac{b}{a}x) + c = a(x^2 + \frac{b}{a}x + \frac{b^2}{4a^2}) - \frac{b^2}{4a} + c = a(x + \frac{b}{2a})^2 + (c - \frac{b^2}{4a})$$

$$y = a(x - h)^2 + k; \text{ where } h = \frac{b}{2a} \text{ and } k = c - \frac{b^2}{4a}$$

Examples: Apply completing the square procedure to each of the following functions:

(i) $f(x) = 2x^2 - 12x + 3$

(ii) $f(x) = -3x^2 - 6x + 1$

Solution:

(a) $f(x) = 2x^2 - 12x + 3 = 2(x^2 - 6x) + 3 = 2(x^2 - 6x + 9) - 18 + 3 = 2(x - 3)^2 - 15$

(b) $-3x^2 - 6x + 1 = -3(x^2 + 2x) + 1 = -3(x^2 + 2x + 1) + 3 + 1 = -3(x + 1)^2 + 4$

Inverses of Specific Functions

Example: Find the inverse of each of the following functions:

(a) $f(x) = \frac{2x - 3}{4x + 7}$ (b) $f(x) = \frac{2}{3x + 5}$ (c) $f(x) = \frac{2x + 3}{4}$

(d) $f(x) = 3^x$ (e) $f(x) = \frac{2}{3}.4^{5x-6} + 8$ (f) $f(x) = 3.10^{2x} + 4$

(g) $f(x) = 3.\ln\frac{2x + 1}{4} + 5$ (h) $f(x) = 2\log_3(3x - 5) + 6$ (i) $f(x) = 3\log(2x - 1) + 4$

(j) $f(x) = x^2 - 12$ (k) $f(x) = -3x^2 - 6x + 1$ (l) $f(x) = 2x^2 - 12x + 3$

Solution:

(a) $f(x) = \frac{2x - 3}{4x + 7} \Rightarrow f^{-1}(x) = \frac{-7x - 3}{4x - 2}$

(b) $f(x) = \frac{2}{3x + 5} = \frac{0x + 2}{3x + 5} \Rightarrow f^{-1}(x) = \frac{-5x + 2}{3x}$

(c) $f(x) = \frac{2x + 3}{4} = \frac{2x + 3}{0x + 4} \Rightarrow f^{-1}(x) = \frac{-4x + 3}{-2}$

(d) $f(x) = 3^x \Rightarrow f^{-1}(x) = \log_3 x$

(e) $f(x) = \frac{2}{3}.4^{5x-6} + 8 \Rightarrow$

$$y = \frac{2}{3}.4^{5x-6} + 8$$

$$x = \frac{2}{3}.4^{5y-6} + 8$$

$$\frac{3}{2}(x - 8) = 4^{5y-6} \Rightarrow 5y - 6 = \log_4[\frac{3}{2}(x - 8)] \Rightarrow y = \frac{6 + \log_4[\frac{3}{2}(x - 8)]}{5} \Rightarrow f^{-1}(x) = \frac{6}{5} + \frac{1}{5}.\log_4[\frac{3}{2}(x - 8)]$$

(f) $f(x) = 3.10^{2x} + 4$

$y = 3.10^{2x} + 4$

$x = 3.10^{2y} + 4$

$\dfrac{x-4}{3} = 10^{2y} \Rightarrow 2y = \log \dfrac{x-4}{3} \Rightarrow y = \dfrac{1}{2}\log\dfrac{x-4}{3} \Rightarrow f^{-1}(x) = \dfrac{1}{2}\log\dfrac{x-4}{3}$

(g) $f(x) = 3.\ln\dfrac{2x+1}{4} + 5$

$y = 3.\ln\dfrac{2x+1}{4} + 5 \Rightarrow x = 3\ln\dfrac{2y+1}{4} + 5 \Rightarrow \dfrac{x-5}{3} = \ln\dfrac{2y+1}{4}$

$\dfrac{2y+1}{4} = e^{\frac{x-5}{3}} \Rightarrow y = \dfrac{4.e^{\frac{x-5}{3}}-1}{2} \Rightarrow f^{-1}(x) = \dfrac{4.e^{\frac{x-5}{3}}-1}{2}$

(h) $f(x) = 2\log_3(3x-5) + 6 \Rightarrow y = 2\log_3(3x-5) + 6 \Rightarrow x = 2\log_3(3y-5) + 6$

$\dfrac{x-6}{2} = \log_3(3y-5) \Rightarrow 3y - 5 = 3^{\frac{x-6}{2}} \Rightarrow y = \dfrac{5 + 3^{\frac{x-6}{2}}}{3} \Rightarrow f^{-1}(x) = \dfrac{5 + 3^{\frac{x-6}{2}}}{3}$

(i) $f(x) = 3\log(2x-1) + 4 \Rightarrow y = 3\log(2x-1) + 4 \Rightarrow x = 3\log(2y-1) + 4$

$\dfrac{x-4}{3} = \log(2y-1) \Rightarrow 2y - 1 = 10^{\frac{x-4}{3}} \Rightarrow y = \dfrac{1 + 10^{\frac{x-4}{3}}}{2} \Rightarrow f^{-1}(x) = \dfrac{1 + 10^{\frac{x-4}{3}}}{2}$

(j) $f(x) = x^2 - 12 \Rightarrow y = x^2 - 12 \Rightarrow x = y^2 - 12 \Rightarrow y = \pm\sqrt{x+12}$

If Domain of f(x) is R then $f^{-1}(x) = \pm\sqrt{x+12}$ and $f^{-1}(x)$ is not a function.

If Domain of f(x) is $x \geq 0$ (or a subset of $x \geq 0$) then $f^{-1}(x) = \sqrt{x+12}$ and $f^{-1}(x)$ is a function.

If Domain of f(x) is $x \leq 0$ (or a subset of $x \leq 0$) then $f^{-1}(x) = -\sqrt{x+12}$ and $f^{-1}(x)$ is a function.

(k) $f(x) = -3x^2 - 6x + 1 = -3(x+1)^2 + 4$

$y = -3(x+1)^2 + 4 \Rightarrow x = -3(y+1)^2 + 4 \Rightarrow \dfrac{x-4}{-3} = (y+1)^2 \Rightarrow (y+1) = \pm\sqrt{\dfrac{x-4}{-3}} \Rightarrow y = -1 \pm\sqrt{\dfrac{x-4}{-3}}$

If Domain of f(x) is R then $f^{-1}(x) = -1\pm\sqrt{\dfrac{x-4}{-3}}$ and $f^{-1}(x)$ is not a function.

If Domain of f(x) is $x \geq -1$ then $f^{-1}(x) = -1+\sqrt{\dfrac{x-4}{-3}}$.

If Domain of f(x) is $x \leq -1$ then $f^{-1}(x) = -1-\sqrt{\dfrac{x-4}{-3}}$.

(l) $f(x) = 2x^2 - 12x + 3 = 2(x-3)^2 - 15$

$y = 2(x-3)^2 - 15 \Rightarrow x = 2(y-3)^2 - 15 \Rightarrow \dfrac{x+15}{2} = (y-3)^2 \Rightarrow (y-3) = \pm\sqrt{\dfrac{x+15}{2}} \Rightarrow y = 3\pm\sqrt{\dfrac{x+15}{2}}$

If Domain of f(x) is R then $f^{-1}(x) = 3\pm\sqrt{\dfrac{x+15}{2}}$ and $f^{-1}(x)$ is not a function.

If Domain of f(x) is $x \geq 3$ then $f^{-1}(x) = 3+\sqrt{\dfrac{x+15}{2}}$.

If Domain of f(x) is $x \leq 3$ then $f^{-1}(x) = 3-\sqrt{\dfrac{x+15}{2}}$.

Reflections

When you reflect a function y = f(x)

- in the **x – axis**: replace (x, y) by **(x, –y)**
- in the **y – axis**: replace (x, y) by **(–x, y)**
- in the **origin**: replace (x, y) by **(–x, –y)**
- in the line **x = a**: replace (x, y) by **(2a – x, y)**

- in the line **y = b**: replace (x, y) by **(x, 2b – y)**
- in the point **(a, b)**: replace (x, y) by **(2a – x, 2b – y)**
- in the line **y = x**: replace (x, y) by **(y, x)**
- in the line **y = –x**: replace (x, y) by **(–y, –x)**

Example: The function given by $f(x) = 2x^2 + 3$ is reflected in the line x = 3. What is the resulting function?

Solution: When we replace (x, y) by (6 – x, y) ; the function becomes $y = 2(6 – x)^2 + 3$

Periodic Functions

For a function f(x) if there exists a positive real number P such that f(x) = f(x + P) then f(x) is called a **periodic function** and the minimum value of P is called the **period** of the function f(x). Please note the following definitions for periodic functions as well:

Frequency = $\frac{1}{\text{Period}} = \frac{1}{P}$

Amplitude = $\frac{y_{max} - y_{min}}{2}$

Offset = $\frac{y_{max} + y_{min}}{2}$

Axis of wave is the line given by **y = offset**

Example:

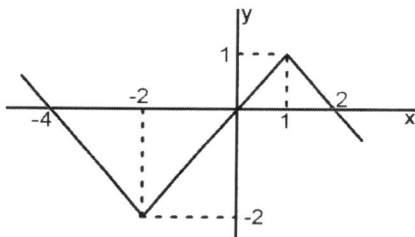

Graph of a periodic function is given above such that one period is plotted and the period is 6. Find the x – coordinates of the first 6 maxima, minima and zeros whose x coordinates are positive. Find the domain, range, amplitude, offset, axis of wave, and frequency.

Solution: Maxima → 1, 7, 13, 19, 25, 31; Minima → 4, 10, 16, 22, 28, 34; Zeros → 2, 6, 8, 12, 14, 18

Domain: R, Range: $-2 \le y \le 1$; Amplitude = $\frac{1--2}{2} = 1.5$, Offset = $\frac{1+(-2)}{2} = -0.5$

Axis of wave: the line given by y = –0.5; Frequency = $\frac{1}{6}$.

Tests for Symmetry

A relation is symmetric

- across the **x axis** if its equation undergoes no change when (x, y) is replaced by **(x, –y)**.
- across the **y axis** if its equation undergoes no change when (x, y) is replaced by **(–x, y)**.
- across the **origin** if its equation undergoes no change when (x, y) is replaced by **(–x, –y)**.
- across the line **y = x** if its equation undergoes no change when (x, y) is replaced by **(y, x)**.
- across the line **y = –x** if its equation undergoes no change when (x, y) is replaced by **(–y, –x)**.

Evenness and Oddness

EVEN	ODD
Algebraically	
$f(-x) = f(x)$	$f(-x) = -f(x)$
Graphically	
$f(x) = f(-x) = A$ $\Rightarrow$ (x, A) and (−x, A) are on the same graph Graph is symmetric with respect to the y − axis.	$f(x) = A$ and $f(-x) = -A$ $\Rightarrow$ (x, A) and (−x, −A) are on the same graph Graph is symmetric with respect to the origin.
Polynomial Functions	
If a polynomial function contains only even powers of x with or without a constant term, then it is even.	If a polynomial function contains only odd powers of x and no constant term, then it is odd.
Relations Given as Sets	
If a relation contains (x, A) and (−x, A) pairs with or without (0, B), then the relation is even.	If a relation contains (x, A), (−x, −A) pairs with or without (0,0), then the relations is odd.
Relations Given Algebraically	
When x is replaced by − x, if no change occurs in relation then the relation is even. (Replace x by − x; if no change then even).	When x is replaced by − x and y is replaced by − y, if no change occurs in the relation, then the relation is odd. (Replace x by − x and y by − y, if no change then odd.)

Basic Functions

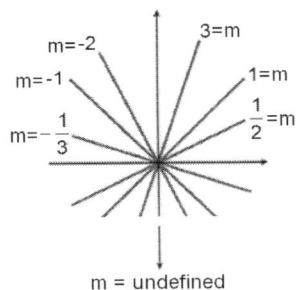

Line Passing Through the Origin

$f(x) = mx$; odd

Domain = R; Range = R

Inverse is a function.

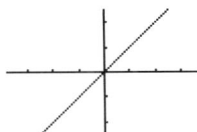

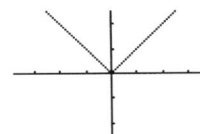

Identity Function

$f(x) = x$; odd

Domain = R; Range = R

Inverse is a function.

Absolute Value Function

$f(x) = |x| = abs(x)$; even

Domain = R; Range = [0, ∞)

Inverse is not a function.

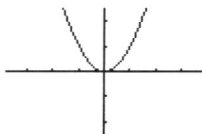

Square Function

$f(x) = x^2$; even

Domain = R; Range = $[0, \infty)$

Inverse is not a function.

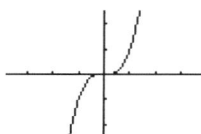

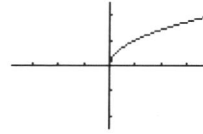

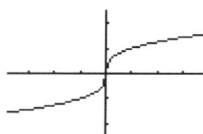

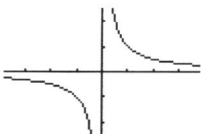

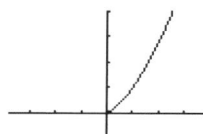

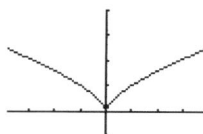

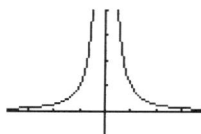

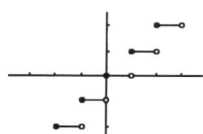

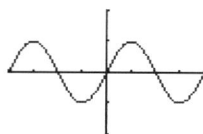

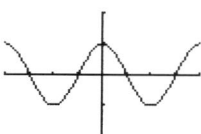

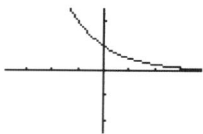

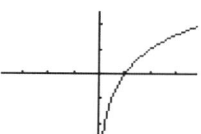

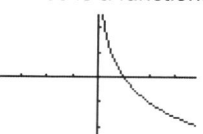

Cube Function

$f(x) = x^3$; odd

Domain = R; Range = R

Inverse is a function.

Square Root Function

$f(x) = \sqrt{x}$; neither odd nor even

Domain = $[0, \infty)$; Range = $[0, \infty)$

Inverse is a function.

Cube–Root Function

$f(x) = \sqrt[3]{x}$: odd

Domain = R; Range = R

Inverse is a function.

Reciprocal Function

$f(x) = \dfrac{1}{x}$; odd

Domain = R − {0}; Range = R − {0}

Inverse is a function.

$f(x) = \sqrt{x^3} = x^{3/2}$

neither odd nor even

Domain = $[0, \infty)$; Range = $[0, \infty)$

Inverse is a function.

$f(x) = \sqrt[3]{x^2} = x^{2/3}$

even

Domain = R; Range = $[0, \infty)$

Inverse is not a function.

Chimney Function

$f(x) = \dfrac{1}{x^2}$; even

Domain = R − {0}; Range = $(0, \infty)$

Inverse is not a function.

Greatest Integer Function

$f(x) = [[x]] = [x] = int(x)$

neither odd nor even

Domain = R; Range = all integers

Inverse is not a function.

Sine Function

$f(x) = \sin(x)$; odd

Domain = R; Range = $[-1, 1]$

Inverse is not a function.

Cosine Function

$f(x) = \cos(x)$; even

Domain = R; Range = $[-1, 1]$

Inverse is not a function.

Exponential Growth Function

$f(x) = b^x$, b > 1

neither odd nor even

Domain = R; Range = $(0, \infty)$

Inverse is a function.

Exponential Decay Function

$f(x) = b^x$, 0 < b < 1

neither odd nor even

Domain = R; Range = $(0, \infty)$

Inverse is a function.

Logarithmic Function (Increasing)

$f(x) = \log_b(x)$, b > 1

neither odd nor even

Domain = $(0, \infty)$; Range = R

Inverse is a function.

Logarithmic Function (Decreasing)

$f(x) = \log_b(x)$, 0 < b < 1

neither odd nor even

Domain = $(0, \infty)$; Range = R

Inverse is a function.

Hyperbolic Rational Function: $f(x) = \dfrac{ax + b}{cx + d}$

Domain $= R - \left\{\dfrac{-d}{c}\right\}$ and Range $= R - \left\{\dfrac{a}{c}\right\}$

Horizontal asymptote: $y = a/c$; Vertical asymptote: $x = -d/c$

It is odd provided that $-d/c = a/c = 0$; otherwise neither odd nor even.

Inverse is a function.

Increasing   **Decreasing**

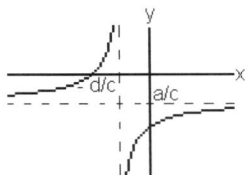   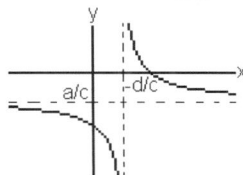   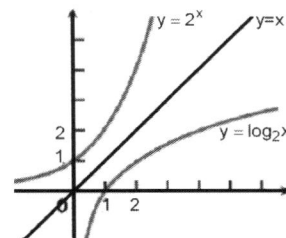

$f(x) = 2^x$ and $f(x) = \log_2 x$ are inverses of each other.

1.4 GEOMETRIC TRANSFORMATIONS

A geometric transformation is a change to a shape that changes it. The common transformations are reflection, rotation, translation, enlargement and stretch. The following definitions need to be known:

An **isometry** is a distance–preserving mapping between two figures; meaning that the resulting figure is congruent to the original one, and all relative distances are preserved.

Types of Transformations

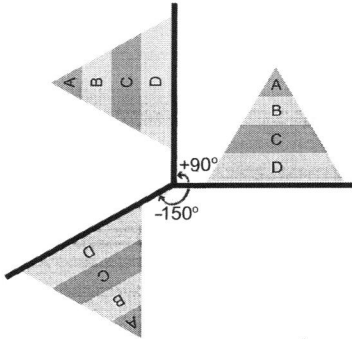

Rotation is defined by a center and an angle (including direction); and points are rotated about the center through the same angle; rotation is a direct isometry and center is the only invariant point.

Example of Rotation

Stretch is defined by an invariant line and a scale factor; points move perpendicular to the invariant line and their distances are multiplied away by the scale factor; neither shape nor size is preserved, but area is multiplied by the scale factor; the invariant line is a line of invariant points.

Example of Horizontal Stretch   **Example of Vertical Stretch**

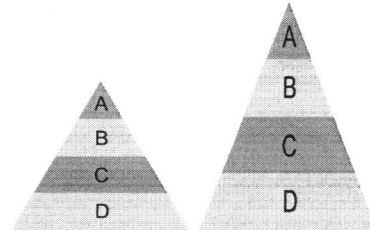

Reflection is defined by a line (the mirror line) or a point; the mirror becomes the perpendicular bisector of every point and its image; it is an opposite isometry and mirror line is a line of invariant points. In point reflection, the point becomes the midpoint of every line segment that connects the point and its image.

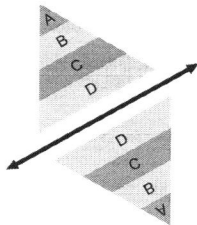

Example of Line Reflection   **Example of Point reflection**

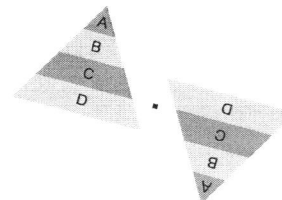

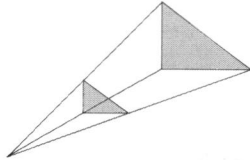

Example of Enlargement

Enlargement is defined by a center and a scale factor; the distance of the points from the center are multiplied by the scale factor; shape is preserved, but not size, area is multiplied by the square of the scale factor i.e. (scale factor)^2; center is the only invariant point.

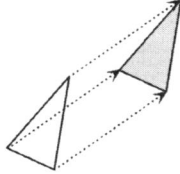

Example of Translation

Translation is defined by a vector along which all points slide; it is a direct isometry with no invariant points.

Example:

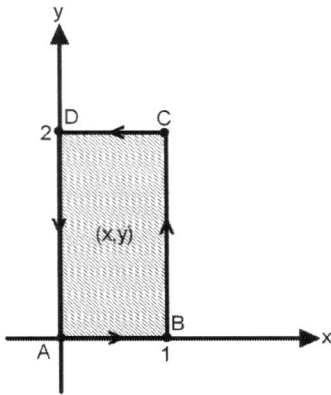

The points shown in the shaded region above are (x, y). Plot the region that would be represented by (−2x, x + y)

Solution:

(x, y)	(−2x, x + y)
(0,0)	(0,0)
(1,0)	(−2, 1)
(1, 2)	(−2, 3)
(0, 2)	(0, 2)
(0,0)	(0,0)

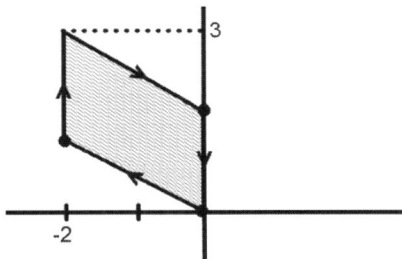

Example: The points on the graph of y = x + 2 are denoted as (x, y). Plot the graph of the points (x + 2, $\sqrt{y}$)

Solution:

Method 1:

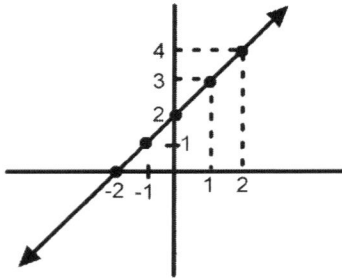

(x, y)	(x + 2, $\sqrt{y}$)
(−2, 0)	(0, 0)
(−1, 1)	(1, 1)
(0, 2)	(2, $\sqrt{2}$)
(1, 3)	(3, $\sqrt{3}$)
(2, 4)	(4, 2)

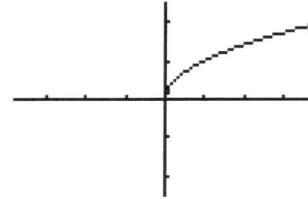

Method 2:

$x' = x + 2$

$y' = \sqrt{y} = \sqrt{x+2}$

Mode: Parametric;

$x_{1T} = x' = t + 2$;

$y_{1T} = y' = \sqrt{t+2}$;

$t_{min} = -2\pi$

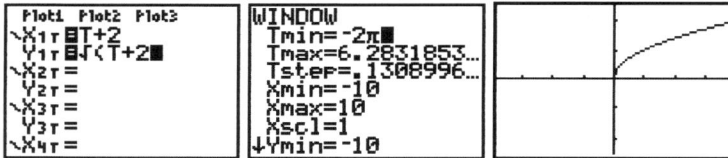

1.5 SYMMETRY AND ROTATIONS

Types of Symmetry

Line Symmetry: A figure has line symmetry if a line can be drawn that divides the figure into two parts that are mirror images. The line of symmetry may be a horizontal line, a vertical line, or neither.

XOX IO ▭	
The examples in the figure above have **horizontal line symmetry**.	
ETƎ PVꟼ	
The examples in the figure above have **vertical line symmetry**.	
G P J	A figure may have **neither horizontal nor vertical line symmetry**, as shown in the figure to the left.
XOX ▭	The figure illustrates that a figure may have **both horizontal and vertical line symmetry**.

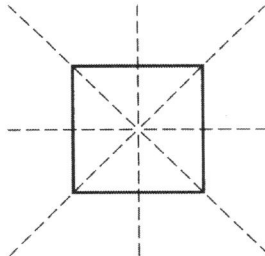

Four lines of symmetry   An infinite number of lines of symmetry   No line of symmetry

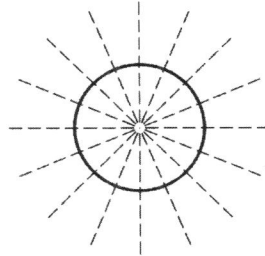

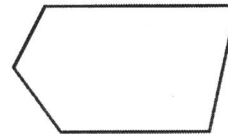

As shown in the figure above, a figure may have more than one line of symmetry or may have no line of symmetry.

Point Symmetry: A figure has point symmetry if it is possible to locate a point, P, such that, if any line is drawn through point P and intersects the figure in another point, A, it will also intersect the figure in a different point, call it B, so that AP = BP.

The letter Z has point symmetry, as shown in the figure to the left. Since the letter Z has point symmetry about point P, turning this figure 180° about point P does not change how the figure looks.

Example:

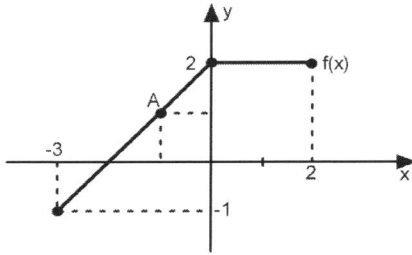

Graph of f(x) is

a) reflected across the line y = 3;

b) reflected across the line x = 3;

c) reflected across the point (3, −1);

d) reflected across origin (0,0);

e) reflected across the line y = x;

f) reflected across the line y = −x;

g) rotated counter clock wise for 90° about the point (2, −1)

Plot the corresponding graphs

Solution:

a)

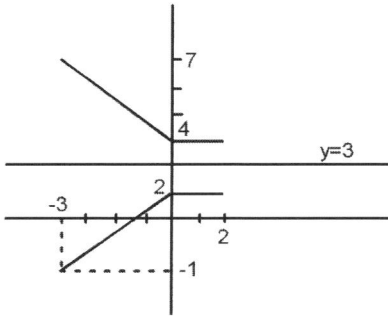

b)

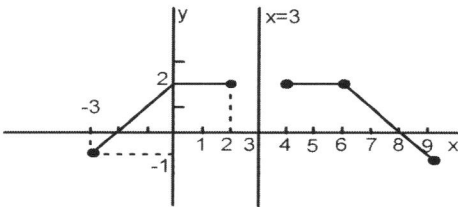

c)

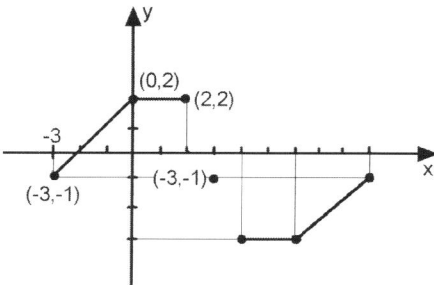

d)

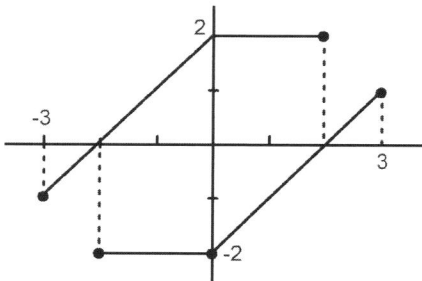

e)

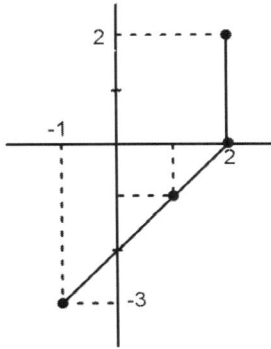

f)

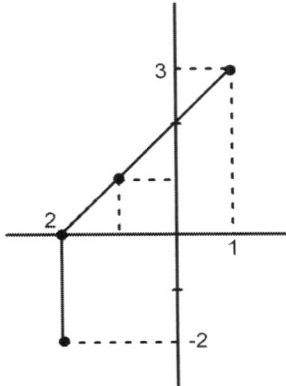

g)

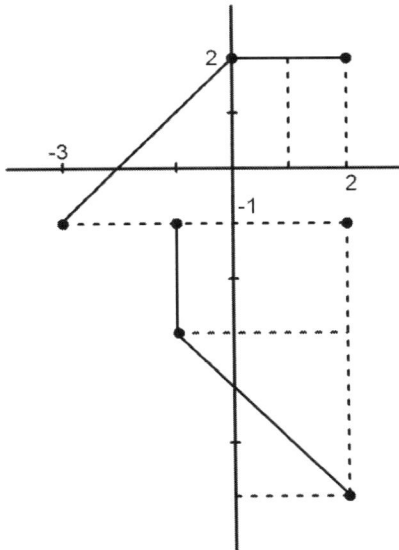

1.6 ADVANCED GRAPHING OF TRANSFORMATIONS ON FUNCTIONS

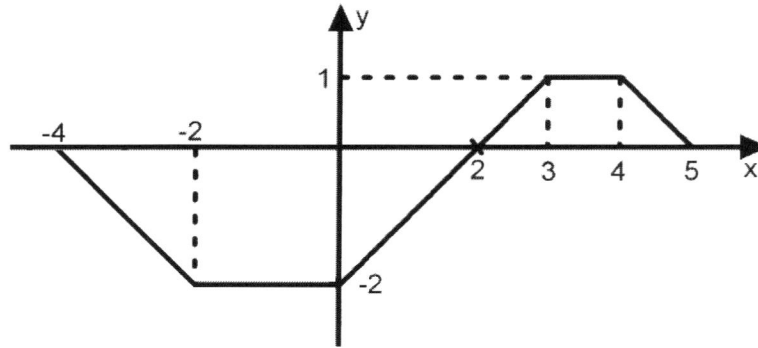

Example: Graph of f(x) is given above, plot the graphs of the following:

a) f(x − 2)   e) f(−x)   l) f(x) + 2   m) | f(x) | q) $\dfrac{1}{f(x)}$

b) f(x + 2)   f) f(|x|)   j) 2f(x)   n) −| f(x) |

c) f(2x)   g) f(−|x|)   k) $\dfrac{f(x)}{2}$ o) f(2x − 6)

d) $f(\dfrac{x}{2})$ h) f(x) − 1   l) −f(x)   p) f $^{-1}$(x)

Solution:

(Horizontal Shifts)

a)

Graph of:	f(x − 2)
Action:	x: x − 2
Sample:	x = 0 → x = 2
Summary:	Shift right for 2 units

b)

Graph of:	f(x + 2)
Action:	x: x + 2
Sample:	x = 0 → x = −2
Summary:	Shift left for 2 units

(Horizontal Shrink − Stretch)

c)

Graph of:	f(2x)
Action:	x: 2x
Sample:	x = 0 → x = 0
	x = 1 → x = $\dfrac{1}{2}$
Summary:	Shrink horizontally by a factor of $\dfrac{1}{2}$

d)

Graph of:	$f(\frac{x}{2})$
Action:	x: $\frac{x}{2}$
Sample:	x = 0 → x = 0 x = 1 → x = 2
Summary:	Stretch horizontally by a factor of 2

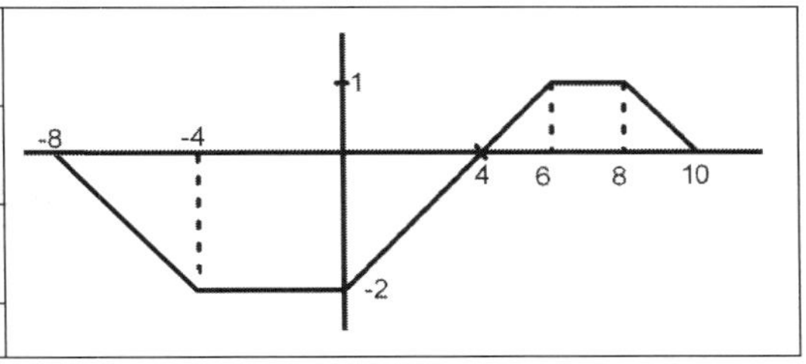

(Reflections in the y – axis)

e)

Graph of:	f(–x)
Action:	x: – x
Sample:	x = 0 → x = 0 x = 1 → x = –1 x = –1 → x = 1
Summary:	Reflect in the y – axis

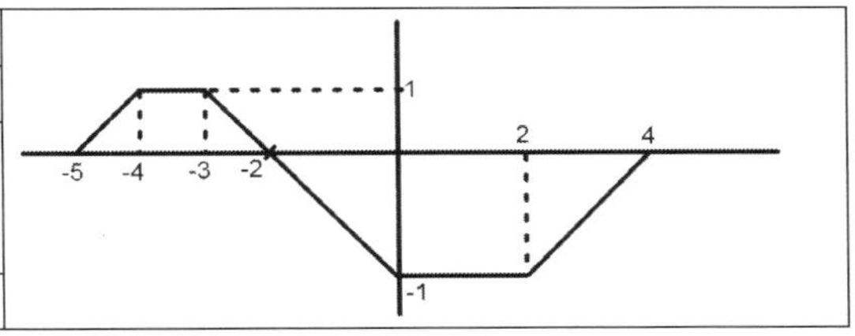

f) $f(|x|) = \begin{cases} f(x) & x \ge 0 \\ f(-x) & x < 0 \end{cases}$

Graph of:	f(|x|)
Action:	x: |x|
Summary:	• Suppress negative x portion of f(x). • Reflect and duplicate positive x portion of f(x). Resulting function becomes even (i.e. symmetric in the y – axis) **Even: f(–x) = f(x); symmetry in the y – axis**

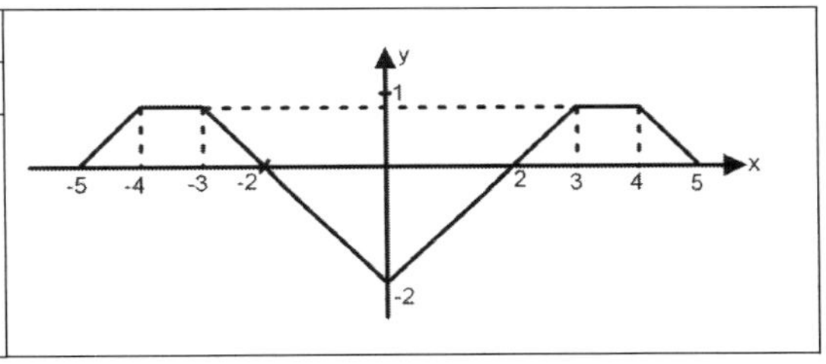

g) $f(-|x|) = \begin{cases} f(-x) & x \ge 0 \\ f(x) & x < 0 \end{cases}$

Graph of:	f(–|x|)
Action:	x: – |x|
Summary:	• Suppress positive x portion of f(x). • Reflect and duplicate negative x portion of f(x). Resulting function becomes even (i.e. symmetric in the y – axis)

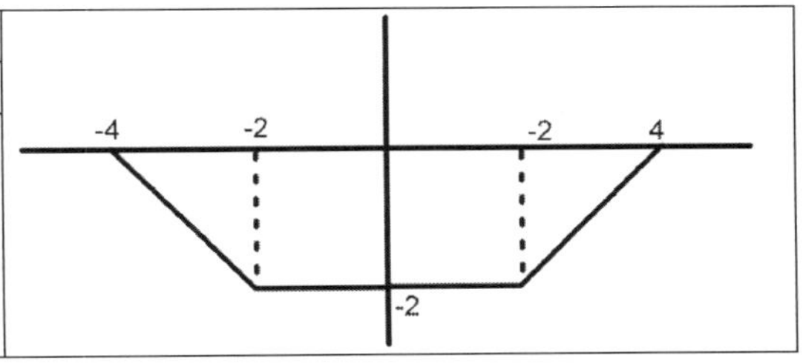

(Vertical Shifts)

h)

Graph of:	f(x) – 1
Action:	y: y + 1 f(x) – 1 = y f(x) = y + 1
Sample:	y = 0 → y = –1
Summary:	Shift down for 1 unit.

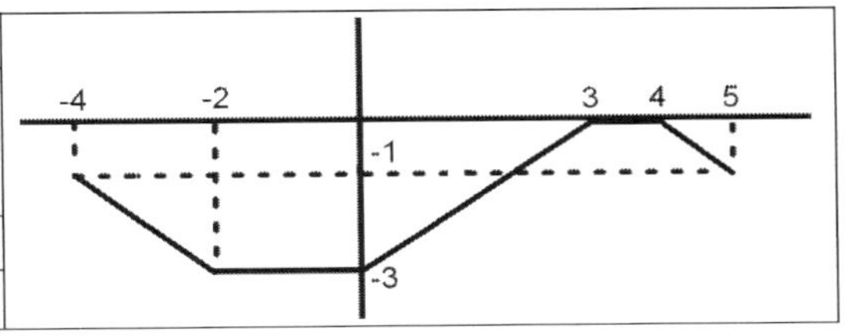

i)

Graph of:	f(x) + 2
Action:	y: y − 2 f(x) + 2 = y f(x) = y − 2
Sample:	y = 0→y = 2
Summary:	Shift up for 2 units.

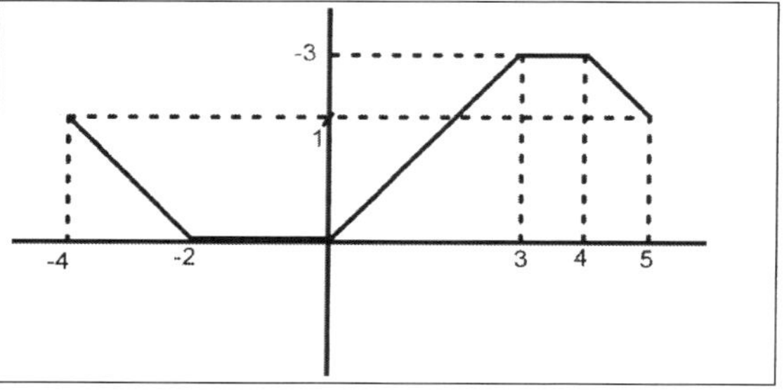

(Vertical Shrink – Stretch)

j)

Graph of:	2f(x)
Action:	y: $\dfrac{y}{2}$ 2f(x) = y f(x) = $\dfrac{y}{2}$
Sample:	y = 0→y = 2
Summary:	Stretch vertically by a factor of 2

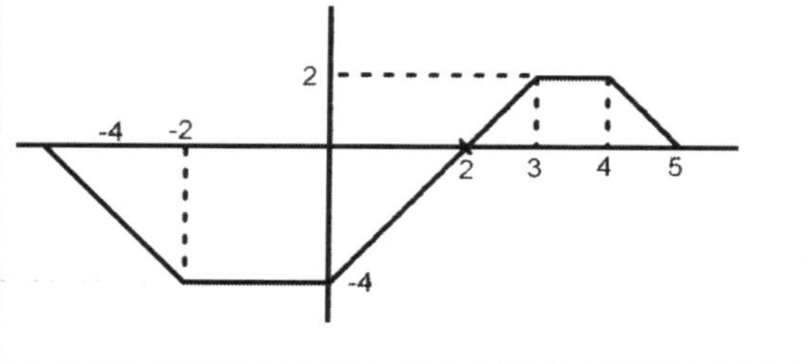

k)

Graph of:	$\dfrac{f(x)}{2}$
Action:	y: 2y $\dfrac{f(x)}{2} = y$ f(x) = 2y
Sample:	y = 0→y = 0 y = 1→y = 1/2
Summary:	Shrink vertically by a factor of $\dfrac{1}{2}$

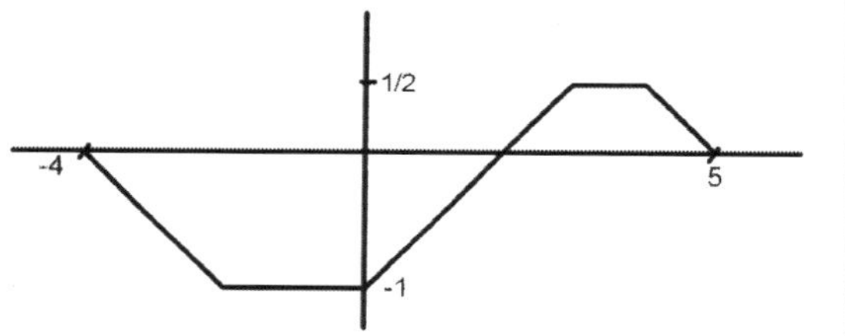

(Reflections in the x – axis)

l)

Graph of:	− f(x)
Action:	y: − y − f(x) = y f(x) = −y
Sample:	y = 0→y = 0 y = 1→y = −1 y = −1→y = 1
Summary:	Reflect in the x – axis

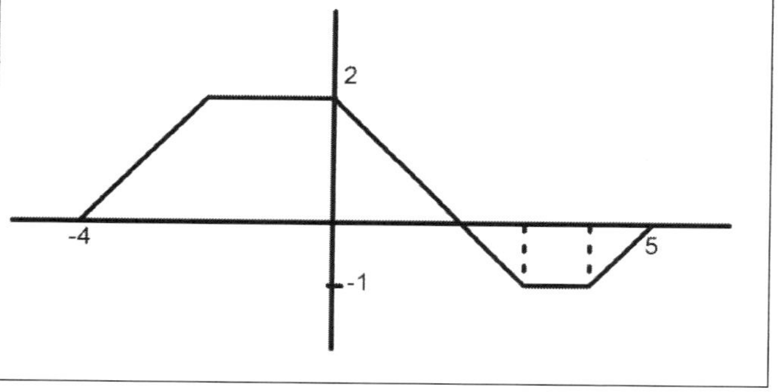

(Absolute Values)

m)

Graph of:	|f(x)|
Summary:	Reflect only the negative y portion of f(x) in the x − axis. The resulting function becomes nonnegative throughout: |f(x)| ≥ 0

n)

Graph of:	−|f(x)|
Summary:	Reflect only the positive y portion of f(x) in the x − axis The resulting function becomes nonpositive throughout: −|f(x)| ≤ 0

o) Graph of: $f(2x − 6) = f(2(x − 3))$: $f(x) \rightarrow f(2x) \rightarrow f(2x − 6)$: **Summary:** Shrink in x by 2; shift in x by 3 (not by 6)

STEP 1: x: 2x

f(2x)

STEP 2: x: x − 3

f(2(x − 3))

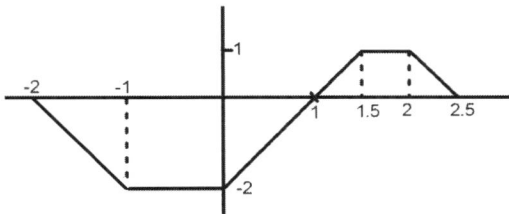

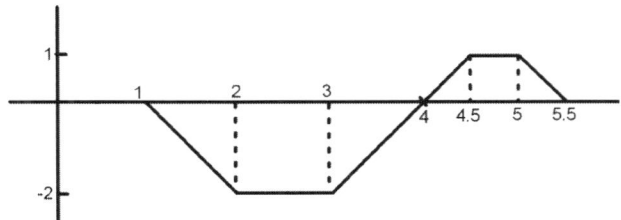

(Inverse of a function)

p) Graph of: $f^{-1}(x)$: **Summary:** Reflect in the line y = x

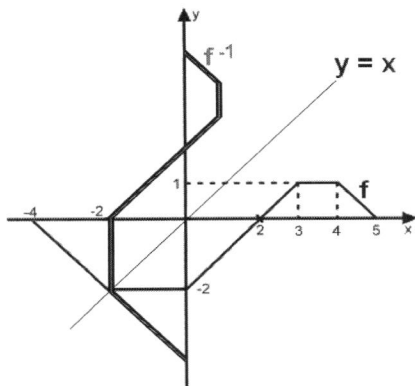

Resulting graph may not correspond to a function.

(Reciprocal of a function)

q) Graph of: $\dfrac{1}{f(x)}$

Domain of f: $-4 \le x \le 5$

Range f: $-2 \le y \le 1$

Domain of $\dfrac{1}{f}$: $-4 < x < 2$ or $2 < x < 5$

Range of $\dfrac{1}{f}$: $y \ge 1$ or $y \le -1/2$

1. $f(x) = 0 \Rightarrow \dfrac{1}{f(x)} = \dfrac{1}{0}$ = undefined $\Rightarrow$ vertical asymptotes (A, B, C) x = -4, 2, 5

2. $f(x) = -2 \Rightarrow \dfrac{1}{f(x)} = \dfrac{1}{-2} = -0, 5$ (D $\leftrightarrow$ E) $-2 \le x \le 0$

3. $f(x) = -1 \Rightarrow \dfrac{1}{f(x)} = \dfrac{1}{-1} = -1$ (F, G)

4. $f(x) = 1 \Rightarrow \dfrac{1}{f(x)} = \dfrac{1}{1} = 1$ (H $\leftrightarrow$ I) $3 \le x \le 4$

5. $f(x) \to 0^{+} \Rightarrow \dfrac{1}{f(x)} \to +\infty$ RHS of x = 2 & LHS of x = 5

    $f(x) \to 0^{-} \Rightarrow \dfrac{1}{f(x)} \to -\infty$ RHS of x = -4 & LHS of x = 2

    (RHS: Right Hand Side; LHS: Left Hand Side)

Please note that the graph of a function can never intersect with the vertical asymptotes.

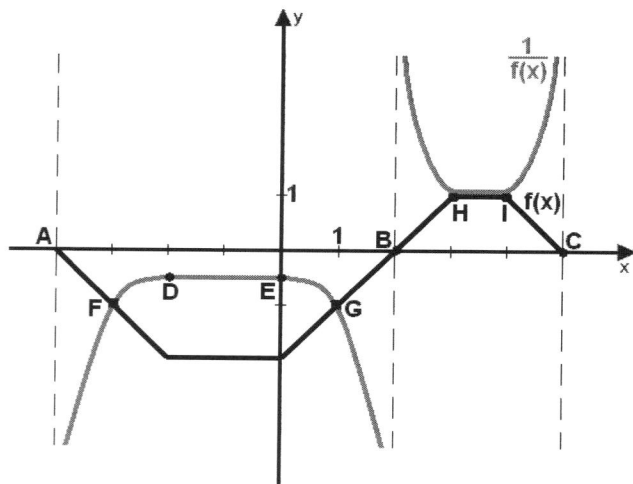

A variety of transformations can be applied on a function given by y = f(x). A partial list of the most common transformations is given in the following table.

Table of Transformations

a and **b** are positive real numbers greater than 1

f(x − **a**)	Shift right for **a** units
f(x + **a**)	Shift left for **a** units
f(**a**x)	Shrink horizontally by a factor of $\dfrac{1}{a}$
f($\dfrac{x}{a}$)	Stretch horizontally by a factor of **a**
f(−x)	Reflect in the y − axis
f(|x|)	Suppress negative x portion of f(x), reflect and duplicate positive x portion of f(x)
f(−|x|)	Suppress positive x portion of f(x), reflect and duplicate negative x portion of f(x)
f(x) − **a**	Shift down for **a** units
f(x) + **a**	Shift up for **a** units
a · f(x)	Stretch vertically by a factor of **a**
$\dfrac{f(x)}{a}$	Shrink vertically by a factor of $\dfrac{1}{a}$
−f(x)	Reflect in the x − axis
|f(x)|	Reflect only the negative y portion of f(x) in the x − axis
− |f(x)|	Reflect only the positive y portion of f(x) in the x − axis
f(**a**x ± **b**)	Shrink in x by **a**; shift in x by $\dfrac{b}{a}$ (not by b)
f^{-1}(x)	Reflect in the line y = x

When f(x, y) = 0 is replaced by f(**a**x, **b**y) = 0 given that **a** and **b** are both greater than 1, x values are divided by **a** and y values are divided by **b**.

Example:

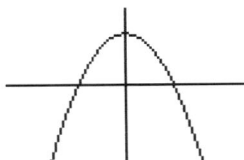

Graph of f(x) is given above. Plot the graph of the slopes of tangents to f(x) at each point.

Solution:

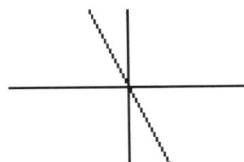

Example:

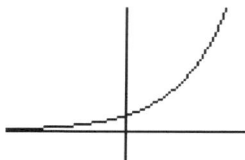

Graph of f(x) is given. Plot the graph of $\dfrac{1}{f(x)}$

Solution:

Example: $f(x) = x^2$

1. Shift right for 3 units
2. Shift down for 1 unit
3. Reflect in the x axis
4. Reflect in the y axis

If steps 1 through 4 are applied to f(x) successively, what will be the resulting function?

Solution: $x^2 \to (x-3)^2 \to (x-3)^2 - 1 \to -(x-3)^2 + 1 \to -(-x-3)^2 + 1 = -(x^2 + 6x + 9) + 1 = -x^2 - 6x - 8$

Example: If the function $f(x) = x^2 + 3x - 6$ is reflected across the point $(2, -3)$ what will be resulting function?

Solution: Each point (x, y) on the curve when reflected across $(2, -3)$ gives the point $(4 - x, -6 - y)$. Therefore the resulting curve is obtained by replacing x with $(4 - x)$ and y with $(-6 - y)$ in

$y = x^2 + 3x - 6. \Rightarrow -6 - y = (4 - x)^2 + 3(4 - x) - 6 \Rightarrow y = -x^2 + 11x - 28$.

Example:

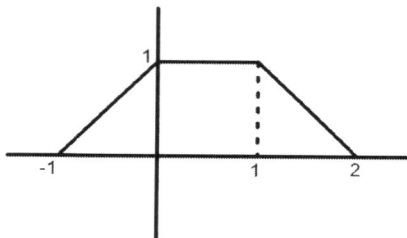

f(x) whose graph is given is reflected across the point $(3, -1/2)$ to get $a \cdot f(x + b) + c$. Find a, b, and c.

Solution:

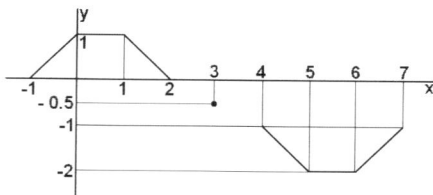

Shift right for 5 units; reflect across the x – axis and shift down for one unit.

$\Rightarrow -f(x - 5) - 1 = a \cdot f(x + b) + c \Rightarrow a = -1; b = -5; c = -1$

1.7 LINEAR FUNCTIONS

A function is called **linear** if it is in the form **f(x) = mx + b** where m and b are constants; and **y = mx + b** is the equation of a **line**.

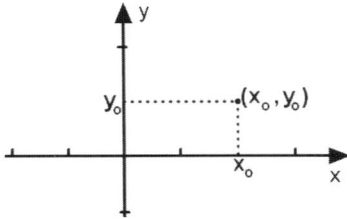

(x_o , y_o) $\Rightarrow x_o$ = x – coordinate or abscissa; y_o = y – coordinate or ordinate

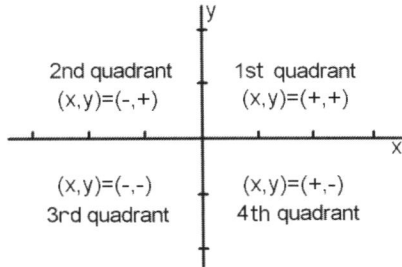

Distance between two points

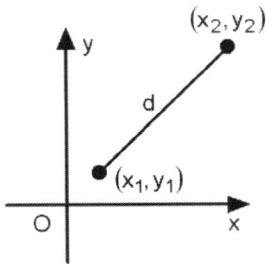

Distance d between the points (x_1, y_1) and (x_2, y_2) is found by: $d = \sqrt{(x_1 - x_2)^2 + (y_1 - y_2)^2}$

Midpoint of a line segment

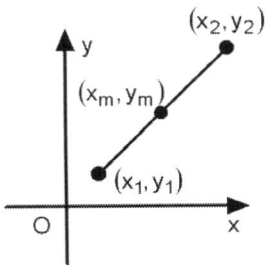

Midpoint (x_m , y_m) of the line segment whose endpoints are (x_1, y_1) and (x_2, y_2) is found by:

$$(x_m, y_m) = \left(\frac{x_1 + x_2}{2}, \frac{y_1 + y_2}{2} \right)$$

Parallelogram

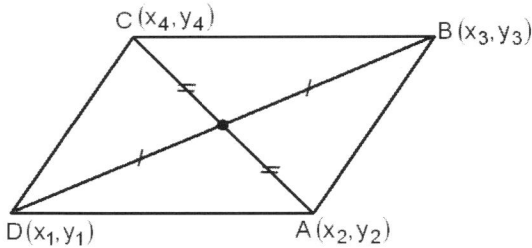

In a parallelogram, the diagonals bisect each other. Therefore the midpoint of line segment AC and the line segment BD is the same point P.

Therefore $\left(\dfrac{x_4 + x_2}{2}, \dfrac{y_4 + y_2}{2} \right) = \left(\dfrac{x_1 + x_3}{2}, \dfrac{y_1 + y_3}{2} \right)$

which implies the following:

$x_4 + x_2 = x_1 + x_3$ and $y_4 + y_2 = y_1 + y_3$

Example: Three vertices of a parallelogram are given by (2, 3), (5, 6) and (−1, −7). Find all possible coordinates of the fourth vertex.

Solution:

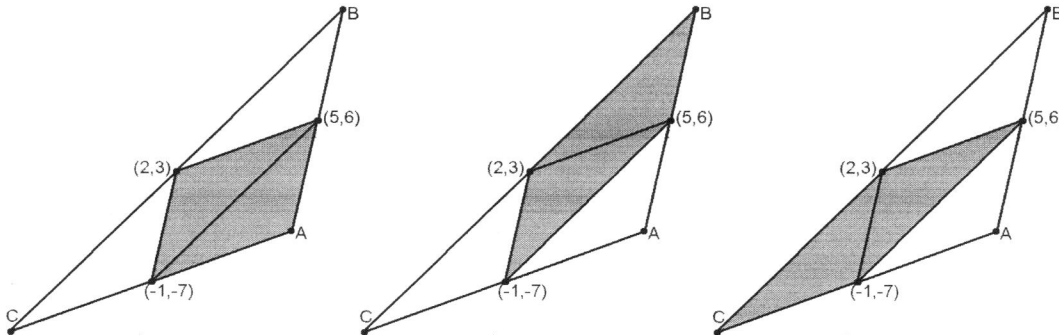

The third vertex can be any of the points A, B, and C given above. Please notice that each shaded region is a parallelogram in the figures given above.

Coordinates of A are (5 − 3, 6 − 10) = (2, -4).

Coordinates of B are (5 + 3, 6 + 10) = (8, 16).

Coordinates of C are (−1 − 3, −7 − 3) = (-4, −10).

Slope of a line segment

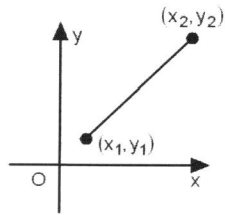

Slope m of the line segment whose endpoints are (x_1, y_1) and (x_2, y_2) is found by the following formula:

$m = \dfrac{\text{rise}}{\text{run}} = \dfrac{\Delta y}{\Delta x} = \dfrac{y_2 - y_1}{x_2 - x_1}$

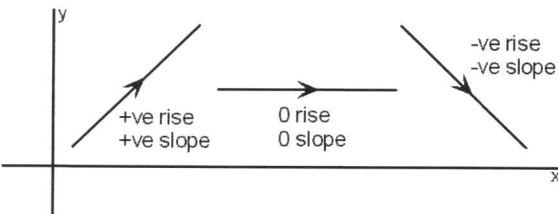

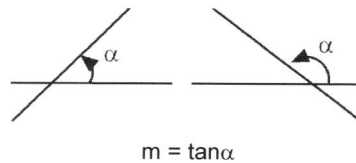

$m = \tan\alpha$

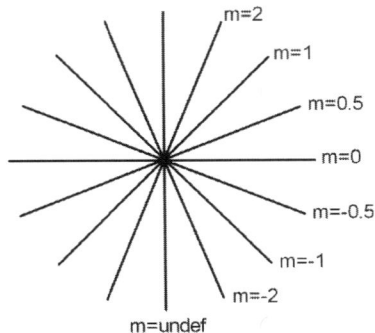

General Form of a Line: $Ax + By + C = 0$

Slope – Intercept Form of a Line: $y = mx + b$ where m = slope and b = y – intercept

$$Ax + By + C = 0 \Rightarrow By = -Ax - C \Rightarrow y = \frac{-A}{B}x - \frac{C}{B}$$

$$y = \frac{-A}{B}x - \frac{C}{B} = mx + b \Rightarrow m = \frac{-A}{B} \text{ and } b = -\frac{C}{B}$$

If $B = 0$ (if there is no y term) $\Rightarrow$ the line cannot be expressed in slope – intercept form. Therefore $Ax + By + C = 0$ is more general than $y = mx + b$.

Two Lines (Slope – Intercept Form)

l_1: $y = m_1x + b_1$

l_2: $y = m_2x + b_2$

- $l_1 = l_2 \Rightarrow m_1 = m_2$ and $b_1 = b_2$
- $l_1 \parallel l_2 \Rightarrow m_1 = m_2$ and $b_1 \neq b_2$
- l_1 and l_2 intersect at a single point $\Rightarrow m_1 \neq m_2$

  l_1 and l_2 intersect at right angles $\Rightarrow m_1 . m_2 = -1$

Two Lines (General Form)

l_1: $a_1x + b_1y + c_1 = 0$

l_2: $a_2x + b_2y + c_2 = 0$

- $\dfrac{a_1}{a_2} = \dfrac{b_1}{b_2} = \dfrac{c_1}{c_2} \Rightarrow l_1 = l_2$; since lines are the same then they intersect at infinitely many points therefore infinitely many

  solutions exist for the system of equations.

- $\dfrac{a_1}{a_2} = \dfrac{b_1}{b_2} \neq \dfrac{c_1}{c_2} \Rightarrow l_1 \parallel l_2$; since lines are parallel then they do not intersect therefore no solution exists for the system of

  equations.

- $\dfrac{a_1}{a_2} \neq \dfrac{b_1}{b_2} \Rightarrow l_1$ and l_2 intersect at a single point; then there exists one unique solution for the system of equations.

Example: l_1: $2x - my + 3 = 0$; l_2: $3x + 2y + n = 0$. Find all possible values for m and n if:

a. l_1 and l_2 are // lines.

b. l_1 and l_2 are the same lines.

c. l_1 and l_2 are $\perp$.

d. l_1 and l_2 intersect at a single point.

Solution:

a. The following condition must hold: $\frac{2}{3}=\frac{-m}{2}\neq\frac{3}{n}$; therefore m = -4/3 and n ≠ 9/2

b. The following condition must hold: $\frac{2}{3}=\frac{-m}{2}=\frac{3}{n}$; therefore m = -4/3 and n = 9/2

c. The following condition must hold: $\frac{2}{m}\cdot\frac{-3}{2}=-1$; therefore m = 3

d. The following condition must hold: $\frac{2}{3}\neq\frac{-m}{2}$ therefore m ≠ -4/3

Distance from a point to a line

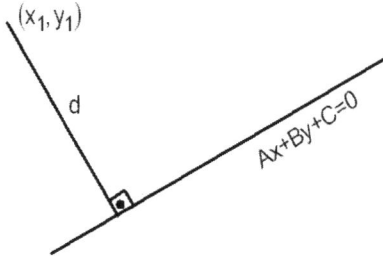

Distance **d** from the point (x_1, y_1) to the line Ax + By + C = 0 is found by: $d = \frac{|Ax_1 + By_1 + C|}{\sqrt{A^2 + B^2}}$

Example: What is the distance from the point (2, −3) to the line 5x − 12y + 3 = 0?

Solution: $d = \frac{|5\cdot 2 - 12\cdot -3 + 3|}{\sqrt{5^2 + (-12)^2}} = 3.769$

Angle between two lines

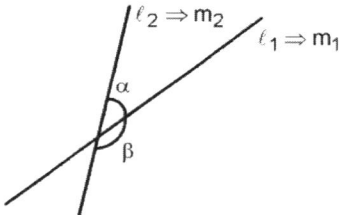

The tangent of the **acute angle** α between the lines l_1 and l_2 whose slopes respectively are m_1 and m_2 is found by: $\tan\alpha = \left|\frac{m_1 - m_2}{1 + m_1 m_2}\right|$

There are three cases about the angle between two lines l_1 and l_2 whose slopes are m_1 and m_2 respectively:

Case 1: $\tan\alpha = 0 \Rightarrow \alpha = 0 \Rightarrow m_1 = m_2 \Rightarrow$ lines are the same or ||

Case 2: $\tan\alpha > 0 \Rightarrow \alpha$ is the acute angle between the lines

If β is the obtuse angle between the lines then $\beta = 180° - \alpha$

Case 3: $\tan\alpha$ = undefined $\Rightarrow \alpha = 90°$ or the lines are perpendicular to each other.

$\Rightarrow 1 + m_1 m_2 = 0 \Rightarrow m_1.m_2 = -1$

Example: What is the obtuse angle between the lines given by y = 2x − 4 and y = −3x + 5?

Solution: If α is the acute angle between the lines then $\tan\alpha = \left|\frac{m_1 - m_2}{1 + m_1 m_2}\right| = \left|\frac{2 - -3}{1 + 2\cdot -3}\right| = 1.$

Therefore $\alpha = \tan^{-1}(1) = 45°$ and the obtuse angle between the lines is $180° - 45° = 135°$.

Area of a closed convex figure

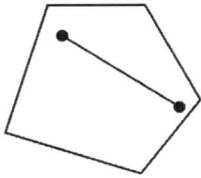 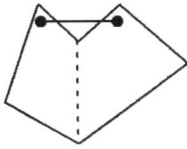

When any two points in a region are connected to give a line segment that lies entirely within that region, the region is called convex.

Convex   **Not Convex**

The following method can be used to calculate the area of any closed convex region regardless of the number of sides that it has. When the region is not convex, it is possible to partition the region to two or more non – overlapping convex regions and use this method for each of the convex regions that result and sum them up to get the whole area.

Rules

1. The region must be convex; however it can have any number of sides.
2. Counter – clockwise direction must be followed when selecting the points.
3. First point must be used twice.
4. The numbers on the same line are multiplied
5. Left Hand Side → –
   Right Hand Side → +
6. $\frac{1}{2}$ must not be forgotten.

Example:

Find the area of the quadrilateral given below:

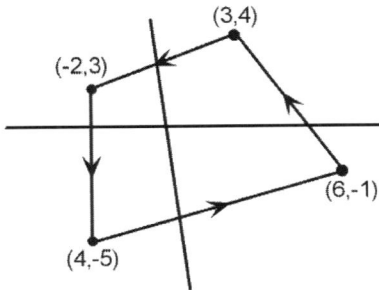

Solution:

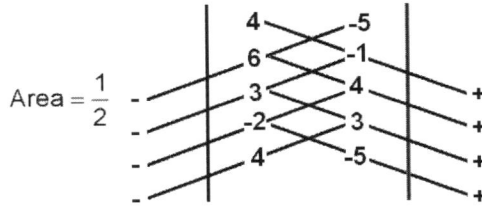

$$\text{Area} = \frac{1}{2}(30 + 3 + 8 - 12 - 4 + 24 + 9 + 10) = \frac{1}{2}(68) = 34$$

Line Equations

line equation 1:

slope intercept form: $y = mx + b$

givens:

slope = $\mathbf{m}$ = $\tan \alpha$ and y – intercept = $\mathbf{b}$

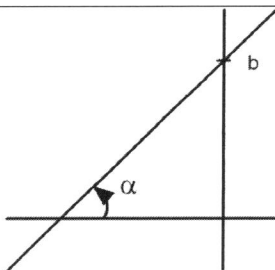
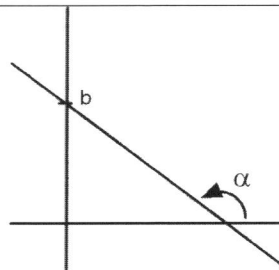

$m = \tan \alpha > 0$ $m = \tan \alpha < 0$

line equation 2:

slope point form: $y - y_1 = m(x - x_1)$

givens:

slope = $\mathbf{m}$ = $\tan \alpha$ and point = $\mathbf{(x_1, y_1)}$

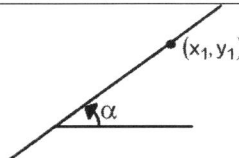

$m = \tan \alpha$

line equation 3:

two point form: $\dfrac{y - y_1}{y_1 - y_2} = \dfrac{x - x_1}{x_1 - x_2}$

givens:

the points $\mathbf{(x_1, y_1)}$ and $\mathbf{(x_2, y_2)}$ that are both on the line

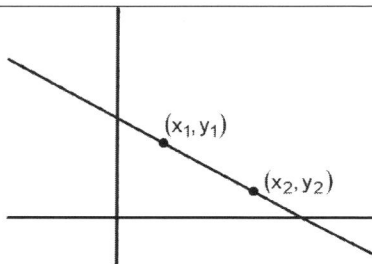

line equation 4:

x – y intercepts form $\dfrac{x}{A} + \dfrac{y}{B} = 1$

givens:

the x and y intercepts, $\mathbf{A}$ and $\mathbf{B}$

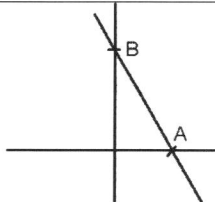

Example: Find equation of the line that

(a) has the slope of 2 and passes through (–1, 3).

(b) has the slope of – 2 and the y intercept of 4.

(c) makes $60°$ with the positive x axis and passes through (2, –3).

(d) passes through the points (1, 3) & (2, 4).

(e) intersects the y axis at (0, -4) and x axis at (3,0).

Solution:

(a) slope point form: $y - 3 = 2 \cdot (x + 1)$

(b) slope intercept form: $y = -2x + 4$

(c) slope = $\tan 60° = \sqrt{3}$; slope point form: $y + 3 = \sqrt{3}\,(x - 2)$

(d) two point form: $\dfrac{y - 4}{4 - 3} = \dfrac{x - 2}{2 - 1}$.

(e) x – y intercepts form: $\dfrac{x}{3} + \dfrac{y}{-4} = 1$

Example: In the figure given, AH $\perp$ BC and M is the midpoint of line segment BC. Find the equation of each of the lines HA and MA.

Solution:

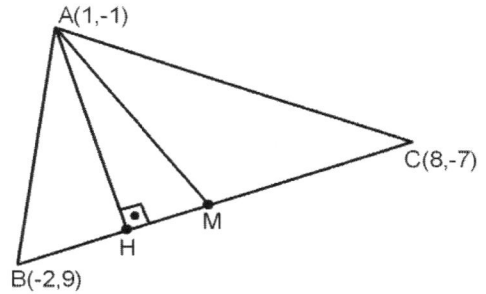

- In order to find the equation of MA we first find point M by the midpoint formula, then use line equation 3 given above.

$$M\left(\frac{-2+8}{2},\frac{9-7}{2}\right) = M(3,1)$$

Equation of MA: $\dfrac{y-1}{1--1} = \dfrac{x-3}{3-1} \Rightarrow y = x - 2$

- In order to find the equation of HA we first find the slope of segment CB then the slope of HA, which is the negative reciprocal of the slope of CB. Then we use line equation 2.

Slope of BC = $\dfrac{9--7}{-2-8} = \dfrac{16}{-10} = -\dfrac{8}{5}$; therefore slope of HA = 5/8.

Equation of HA: y $--$ 1 = 5/8$\cdot$(x $-$ 1)

Perpendicular Bisector of a Line Segment

The locus of points equidistant from two given points in a plane is the line that perpendicularly bisects the line segment that joins those points.

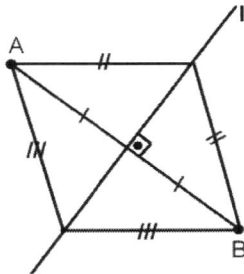

In order to find the equation of line l,

i.   Find the slope m_{AB} of line AB and the slope m_l of line l using the relation $m_{AB} \cdot m_l = -1$

ii. Find the midpoint of line AB.

iii. Use line equation 2 to find the equation of line l.

Example: What is the equation of the perpendicular bisector of segment AB whose endpoints are given by A(1, 5) and B(7, $-$3)?

Solution: Midpoint of AB: $\left(\dfrac{1+7}{2},\dfrac{5-3}{2}\right) = (4,1)$; Slope of AB: $\dfrac{5--3}{1-7} = -\dfrac{8}{6} = -\dfrac{4}{3}$;

Slope of the perpendicular bisector = 3/4

Equation of the perpendicular bisector is y $-$ 1 = 3/4$\cdot$(x $-$ 4)

Reflections

Reflection of the point **(x, y)** in the **x $-$ axis: (x, $-$y)**

Reflection of the point **(x, y)** in the **y $-$ axis: ($-$x, y)**

Reflection of the point **(x, y)** in the **origin: ($-$x, $-$y)**

Reflection of the point **(x, y)** in the line **x = a: (2a $-$ x, y)**

Reflection of the point **(x, y)** in the line **y = b: (x, 2b $-$ y)**

Reflection of the point **(x, y)** in the point **(a, b): (2a $-$ x, 2b $-$ y)**

Reflection of the point **(x, y)** in the line **y = x: (y, x)**

Reflection of the point **(x, y)** in the line **y = $-$x: ($-$y, $-$x)**

Please note that when a line **y = mx + b** is reflected across

- **the x axis** it becomes: **y = –mx – b.**
- **the y axis** it becomes: **y = –mx + b.**
- **the origin** it becomes: **y = mx – b.**
- **the line y = x** it becomes: **x = my + b.**
- **the line y = –x** it becomes: **– x = –my + b.**

Linear Models

A mathematical model is a set of equations, inequalities, functions, graphs, tables, etc. used to describe a real world problem. **A linear model** is an input output model of the form **f(x) = ax + b** where **x** is the input and **f(x)** is the output.

Example: In a production plant the cost C of producing n items is defined by a linear function as C(n) = An + B. If the cost of producing 800 items is 2,000 dollars and that of 1400 items is 3,200 dollars then what will be the cost of producing

(a) 500 items;

(b) no items.

Solution:

2000 = 800 A + B

3200 = 1400 A + B

$\Rightarrow$ 1200 = 600 A; A = 2 and B = 400

Therefore C(n) = 2n + 400

(a) C(500) = 2 · 500 + 400 = 1400

(b) C(0) = 400

Finding the Equation of a Line Using Regression

Example: Find the equation of the line through the points (1, 3) and (2, -4)?

Solution:

Answer: y = –7x + 10

Linear Interpolation

Suppose that **(a, f(a))** and **(b, f(b))** are two points on a continuous function. We are given that f(x) continuously increases or decreases when **a < x < b** and we would like to calculate $f\left(\dfrac{a+b}{2}\right)$. In order to accomplish such a task, we can find the midpoint of the points **(a, f(a))** and **(b, f(b))** in order to get an estimate of $f\left(\dfrac{a+b}{2}\right)$ which is $f\left(\dfrac{a+b}{2}\right) = \dfrac{f(a)+f(b)}{2}$. We have assumed that **f(x)** is a linear function of x when **a < x < b**. This is called linear interpolation.

Example: (0.5, 0.479) and (0.9, 0.783) are two points on y = sin(x). What will be the error associated if sin(0.7) were calculated using linear interpolation?

Solution: Midpoint will be calculated as (0.7, 0.631). The actual value of sin(0.7) is 0.644. The error that has been done can be calculated by $\dfrac{0.644 - 0.631}{0.644} \cdot 100$ and it equals 2.02%.

1.8 QUADRATIC FUNCTIONS

$y = f(x) = ax^2 + bx + c$; $a \neq 0$; $a, b, c \in \mathbb{R}$

$y = ax^2 + bx + c \Rightarrow y = a(x - h)^2 + k$ where (h, k) is the vertex and it can be found using one of the following ways:

- By completing the square

- By using the following set of formulas: $h = \dfrac{-b}{2a}$ and $k = \dfrac{4ac - b^2}{4a}$

- By using the following set of formulas: $h = \dfrac{-b}{2a}$ and $k = f(h)$

- By using derivatives: The derivative at the vertex is zero, thus $f'(x) = 2ax + b = 0 \Rightarrow x = \dfrac{-b}{2a} = h$ and $k = f(h)$.

- By using a graphing calculator: Find the maximum or the minimum point on the graph of the function (which is a parabola that is U or ∩ shaped); this will be the point (h, k).

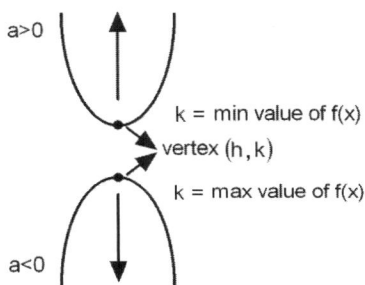

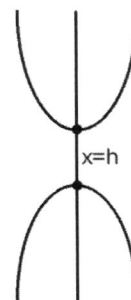

a>0

k = min value of f(x)

vertex (h, k)

k = max value of f(x)

a<0

The larger the value of |a|, the narrower the parabola will be.

x=h

x = h: axis of symmetry

Roots of a quadratic equation

$f(x) = ax^2 + bx + c = 0 \Rightarrow \Delta = b^2 - 4ac$: discriminant; $x_1 = \dfrac{-b + \sqrt{\Delta}}{2a}$ and $x_2 = \dfrac{-b - \sqrt{\Delta}}{2a}$

Case 1: $\Delta < 0$

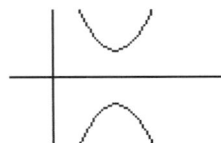

two complex conjugate zeros

- If one root is **p + qi** then the other is **p − qi**, or vice versa.
- f(x) is always positive (when a > 0) or always negative (when a < 0).

Case 2: $\Delta = 0$

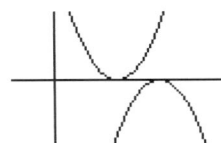

two real equal zeros, one double root

$\Rightarrow$ f(x) is always non − negative (when a > 0) or always non − positive (when a < 0).

$x_1 = x_2 = \dfrac{-b}{2a}$

Case 3: $\Delta > 0$

two real unequal (distinct, different) roots

$x_1 = \dfrac{-b + \sqrt{\Delta}}{2a}$ and $x_2 = \dfrac{-b - \sqrt{\Delta}}{2a}$

- f(x) is not always positive or negative.
- If a > 0 then f(x) is negative when x lies between the roots and positive when x lies outside the roots. If a < 0 then f(x) is positive when x lies between the roots and negative when x lies outside the roots.
- If Δ is nonzero and perfect square $\Rightarrow$ roots are distinct and rational.
- If Δ is positive and not a perfect square $\Rightarrow$ roots are distinct and irrational. If one root is $p + \sqrt{q}$ then the other is $p - \sqrt{q}$ or vice versa, where b is positive and not a perfect square.
- If $\Delta \geq 0$ then the roots are real (they may be equal or distinct).

Sum and product of the roots of a quadratic equation

$$P(x) = ax^2 + bx + c = 0 \Rightarrow x^2 + \frac{b}{a}x + \frac{c}{a} = 0$$

$$(x - x_1)(x - x_2) = x^2 - x_1 x - x_2 x + x_1 x_2 = x^2 - (x_1 + x_2)x + x_1 x_2 \Rightarrow x^2 - (x_1 + x_2)x + x_1 x_2 = x^2 + \frac{b}{a}x + \frac{c}{a}$$

$$S = x_1 + x_2 = \frac{-b}{a} = \text{sum of the roots}$$

$$P = x_1 \cdot x_2 = \frac{c}{a} = \text{product of the roots}$$

Given the roots, construct the equation

$$S = x_1 + x_2 \text{ and } P = x_1 \cdot x_2 \Rightarrow x^2 - Sx + P = 0$$

Example: For the function $f(x) = x^2 - 4x - 5$; find the vertex, the x and y intercepts, the axis of symmetry, the max or min value of the function, the domain and range of the function.

Solution: $y = x^2 - 4x - 5 = x^2 - 4x + 4 - 9 = (x - 2)^2 - 9 \Rightarrow$ vertex is (2, −9)

$x = 0 \Rightarrow y = -5$ therefore y intercept is − 5 (the point whose coordinates are (0, −5))

$y = 0 \Rightarrow (x - 5)(x + 1) = 0 \Rightarrow x = 5$ or $x = -1$ therefore x intercepts are 5 and − 1; (the points (5, 0) and (−1, 0))

axis of symmetry is the line given by x = 2

minimum value of the function is − 9

domain is all real numbers; range is y ≥ − 9.

Example: Domain of f(x) is given by $x^2 + 3x - 4 < 0$ and $f(x) = x^2 + 4x + 5$. Find range of f(x).

Solution:

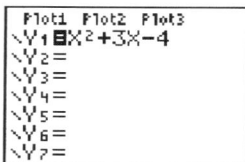 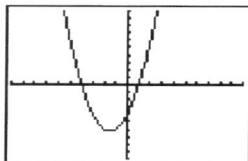 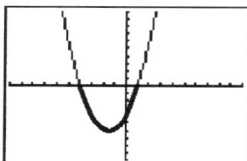

Domain: − 4 < x < 1

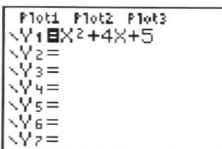 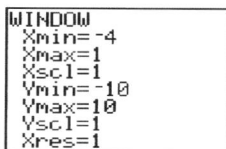 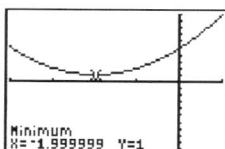 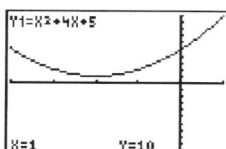

Answer: 1 ≤ y < 10

Example: Construct a quadratic equation that has

a. two roots − 3 and 5.

b. two roots 0 and 2.

c. two roots $3 + \sqrt{5}$ and $3 - \sqrt{5}$.

d. two roots 3 − i and 3 + i.

e. the only root of $\dfrac{4}{3}$.

Solution:

a. $S = -3 + 5 = 2$; $P = -3 \cdot 5 = -15$; $x^2 - 2x - 15 = 0$

b. $S = 0 + 2 = 2$; $P = 0 \cdot 2 = 0$; $x^2 - 2x = 0$

c. $S = 3 + \sqrt{5} + 3 - \sqrt{5} = 6$; $P = (3 + \sqrt{5})(3 - \sqrt{5}) = 9 - 5 = 4$; $x^2 - 6x + 4 = 0$

d. $S = 3 - i + 3 + i = 6$; $P = (3 - i)(3 + i) = 9 + 1 = 10$; $x^2 - 6x + 10 = 0$

e. $S = \dfrac{4}{3} + \dfrac{4}{3} = \dfrac{8}{3}$; $P = \dfrac{4}{3} \cdot \dfrac{4}{3} = \dfrac{16}{9}$; $x^2 - \dfrac{8}{3}x + \dfrac{16}{9} = 0 \Rightarrow 9x^2 - 24x + 16 = 0$

Example: $f(x) = 2x^2 - mx + 3$. Find all possible values for m if

a. f(x) intersects the x axis at two distinct points.

b. f(x) is tangent to the x axis.

c. f(x) does not intersect the x axis.

Solution:

$\Delta = b^2 - 4ac = m^2 - 4 \cdot 2 \cdot 3 = m^2 - 24$

a. $m^2 - 24 > 0 \Rightarrow |m| > \sqrt{24} = 2\sqrt{6} \Rightarrow m > 2\sqrt{6}$ or $m < -2\sqrt{6}$

b. $m^2 - 24 = 0 \Rightarrow m = 2\sqrt{6}$ or $m = -2\sqrt{6}$

c. $m^2 - 24 < 0 \Rightarrow |m| < \sqrt{24} = 2\sqrt{6} \Rightarrow -2\sqrt{6} < m < 2\sqrt{6}$

Example: $f(x) = -(x - 1)^2 + 3$ and $-2 \le x \le 2$. Find the range of f(x).

Solution:

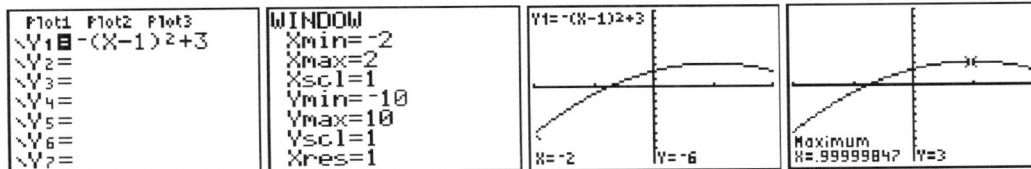

Answer: $-6 \le y \le 3$.

Completing the square (revisited)

$y = ax^2 + bx + c$

$= a(x^2 + \dfrac{b}{a}x) + c$

$= a(x^2 + \dfrac{b}{a}x + \dfrac{b^2}{4a^2}) - \dfrac{b^2}{4a} + c$

$= a(x + \dfrac{b}{2a})^2 + (c - \dfrac{b^2}{4a})$

$y = a(x - h)^2 + k$

where $h = \dfrac{b}{2a}$ and $k = c - \dfrac{b^2}{4a}$

A parabola and a line:

$y = f_1(x) = ax^2 + bx + c$

$y = f_2(x) = mx + p$

$f_1(x) = f_2(x) \Rightarrow mx + p = ax^2 + bx + c \Rightarrow ax^2 + (b - m)x + (c - p) = 0$

A quadratic equation is obtained and depending on the roots of this equation there will be three cases:

$Ax^2 + Bx + C = 0$ where $A = a$; $B = b - m$; $C = c - p$ (1)

$\Delta = B^2 - 4AC$

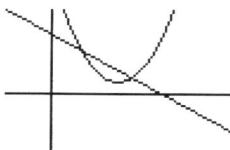

$\Delta > 0 \Rightarrow$ The parabola and the line intersect at two points whose x – coordinates are the roots of equation (1).

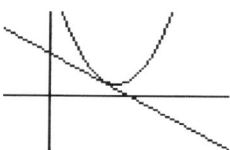

$\Delta = 0 \Rightarrow$ The parabola and the line are tangent (they intersect at a single point). The point of tangency has an x – coordinate, which is the root of equation (1).

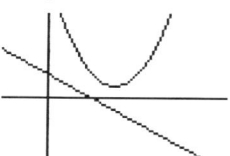

$\Delta < 0 \Rightarrow$ The parabola and the line don't intersect; equation (1) has no real roots.

Example: A parabola p and a line l are given by p: $y = mx^2 + x + 1$ and l: $y = 2x + 3$. Find all possible values for m if

a. parabola and line are tangent;

b. parabola and line don't intersect;

c. parabola and line intersect;

d. line cuts the parabola at two distinct points.

Solution:

$mx^2 + x + 1 = 2x + 3 \Rightarrow mx^2 - x - 2 = 0$

$\Delta = 1 - 4 \cdot m \cdot (-2) = 1 + 8m$

a. $1 + 8m = 0 \Rightarrow m = -1/8$

b. $1 + 8m < 0 \Rightarrow m < -1/8$

c. $1 + 8m \geq 0 \Rightarrow m \geq -1/8$

d. $1 + 8m > 0 \Rightarrow m > -1/8$

Finding the Equation of a Parabola Using Regression

Example: Find the equation of the parabola through the points (1, 4), (0, 3), and (−1, 6)?

Solution:

Answer: $y = 2x^2 - x + 3$

Quadratic Models

A quadratic model is an input output model of the form $f(x) = ax^2 + bx + c$ where x is the input and $f(x)$ is the output.

Example: The cost of production in a certain factory is a quadratic function of the production. The fixed costs, i.e. the cost of producing no items is $500; the cost of producing 100 items is $30, 500 and the cost of producing 150 items is $38,000. What is the cost of producing 180 items in this factory?

Solution: $f(x) = ax^2 + bx + c$

$f(0) = 500 = c$

$f(100) = 30,500 = 10,000a + 100b + c$

$f(150) = 38,000 = 22,500a + 150b + c$

$10,000a + 100b = 30,000$

$22,500a + 150b = 37,500$

Solving the above system yields $a = -1$ and $b = 400$.

Therefore $f(x) = -x^2 + 400x + 500$ and $f(180) = -180^2 + 400 \cdot 180 + 500 = 40,100$

1.9 POLYNOMIAL FUNCTIONS

A **monomial** has only **one term**: $2x^4$; $5x^3y^2$; $-8x^4yz^3$

A **binomial** has only **two terms**: $2x - 4y$; $1 - 5x$; $9x^2yz - st^3$

A **trinomial** has only **three terms**: $3x + y - z$, $2x^2 + 15y^3 - z^5$

$P(x) = a_nx^n + a_{n-1}x^{n-1} + a_{n-2}x^{n-2} + \dots + a_5x^5 + a_4x^4 + a_3x^3 + a_2x^2 + a_1x + a_0$

for $P(x)$ to be a polynomial function:

- a_n values must be complex numbers (in SAT II context they will all be real numbers) and

- n values must be nonnegative integers.

a_n 's are called **coefficients**.

a_0 is called the **constant** term

a_1x is called the **linear** term

a_2x^2 is called the **quadratic** term

a_3x^3 is called the **cubic** term

a_4x^4 is called the **quartic** term

a_5x^5 is called the **quintic** term

a_nx^n is called the **leading** term (the term with the greatest exponent).

The **greatest exponent** is called the **degree of the polynomial**.

Coefficient of the leading term is called the **leading coefficient**.

Two terms of a polynomial are like terms if they have the same variables and each variable has the same exponent.

$P(x) = \mathbf{0}$: **zero polynomial**.

$P(x) = a_0$: **constant polynomial**.

$P(x) = a_1x + a_0$: **linear polynomial**, $a_1 \neq 0$

$P(x) = a_2x^2 + a_1x + a_0$: **quadratic polynomial**, $a_2 \neq 0$

$P(x) = a_3x^3 + a_2x^2 + a_1x + a_0$: **cubic polynomial**, $a_3 \neq 0$

$P(x) = a_4x^4 + a_3x^3 + a_2x^2 + a_1x + a_0$: **quartic polynomial**, $a_4 \neq 0$

$P(x) = a_5x^5 + a_4x^4 + a_3x^3 + a_2x^2 + a_1x + a_0$: **quintic polynomial**, $a_5 \neq 0$

If all **coefficients** are **real**, then the polynomial is a **real polynomial**.

If all **coefficients** are **rational**, then the polynomial is a **rational polynomial**.

If all **coefficients** are **integers**, then the polynomial is an **integral polynomial**.

Polynomial Identities

$(A + B)^2 = A^2 + 2AB + B^2$

$(A - B)^2 = A^2 - 2AB + B^2$

$A^2 - B^2 = (A - B)(A + B)$

$(A + B + C)^2 = A^2 + B^2 + C^2 + 2AB + 2AC + 2BC$

$(A + B)^3 = A^3 + 3A^2B + 3AB^2 + B^3$

$(A - B)^3 = A^3 - 3A^2B + 3AB^2 - B^3$

$A^3 + B^3 = (A + B)(A^2 - AB + B^2)$

$A^3 - B^3 = (A - B)(A^2 + AB + B^2)$,

$A^n - B^n = (A - B)(A^{n-1} + A^{n-2}B + A^{n-3}B^2 + \dots + AB^{n-2} + B^{n-1})$ where $n > 1$

$A^n + B^n = (A + B)(A^{n-1} - A^{n-2}B + A^{n-3}B^2 - \dots)$ where $n > 1$ and n is odd.

Examples:

$x^5 + y^5 = (x + y)(x^4 - x^3y + x^2y^2 - xy^3 + y^4)$ $x^5 - y^5 = (x - y)(x^4 + x^3y + x^2y^2 + xy^3 + y^4)$

Please note that the coefficients of the terms in $(x + y)^n$ are the same as the numbers in **Pascal's Triangle**.

$(x + y)^0 = 1$

$(x + y)^1 = x + y$

$(x + y)^2 = x^2 + 2xy + y^2$

$(x + y)^3 = x^3 + 3x^2y + 3xy^2 + y^3$

$(x + y)^4 = x^4 + 4x^3y + 6x^2y^2 + 4xy^3 + y^4$

$(x + y)^5 = x^5 + 5x^4y + 10x^3y^2 + 10x^2y^3 + 5xy^4 + y^5$

1

1x + 1y

1x² + 2xy + 1y²

1x³ + 3x²y + 3xy² + 1y³

1x⁴ + 4x³y + 6x²y² + 4xy³ + 1y⁴

1x⁵ + 5x⁴y + 10x³y² + 10x²y³ + 5xy⁴ + 1y⁵

Examples:

$(x + y)^3 = x^3 + 3x^2y + 3xy^2 + y^3$ $(x + y)^4 = x^4 + 4x^3y + 6x^2y^2 + 4xy^3 + y^4$

Please also note that when expanding $(x - y)^n$ the signs of terms should alternate.

$(x - y)^3 = x^3 - 3x^2y + 3xy^2 - y^3$ $(x - y)^4 = x^4 - 4x^3y + 6x^2y^2 - 4xy^3 + y^4$

Properties of Higher Degree Polynomial Functions

1. Polynomial functions are always continuous curves whose graphs can be drawn without your hand leaving the paper.

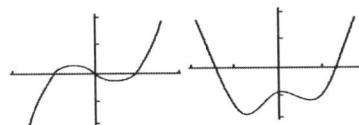

2. If the largest exponent is even (polynomial has an even degree), the both ends leave from top or from bottom; end behavior is the same at both ends.

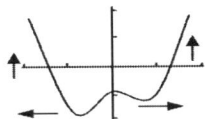

When x increases or decreases without bound, y increases without bound: $\lim_{x \to \pm\infty} f(x) = +\infty$.

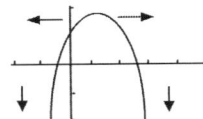

When x increases or decreases without bound, y decreases without bound: $\lim_{x \to \pm\infty} f(x) = -\infty$.

3. If the largest exponent is odd (polynomial has an odd degree), then the ends leave from opposite sides; end behavior is opposite at the ends.

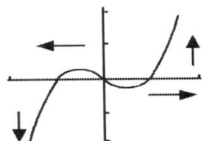

When x increases or decreases without bound, y either increases or decreases without bound: $\lim_{x \to \pm\infty} f(x) = \pm\infty$.

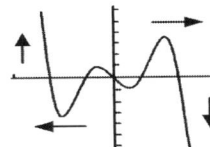

When x increases or decreases without bound, y either decreases or increases without bound: $\lim_{x \to \pm\infty} f(x) = \mp\infty$.

4. If all exponents are even, with or without a constant term $\Rightarrow$ polynomial is even.

Example: $P(x) = 3x^6 + 5x^4 - 3x^2$ or $Q(x) = 3x^6 + 5x^4 - 3x^2 + 1$; both P(x) and Q(x) are even.

5. If all exponents are odd and there is no constant term $\Rightarrow$ polynomial is odd.

    Example: $P(x) = 2x^5 + 5x^3 - 4x$ is odd; however $Q(x) = 2x^5 + 5x^3 - 4$ and $R(x) = 2x^5 + 5x^3 - 4x^2$ are neither odd nor even.

6. **Remainder theorem:** When $P(x)$ is divided by $(x - a)$, remainder is $P(a)$.

    $$
    \begin{array}{c|c}
    P(x) & x - a \\
    \hline
     & Q(x) \\
    \hline
    P(a) &
    \end{array}
    \qquad
    \begin{array}{r}
    Q(x) \\
    x-a \overline{)\; P(x)} \\
    \hline
    P(a)
    \end{array}
    $$

    $P(x) = (x - a)\cdot Q(x) + P(a)$

    For example, the remainder when the polynomial $P(x) = x^3 - 3x^2 + 5x - 6$ is divided by $x - 1$ is given by $P(1) = 1 - 3 + 5 - 6 = -3$.

7. **Factor theorem:** $P(a) = 0 \Leftrightarrow P(x) = (x - a)\, Q(x)$

    If $P(x)$ has a zero which is equal to **a**, it has a factor of **$(x - a)$** or vice – versa.

8. Every polynomial with a degree of n has exactly n zeros.

    Some can be real, some can be complex, some can be positive, some can be negative, some can be integers or rational or irrational, some can be the same and some can be different. However the total number of zeros is always n.

    Example: The sum and product of the zeros of $P(x) = (x - 2)^2 \cdot (x + 3)$:
    Sum of the zeros $= 2 + 2 - 3 = 1$; Product of the zeros $= 2 \cdot 2 \cdot (-3) = -12$.

    Example: The sum and product of the **distinct** zeros of $P(x) = (x - 2)^2 \cdot (x + 3)$:
    Sum of the zeros $= 2 - 3 = -1$; Product of the zeros $= 2 \cdot (-3) = -6$.

9. **Rational root theorem:** If $\dfrac{p}{q}$ is a rational zero of the polynomial $P(x) = a_n x^n + a_{n-1} x^{n-1} + \dots + a_1 x + a_0,$ reduced to its lowest terms, then p is a factor of a_0 and q is a factor of a_n. However; $\dfrac{p}{q}$ may or may not be a zero of $P(x)$.

    Example: $P(x) = 2x^3 + 13x^2 - 15kx + 6$; the possible rational zeros are: $\dfrac{p}{q}$ where p is a factor of 6: $\pm 1, \pm 2, \pm 3, \pm 6$ and q is a factor of 2: $\pm 1, \pm 2$. Therefore $\dfrac{p}{q} \Rightarrow \pm 1, \pm 2, \pm 3, \pm 6, \pm \dfrac{1}{2}, \pm \dfrac{3}{2}$, are all of the possible zeros. However it is also possible that none of the above appear as zeros.

10. **Irrational roots of a rational polynomial:** If $P(x)$ is a rational polynomial (a polynomial with rational coefficients) then irrational zeros appear in conjugate pairs.$\Rightarrow$ If $p + \sqrt{q}$ is a zero of $P(x)$ so is $p - \sqrt{q}$ or vice versa. For example if $3 + \sqrt{2}$ is a zero, $3 - \sqrt{2}$ is also a zero or vice versa. Therefore a rational polynomial has definitely an even number of irrational zeros.

11. **Conjugate roots theorem – complex roots of a real polynomial:** If $P(x)$ is a real polynomial (a polynomial with real coefficient) then complex (non – real) zeros appear in conjugate pairs. $\Rightarrow$ If $p + qi$ is a root so is $p - qi$ or vice versa where $i = \sqrt{-1}$. For example if $3 + 2i$ is a zero, $3 - 2i$ is also a zero or vice versa. Therefore a real polynomial has definitely an even number of complex zeros.

Degree of polynomial with real coefficients	Number of real zeros	Number of complex zeros
1	1	0
2	2	0
	0	2
3	3	0
	1	2
4	4	0
	2	2
	0	4
5	5	0
	3	2
	1	4

Observation 1: A polynomial with real coefficients and odd degree has at least one real root definitely.

Observation 2: A polynomial with real coefficients but no real zeros must have even degree.

12. **Relation between zeros & coefficients**

$P(x) = ax + b$ $\qquad\qquad x_1 = \dfrac{-b}{a}$ $\qquad\qquad\qquad (-)$

$P(x) = ax^2 + bx + c$ $\qquad x_1 + x_2 = \dfrac{-b}{a}$ $\qquad\qquad (-)$

$\qquad\qquad\qquad\qquad\qquad x_1 . x_2 = \dfrac{c}{a}$ $\qquad\qquad\quad (+)$

$P(x) = ax^3 + bx^2 + cx + d$ $\qquad x_1 + x_2 + x_3 = \dfrac{-b}{a}$ $\qquad (-)$

$\qquad\qquad\qquad\qquad\qquad x_1 x_2 + x_1 x_3 + x_2 x_3 = \dfrac{c}{a}$ $\qquad (+)$

$\qquad\qquad\qquad\qquad\qquad x_1 x_2 x_3 = \dfrac{-d}{a}$ $\qquad\qquad (-)$

$P(x) = ax^4 + bx^3 + cx^2 + dx + e$ $\qquad x_1 + x_2 + x_3 + x_4 = \dfrac{-b}{a}$ $\qquad (-)$

$\qquad\qquad\qquad\qquad\qquad x_1 x_2 + \ldots\ldots + x_3 x_4 = \dfrac{c}{a}$ $\qquad (+)$

$\qquad\qquad\qquad\qquad\qquad x_1 x_2 x_3 + \ldots + x_2 x_3 x_4 = \dfrac{-d}{a}$ $\qquad (-)$

$\qquad\qquad\qquad\qquad\qquad x_1 x_2 x_3 x_4 = \dfrac{e}{a}$ $\qquad\qquad (+)$

Example: If x_1, x_2 and x_3 are the roots of the equation $3x^3 + 5x^2 - 7x + 6 = 0$ then $\dfrac{1}{x_1} + \dfrac{1}{x_2} + \dfrac{1}{x_3} = ?$

Solution: $\dfrac{1}{x_1} + \dfrac{1}{x_2} + \dfrac{1}{x_3} = \dfrac{x_2 x_3 + x_1 x_3 + x_1 x_2}{x_1 x_2 x_3} = \dfrac{\dfrac{-7}{3}}{\dfrac{-6}{3}} = \dfrac{7}{6}$

13. **Descartes' Rule of Signs:**

Number of the positive real zeros of a real polynomial $P(x)$

= Number of sign changes in $P(x)$ – (an even number less)

Number of the negative real zeros of a real polynomial $P(x)$

= Number of sign changes in $P(-x)$ – (an even number less)

Example: How many positive or negative real zeros does the polynomial $P(x) = 18x^4 - bx^3 + 7x^2 + 8x - 5$ have where $b > 0$?

Solution: First order the terms in decreasing powers of x:

$$P(x) = +18x^4 \underbrace{-bx^3}_{1} \underbrace{+7x^2}_{2} \underbrace{+8x \quad -5}_{3}$$

3 sign changes exist in $P(x)$ therefore $P(x)$ has 3 or 1 positive real zeros

$$P(-x) = +18x^4 +bx^3 \quad +7x^2 \underbrace{+8x \quad -5}_{1}$$

1 sign change exists in $P(-x)$ therefore $P(x)$ has 1 negative real zero.

14. **Long Division:**

15. **Synthetic Division:** This method can be used while dividing a polynomial by a linear polynomial of the form $ax + b$.

Example: Divide $P(x) = 3x^5 + 2x^4 + 13x^2 - 7x - 10$ by $x + 2$. Find quotient and remainder.

Solution: $x + 2 = 0 \Rightarrow x = -2$

	3	2	0	13	-7	-10
-2		-6	8	-16	6	2
	3	-4	8	-3	-1	$-8 = P(-2) =$ Remainder of the division

$Q(x)$ is a polynomial with a degree 1 less than $P(x)$ as the degree of $(x + 2)$ is 1 and coefficients of $Q(x)$ are 3, -4, 8, -3, and -1. Therefore $Q(x) = 3x^4 - 4x^3 + 8x^2 - 3x - 1$.

Remainder is given by $R(x) = -8$

Example: Divide $P(x) = 3x^5 + 2x^4 + 13x^2 - 7x - 10$ by $3x + 6$. Find quotient and remainder.

Solution: Quotient changes; it is divided by the **3** of **$3x + 6$** $\Rightarrow Q(x) = \dfrac{3x^4 - 4x^3 + 8x^2 - 3x - 1}{3}$

Remainder does not change $\Rightarrow R(x) = -8$

16. When roots are given and equation is required; find the sum and the product of the roots, then construct the following equation: $x_1 + x_2 = S$; $x_1 . x_2 = P$; and $x^2 - Sx + P = 0$

   Example: Construct the real polynomial of lowest degree that has the roots of 2 and $2 - i$.

   Solution: $P(x) = (x - 2)Q(x)$ where $Q(x) = x^2 - Sx + P$.

   $S = 2 - i + 2 + i = 4$; $P = (2 - i)(2 + i) = 4 - i^2 = 4 - -1 = 5$

   $P(x) = (x - 2)(x^2 - 4x + 5) = x^3 - 6x^2 + 13x - 10$

17. **Sum of the coefficients** of $P(x) = P(1)$. When there are more variables than one variable, replace all variables by 1 to find the sum of the coefficients.

   Sum of the coefficients of the even degree terms in P(x) is $\dfrac{P(1) + P(-1)}{2}$.

   Sum of the coefficients of the odd degree terms in P(x) is $\dfrac{P(1) - P(-1)}{2}$.

18. **Constant term** of $P(x) = P(0)$. When there are more variables than one variable, replace all variables by 0 to find the constant term.

   Example: Find the sum of the coefficients and the constant term for each of the following expansions.

   a. $P(x) = (x^2 - 3x - 1)^{20}$

   b. $P(x, y) = (2x - 3y + 1)^{30}$

   Solution:

   a. Sum of the coefficients of $P(x) = P(1) = (1 - 3 - 1)^{20} = 3^{20}$; Constant term of $P(x)$ is $P(0) = (0 - 0 - 1)^{20} = 1$.

   b. Sum of the coefficients of $P(x, y) = P(1, 1) = (2 - 3 + 1)^{30} = 0$;

   Constant term of $P(x, y)$ is $P(0, 0) = (0 - 0 + 1)^{30} = 1$.

19.
$$
\begin{array}{r|l}
P(x) & D(x) \\
\hline
 & Q(x) \\
- & \\
\hline
R(x) &
\end{array}
\qquad
\begin{array}{r}
Q(x) \\
\hline
D(x) \overline{)\, P(x)} \\
- \\
\hline
R(x)
\end{array}
$$

   degree of $D(x) >$ degree of $R(x) \geq 0$

   degree of $P(x) =$ degree of $D(x) +$ degree of $Q(x)$

20. If two polynomials, $P(x)$ and $Q(x)$ are equal, then the coefficients of the same degree terms are equal on both polynomials.

   Example: If $(x - 2)(x^2 - cx + d) = x^3 - 5x^2 + ex + 4$ then $c + 2d - 3e = ?$

   Solution: $(x - 2)(x^2 - cx + d) = x^3 - cx^2 + dx - 2x^2 + 2cx - 2d = x^3 - (c + 2) x^2 + (d + 2c)x - 2d$

   $x^3 - (c + 2) x^2 + (d + 2c)x - 2d = x^3 - 5x^2 + ex + 4$

   $- 2d = 4$ so $d = -2$;

   $- c - 2 = -5$ so $c = 3$;

   $d + 2c = e$ so $e = -2 + 6 = 4$.

   Therefore $c + 2d - 3e = 3 - 4 - 12 = -13$.

21. For a polynomial function $P(x)$ if $P(a)$ and $P(b)$ have opposite signs then $P(x)$ definitely has a zero that is between a and b. For example for the polynomial function $P(x)$ if $P(-2) = 3$ and $P(4) = -7$ then $P(x)$ surely has a zero between $- 2$ and 4.

Constructing a polynomial from its graph

- When a polynomial has a **single zero**, it intersects the x axis as follows:

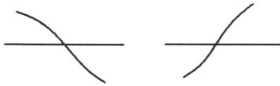

Single zero at x = a means that the polynomial has the factor of (x – a).

- When a polynomial has a **double zero**, it intersects the x axis as follows:

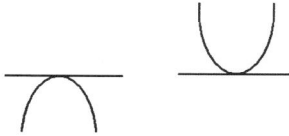

Double zero at x = a means that the polynomial has the factor of $(x - a)^2$.

- When a polynomial has a **triple zero**, it intersects the x axis as follows:

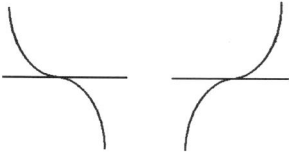

Triple zero at x = a means that the polynomial has the factor of $(x - a)^3$.

Example: Find the polynomial of lowest degree that gives each of the following graphs.

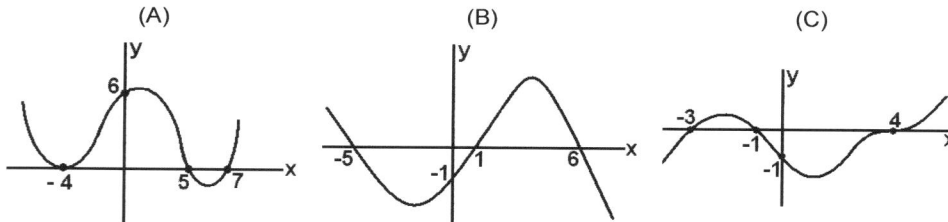

Solution:

(A) $P(x) = a \cdot (x + 4)^2(x - 5)(x - 7)$; $P(0) = 6 = a \cdot 16(-5)(-7) \Rightarrow a = 6/560$

(B) $P(x) = a \cdot (x + 5)(x - 1)(x - 6)$; $P(0) = -1 = a \cdot 5(-1)(-6) \Rightarrow a = -1/30$

(C) $P(x) = a \cdot (x + 3)(x + 1)(x - 4)^3$; $P(0) = -1 = a \cdot 3(1)(-4)^3 \Rightarrow a = 1/192$

1.10 TRIGONOMETRY

Definition of an Angle

Two rays emerging from the same point.

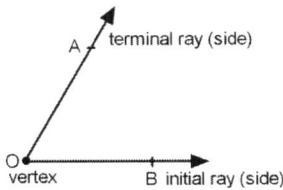

$\angle AOB = [OA \cup [OB$

Angle in standard position

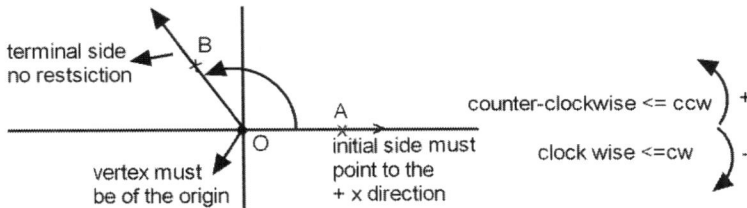

Point B is on the terminal side of angle AOB that is in standard position.

Circle Equation

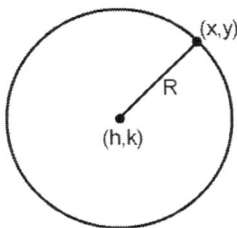

Circle is the locus of points that are equidistant (distance = radius = R) from a fixed point (center = (h, k)) in a plane.

$$R = \sqrt{(x-h)^2 + (y-k)^2} \Rightarrow (x-h)^2 + (y-k)^2 = R^2$$

If equation of the circle is given by $x^2 + y^2 + Dx + Ey + F = 0$ then the center and radius can be found by completing squares or by the following

formulas: center = $(-\dfrac{D}{2}, -\dfrac{E}{2})$; radius = $\dfrac{1}{2}\sqrt{D^2 + E^2 - 4F}$

Example: Find center and radius of the following circle: $x^2 - 6x + y^2 + 4y = 1$.

Solution:

$x^2 - 6x + 9 + y^2 + 4y + 4 = 1 + 9 + 4$

$(x - 3)^2 + (y + 2)^2 = 14 \Rightarrow$ Center C(3, −2); Radius = $\sqrt{14}$

Trigonometric Ratios in the Right Triangle

SOH – CAH – TOA

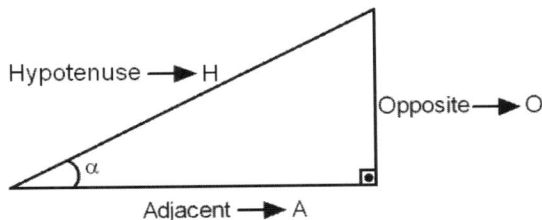

$$SOH : \sin\alpha = \frac{O}{H}$$

$$CAH : \cos\alpha = \frac{A}{H}$$

$$TOA : \tan\alpha = \frac{O}{A}$$

$$\cot\alpha = \frac{1}{\tan\alpha} = \frac{A}{O}$$

$$\sec\alpha = \frac{1}{\cos\alpha} = \frac{H}{A}$$

$$\csc\alpha = \frac{1}{\sin\alpha} = \frac{H}{O}$$

Reminders

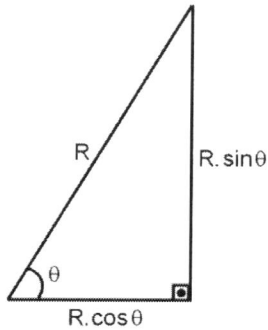

The **adjacent leg** has the length of **R·cos(θ)** whereas

the **opposite leg** has the length of **R·sin(θ)**.

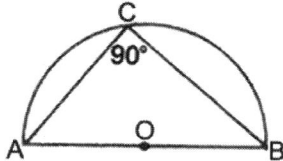

The angle ∠C that "sees" the diameter is 90°.

Angle of Elevation and Angle of Depression

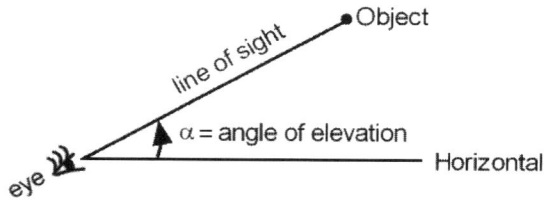

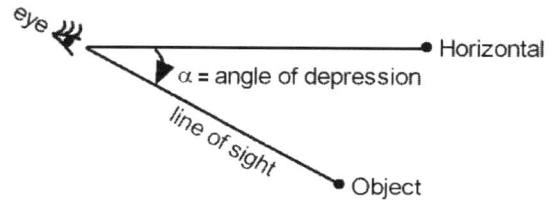

Example:

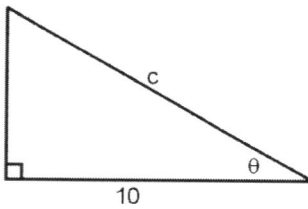

θ = 49°; c = ?

Solution:

$$\cos 49° = \frac{10}{c} \Rightarrow c = \frac{10}{\cos 49°} = 15.24$$

Example: From a plane flying at a height of 4000 feet, the angle of depression to a landmark on the ground is 55°. What is the horizontal distance the plane has to fly to be directly over the mark?

Solution:

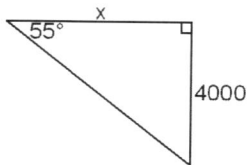

$$\tan 55° = \frac{4000}{x} \Rightarrow x = \frac{4000}{\tan 55°} = 2800.8$$

Unit Circle

$x^2 + y^2 = 1 \Rightarrow$ center $= (0,0)$ and radius $= R = 1$

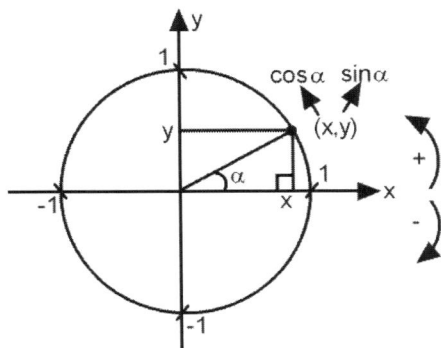

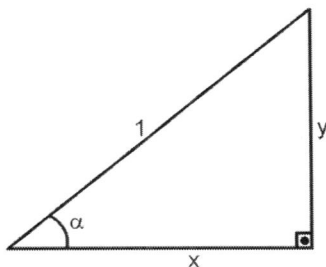

$$\sin\alpha = \frac{O}{H} = \frac{y}{1} = y$$

$$\cos\alpha = \frac{A}{H} = \frac{x}{1} = x$$

For every angle α on the unit circle, **x = cos α** and **y = sin α**, therefore:

- $x^2 + y^2 = 1 \Rightarrow \cos^2\alpha + \sin^2\alpha = 1$

- $-1 \le x \le 1 \Rightarrow -1 \le \cos\alpha \le 1$

- $-1 \le y \le 1 \Rightarrow -1 \le \sin\alpha \le 1$

Signs of Trigonometric Functions

SILVER				**ALL**
Sinx +			Sinx +	
Cosx −			Cosx +	
Tanx −	II	I	Tanx +	
Sinx −	III	IV	Sinx −	
Cosx −			Cosx +	
TEA	Tanx +		Tanx −	**C**UPS

Please note that:

tanx and **cotx** have the same sign;

cosx and **secx** have the same sign;

sinx and **cscx** have the same sign.

Special Angles

45°

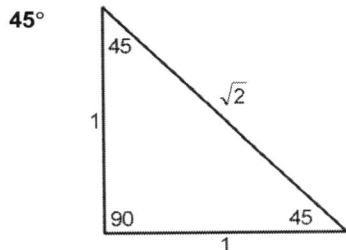

$$\sin 45^\circ = \frac{1}{\sqrt{2}} = \frac{\sqrt{2}}{2} = \cos 45^\circ$$

$$\tan 45^\circ = 1 = \cot 45^\circ$$

30° and 60°

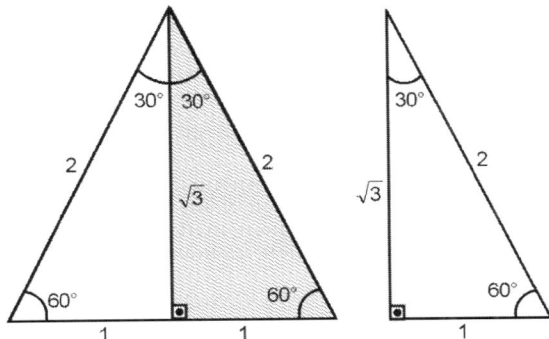

$$\sin 30^\circ = \frac{1}{2} = \cos 60^\circ$$

$$\cos 30^\circ = \frac{\sqrt{3}}{2} = \sin 60^\circ$$

$$\tan 30^\circ = \frac{1}{\sqrt{3}} = \frac{\sqrt{3}}{3} = \cot 60^\circ$$

$$\cot 30^\circ = \sqrt{3} = \tan 60^\circ$$

0°, 90°, 180°, 270°, 360°

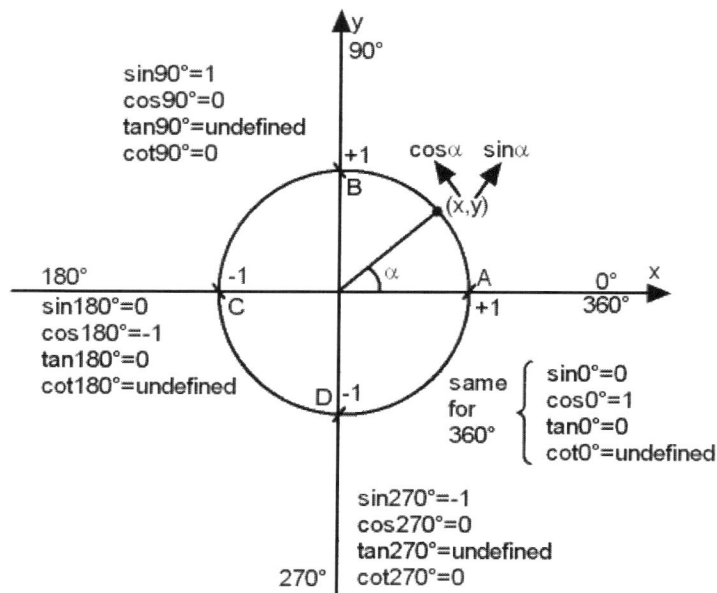

sin90°=1
cos90°=0
tan90°=undefined
cot90°=0

$x = \cos \alpha$

$y = \sin \alpha$

$\tan \alpha = \dfrac{\sin \alpha}{\cos \alpha} = \dfrac{y}{x}$

$\cot \alpha = \dfrac{\cos \alpha}{\sin \alpha} = \dfrac{x}{y}$

$\sec \alpha = \dfrac{1}{\cos \alpha} = \dfrac{1}{x}$

$\csc \alpha = \dfrac{1}{\sin \alpha} = \dfrac{1}{y}$

180°
sin180°=0
cos180°=-1
tan180°=0
cot180°=undefined

same for 360°

sin0°=0
cos0°=1
tan0°=0
cot0°=undefined

sin270°=-1
cos270°=0
tan270°=undefined
cot270°=0

Example: It is given that $\sin x = \dfrac{5}{13}$ where $90° \le x \le 180°$ and $\cos y = \dfrac{4}{9}$ where y is in 4'th quadrant. $\sin (x + y) = ?$

Solution: Angle Mode: Degrees

```
sin⁻¹(5/13
         22.61986495
180-Ans
         157.3801351
Ans→X
         157.3801351
```
```
cos⁻¹(4/9
         63.61220004
360-Ans
         296.3878
Ans→Y
         296.3878
```
```
sin(X+Y
         .9978384015
```

Answer: 0.9978

	0°	30°	45°	60°	90°
sin	$\dfrac{\sqrt{0}}{2} = 0$	$\dfrac{\sqrt{1}}{2} = \dfrac{1}{2}$	$\dfrac{\sqrt{2}}{2}$	$\dfrac{\sqrt{3}}{2}$	$\dfrac{\sqrt{4}}{2} = 1$
cos	1	$\dfrac{\sqrt{3}}{2}$	$\dfrac{\sqrt{2}}{2}$	$\dfrac{1}{2}$	0
tan	0	$\dfrac{1}{\sqrt{3}} = \dfrac{\sqrt{3}}{3}$	1	$\sqrt{3}$	undefined
cot	undefined	$\sqrt{3}$	1	$\dfrac{\sqrt{3}}{3}$	0

Please note the sequence

$\dfrac{\sqrt{0}}{2}, \dfrac{\sqrt{1}}{2}, \dfrac{\sqrt{2}}{2}, \dfrac{\sqrt{3}}{2}, \dfrac{\sqrt{4}}{2}$

Reverse the **sin** row to get the **cos** row.

Divide **sin** row by the **cos** row to get the **tan** row.

Reverse the **tan** row to get the **cot** row.

Radian and Degree

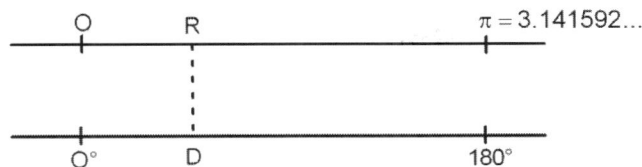

$$\pi = 3.141592...$$

$$\boxed{\dfrac{R}{\pi} = \dfrac{D}{180°}}$$

Degree to Radian Conversion: $D \cdot \dfrac{\pi}{180°} = R$

Radian to Degree Conversion: $R \cdot \dfrac{180°}{\pi} = D$

Example: $f(x) = e^x$; $g(x) = \cos x$; $(f \circ g)(\sqrt{3}) = ?$

Solution: Angle Mode: Radians

```
e^(cos(√(3
           .85166967
```

Answer: 0.85

Functions and Cofunctions

The function pairs, sinx and cosx; tanx and cotx; secx and cscx are cofunctions of each other.

Arc Length and Area of a Sector

l: length of arc $\overset{\frown}{AB}$

S: area of the minor sector AOB

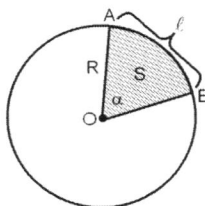

α in degrees:

$l = 2\pi R \cdot \dfrac{\alpha}{360°}$

$S = \pi R^2 \cdot \dfrac{\alpha}{360°}$

α in radians:

$l = 2\pi R \cdot \dfrac{\alpha}{2\pi} = R.\alpha \Rightarrow \boxed{l = R\,\alpha}$

$S = \pi R^2 \cdot \dfrac{\alpha}{2\pi} = \dfrac{1}{2}R^2.\alpha = \dfrac{1}{2}.R\alpha.R = \dfrac{1}{2}l.R$

$\Rightarrow \boxed{S = \dfrac{l.R}{2} = \dfrac{1}{2}.R^2\alpha}$

Trigonometric Identities

BASIC	ADVANCED
$tanx = \dfrac{sinx}{cosx}$ and $cotx = \dfrac{cosx}{sinx} \Rightarrow tanx \cdot cotx = 1 \Rightarrow tanx = \dfrac{1}{cotx}$ and $cotx = \dfrac{1}{tanx}$ $secx = \dfrac{1}{cosx}$ and $cscx = \dfrac{1}{sinx}$	$\sin^2 x + \cos^2 x = 1$ $1 + \tan^2 x = \sec^2 x$ $1 + \cot^2 x = \csc^2 x$

Reference Angle

The acute angle that the given angle makes with the x axis:

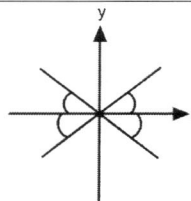

$\alpha = 30° \Rightarrow \alpha_{ref} = 30°$ $\alpha_{ref} = \alpha$	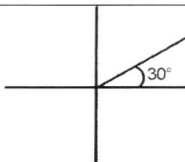	$\alpha = 155° \Rightarrow \alpha_{ref} = 25°$ $\alpha_{ref} = 180° - \alpha$	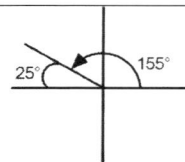
$\alpha = 215° \Rightarrow \alpha_{ref} = 35°$ $\alpha_{ref} = \alpha - 180°$	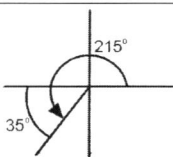	$\alpha = 340° \Rightarrow \alpha_{ref} = 20°$ $\alpha_{ref} = 360° - \alpha$	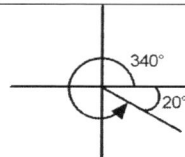

Common Transformations on Trigonometric Functions

Function	→ Function if π, 2π	
$\sin(\mp x \mp \pi)$	→ ? $\sin x$	
$\mp x \mp 2\pi$		
$\cos(\mp x \mp 2\pi)$	→ ? $\cos x$	
$\tan(\mp x \mp 2\pi)$	→ ? $\tan x$	
$\cot(\mp x \mp 2\pi)$	→ ? $\cot x$	
Function	→ **Cofunction if $\pi/2$, $3\pi/2$**	**?**: Means the sign, **+** or **−**. While determining sign:
$\sin(\mp x \mp \dfrac{\pi}{2})$	→ ? $\cos x$	• x must be assumed as an acute angle
$\mp x \mp \dfrac{3\pi}{2}$		• the given function (not the function that it is transformed to) and its region must be used in determining the sign.
$\cos(\mp x \mp \dfrac{\pi}{2})$	→ ? $\sin x$	
$\tan(\mp x \mp \dfrac{\pi}{2})$	→ ? $\cot x$	
$\cot(\mp x \mp \dfrac{\pi}{2})$	→ ? $\tan x$	

Special Cases

$\sin(-x) = -\sin x$

$\cos(-x) = \cos x$

$\tan(-x) = -\tan x$

$\cot(-x) = -\cot x$

$\cos(\pi - x) = -\cos x$

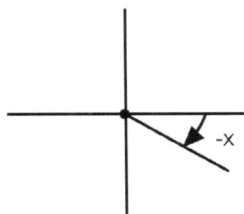

$-x \cong 2\pi - x$

$\sin\left(\dfrac{\pi}{2} - x\right) = \cos x$

$\cos\left(\dfrac{\pi}{2} - x\right) = \sin x$

$\tan\left(\dfrac{\pi}{2} - x\right) = \cot x$

$\cot\left(\dfrac{\pi}{2} - x\right) = \tan x$

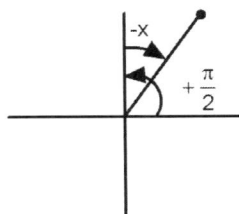

This means when $\alpha + \beta = 90°$

$\sin\alpha = \cos\beta$

$\tan\alpha = \cot\beta$

$\sec\alpha = \csc\beta$

Examples:

$\sin\left(\dfrac{\pi}{2} + x\right) = \cos x$	$\cot(\pi - x) = -\cot x$	$\tan(\pi + x) = \tan x$

Trigonometric Equations

- $\sin x = \sin\alpha \Rightarrow x = \alpha + k \cdot 2\pi$ OR $x = \pi - \alpha + k \cdot 2\pi$ (a direct result of the fact that $\sin(x) = \sin(\pi - x)$)

- $\cos x = \cos\alpha \Rightarrow x = \mp\alpha + k \cdot 2\pi$ (a direct result of the fact that $\cos(x) = \cos(-x)$)

- $\tan x = \tan\alpha$ or $\cot x = \cot\alpha \Rightarrow x = \alpha + k\pi$ (a direct result of the fact that period of the tangent and cotangent functions are each π)

Solving Trigonometric Equations with the TI

When solving a trigonometric equation in the form **f(x) = g(x),** perform the following steps:

i.   Write the equation in the form: **f(x) – g(x) = 0**.

ii.   While writing the trigonometric expressions please observe the rules given in parts 1.17 and 1.18 that involve the trigonometric functions that are built in TI or otherwise.

iii.   Plot the graph of **y = f(x) – g(x)**.

iv.   Set the **angle mode to radians or degrees** depending on which angle measure is used in the question. If no degree signs (like in 90°) are used then the mode should be radians. However when exact values are required you may wish to solve the equation in degrees and convert the answer to radians using the following formula $\dfrac{R}{\pi} = \dfrac{D}{180°}$. In such a case finding the answer in radians and then trying to find which answer choice matches this answer can also be an option; while doing so you may directly replace π with $180°$

v. If x is limited to a certain interval then set **Xmin**; **Xmax** and **Xscl** accordingly. For example, if x is an acute angle and the angle mode is degrees, then **Xmin** must be set to 0°; **Xmax** must be set to 90° and **Xscl** must be set so that the grids will be placed on the x – axis properly. In such a case **Xscl** being 30° would be fine. If x is an acute angle and the angle mode is radians, then **Xmin** must be set to 0; **Xmax** must be set to $\pi/2$ and **Xscl** may be set to 1.

vi. When only sines and cosines are involved, **ZoomFit** option may give a clearer graph. However, since only the x – intercepts are required, the window setting parameters **Ymin = –1** and **Ymax = 1** can give a clear view of the zeros.

vii. Find the x – intercepts using the **Calc Zero** of TI – 84 Plus. However when the graph seems to be tangent to the x – axis at a certain point, you may use the **Calc Min** or **Calc Max** facilities but you should make sure that the y – coordinate of the minimum or maximum point is zero.

viii. Any value like **–6.61E–10** or **7.2E–11** can be interpreted as 0 as they mean **–6.6x10^{-10}** and **7.2x10^{-11}** respectively.

Example: $\cos(2x) = 2\sin(90° - x)$. What are all possible values of x between 0° & 360°?

Solution: Mode: Degrees

$\cos(2x) - 2\sin(90° - x) = 0$

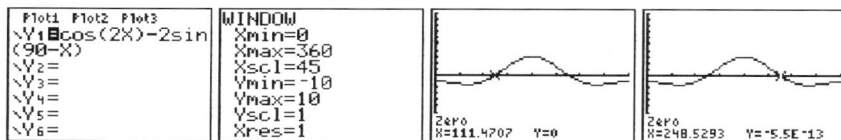

Answer: 111.47°, 248.53°

Example: $2\sin x + \cos(2x) = 2\sin^2 x - 1$ and $0 \leq x < 2\pi \Rightarrow x = ?$

Solution: Mode: Radians

$2\sin x + \cos(2x) - 2\sin^2 x + 1 = 0$

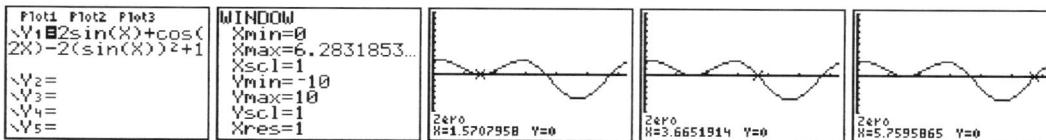

Answer: 1.57, 3.67, 5.76

Solving Trigonometric Inequalities with TI

When solving a trigonometric inequality in the form **f(x) < g(x), or f(x) ≤ g(x), or f(x) > g(x), or f(x) ≥ g(x)** perform the following steps:

i. Write the inequality in the form: **f(x) – g(x) < 0 or f(x) – g(x) ≤ 0 or f(x) – g(x) > 0 or f(x) – g(x) ≥ 0.**

ii. While writing the trigonometric expressions please observe the rules given in parts 1.17 and 1.18 that involve the trigonometric functions that are built in TI or otherwise.

iii. Plot the graph of **y = f(x) – g(x).**

iv. Set the **angle mode to radians or degrees** depending on which angle measure is used in the question. If no degree signs (like in 90°) are used then the mode should be radians. However when exact values are required you may wish to solve the equation in degrees and convert the answer to radians using the following formula $\dfrac{R}{\pi} = \dfrac{D}{180°}$. In such a case finding the answer in radians and then trying to find which answer choice matches this answer can also be an option; while doing so you may directly replace π with 180°

v. If x is limited to a certain interval then set **Xmin**; **Xmax** and **Xscl** accordingly. For example, if x is an acute angle and the angle mode is degrees, then **Xmin** must be set to 0°; **Xmax** must be set to 90° and **Xscl** must be set so that the grids will be placed on the x – axis properly. In such a case **Xscl** being 30° would be fine. If x is an acute angle and the angle mode is radians, then **Xmin** must be set to 0; **Xmax** must be set to $\pi/2$ and **Xscl** may be set to 1.

vi. When only sines and cosines are involved, **ZoomFit** option may give a clearer graph. However, since only the x – intercepts are required, the window setting parameters **Ymin = –1** and **Ymax = 1** can give a clear view of the zeros.

vii. Find the x – intercepts using the **Calc Zero** of TI – 84 Plus. However when the graph seems to be tangent to the x – axis at a certain point, you may use the **Calc Min** or **Calc Max** facilities but you should make sure that the y – coordinate of the minimum or maximum point is zero.

viii. Any value like **–6.61E–10** or **7.2E–11** can be interpreted as 0 as they mean **-6.6×10^{-10}** and **7.2×10^{-11}** respectively.

ix. The solution of the inequality will be the set of values of x for which the graph of f(x) – g(x) lies below the x axis if the inequality is in one of the forms **f(x) – g(x) < 0** or **f(x) – g(x) ≤ 0**. The solution of the inequality will be the set of values of x for which the graph of f(x) – g(x) lies above the x axis if the inequality is in one of the forms **f(x) – g(x) > 0** or **f(x) – g(x) ≥ 0**. If $\leq$ or $\geq$ symbols are involved, then the x – intercepts are also included within the solution set.

x. Please note that the x – values that correspond to asymptotes are never included in the solution set.

Example: sin(2x) > sinx

Find the set of values of x that satisfy the above inequality in the interval $0 < x < 2\pi$.

Solution: Mode: Radians and sin(2x) – sinx > 0

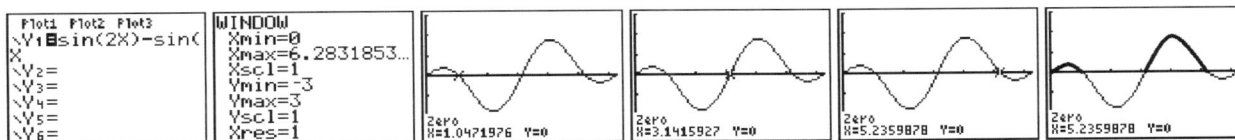

Answer: (0, 1.05) or (3.14, 5.24)

Example: Find the set of values of x that satisfy the inequality cos(2x) ≥ cosx in the interval $0 \leq x \leq 360°$.

Solution: Mode: Degrees and cos(2x) – cosx ≥ 0

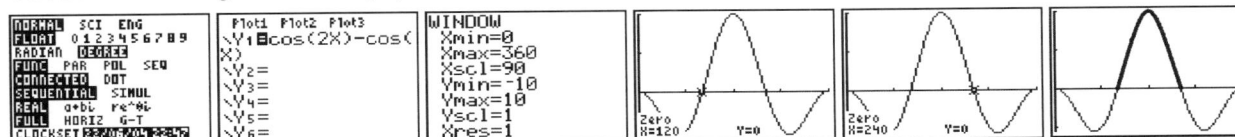

Answer: [120°, 240°] or {0°, 360°}

Sum and Difference Formulas

$\sin(x \mp y) = \sin x \cos y \mp \cos x \sin y$ (same sign)

$\cos(x \mp y) = \cos x \cos y \pm \sin x \sin y$ (opposite sign)

$$\tan(x + y) = \frac{\tan x + \tan y}{1 - \tan x \tan y} \qquad \cot(x + y) = \frac{\cot x \cot y - 1}{\cot x + \cot y}$$

$$\tan(x - y) = \frac{\tan x - \tan y}{1 + \tan x \tan y} \qquad \cot(x - y) = \frac{-\cot x \cot y - 1}{\cot x - \cot y}$$

Double Angle Formulas

$$\sin(2x) = 2 \cdot \sin x \cdot \cos x$$

$$\cos(2x) = \cos^2 x - \sin^2 x$$
$$= 1 - 2 \cdot \sin^2 x$$
$$= 2 \cdot \cos^2 x - 1$$

$$\tan(2x) = \frac{2 \tan x}{1 - \tan^2 x}$$

$$\cot(2x) = \frac{\cot^2 x - 1}{2 \cot x}$$

Sine Rule

When

(i)   two sides and an angle opposite one of them are given or

(ii)   two angles and a side opposite one of them are given;

use the sine rule to find the other sides and angles. Please note that due to the identity **sin(180° − x) = sin(x)** there may be degenerate cases when there are two triangles that satisfy the given conditions. Moreover, the triangle inequality requires that opposite a large angle lies the opposite side or vice versa; this has to hold in every case.

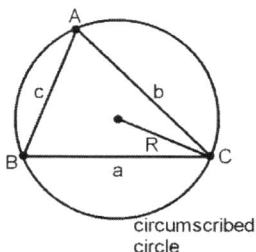
circumscribed circle

$$\frac{a}{\sin \hat{A}} = \frac{b}{\sin \hat{B}} = \frac{c}{\sin \hat{C}} = 2R$$

Please note that **R** is the radius of the circumscribed circle.

Cosine Rule

(i)   When three sides are given and an angle opposite one of them is to be calculated, or

(ii)   when two sides and the angle between them are given and the side opposite the given angle is to be calculated; use the cosine rule.

It may be necessary to note that: **cos(180° − x) = −cos(x)**

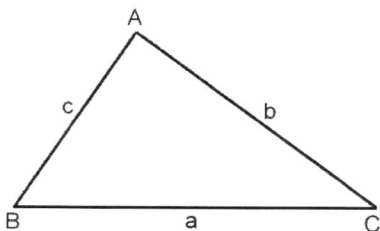

$$a^2 = b^2 + c^2 - 2bc \cdot \cos \hat{A}$$

$$b^2 = a^2 + c^2 - 2ac \cdot \cos \hat{B}$$

$$c^2 = a^2 + b^2 - 2ab \cdot \cos \hat{C}$$

Area of a Triangle

$$\text{Area} = \frac{1}{2} bc \sin \hat{A} = \frac{1}{2} ac \sin \hat{B} = \frac{1}{2} ab \sin \hat{C} : \text{Use when two sides and the angle between them are given in a triangle.}$$

$$\text{Area} = \sqrt{u(u-a)(u-b)(u-c)} \quad \text{where} \quad u = \frac{a+b+c}{2} \quad \text{is the semi} - \text{perimeter: Use when all three sides of a triangle are given.}$$

Example:

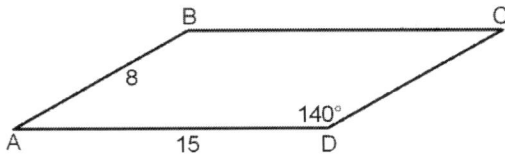

Find area of the parallelogram ABCD given in figure

Solution:

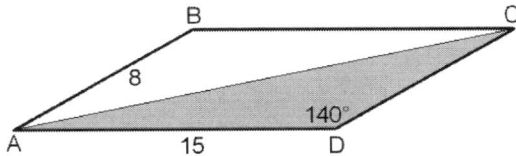

Area of parallelogram is twice the area of the shaded region and it is given by

$$2 \cdot \frac{1}{2} \cdot 8 \cdot 15 \cdot \sin 140° = 77.13$$

Example:

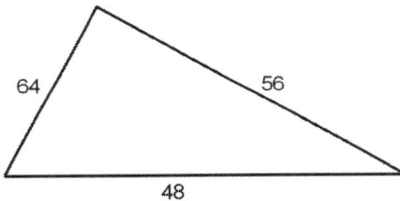

Largest angle = ?

Area of the triangle = ?

Radius of the circumscribed circle = ?

Solution: Largest angle is opposite 64 and it is denoted by x as it is given in the following figure: You should use cosine rule to find this angle.

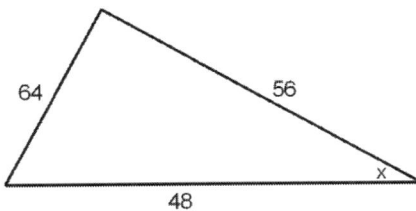
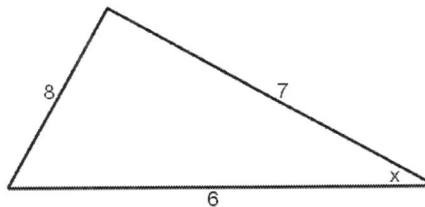

However, if two triangles are similar, then the corresponding angle measures are the same. So for simplicity you can reduce each side by the greatest common factor and find the angle in the simplified triangle that will give smaller numbers easier to manipulate.

$$8^2 = 7^2 + 6^2 - 2 \cdot 7 \cdot 6 \cdot \cos x \Rightarrow \cos x = 0.25 \Rightarrow x = 75.5°$$

Area of the triangle is: $\frac{1}{2} \cdot 56 \cdot 48 \cdot \sin 75.5 = 1301.32$

If R = radius of the circumscribed triangle then $\frac{64}{\sin x} = \frac{64}{\sin 75.5°} = 2R$ and R = 33.05.

Domains and Ranges of Trigonometric Functions

Function	Domain	Range	Period
sinx cosx	R	$-1 \le y \le 1$	2π
tanx	$R - \left\{ \mp\dfrac{\pi}{2}, \mp\dfrac{3\pi}{2}, \mp\dfrac{5\pi}{2}, ... \right\} = R - \left\{ \mp(2k+1)\dfrac{\pi}{2} \mid k = \text{integer} \right\}$ All real numbers except for the odd multiples of $\dfrac{\pi}{2}$.	R	π
cotx	$R - \left\{ 0, \mp\pi, \mp2\pi, \mp3\pi, ... \right\} = R - \left\{ \pi k \mid k = \text{integer} \right\}$ All real numbers except for the integer multiples of π.	R	π
secx	Same as tanx	$y \le -1$ or $y \ge 1$	2π
cscx	Same as cotx	$y \le -1$ or $y \ge 1$	2π

Even and Odd Trigonometric Functions

f(−x) = −f(x):	**odd**	**f(−x) = f(x):**	**even**
sin(−x) = −sinx	odd	cos(−x) = cosx	even
tan(−x) = −tanx	odd	sec(−x) = secx	even
cot(−x) = −cotx	odd		
csc(−x) = −cscx	odd		

Graphs of Trigonometric Functions

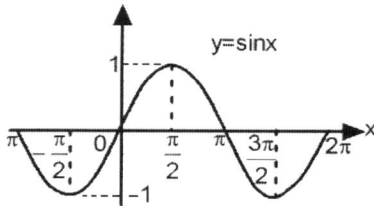

Domain: $-\infty < x < \infty$
Range: $-1 \le y \le 1$
Period: 2π

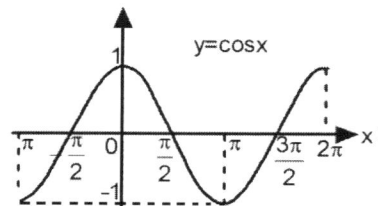

Domain: $-\infty < x < \infty$
Range: $-1 \le y \le 1$
Period: 2π

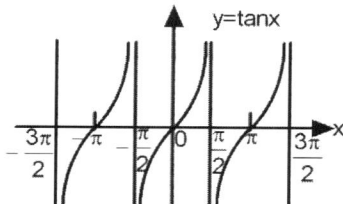

Domain: $x \ne \pm\dfrac{\pi}{2}, \pm\dfrac{3\pi}{2}, ...$
Range: $-\infty < y < \infty$
Period: π

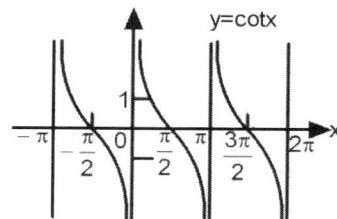

Domain: $x \ne 0, \pm\pi, \pm2\pi, ...$
Range: $-\infty < y < \infty$
Period: π

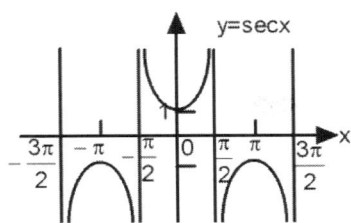

$y=\sec x$

Domain: $x \neq \pm\dfrac{\pi}{2}, \pm\dfrac{3\pi}{2}, \ldots$

Range: $y \leq -1$ or $y \geq 1$

Period: 2π

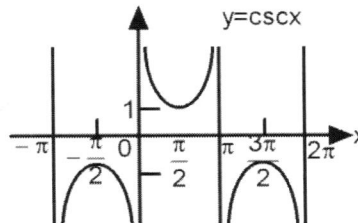

$y=\csc x$

Domain: $x \neq 0, \pm\pi, \pm 2\pi, \ldots$

Range: $y \leq -1$ or $y \geq 1$

Period: 2π

Periodicity

If there exists a positive real number P such that f(x + P) = f(x); then f(x) is called a periodic function and the smallest possible value of P is called the period of f(x).

$\sin(x + 2\pi) = \sin x$ $\qquad$ $\tan(x + \pi) = \tan x$ $\qquad$ $\sec(x + 2\pi) = \sec x$

$\cos(x + 2\pi) = \cos x$ $\qquad$ $\cot(x + \pi) = \cot x$ $\qquad$ $\csc(x + 2\pi) = \csc x$

sin(x), cos(x), sec(x) and csc(x) are periodic with P = 2π; tan(x) and cot(x) are periodic with P = π.

Odd powers of sine and cosine: $\sin^{2n+1}(Ax + B)$ or $\cos^{2n+1}(Ax + B) \Rightarrow P = \dfrac{2\pi}{|A|}$

Even powers of sine and cosine: $\sin^{2n}(Ax + B)$ or $\cos^{2n}(Ax + B) \Rightarrow P = \dfrac{\pi}{|A|}$

All powers of tangent and cotangent: $\tan^{n}(Ax + B)$ or $\cot^{n}(Ax + B) \Rightarrow P = \dfrac{\pi}{|A|}$

If there are more than one periodic functions that are added up, the common period is found by taking the LCM (Least Common Multiple) of the individual periods. If some of the individual periods are fractions then, their LCM is found by first reducing each of them into its lowest terms and then by taking the LCM of only the numerators of the individual periods.

Finding a Trigonometric Model

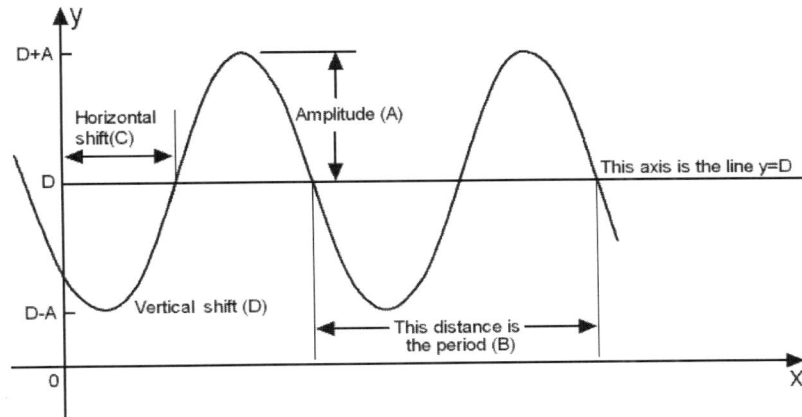

$$f(x) = A \sin\left[\dfrac{2\pi}{|B|}(x - C)\right] + D \quad \text{where}$$

- $|A|$ = **Amplitude** = $\dfrac{y_{max} - y_{min}}{2}$. If the function is upside down then A will be negative.

- $|B|$ = **Period**; **Frequency** = $\dfrac{1}{\text{Period}}$

- C = **Phase Shift** (horizontal shift)

  If positive, indicates rightward shift for $|C|$ units; if negative indicates leftward shift for $|C|$ units.

  For a function f(Bx + C) where f is a trigonometric function, phase shift = $-\dfrac{C}{B}$

  (if positive, indicates rightward shift and if negative indicates leftward shift).

- D = **Offset** = $\dfrac{y_{max} + y_{min}}{2}$, offset is the vertical shift.

- **Axis of wave** is the line given by y = D.

- **Range**: $y_{min} \le y \le y_{max}$

Please also note that: For a trigonometric function given by f(x) = A · sin(Bx + C) + D or f(x) = A · cos(Bx + C) + D

- If A is changed then **amplitude** will be changed. (narrower or wider vertically)

- If B is changed then **period**, **frequency** and **phase shift** will be changed. (narrower or wider horizontally).

- If **phase shift** should remain the same, then both B and C should be changed.

- If C is changed then **phase shift** (or **horizontal shift**) will be changed. (rightward – leftward shifts)

- If D is changed then **offset** (or **vertical shift**) will be changed (upward – downward shifts)

Example: y = 2 cos^3(3x – 5) + 4

Offset is 4 units up

Axis of wave is y = 4

Amplitude = $|2|$ = 2

Phase shift = $\dfrac{-\,-5}{3} = \dfrac{5}{3} \Rightarrow$ Rightward shift for $\dfrac{5}{3}$ units.

Period = $\dfrac{2\pi}{|3|} = \dfrac{2\pi}{3}$

Frequency = $\dfrac{3}{2\pi}$

Inverse Trigonometric Functions

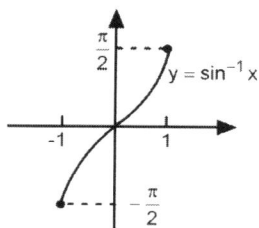

Domain : $-1 \le x \le 1$

Range : $-\dfrac{\pi}{2} \le y \le \dfrac{\pi}{2}$

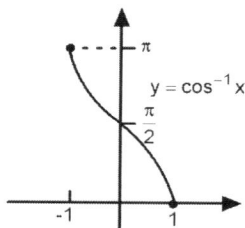

Domain : $-1 \le x \le 1$

Range : $0 \le y \le \pi$

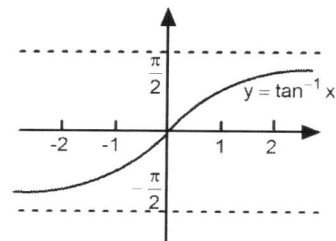

Domain : $-\infty < x < \infty$

Range : $-\dfrac{\pi}{2} < y < \dfrac{\pi}{2}$

Domain : $x \leq -1$ or $x \geq 1$

Range : $0 \leq y \leq \pi, y \neq \dfrac{\pi}{2}$

Domain : $-\infty < x < \infty$

Range : $0 < y < \pi$

Domain : $x \leq -1$ or $x \geq 1$

Range : $-\dfrac{\pi}{2} \leq y \leq \dfrac{\pi}{2}, y \neq 0$

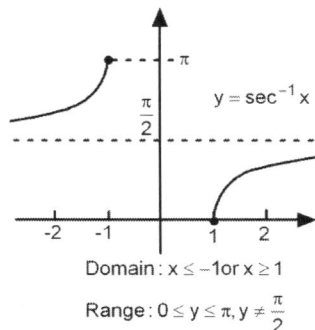

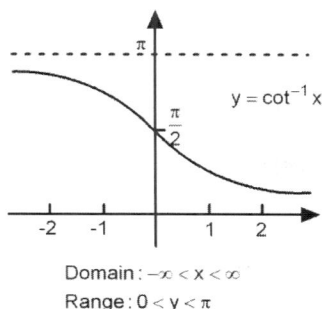

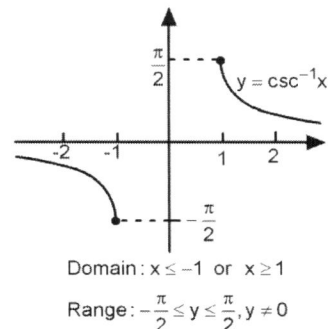

Domains and Ranges of Inverse Trigonometric Functions

Function	Domain	Range
$\sin^{-1}(x) = \text{Arcsin}(x)$	$-1 \leq x \leq 1$ $|x| \leq 1$	$-\dfrac{\pi}{2} \leq y \leq \dfrac{\pi}{2}$ $|y| \leq \dfrac{\pi}{2}$
$\cos^{-1}(x) = \text{Arccos}x$	$-1 \leq x \leq 1$	$0 \leq y \leq \pi$
$\tan^{-1}(x) = \text{Arctan}(x)$	R	$-\dfrac{\pi}{2} < y < \dfrac{\pi}{2}$ $|y| < \dfrac{\pi}{2}$
$\cot^{-1}(x) = \text{Arccot}(x)$	R	$0 < y < \pi$
$\sec^{-1}(x) = \text{Arcsec}(x)$	$x \leq -1$ or $x \geq 1$ $|x| \geq 1$	$0 \leq y \leq \pi$ $y \neq \dfrac{\pi}{2}$
$\csc^{-1}(x) = \text{Arccsc}(x)$	$x \leq -1$ or $x \geq 1$ $|x| \geq 1$	$\dfrac{-\pi}{2} \leq y \leq \dfrac{\pi}{2}$ $y \neq 0$

Please note the following:

- $\cot x = \dfrac{1}{\tan x}$ however $\cot^{-1}(x) \neq \dfrac{1}{\tan^{-1}(x)}$
- $\sec x = \dfrac{1}{\cos x}$ however $\sec^{-1}(x) \neq \dfrac{1}{\cos^{-1}(x)}$
- $\csc x = \dfrac{1}{\sin x}$ however $\csc^{-1}(x) \neq \dfrac{1}{\cos^{-1}(x)}$
- $\cot^{-1}(x) = \tan^{-1}(\dfrac{1}{x})$ is correct if and only if x is positive
- $\cot^{-1}(x) = \dfrac{\pi}{2} - \tan^{-1}(x)$ (in radians)
- $\cot^{-1}(x) = 90° - \tan^{-1}(x)$ (in degrees)
- $\sec^{-1}(x) = \cos^{-1}\left(\dfrac{1}{x}\right)$
- $\csc^{-1}(x) = \sin^{-1}\left(\dfrac{1}{x}\right)$

Solving Inverse Trigonometric Equations with TI

When solving an inverse trigonometric equation in the form **f(x) = g(x),** perform the following steps:

i. Write the equation in the form: **f(x) – g(x) = 0**.

ii. While writing the trigonometric expressions please observe the rules given in parts 1.17 and 1.18 that involve the trigonometric functions that are built in TI or otherwise.

iii. Plot the graph of **y = f(x) – g(x)**.

iv. Set the **angle mode to radians or degrees** depending on which angle measure is used in the question. If no degree signs (like in 90°) are used then the mode should be radians. However when exact values are required you may wish to solve the equation in degrees and convert the answer to radians using the following formula $\dfrac{R}{\pi} = \dfrac{D}{180°}$. In such a case finding the answer in radians and then trying to find which answer choice matches this answer can also be an option; while doing so you may directly replace π with 180°

v. Find the x – intercepts using the **Calc Zero** of TI – 84 Plus. However when the graph seems to be tangent to the x – axis at a certain point, you may use the **Calc Min** or **Calc Max** facilities but you should make sure that the y – coordinate of the minimum or maximum point is zero.

vi. Any value like **–6.61E–10** or **7.2E–11** can be interpreted as 0 as they mean **–6.6x10^{-10}** and **7.2x10^{-11}** respectively.

Example: Solve for x: $\cos^{-1}(2x - 2x^2) = \dfrac{2\pi}{3}$

Solution: Angle Mode: Radians

$$\cos^{-1}(2x - 2x^2) - \dfrac{2\pi}{3} = 0$$

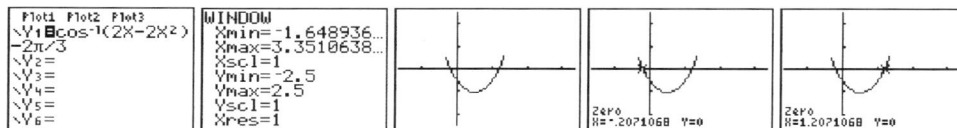

Answer: -0.207 or 1.207

Example: $\cos\left(\text{Arcsin}\ \dfrac{-4}{5}\ +\ \text{Arccos}\ \dfrac{12}{13}\right) = ?$

Solution:

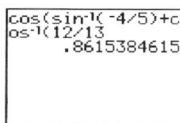

Answer: 0.86

Built in Trigonometric Functions in TI

FUNCTION	DESCRIPTION	ABBREVIATION
sin(	Sine function	
cos(	Cosine function	
tan(	Tangent function	
$\sin^{-1}($	Arcsine or sine inverse function	Arcsin
$\cos^{-1}($	Arccosine or cosine inverse function	Arccos
$\tan^{-1}($	Arctangent or tangent inverse function	Arctan

Additional Trigonometric Functions with TI

WHEN YOU NEED	USE THE FOLLOWING DEFINITION	WARNING
sec(x)	1 / cos(x)	
csc(x)	1 / sin(x)	
cot(x)	cos(x) / sin(x)	Although mathematically correct, DO NOT USE 1 / tan(x) for cot(x) because when tan(x) is undefined, TI will interpret 1 / tan(x) as undefined, too, which is not correct.
$\sec^{-1}(x)$	$\cos^{-1}(1/x)$	Do NOT use 1 / $\cos^{-1}(x)$, mathematically incorrect.
$\csc^{-1}(x)$	$\sin^{-1}(1/x)$	Do NOT use 1 / $\sin^{-1}(x)$, mathematically incorrect.
$\cot^{-1}(x)$	$\pi/2 - \tan^{-1}(x)$ if in radians $90° - \tan^{-1}(x)$ if in degrees	Do NOT use 1 / $\tan^{-1}(x)$, mathematically incorrect.

1.11 EXPONENTIAL AND LOGARITHMIC FUNCTIONS

Exponents

1. $x^a \cdot x^b = x^{a+b}$ and $\dfrac{x^a}{x^b} = x^{a-b}$

2. $(x^a)^b = x^{ab}$

3. $x^a \cdot y^a = (xy)^a$ and $\dfrac{x^a}{y^a} = \left(\dfrac{x}{y}\right)^a$

4. $x^0 = 1$ where $x \neq 0$; $x^1 = x$; $x - 1 = \dfrac{1}{x}$

5. $x^{\frac{a}{b}} = \sqrt[b]{x^a}$

6. $\sqrt{x^2} = |x|$ and $\sqrt[2n]{x^{2n}} = |x|$

    Please note that $\sqrt{9} = +3$ however the solution of $x^2 = 9$ is ± 3 and that these two cases should not be mixed up.

7. $\sqrt[3]{x^3} = x$ and $\sqrt[2n+1]{x^{2n+1}} = x$

8. $f(a)\,f(b) = f(a+b)$; $\dfrac{f(a)}{f(b)} = f(a-b)$; $f(a)^n = f(an)$

    All of the above can be satisfied by a function defined as $f(x) = c^x$.

9. If $a^x = a^y$ then one of the following conditions holds:

    * $a = 1 \Rightarrow x$ and y are any real numbers.
    * $a = -1 \Rightarrow x$ and y are both odd or both even.
    * $a = 0 \Rightarrow x$ and y are both positive.
    * $a \notin \{1, -1, 0\} \Rightarrow x = y$

10. If $a^x = b^x$ and x is an integer then one of the following conditions holds:

    * $x = 0 \Rightarrow a$ and b are any nonzero real numbers
    * $x = \text{even} \Rightarrow |a| = |b|$
    * $x = \text{odd} \Rightarrow a = b$

Exponential Growth

$A = B \cdot (1+r)^t$ or $A = B.e^{rt}$

Exponential Decay

$A = B \cdot (1-r)^t$ or $A = B \cdot e^{-rt}$

where

B: Initial amount

A: Final amount

r: Growth or Decay rate as a decimal

t: number of periods of Growth or Decay

Example: Population Growth

At the beginning of 2000, the population of a certain city was 1,096,250. If the population increases at the rate 2.5 percent each year, what will the population of the city be at the end of 2004?

Solution: $A = 1{,}096{,}250 \cdot \left(1 + \dfrac{2.5}{100}\right)^5 = 1{,}240{,}306$

Example: Compound Interest

1000$ is invested for 2 years in a bank that pays 8% interest each year. Find the total interest earned if the investment is compounded

a. yearly.

b. semi – annually.

c. quarterly.

d. monthly.

e. weekly (1 year = 52 weeks).

f. daily (1 year = 365 days).

g. continuously.

Solution:

a. $1000 \cdot (1 + 0.08)^2 = 1,166.4$

b. $1000 \cdot \left(1 + \dfrac{0.08}{2}\right)^4 = 1,169.9$

c. $1000 \cdot \left(1 + \dfrac{0.08}{4}\right)^8 = 1,171.7$

d. $1000 \cdot \left(1 + \dfrac{0.08}{12}\right)^{24} = 1,172.9$

e. $1000 \cdot \left(1 + \dfrac{0.08}{52}\right)^{104} = 1,173.4$

f. $1000 \cdot \left(1 + \dfrac{0.08}{365}\right)^{730} = 1,173.5$

g. $1000 \cdot e^{0.08 \cdot 2} = 1,173.5$

Example: If a certain car now worth $45,000 decreases in value at the rate of 8 percent per year, how much will it be worth 3 years from now?

Solution: $45,000 \cdot (1 - 0.08)^3 = 35,041$

Properties of Logarithms

1. $\log_a b = x \Rightarrow a^x = b$

2. $\log_{10} x = \log x;\ \log_e x = \ln x$

3. $\log_a a = 1;\ \log 10 = 1;\ \ln(e) = 1$

   $\log_a 1 = 0;\ \log 1 = 0;\ \ln(1) = 0$

4. $\log_a(xy) = \log_a x + \log_a y$

5. $\log_a\left(\dfrac{x}{y}\right) = \log_a x - \log_a y$

6. $\log_{a^x}(b^y) = \dfrac{y}{x}\log_a b$

7. $e = \lim\limits_{n \to \infty}\left(1 + \dfrac{1}{n}\right)^n$

8. $\log_a b = \dfrac{\log_x b}{\log_x a} = \dfrac{\log\ b}{\log\ a} = \dfrac{\log_{10} b}{\log_{10} a} = \dfrac{\ln b}{\ln a} = \dfrac{\log_e b}{\log_e a}$

   $\log_3 7 = \dfrac{\ln 7}{\ln 3} = \dfrac{\log(7)}{\log(3)}$ (for the logarithms with respect to different bases than 10 and e via the calculator)

9. $a^{\log_a b} = b;\ 10^{\log b} = b;\ e^{\ln(b)} = b$

   $3^{\log_3 9} = 9;\ 10^{\log 9} = 9;\ e^{\ln 9} = 9$

10. $f(ab) = f(a) + f(b);\ f\left(\dfrac{a}{b}\right) = f(a) - f(b);\ f(a^n) = n \cdot f(a)$

    All of the above can be satisfied by a function defined as $f(x) = \log_c x$.

11. The logarithm (base 10) of a positive number can be expressed as the sum of an integer (called the characteristic) and the log of a number (called the mantissa) between 1 and 0. The characteristic, when it is positive, is 1 less than the number of digits before the decimal point of the given number.

12. $f(x) = a^x \Leftrightarrow f^{-1}(x) = \log_a x$

$f(x) = 10^x \Leftrightarrow f^{-1}(x) = \log_{10} x = \log x$

$f(x) = e^x \Leftrightarrow f^{-1}(x) = \log_e x = \ln x$

Logarithmic Inequalities

$\log_a x < \log_a y$ implies that

Case 1: If $a > 1$ $\Rightarrow$ $0 < x < y$

Case 2: If $0 < a < 1$ $\Rightarrow$ $x > y > 0$

Domain of Logarithms

$y = \log_{A(x)} B(x)$

Domain: $A(x) > 0$, $A(x) \neq 1$, $B(x) > 0$

Example: $\log_{36} 6 - \log_3 27 + \log_2 (0.25)^{1/3} = ?$

Solution:

$$\log_{36} 6 - \log_3 27 + \log_2 (0.25)^{1/3} = \log_{6^2} 6 - \log_3 3^3 + \log_2 \left(2^{-2}\right)^{\frac{1}{3}} = \log_{6^2} 6 - \log_3 3^3 + \log_2 \left(2^{-\frac{2}{3}}\right) = \frac{1}{2} - 3 - \frac{2}{3} = -\frac{19}{6}$$

Example: $2^{x+3} = 3^x \Rightarrow x = ?$

Solution: $2^{x+3} - 3^x = 0$; we would like to find the zero of the function $y = 2^{x+3} - 3^x$

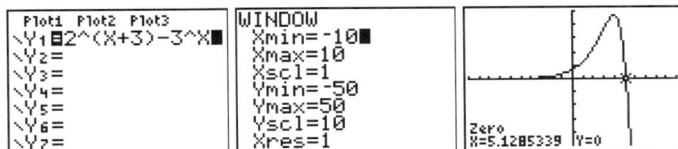

Answer: 5.13

Example: $e^{-x} - e^x = 2 \Rightarrow x = ?$

Solution: $e^{-x} - e^x - 2 = 0$; we would like to find the zero of the function $y = e^{-x} - e^x - 2$

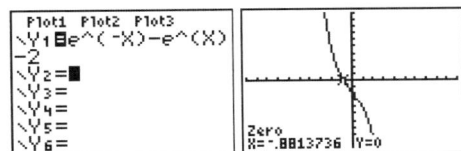

Answer: -0.88

Example: $\log(\sin 2) + \log(\sin 20) + \log(\sin 20°) = ?$

Solution:

The following calculation is carried out in the radian mode of TI 84.

The following calculation is carried out in the degree mode of TI 84.

Answer: $-0.808493 - 0.4659483 \approx -0.547$

Inverses of Exponential and Logarithmic Functions

Example: Find the inverse of $f(x) = 3 \cdot 2^{x+1}$

Solution:

$f(x) = 3 \cdot 2^{x+1} \Rightarrow y = 3 \cdot 2^{x+1}$

$x = 3 \cdot 2^{y+1} \Rightarrow \dfrac{x}{3} = 2^{y+1} \Rightarrow \log\dfrac{x}{3} = \log 2^{y+1} \Rightarrow \log\dfrac{x}{3} = (y+1)\log 2$

$y + 1 = \dfrac{\log\dfrac{x}{3}}{\log 2} = \log_2\left(\dfrac{x}{3}\right) \Rightarrow y = \log_2\left(\dfrac{x}{3}\right) - 1$

$f^{-1}(x) = \log_2\left(\dfrac{x}{3}\right) - 1$

Example: Find the inverse of $f(x) = 4\ln(x + 2)$

Solution:

$f(x) = 4\ln(x + 2) \Rightarrow y = 4\ln(x + 2)$

$x = 4\ln(y + 2) \Rightarrow \dfrac{x}{4} = \ln(y + 2)$

$y + 2 = e^{\frac{x}{4}} \Rightarrow y = e^{\frac{x}{4}} - 2 \Rightarrow f^{-1}(x) = e^{\frac{x}{4}} - 2$

Example: What is the approximate value of $\log_3 8$ correct to the nearest hundredth?

Solution: $\log_3 8 = \dfrac{\log 8}{\log 3} = 1.89$

Example: How many digits does the number 777^{777} have?

Solution: $\log 777^{777} = 777 \cdot \log 777 = 2245.85 \Rightarrow$ Therefore 777^{777} has 2246 digits.

Example: $\log 2 = A$ and $\log 3 = B$. In terms of A and B calculate the following:

a. $\log\left(\dfrac{20}{9}\right)$

b. $\log(3.6)$

Solution:

a. $\log\left(\dfrac{20}{9}\right) = \log\left(\dfrac{10 \cdot 2}{3^2}\right) = \log 10 + \log 2 - \log 3^2 = \log 10 + \log 2 - 2\log 3 = 1 + A - 2B$

b. $\log(3.6) = \log\dfrac{36}{10} = \log\dfrac{2^2 \cdot 3^2}{10} = \log 2^2 + \log 3^2 - \log 10 = 2\log 2 + 2\log 3 - \log 10 = 2A + 2B - 1$

1.12 RATIONAL FUNCTIONS

A rational function f(x) is defined as $f(x) = \dfrac{P(x)}{Q(x)}$ where P(x) and Q(x) are both polynomial functions.

Zero: If $P(x_o) = 0$ and $Q(x_o) \neq 0$ then f(x) has a zero at $x = x_o$.

Hole: If $P(x_o) = 0$ and $Q(x_o) = 0$, and the multiplicity of x_o is the same in both polynomials, then f (x) has a hole at $x = x_o$

Vertical asymptote: If $P(x_o) \neq 0$ but $Q(x_o) = 0$, then f (x) has a vertical asymptote at $x = x_o$

Horizontal asymptote: If the limit of $\dfrac{P(x)}{Q(x)}$ equals b as x goes to $\pm\infty$ then y = b is the horizontal asymptote.

Remark: The graph of a function can intersect the horizontal asymptote; but it can not intersect the vertical asymptote.

Existence of Limit: For a function to have a limit for a given value of x = a, the right hand limit at a^+ and the left hand limit at a^- must be the same and each limit must be equal to a real number L other than infinity:

If $\lim\limits_{x \to a^+} f(x) = \lim\limits_{x \to a^-} f(x) = L$ and $L \in R$ then $\lim\limits_{x \to a} f(x) = L$.

Continuity: If $\lim\limits_{x \to a^+} f(x) = \lim\limits_{x \to a^-} f(x) = f(a) \in R$ then f(x) is continuous at x = a.

Limits at infinity:

$$\lim_{x \to \pm\infty} \frac{P(x)}{Q(x)} = \begin{cases} 0 & \text{if } d(P(x)) < d(Q(x)) \\ \pm\infty & \text{if } d(P(x)) > d(Q(x)) \\ \text{ratio of leading coefficient of P(x) to that of Q(x)} & \text{if } d(P(x)) = d(Q(x)) \end{cases}$$

where d(P(x)) = degree of P(x) and d(Q(x)) = degree of Q(x).

Hyperbolic Rational Functions

$f(x) = \dfrac{ax + b}{cx + d}$

Domain $= R - \left\{\dfrac{-d}{c}\right\}$; Range $= R - \left\{\dfrac{a}{c}\right\}$

Horizontal asymptote: y = a/c

Vertical asymptote: x = –d/c

Increasing

Decreasing

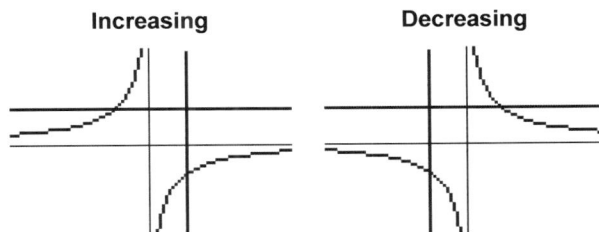

Examples:

$\lim\limits_{x \to -\infty} \dfrac{3x^3 - 5x^2 + 2}{2x^2 - 4x + 2} = \dfrac{3x^3}{2x^2} = \dfrac{3x}{2} = -\infty$

$\lim\limits_{x \to +\infty} \dfrac{3x^3 - 5x^2 + 2}{-2x^3 - 4x + 7} = \dfrac{3}{-2}$

$\lim\limits_{x \to +\infty} \dfrac{2x^2 - 5x - 7}{-3x^3 + 1} = 0$

Example: Find all asymptotes of the function given by $y = \dfrac{2x^2 - 18}{x^2 - 4}$.

Solution: $y = \dfrac{2x^2 - 18}{x^2 - 4} = \dfrac{2x^2 - 18}{(x - 2) \cdot (x + 2)} \Rightarrow$ Vertical asymptotes are x = 2 and x = –2.

$\lim\limits_{x \to \infty} \dfrac{2x^2 - 18}{x^2 - 4} = 2$; therefore y = 2 is the horizontal asymptote.

Example: $f(x) = \begin{cases} \dfrac{4x^2 + 3x}{x} & \text{if } x \neq 0 \\ m & \text{if } x = 0 \end{cases}$; if f(x) is a continuous function then m = ?

Solution: $m = \lim_{x \to 0} \dfrac{4x^2 + 3x}{x} = \lim_{x \to 0} \dfrac{x \cdot (4x + 3)}{x} = \lim_{x \to 0} (4x + 3) = 3$

Example: $f(x) = \begin{cases} x + 4 & x > 3 \\ 6 & x = 3 \\ x + 2 & x < 3 \end{cases}$

a. $\lim_{x \to 3^+} f(x) = ?$

b. $\lim_{x \to 3^-} f(x) = ?$

c. f(3) = ?

Solution:

$\lim_{x \to 3^+} f(x) = 3 + 4 = 7$; $\lim_{x \to 3^-} f(x) = 3 + 2 = 5$; f(3) = 6

Example: At which point does the graph of f(x) = $\dfrac{x^2 - 1}{x - 1}$ have a hole?

Solution: f(x) = $\dfrac{x^2 - 1}{x - 1} = \dfrac{(x - 1) \cdot (x + 1)}{x - 1}$

The function f(x) = $\dfrac{x^2 - 1}{x - 1}$ has a hole at x = 1.

$\lim_{x \to 1} \dfrac{x^2 - 1}{x - 1} = \dfrac{(x - 1) \cdot (x + 1)}{x - 1} = \lim_{x \to 1} x + 1 = 2$. Therefore the hole is at (1, 2).

Exploring Limits with TI

- Limit for a certain value of x or limit at infinity can be calculated by using the **STO**re facility of TI. What must be done is simply to store a value in x and calculate the value of the expression for this x – value.

- ∞ can be replaced by 100,000,000,000; and $-\infty$ can be replaced by $-$ 100,000,000,000.

- Limit at a value of x other than $\pm \infty$ must be calculated as follows: If for example the limit at x = 3 will be calculated, 3.000000001 (which means the right hand limit at 3^+) must be stored in x and the expression must be evaluated; then 2.999999999 (which means the left hand limit at 3^-) must be stored in x and the expression must be evaluated again. If both limits are the same, say L, then the limit is equal to L, otherwise there is no limit.

Example: $\lim_{x \to 3} \dfrac{x^3 - 27}{x^4 - 81} = ?$

Solution:

```
3.0000001→X
        3.0000001
(X^3-27)/(X^4-81
)
            .25
```
```
2.999999→X
        2.999999
(X^3-27)/(X^4-81
)
        .2500000417
```

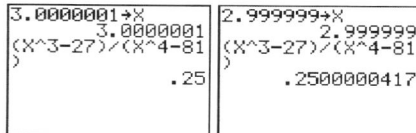

Limit at x = 3 is 0.25.

1.13 GREATEST INTEGER FUNCTION

[x] = [|x|] = The greatest integer less than or equal to x.

f(x) = k if k ≤ x < k + 1 and k = integer ⇒ f(x) = [x]

⌈x⌉ = The least integer greater than or equal to x: The **ceiling function**.

⌊x⌋ = The greatest integer less than or equal to x: The **floor function** is the same as the greatest integer function.

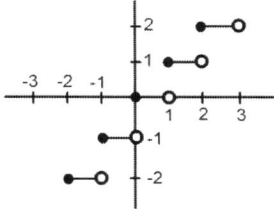

[4] = 4   [0.5] = 0   [9.76] = 9   [−3] = −3   [−8.67] = −9   [−0.32] = −1

TI Usage:

y = int(x) and style must be set to dot

Properties:

If [x + k] = [x] + k then k must be integer

y = [x]: {Domain = All real numbers} and {Range = Set of integers}

Example: f(x) = k where k is an integer for which k ≤ x < k + 1 and g(x) = |f(x)| − f(x) + 1. What is the minimum value for g(x)?

Solution:

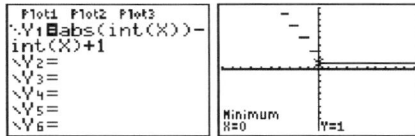

Answer: 1

Example: f(x) = |1 − 2x + 2[x]|

What is the period and frequency of the above function if [x] represents the greatest integer less than or equal to x? What are the maximum and the minimum values of f(x)? What is the amplitude, offset, and equation of the Axis of wave? What is the domain and range?

Solution:

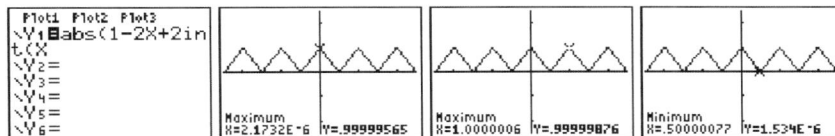

Min = 0; Max = 1

Period = | 1 − 0 | = 1 → (The distance between two adjacent maxima or minima)

Frequency = 1 → (Frequency = 1 / Period)

Amplitude = (1 − 0) / 2 = 1/2 → (Amplitude = (Ymax − Ymin) / 2)

Offset: (1 + 0) / 2 = 1/2 → (Offset = (Ymax + Ymin) / 2)

Axis of wave: y = 1/2 → (Axis of wave equation is y = Offset)

Domain: R, Range: 0 ≤ y ≤ 1.

Example: f(x) = [x] where [x] represents the greatest integer function. What is the range of f(x)?

Solution:

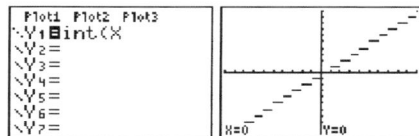

Answer: The range is all integers. The domain is all real numbers.

Example: [4.6] − [−5.4] + 2[0.3] + [4] − [0] = ?

Solution:

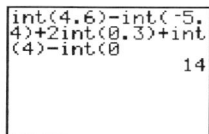

Answer: 14

If at first an idea is not absurd, then there is no hope for it.

Albert Einstein

CHAPTER 2 – Combinatorics

Permutations and Combinations

Binomial Theorem

Probability

Statistics

Data Analysis, Tables and Graphs

2.1 PERMUTATIONS AND COMBINATIONS

Factorial Notation

n! = n (n − 1) (n − 2) (n − 3)………. 3·2·1

1! = 1

0! = 1

Counting by Multiplication

Example: T – shirts at the school store are sold at 15 different models, 8 different colors and 4 different sizes. How many unique types of T – shirts does the school store sell?

Solution:

15 models
8 colors $\Big\}$ $15 \cdot 8 \cdot 4 = 480$
4 sizes

Example: In how many ways can 9 unique books be arranged on a shelf?

Solution: 9!

Example: In how many ways can three of 9 unique books be arranged on a shelf?

Solution: $9 \cdot 8 \cdot 7$

Example:

a. How many unique 4 digit integers are there?

b. How many unique 4 digit odd integers are there?

c. How many unique 4 digit even integers are there?

d. How many unique 4 digit integers contain distinct digits?

e. How many unique 4 digit odd integers contain distinct digits?

f. How many unique 4 digit even integers contain distinct digits?

Solution:

a. There are $9 \cdot 10 \cdot 10 \cdot 10 = 9000$ unique 4 digit integers.

b. There are $9 \cdot 10 \cdot 10 \cdot 5 = 4500$ unique 4 digit odd integers.

c. There are $9 \cdot 10 \cdot 10 \cdot 5 = 4500$ unique 4 digit even integers.

d. There are $9 \cdot 9 \cdot 8 \cdot 7 = 4536$ unique 4 digit integers with distinct digits.

e. There are $8 \cdot 8 \cdot 7 \cdot 5 = 2240$ unique 4 digit odd integers with distinct digits.

f. There are $9 \cdot 8 \cdot 7 \cdot 1 = 504$ unique 4 digit integers each having distinct digits and a units digit of 0. There are $8 \cdot 8 \cdot 7 \cdot 4 = 1792$ unique 4 digit integers each having distinct digits and a nonzero units digit. So totally there are 1792 + 504 = 2296 unique 4 digit even integers with distinct digits

Example: There are 3 roads from Ankara to Istanbul and 4 roads from Istanbul to Edirne.

a. Naz wants to go from Ankara to Edirne passing through Istanbul only once. How many unique routes can she take?

b. Naz wants to go from Ankara to Edirne and back passing through Istanbul once in each direction. How many unique routes can she take?

c. Naz wants to go from Ankara to Edirne and back passing through Istanbul once in each direction and she cannot take ant road more than once. How many unique routes can she take?

Solution:

a. She can take $3 \cdot 4 = 12$ unique routes.

b. She can take $3 \cdot 4 \cdot 4 \cdot 3 = 144$ unique routes.

c. She can take $3 \cdot 4 \cdot 3 \cdot 2 = 72$ unique routes.

Example: There are 3 roads from Ankara to Izmir; 4 roads from Izmir to Mugla; and 2 roads from Mugla to Ankara. Muge wants to make a round trip starting at Ankara, and visiting Mugla and Izmir only once and she will not take any road more than once. How many different routes are there for her round trip?

Solution: $A - I - M - A$: $3 \cdot 4 \cdot 2 = 24$; $A - M - I - A$: $3 \cdot 2 \cdot 4 = 24$; She can take a total of 48 unique routes.

Example: In a restaurant, 4 different soups, 5 different salads, 6 different main meals, 7 different pizzas, 3 different sweets, 10 different beverages are served along with coffee and tea. Emre would like to eat in this restaurant and his meal will consist of a soup or salad, a pizza or a main meal, a sweet, a beverage and coffee or tea. How many different meals can he choose from?

Solution: Soup or salad: 9 choices; pizza or a main meal: 13 choices; sweet: 3 choices; beverage: 10 choices; coffee or tea: 2 choices. So he can make $9 \cdot 13 \cdot 3 \cdot 10 \cdot 2 = 7020$ different choices.

Definition of Permutation

$$P(n, r) = {}^nPr = nPr = P_r^n = \frac{n!}{(n-r)!}$$

Definition of Combination

$$C(n,r) = \frac{n!}{(n-r)! \cdot r!} = \frac{P(n,r)}{r!} = \binom{n}{r} = C_r^n = {}^nC_r = {}_nC_r$$

Examples:

$P(9, 4) = 9 \cdot 8 \cdot 7 \cdot 6$: (Write 4 consecutive integers in decreasing order starting with 9)

$C(9, 4) = \dfrac{9 \cdot 8 \cdot 7 \cdot 6}{4 \cdot 3 \cdot 2 \cdot 1}$: (Write 4 consecutive integers in decreasing order, starting with 9; and divide by a sequence of 4 consecutive integers in decreasing order starting with 4)

$\dfrac{(5+3)!}{5!+3!} = 320$; $C(9,3) = \binom{9}{3} = 9 \text{ nCr } 3 = nCr(9,3) = 84$; $P(9,3) = 9 \text{ nPr } 3 = nPr(9,3) = 504$

Round Table Problem

If **n** people will sit at a round table and rotations do not make a difference then there are **(n − 1)!** different seating schemes.

Example: In how many ways can 4 people be seated at a round table?

Solution:

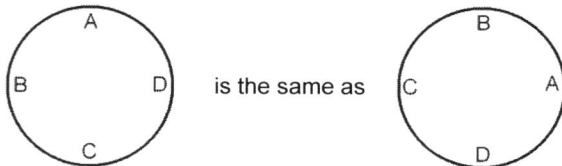

Rotations do not make any difference in round tables as the relative positions of the people do not change. The seating scheme changes only if the relative positions change. Therefore we choose 1 person and keep that person's position fixed; the remaining 3 people can be seated in 3! ways.

Necklace – Bracelet Problem

If a necklace or a bracelet will be made using **n** different beads the number of different necklaces is: $\dfrac{(n-1)!}{2}$

Example: 4 seashells will be used to make bracelets, how many different bracelets can be made?

Solution: This is similar to the round table problem however when the bracelet is turned upside down, a different arrangement is not obtained, so every arrangement is actually counted twice so the round table approach must be divided by two.

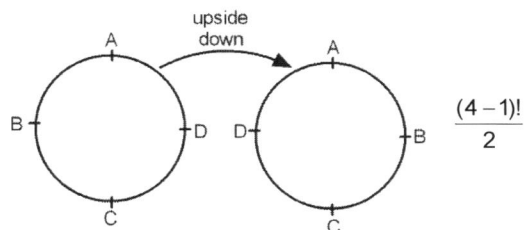

$$\frac{(4-1)!}{2}$$

Example: With 6 stones each having different colors, how many different necklaces can be made?

Solution: $\dfrac{(6-1)!}{2}$

Repeated Permutations

Example: Using all letters of the word MASSACHUSETTS, how many different words can be obtained?

Solution: When S's are shuffled, a different word is not obtained; the same applies for A's and T's as well. Therefore there are $\dfrac{13!}{2!\cdot 4!\cdot 2!}$ different words.

Example: Using all letters of the word UUURR, how many different words can be obtained?

Solution: $\dfrac{5!}{3!\cdot 2!} = \dbinom{5}{3} = \dbinom{5}{2}$

Example: Using all letters of the word HHHHTT, how many different words can be obtained?

Solution: $\dfrac{6!}{4!\cdot 2!}$

Example: In how many ways can 9 apples be distributed to 3 friends if apples are considered to be identical?

Solution: AAAASAASAAA: This notation symbolizes that the 1st person gets 4 apples; 2nd one gets 2 apples and the 3rd one gets 3 apples. Each S letter stands for a separator: $\dfrac{11!}{9!\cdot 2!}$

Example: How many different paths are there from A to B going one unit upward or one unit rightward in a single move?

Solution: UUURR $\Rightarrow \dfrac{5!}{3!\cdot 2!}$ = 10 different paths

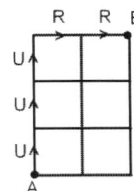

Difference between Permutation and Combination

P(n, r) = There are n people and r different seats available where n≥r. In how many ways can these people be seated leaving no empty space?

Example: 4 of 9 people will be seated at 4 seats available; in how many ways can they be seated?

Solution: $\underline{9}\cdot\underline{8}\cdot\underline{7}\cdot\underline{6}$ = P(9, 4)

$C(n, r) = \binom{n}{r} =$ There are n different people. In how many ways can a team of r people be made?

Example: From 9 people how many different teams with 4 members can be made?

Solution: $\binom{9}{4} = \dfrac{9 \cdot 8 \cdot 7 \cdot 6}{4 \cdot 3 \cdot 2 \cdot 1}$

Example: A, B, C, D

If three of the letters above are chosen to make words how many different words can be made?

Solution:

ABC	ABD	**ACD**	BCD
ACB	ADB	**ADC**	BDC
BAC	**BAD**	CAD	**CBD**
BCA	**BDA**	CDA	**CDB**
CAB	DAB	**DAC**	DBC
CBA	DBA	**DCA**	DCB

$\Rightarrow P(4, 3) = 24$ different words are possible

Example: Among the group of 4 people consisting of Ali, Berk, Cem and Deniz, how many three member teams can be made?

Solution:

A,B,C
A,B,D
A,C,D   } 4 teams $\Rightarrow$ C (4, 3) = $\dfrac{4!}{1! \cdot 3!}$ = 4 different teams are possible
B,C,D

ABC is a word;	Ali, Berk, Cem is a team;
Switch places of B and C:	Switch places of Berk & Cem:
ACB is different from the word ABC.	Ali, Cem, Berk is the SAME team as Ali, Berk, Cem
Different orders are considered to be different.	Different orders are NOT considered to be different.
$\Rightarrow$ PERMUTATION	$\Rightarrow$ COMBINATION

Properties of Combinations

1. C (0,0) = 1
2. C (n,0) = 1
3. C (n, 1) = n
4. C (n, n) = 1
5. C (n, r) = C (n, n − r)
6. C (n, r) + C (n, r + 1) = C (n + 1, r + 1)
7. C (n,0) + C (n, 1) + C (n, 2) + ……. + C (n, n) = 2^n
8. The total number of subsets of a set having n elements is 2^n.
9. The total number of combinations of a set of n elements is the total number of those subsets that contain at least one element, and this number is $2^n - 1$.

Examples: $\binom{9}{3} = \binom{9}{6}$; $\binom{9}{2} + \binom{9}{3} = \binom{10}{3}$; $\binom{16}{x} = \binom{12}{x} \Rightarrow x = 0$; $\binom{x}{6} = \binom{x}{9} \Rightarrow x = 15$

Example: From 1 penny, 1 nickel, 1 dime, 1 quarter and 1 dollar, how many different sums of money can be made?

Solution: $\binom{5}{1} + \binom{5}{2} + \binom{5}{3} + \binom{5}{4} + \binom{5}{5} = 2^5 - 1 = 31$

Ace, King, Queen, Jack, 10, ..., 2: Totally 13 cards		**Black cards: Spades** and **Clubs**
Spades ♠ **Clubs ♣**	**Diamonds ♦** **Hearts ♥**	**Red cards: Diamonds** and **Hearts**
Face cards: King, Queen, Jack		

Example: 40 cards will be selected from a standard deck of 52 cards. How many selections can be made?

Solution: 52 Cards, Choose 40 Cards; $\binom{52}{40}$

Example: From a standard deck of 52 cards; we would like to choose 10 cards so that 3 of them will be spades and 7 of them will be diamonds. In how many ways can this be done?

Solution: $\binom{13}{3}\binom{13}{7}$

Example: 5 cards will be selected from 52 cards and order is not considered to be important. How many different selections are possible?

Solution: Every choice of 5 cards will determine a different hand: $\binom{52}{5}$

Example: There are 10 points no 3 of which are collinear. How many lines do they determine such that each line passes through exactly 2 of the points?

Solution: Every pair of points will determine one line: $\binom{10}{2}$

Example: 10 people will shake hands so that each person shakes hands with every other person exactly once. How many different handshakes are possible?

Solution: Every two people will shake hands once: $\binom{10}{2}$

Example: How many unique diagonals does a regular octagon have?

Solution: Every 2 points determine a side or a diagonal and of these 8 are sides: $\binom{8}{2} - 8$.

(Please note that the number of diagonals of a regular polygon having n sides is $\binom{n}{2} - n = \dfrac{n \cdot (n-3)}{2}$.)

Example: How many unique parallelograms are there in the figure given?

Solution: When a pair of parallel lines are intersected by another pair of parallel lines a parallelogram is obtained. So there are $\binom{5}{2} \cdot \binom{4}{2} = 60$ unique parallelograms in the figure given.

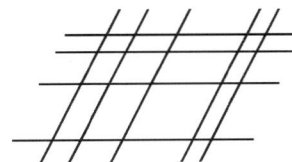

Example: An 8 people committee will be selected from 12 physicists and 8 mathematicians such that each committee will contain 3 mathematicians and 5 physicists. How many different committees can be selected?

Solution: Total number of committees are $\binom{12}{5} \cdot \binom{8}{3}$.

Example: From 12 physicists and 8 biologists and 7 chemists a science board will be selected such that the president has to be a physicist and the vice president has to be a chemist or a biologist. If each board also contains 3 other members then how many different boards can be selected?

Solution: Total number of different boards are: $12 \cdot 15 \cdot \binom{25}{3}$.

2.2 BINOMIAL THEOREM

$$(x + y)^n = \binom{n}{0} x^n$$

$$+ \binom{n}{1} x^{n-1} \cdot y^1$$

$$+ \binom{n}{2} x^{n-2} \cdot y^2$$

$$+ \binom{n}{3} x^{n-3} \cdot y^3 \qquad \rightarrow \qquad \text{4 th term.}$$

$$+ \ldots$$

$$+ \binom{n}{n-1} \cdot x \cdot y^{n-1}$$

$$+ \binom{n}{n} \cdot y^n$$

(r + 1)'th term in the expansion of $(x + y)^n = \binom{n}{r} \cdot x^{n-r} \cdot y^r$ where $r \leq n$

$$\binom{9}{4} = \frac{9 \cdot 8 \cdot 7 \cdot 6}{4 \cdot 3 \cdot 2 \cdot 1}$$

Observation:

$(x + y)^n$:

- Number of terms = (n + 1) if n is a positive integer.

- If n is even; there is a middle term and $r = \dfrac{n}{2}$ for the middle term.

- If n is not a positive integer meaning that if
    i)   n is not positive
    ii) n is not an integer
    iii) n is neither positive nor an integer
    then there are infinitely many terms!

Pascal's Triangle

Please note that the coefficients of the terms in $(x + y)^n$ are the same as the numbers in Pascal's Triangle.

$(x + y)^0 =$	1
$(x + y)^1 =$	$1x + 1y$
$(x + y)^2 =$	$1x^2 + 2xy + 1y^2$
$(x + y)^3 =$	$1x^3 + 3x^2y + 3xy^2 + 1y^3$
$(x + y)^4 =$	$1x^4 + 4x^3y + 6x^2y^2 + 4xy^3 + 1y^4$
$(x + y)^5 =$	$1x^5 + 5x^4y + 10x^3y^2 + 10x^2y^3 + 5xy^4 + 1y^5$

```
            1
          1   1
        1   2   1
      1   3   3   1
    1   4   6   4   1
  1   5  10  10   5   1
```

$(x + y)^3 = x^3 + 3x^2y + 3xy^2 + y^3$

$(x + y)^4 = x^4 + 4x^3y + 6x^2y^2 + 4xy^3 + y^4$

Please also note that when expanding $(x - y)^n$ the signs of terms should alternate.

$(x - y)^3 = x^3 - 3x^2y + 3xy^2 - y^3$

$(x - y)^4 = x^4 - 4x^3y + 6x^2y^2 - 4xy^3 + y^4$

Negative and Fractional Powers of Binomials

Example: $(x - 2y)^{1/4}$; give the first 4 terms.

Solution:

$$\binom{1/4}{0}x^{\frac{1}{4}} + \binom{1/4}{1}x^{\frac{1}{4}-1}(-2y)^1 + \binom{1/4}{2}x^{\frac{1}{4}-2}(-2y)^2 + \binom{1/4}{3}x^{\frac{1}{4}-3}(-2y)^3$$

$$= 1 \cdot x^{\frac{1}{4}} + \frac{1}{4}x^{-\frac{3}{4}}(-2y) + \frac{\frac{1}{4}\cdot\left(\frac{1}{4}-1\right)}{2\cdot 1}x^{-\frac{7}{4}}\left(4y^2\right) + \frac{\frac{1}{4}\cdot\left(\frac{1}{4}-1\right)\cdot\left(\frac{1}{4}-2\right)}{3\cdot 2\cdot 1}x^{-\frac{11}{4}}\left(-8y^3\right)$$

$$= x^{\frac{1}{4}} - \frac{1}{2}x^{-\frac{3}{4}}y - \frac{3}{8}x^{-\frac{7}{4}}y^2 - \frac{7}{16}x^{-\frac{11}{4}}y^3$$

Example: $(x - y)^{-5}$; give the first 4 terms.

Solution:

$$\binom{-5}{0}x^{-5} + \binom{-5}{1}x^{-5-1}(-y)^1 + \binom{-5}{2}x^{-5-2}(-y)^2 + \binom{-5}{3}x^{-5-3}(-y)^3$$

$$= 1 \cdot x^{-5} + (-5)x^{-6}(-y) + \frac{-5\cdot(-5-1)}{2\cdot 1}x^{-7}y^2 + \frac{-5\cdot(-5-1)\cdot(-5-2)}{3\cdot 2\cdot 1}x^{-8}\left(-y^3\right)$$

$$= x^{-5} + 5x^{-6}y + 15x^{-7}y^2 + 35x^{-8}y^3$$

2.3 PROBABILITY

Set Theory in Brief

The term **set** represents a group of objects named so as to provide a check that indicates whether or not some particular object belongs to (symbolized as "$\in$") the set. Objects that belong to a set are called **elements** or **members** of that set. The Universal set denoted by U consists of all elements A and B and possibly the elements other than those of A and B

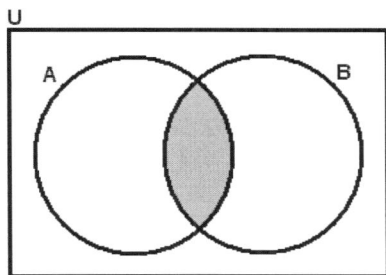

A∩B

A **intersection** B consists of the elements that belong to both sets.

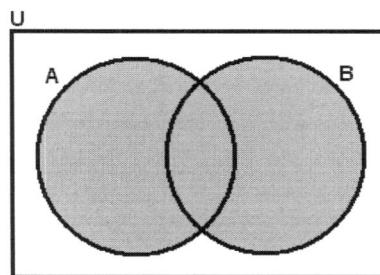

A∪B

A **union** B consists of the elements that belong to either or both sets.

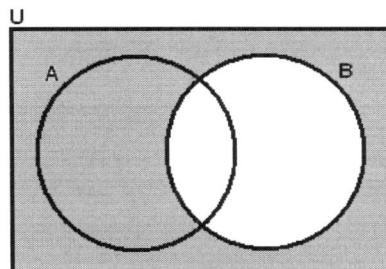

B' = U – B

B **complement** consists of the elements that belong to the universal set but not to B

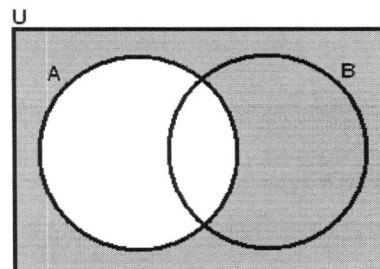

A' = U – A

A **complement** consists of the elements that belong to the universal set but not to A

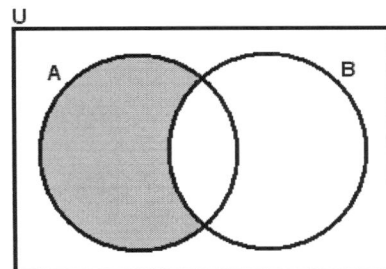

A – B = A / B = A \ B = A ∩ B'

A **difference** B consists of the elements that belong to A but not to B

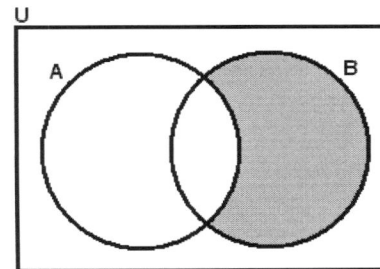

B – A = B / A = B \ A = B ∩ A'

B **difference** A consists of the elements that belong to B but not to A

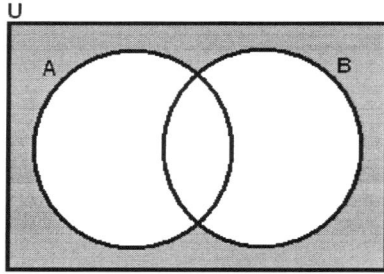

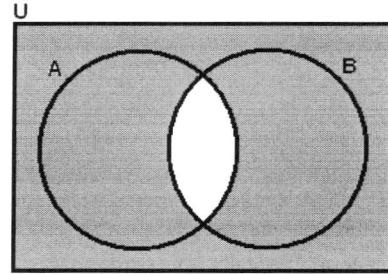

$(A \cup B)' = A' \cap B'$

$(A \cap B)' = A' \cup B'$

The **complement** of A **union** B consists of the elements that belong to the universal set but not to set A or set B.

The **complement** of A **union** B consists of the elements that belong to the universal set or set A or set B but not to both sets.

The **sample space** is the set of everything that can happen and is defined by the letter U (the universal set in set theory).

An **event** is one particular thing that can happen and is given any other capital letter, such as A.

P stands for **probability**, and **P(A)** stands for the **probability of event A**.

The number of ways an event A can happen is denoted by **n(A)**. To find the probability of event A we divide the number of ways event A can happen by the total number of possibilities in the sample space: $P(A) = \dfrac{n(A)}{n(U)}$.

Since A is a subset of U then $n(A) \leq n(U)$ which implies that probabilities are always nonnegative real numbers that cannot be greater than 1: $0 \leq P(A) \leq 1$. P(A) is between **0 (impossible event – the event definitely will not happen)** and **1 (certain event – the event will definitely happen)** inclusive.

The probability that **event A does not happen** is denoted by **P(A')**. It follows that P(A) + P(A') = 1

Odds in favor of an event A = $\dfrac{P\,(\text{event A happens})}{P\,(\text{event A does not happen})}$

Odds against an event A = $\dfrac{P\,(\text{event A does not happen})}{P\,(\text{event A happens})}$

Example: What are the odds in favor of getting a number greater than 1 when one die is thrown?
Solution:

$$\frac{P\,(\text{event happens})}{P\,(\text{event does not happen})} = \frac{P(\text{number is greater than 1})}{P(\text{number is not greater than 1})} = \frac{\frac{5}{6}}{\frac{1}{6}} = \frac{5}{1}$$

Example: What are the odds against getting a number greater than 1 when one die is thrown?
Solution:

$$\frac{P\,(\text{event does not happen})}{P\,(\text{event happens})} = \frac{1}{5}$$

Combined Events: The probability of event A or B or both happening.

The symbols $\cap$ and $\cup$ in the set theory are used for the words "and" and "or" in probability theory respectively. If the events A and B are **mutually exclusive** then they cannot happen at the same time; this implies $P(A \cup B) = P(A) + P(B)$ and $P(A \cap B) = 0$

If two events A and B are mutually exclusive and A can happen in a ways while B can happen in b ways, then one or the other event can occur in a + b ways.

If the events A and B are not mutually exclusive then the following holds: $P(A \cup B) = P(A) + P(B) - P(A \cap B)$

If A and B are **independent events** then the probability of the events A and B both happening is calculated by multiplication: $P(A \cap B) = P(A) \cdot P(B)$

Please note that multiplying simple fractions gives a smaller result and thus it is less likely that both events will happen than just one. If A and B are independent then one of them happening does not affect the probability of the other happening.

If the events are not independent we have to deal with **conditional probability** – i.e. the probability of one event happening given that the other has already happened. This is written as $P(A|B)$, and read as "the probability of A given B."

The related formula is $P(A \mid B) = \dfrac{P(A \cap B)}{P(B)}$.

Note that the definition of independence is $P(A) = P(A|B) = P(A|B')$. In other words, the probability of A is the same whether or not B has happened. But if you are asked to test whether events are independent, just investigate if $P(A \cap B) = P(A) \cdot P(B)$ holds or not.

- Suppose that a bag contains balls of two different colors. One is taken out, then another. The color of the second is independent of the first if the first has been put back.
- If the first is not replaced in the bag then the color of the second depends on the color of the first.

Venn Diagrams

Venn Diagrams can be used to simulate an event. In such a case the symbols $\cap$ and $\cup$ in the set theory are used for the words "and" and "or" in probability theory respectively.

Example:

Among the 107 seniors in **RUSH** academy 68 take math classes and 45 take history classes. If 20 take both classes then what is the probability that a randomly selected student

a) takes math?

b) takes history?

c) takes both math and history?

d) takes math or history or both?

e) does not take math?

f) does not take history?

g) takes neither math nor history?

h) takes math given that he takes history?

i) takes history given that he takes math?

Solution:

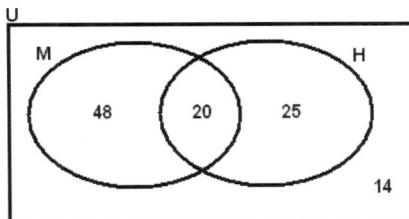

a) $P(M) = \dfrac{68}{107}$ b) $P(H) = \dfrac{45}{107}$ c) $P(M \cap H) = \dfrac{20}{107}$

d) $P(M \cup H) = \dfrac{93}{107}$ e) $P(M') = \dfrac{39}{107}$ f) $P(H') = \dfrac{62}{107}$

g) $P(H') = \dfrac{14}{107}$ h) $P(M \mid H) = \dfrac{20}{45}$ i) $P(H \mid M) = \dfrac{20}{68}$

Example: For the events A and B, P(A) = 0.5, P(B) = 0.4.

a) Find P(A∪B) if A and B are independent.

b) Find P(A'∩B') if A and B are mutually exclusive.

Solution:

a) P(A∩B) = 0.5 . 0.4 = 0.2

   P(A∪B) = P(A) + P(B) − P(A ∩B) = 0.5 + 0.4 − 0.2 = 0.7

b) P(A'∩B') = P((A∪B)') = 1 − P(A∪B) = 1 − (P(A) + P(B)) = 1 − (0.5 + 0.4) = 0.1.

Lists and Charts

Lists: A list of possible outcomes is useful if there aren't too many of them. And it is important to be sure that each outcome in the list is equally likely. For example, when three coins are thrown, the possible combinations of heads and tails are HHH, HHT, HTH, HTT, THH, THT, TTH, and TTT. If we would like to find the probability of getting exactly two heads, we can see that there are three possible ways that are HHT, HTH and THH so the probability is 3/8. As another example, when four coins are thrown, the possible combinations of heads and tails are TTTT, TTTH, TTHT, TTHH, THTT, THTH, THHT, THHH, HTTT, HTTH, HTHT, HTHH, HHTT, HHTH, HHHT, and HHHH.

Possibility Space Chart: This is a way of showing a list of outcomes on a diagram, but can only be used for two events.

Example: The diagram below shows all the possible totals when two six − sided dice (black and white) are thrown:

	6	7	8	9	10	11	12
	5	6	7	8	9	10	11
	4	5	6	7	8	9	10
Black	3	4	5	6	7	8	9
	2	3	4	5	6	7	8
	1	2	3	4	5	6	7
		1	2	3	4	5	6
				White			

Note that there is only one way a double 2, say, can happen − a 2 on the black and a 2 on the white. But a 1 and a 3 can happen in two ways: 1 on the black and 3 on the white, or the other way around. Thus there are 36 possibilities.

Some examples of probabilities are: P(Total of 9) = 4/36; P(Total of 9 or 7) = 10/36; P(Total of 10 or a double) = 8/36

P(Double | Total ≥ 9) = 2/10

Tables of Outcomes: Tables of outcomes show how many ways two events can, or cannot, happen.

Example: In a survey of 400 people, 170 of whom were female, it was found that 120 people were unemployed, including 30 males. If a person is selected at random from the 400, find the probability that this person is

a) An unemployed female.

b) A male, given that the person is employed.

Solution:

	Males	Females	Totals
Unemployed	30	90	120
Employed	200	80	280
Totals	230	170	400

a) There are 90 unemployed females cut of 200.

   Thus P(unemployed female) = 90/400.

b) This is a conditional probability; there are 280 people who are employed and of these, 200 are males. So P(male | employed) = 200/280

Example: In a survey, 100 students were asked "do you prefer to watch television or play sport?" Of the 46 boys in the survey, 33 said they preferred sport, while 29 girls made this choice. Complete the table and find the probability that:

a) A student selected at random prefers to watch television.

b) A student selected at random is a boy.

c) A student selected at random is a boy who prefers to watch television i.e. the student is a boy **and** he prefers to watch television.

d) A student selected at random is a boy **or** he prefers to watch television.

e) A student prefers to watch television, given that the student is a boy.

f) A student is a boy, given that he prefers to watch television.

g) Are the events of being a boy and preferring to watch the television mutually exclusive or not?

h) Are the events of being a boy and preferring to watch the television statistically dependent or independent?

Solution:

	Boys	Girls	Total
Television	13	25	38
Sport	**33**	**29**	62
Total	**46**	54	**100**

B: The event that a randomly selected person is a boy

T: The event that a randomly selected person prefers to watch television

a) $P(T) = \dfrac{38}{100}$

b) $P(B) = \dfrac{46}{100}$

c) $P(B \cap T) = \dfrac{13}{100}$

d) $P(B \cup T) = \dfrac{33 + 13 + 25}{100} = \dfrac{71}{100}$

e) $P(T|B) = \dfrac{13}{46}$

f) $P(B|T) = \dfrac{13}{38}$

g) $P(B \cap T) = \dfrac{13}{100} \neq 0 \Rightarrow$ not mutually exclusive.

h) $P(B \cap T) = \dfrac{13}{100} = 0.13$;

$P(B) \cdot P(T) = \dfrac{38}{100} \cdot \dfrac{46}{100} = 0.1748$

$P(B \cap T) \neq P(B) \cdot P(T) \Rightarrow$ not independent.

Tree Diagrams

Tree diagrams are used to work out the probabilities for a sequence of events. To find the probability of a set of consecutive branches, each individual probability is multiplied. To find the probability of one of several branches that may take place, probabilities of each outcome are added.

Example: The probability that it may be foggy today is 0.8. If it is foggy today, the probability that it will be foggy tomorrow is 0.6. If it is not foggy today, the probability that it will not be foggy tomorrow is 0.7.

Calculate the following probabilities:

a) The probability that both today and tomorrow will be foggy

b) The probability that neither today nor tomorrow is foggy

c) The probability that exactly one of today and tomorrow is foggy

d) The probability that it is foggy today given that it is foggy tomorrow

Solution:

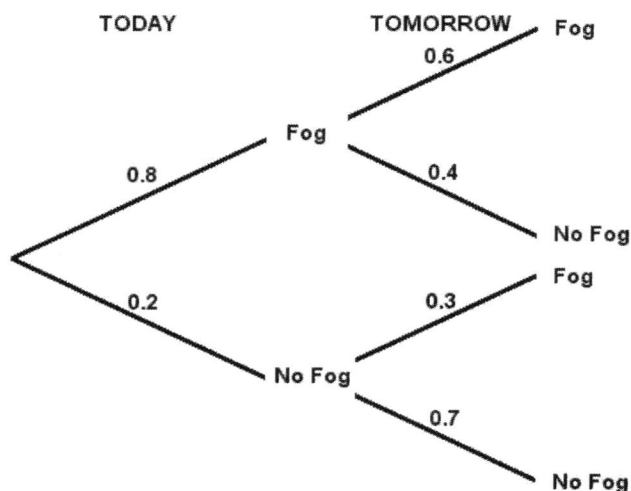

a) $0.8 \cdot 0.6 = 0.48$

b) $0.2 \cdot 0.7 = 0.14$

c) $0.8 \cdot 0.4 + 0.2 \cdot 0.3 = 0.38$

d) $\dfrac{0.8 \cdot 0.6}{0.8 \cdot 0.6 + 0.2 \cdot 0.3} = \dfrac{0.48}{0.54}$

Please note the following:

- Probabilities of branches coming out of one point add up to 1 since they generate all possibilities.
- The overall probabilities also add up to 1.
- The fact that it is foggy tomorrow is not independent of the fact that it is foggy today.

Example: A bag contains 4 red, 6 green and 7 blue balls. Two balls are drawn at random from the bag without replacement. What is the probability that the balls

a) are both blue?

b) are same in color?

c) are different in color?

Solution:

There are two events (1st ball, 2nd ball) with three outcomes each time. So one should end up with nine branches. Please note that drawing two balls at the same time from the bag is the same as drawing two balls from the bag one at a time without replacement.

a) $\dfrac{7}{17} \cdot \dfrac{6}{16}$

b) $\dfrac{7 \cdot 6 + 6 \cdot 5 + 4 \cdot 3}{17 \cdot 16}$

c) $1 - \dfrac{7 \cdot 6 + 6 \cdot 5 + 4 \cdot 3}{17 \cdot 16}$

Binomial Probabilities

Example: In a bag there are 9 red and 7 blue balls. If 5 balls are drawn from the bag one after another **without replacement**, what will be the probability that

a) all will be red

b) all will be blue

c) 3 of them will be red and 2 of them will be blue

Solution:

a) $\dfrac{9}{16} \cdot \dfrac{8}{15} \cdot \dfrac{7}{14} \cdot \dfrac{6}{13} \cdot \dfrac{5}{12}$ or alternatively $\dfrac{\dbinom{9}{5}}{\dbinom{16}{5}}$

c) $\dfrac{9}{16} \cdot \dfrac{8}{15} \cdot \dfrac{7}{14} \cdot \dfrac{7}{13} \cdot \dfrac{6}{12} \cdot \dfrac{5!}{3! \cdot 2!}$ or alternatively $\dfrac{\dbinom{9}{3}\dbinom{7}{2}}{\dbinom{16}{5}}$

b) $\dfrac{7}{16} \cdot \dfrac{6}{15} \cdot \dfrac{5}{14} \cdot \dfrac{4}{13} \cdot \dfrac{3}{12}$ or alternatively $\dfrac{\dbinom{7}{5}}{\dbinom{16}{5}}$

Example: In a bag there are 9 red and 7 blue balls. If 5 balls are drawn from the bag one after another **with replacement**, what will be the probability that

a) all will be red

b) all will be blue

c) 3 of them will be red and 2 of them will be blue

Solution:

a) $\left(\dfrac{9}{16}\right)^5$

b) $\left(\dfrac{7}{16}\right)^5$

c) $\left(\dfrac{9}{16}\right)^3 \cdot \left(\dfrac{7}{16}\right)^2 \cdot \dfrac{5!}{3! \cdot 2!}$

Example: A bag contains a large number of balls of whose 70% are red and 30% are blue. If 5 balls are drawn from the bag one after another (with or without replacement), what will be the probability that

a) all will be red

b) all will be blue

c) 3 of them will be red and 2 of them will be blue

Solution:

a) $(0.7)^5$

b) $(0.3)^5$

c) $(0.7)^3 \cdot (0.3)^2 \cdot \dfrac{5!}{3! \cdot 2!}$

2.4 STATISTICS

A **population** is a group of data for which statistics are calculated.

A **sample** is a subgroup drawn from the population. Sample statistics (such as the mean) can be used to estimate the statistics of the population.

Discrete data are restricted to certain values that are often integers whereas **continuous data** can take any values.

Frequency is the number of times a particular value occurs.

Mean, Median and Mode

These measures can be used as a representative of the entire group of numbers. The most commonly used measures are as follows:

- The **mean** or the **average** of n numbers is the sum of the numbers divided by n:

  Mean = $\bar{x} = \dfrac{x_1 + x_2 + ... + x_n}{n}$

- The **median** of n numbers is the middle number when the numbers are written in increasing or decreasing order. If n is even, the median is the average of the two middle numbers.

- The **mode** of n numbers is the number that is most frequent. If two numbers tie for the most frequent occurrence, the group has two modes and it is called **bimodal**.

- The **range** of a group of data is the difference between the maximum and the minimum values in this group.

Variance and Standard Deviation

These quantities are the **measures of dispersion**, that are different from the mean of the set. These two measures are called the **variance** (σ^2) of the set and the **standard deviation** (σ) of the set. If the data is closely packed about the mean then σ will be small and if the data is loosely packed about the mean then σ will be large. Consider a group of numbers x_1, x_2, ..., x_n with a mean of $\bar{x}$. The **variance** of the set is given by $\sigma^2 = \dfrac{(x_1 - \bar{x})^2 + (x_2 - \bar{x})^2 + ... + (x_n - \bar{x})^2}{n}$ where the **standard deviation** of the set is σ.

Quartiles

The **lower quartile** is the median of the numbers that occur before the median and the **upper quartile** is the median of the numbers that occur after the median. A cruder measure of dispersion is the interquartile range which is calculated by subtracting the lower quartile from the upper quartile.

TI Calculator Usage

The TI 83 – 84 family of graphing calculators is very useful in studying the statistics of the group of data. However before performing any statistical calculations, it may be essential to clear any previous list entries. **MEMory ClrAllLists** option will accomplish this task. The data may be given in two ways, in raw format or in data – frequency format. When data is given in raw format, all data is entered in the list named **L₁** using the **STAT EDIT** option. When data is given in data – frequency format, the data is entered in the list named **L₁** and the individual frequencies are entered in the list named **L₂**, again using the **STAT EDIT** option. When data is in raw format, the command of **1 – Var Stats** or **1 – Var Stats L₁** will calculate the statistics of the data, these commands can be accessed through the **STAT CALC** option. When data is in data – frequency format, the command of **1 – Var Stats L₁, L₂** must be used to calculate the statistics of the data. The calculated statistics and their meanings are as follows:

$\bar{x}$: The arithmetic mean of the data.

$\sum x$: Sum of all individual entries in the data set.

$\sum x^2$: Sum of the squares of all individual entries in the data set.

Sx: The sample standard deviation.

σx: The population standard deviation.

n: number of data

minX: Minimum entry in the data set.

Q_1: Lower Quartile

Med: Median

Q_3: Upper Quartile

MaxX: Maximum entry in the data set.

Example: Find the statistics of the following data: 1, 3, 5, 6, 3, 6, 6.

Solution:

Example: Find the statistics of the following data:

Data	1	3	5	6
Frequency	1	2	1	3

Solution:

Example: 100 people are staying at a hotel: 56 are men and 44 women. The men have a mean height of 1.78 meters and the women have a mean height of 1.65 meters. Find the mean height of the 100 people correct to the nearest hundredth of a meter.

Solution: Mean Height = $\dfrac{56 \cdot 1.78 + 44 \cdot 1.65}{100} = 1.72$

Example:

Score	10	15	20	25	30
Number of students	2	3	5	m	4

The table shows the scores of students in a competition. The mean score is 21.75; find the value of m.

Solution: $\dfrac{10 \cdot 2 + 15 \cdot 3 + 20 \cdot 5 + 25 \cdot m + 30 \cdot 4}{2 + 3 + 5 + m + 4} = 21.75 \Rightarrow m = 6$

Example: Find mean, variance and standard deviation of the numbers 1, 1, 2, 3, 3.

Solution:

Step 1: find **mean** = $\dfrac{1+1+2+3+3}{5} = \dfrac{10}{5} = 2$

Step 2: Find deviation from the mean (subtract mean from each data)

1	1	2	3	3
-2	-2	-2	-2	-2
-1	-1	0	$+1$	$+1$

Step 3. Square the differences and sum them up: 1 + 1 + 0 + 1 + 1 = 4

Step 4: Divide the sum by the number of terms and you get **variance**: $\dfrac{4}{5} = 0.8 = \sigma^2$

Step 5: Find the square root of the result and you get **standard deviation** = $\sqrt{0.8} = 0.89 = \sigma$

Example:

Data	Frequency
0	2
1	3
2	5
3	8
4	2

Find mode, median, mean, range, frequency of each data for the group of data given above.

Solution:

mode = 3; median = $\dfrac{2+3}{2} = 2.5$; mean = $\dfrac{0 \cdot 2 + 1 \cdot 3 + 2 \cdot 5 + 3 \cdot 8 + 4 \cdot 2}{20} = \dfrac{45}{20} = 2.25$; range = max − min = 4 − 0 = 4

frequency of 0 = 2; frequency of 1 = 3; frequency of 2 = 5; frequency of 3 = 8; frequency of 4 = 2

2.5 NORMAL DISTRIBUTION WITH TI

Suppose we are given the mean and standard deviation of a group of data. In the context of SAT math subject test, particularly the level 2, we might be required to determine the following:

- the probability that a randomly chosen item has a value that is greater than a certain value,
- the probability that a randomly chosen item has a value that is less than a certain value,
- the probability that a randomly chosen item has a value that is between two certain values,
- or
- given the probability, we might be required to find what the certain value or what those values are.

In this case we will use the two very useful utilities that are accessible though the $\boxed{\text{2nd}}$ $\overset{\text{DISTR}}{\boxed{\text{VARS}}}$ menu.

```
DISTR DRAW
1:normalpdf(
2:normalcdf(
3:invNorm(
4:tpdf(
5:tcdf(
6:X²pdf(
7↓X²cdf(
```

These utilities are **normalcdf(** and the **invNorm(**. The **normalcdf(** utility can be used in the following two ways:

- **normalcdf(lower limit, upper limit, mean, standard deviation)** or
- **normalcdf(lower limit, upper limit)**

In the latter case, the **normalcdf(** utility assumes the mean of 0 and the standard deviation of 1. The **normalcdf(** utility allows us to compute the probability that a randomly chosen item has a value that is greater than a certain value, or the probability that a randomly chosen item has a value that is less than a certain value, or the probability that a randomly chosen item has a value that is between two certain values,

Similarly, the invnorm(utility can be used in the following two ways:

- **invNorm(probability, mean, standard deviation)** or
- **invNorm(probability)**

In the latter case, the **invNorm(** utility assumes the mean of 0 and the standard deviation of 1.

Please go over the following illustrative examples:

Example: In Geniuseum Academy, the IQ's of the students are randomly distributed with the mean of 125 and the standard deviation of 12. Perform the following calculations:

a. The probability that a randomly selected student has an IQ that is greater than 135.

b. The percentage of students whose IQ's are between 120 and 140.

c. The percentage of students whose IQ's are less than 110.

d. It is given that 80 percent of the students have an IQ that is greater than x; what is the value of x?

Solution:

a.
```
normalcdf(135,10
00000,125,12
        .2023283246
```
Answer: 0.2

b.
```
normalcdf(120,14
0,125,12
        .5558890044
```
Answer: 0.556 · 100 = 55.6 %

c.
```
normalcdf(-10000
0,110,125,12
        .105649839
```
Answer: 0.106 · 100 = 10.6 %

d.
```
invNorm(.2,125,1
2
        114.9005452
```
Answer: 114.9

2.6 DATA ANALYSIS, TABLES AND GRAPHS

Data analysis questions usually require careful examination and manipulation of data given in tables, graphs, or various other forms. In such questions there is usually information hidden in some part of the data or the question and/or redundant information in order to make the question harder. Moreover some questions will require that all pieces of information be used to solve a certain question; such as two graphs given and a question asking for a quantity that should be calculated using both graphs. In this section you will see 20 examples carefully chosen and fully solved. Please pay extra attention on how the hidden information is used.

For examples 1 – 2 please refer to the data given in figure 1 that shows the number of books checked by the crew working in RUSH Publications.

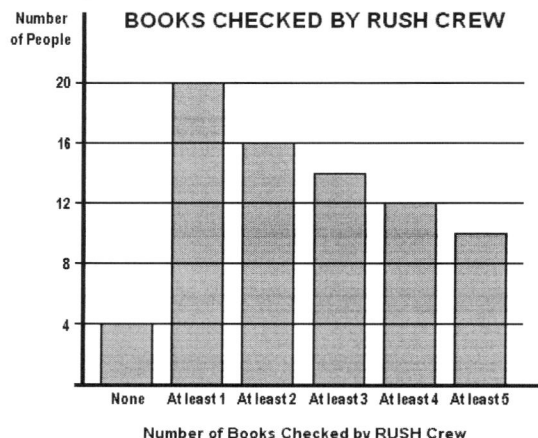

Figure 1

Example 1: How many members of the RUSH crew checked exactly 3 books?

(A) 2 (B) 4 (C) 6

(D) 12 (E) 14

Solution: (The number of RUSH crew members who checked exactly 3 books) equals (the number of RUSH crew members who checked at least 3 books) – (the number of RUSH crew members who checked at least 4 books) = 14 – 12 = 2. Correct answer is (A).

Example 2: How many people are there in the RUSH crew totally?

(A) 20 (B) 24 (C) 54 (D) 66 (E) 74

Solution: RUSH crew consists of 20 + 4 = 24 people (those who checked at least 1 book and no books). Correct answer is (B).

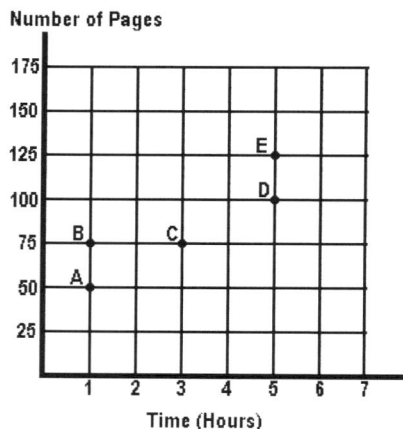

Figure 2

Example 3: In RUSH Publications there are five test controllers Alihan, Berk, Cemal, Deniz, and Enis whose working rates can be calculated using the information given by the graph in figure 2. Which of the following is a correct statement if the lettered points represent the initials of the controllers?

(A) Alihan and Berk work at the same rate.

(B) Berk is the slowest of them all.

(C) Cemal and Enis work at the same rate.

(D) Deniz is the fastest of them all.

(E) Deniz and Enis work at the same rate.

Solution: Individual rates of the controllers are as follows:

A: 50/1 = 50; B: 75/1 = 75; C: 75/3 = 25; D: 100/5 = 20;

E: 125/5 = 25. So C and D work at the same rate; correct answer is (C).

Expenditures of Spendalot Family in 2003

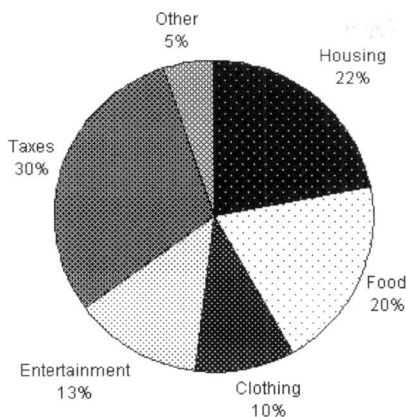

Figure 3

Example 4: The pie chart given in figure 4 shows the classification of the expenditures of Spendalot family whose total household income in 2003 was $240,000. In 2004, the household income increased to $300,000 and the dollar amounts spent on Housing, Food, Clothing and Other stayed the same. However in 2004, taxes increased to %35 of the total household income and the family members decided to decrease their expenditures on entertainment by 25% over the previous year and deposit the remaining money into a savings account. Approximately what percent of the household income went into savings in 2004?

(A) 3.4%   (B) 3.5%

(C) 11.6%   (D) 14.5%

(E) None of the above

Solution:

Expenditures	2003	2004	Notes
Housing	52.8	52.8	Same dollar amount
Food	48	48	Same dollar amount
Clothing	24	24	Same dollar amount
Taxes		105	Increased TO %35 $300 \times 0.35 = 105$
Entertainment	31.2	23.4	Decreased BY %25 $31.2 - 31.2 \times 0.25 = 23.4$
Other	12	12	Same dollar amount
TOTALS	240	300	

Savings in 2004 = $300 - (52.8 + 48 + 24 + 105 + 23.4 + 12) = 34.8 \Rightarrow$ % of savings = $34.8/300 \times 100 = 11.6\%$

For examples 5 and 6 please refer to the data given in the following table:

```
4 | 4 5 6 7
5 | 0 3 5 6 7 7
6 | 0 2 3 5 6 9
7 | 0 1 1 2 3 5 5 5 8
8 | 1 2 4 7 8

5 | 6 =        56 percent
```

Example 5: The stem and leaf plot gives the scores of the students entering a local math contest recently held at RUSH Academy. If only those who scored 75 or above will be admitted to the finals then what percent of the entrants are qualified for the final round?

(A) 24   (B) 27   (C) 30   (D) 33   (E) 35

Solution: Totally 30 students entered the math contest and 9 of them scored 75 or above. So the percentage of the qualified students is $9/30 \times 100 = 30\%$. Correct answer is (C).

Example 6: Which of the following correctly gives the mode, median and mean of the test scores in that order?

(A) 57, 67.5, 63.9   (B) 57, 67.6, 68.9   (C) 72, 68.5, 65.6

(D) 75, 67.5, 65.9   (E) 75, 65.7, 65.9

Solution: Mode is 75; median is $(66 + 69)/2 = 67.5$; mean is 65.9; therefore correct answer is (D).

For examples 7 and 8 please refer to the data given in figure 4:

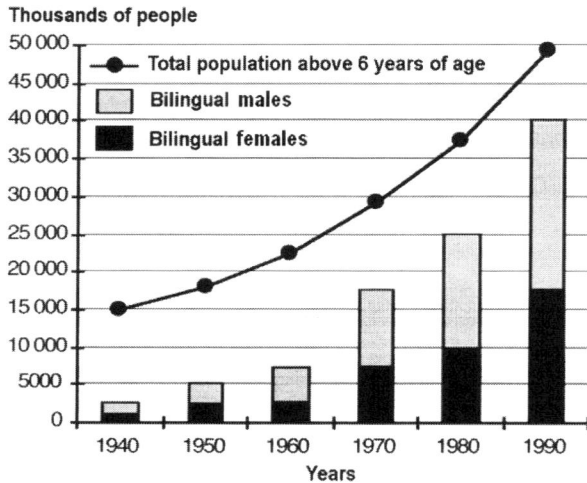

Figure 4

Example 7: In 1980 what percent of the total population above 6 years of age consisted of bilingual males?

(A) 25   (B) 27   (C) 33

(D) 40   (E) 45

Solution: In 1980, the total population was 37, 500 and number of bilingual males was 25,000 − 10,000 = 15,000. % of bilingual males was 15,000/37, 500×100 = 40%. Correct answer is (D).

Example 8: Which of the following cannot be inferred from the data given in the above graph?

(A) Bilingual females never exceeded 50% of the total bilingual population.

(B) In 1970 the number of bilingual females was 200% more than that in 1960.

(C) In 1990 the ratio of the bilingual female population to the bilingual male population was about 7/9.

(D) In the year when the bilingual population was around 18,000 approximately one fourth of all population consisted of bilingual males.

(E) In 1960 there were as many bilingual females as there were in 1950.

Solution: (D) cannot be inferred because in 1970, bilingual population was 18,000; number of bilingual males was 10,000; and total population was 30,000. Thus bilingual males accounted to more than one fourth of all population.

For examples 9 and 10 please refer to the following graph:

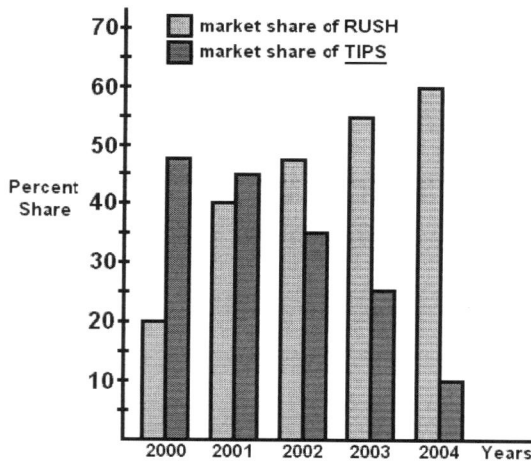

Figure 5

The graph given in figure 5 represents the market shares of two companies RUSH and TIPS in the period 2000 − 2004. Because of continuous efforts of research and development, high quality of service and a reasonable pricing policy, the market share of RUSH tends to increase whereas that of TIPS tends to decrease due to extremely high prices and very poor quality of service.

Example 9: If the market share of a company is above 50 percent, it is considered to be the leader of the market. At the year when RUSH became the leader of the market for the first time, by what percent was the market share of RUSH greater than that of TIPS?

(A) 44%   (B) 45%   (C) 46%

(D) 100%   (E) 120%

Solution: In 2003, RUSH became the leader; market shares of RUSH and TIPS were 55% and 25% respectively. In this year, market share of RUSH was 30/25×100 = 120% greater than that of TIPS. Correct answer is (E).

Example 10: If the market share of a company falls below 1 percent, it is considered to be out of the market. If the percentage decrease in the market share of TIPS over the previous year is projected to be the same after 2004, then at which year will TIPS become out of the market for the first time?

(A) 2005   (B) 2006   (C) 2007   (D) 2008   (E) 2009

Solution: In 2004, market share of TIPS decreased to $10/25 \times 100 = 40\%$. Therefore in 2007, market share of TIPS will become $10 \times 0.4^3 = 0.64\%$; it will fall below 1% and become out of the market. Correct answer is (C).

For examples 11 and 12 please refer to the data given in the following table:

Road	Grade of the road (%)	Length of the road (mi)
A	6.5	7450
B	5.7	3340
C	9.3	6520
D	4.2	9980
E	8.6	5570

A road with a grade of n% means that the height of a car driving on that road changes by n units for every change of 100 units in horizontal distance. For example a car traveling on a road with 5% grade would mean that the car traveling uphill on this road will rise 5 feet for every horizontal distance of 100 feet it covers.

Example 11: What is the angle of elevation of road B?

(A) 2.41°   (B) 3.26°   (C) 3.72°   (D) 4.92°   (E) 5.31°

Solution:

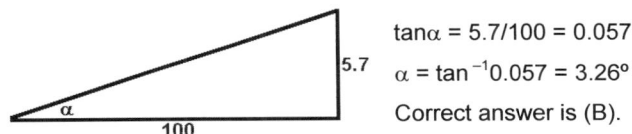

$\tan\alpha = 5.7/100 = 0.057$

$\alpha = \tan^{-1}0.057 = 3.26°$

Correct answer is (B).

Example 12: Road D climbs up a maximum height of

(A) 389 mi   (B) 403 mi   (C) 410 mi   (D) 418 mi   (E) 419 mi

Solution:

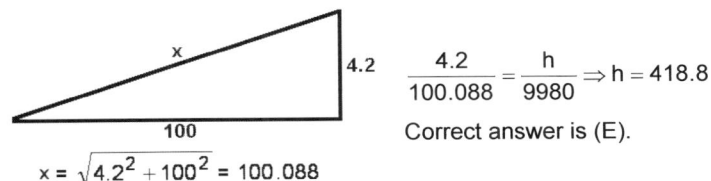

$$\frac{4.2}{100.088} = \frac{h}{9980} \Rightarrow h = 418.8$$

Correct answer is (E).

$x = \sqrt{4.2^2 + 100^2} = 100.088$

For examples 13 through 15 please refer to the following table that shows the preferences of the engineering students by major at the beginning and at the end of the sophomore year of the university.

		Major at the end of the sophomore year					
		Civil	Electrical	Computer	Environmental	Industrial	Totals at the beginning of the year
Major at the beginning of the sophomore year	Civil	45	5	8	2	6	66
	Electrical	6	40	5	0	17	68
	Computer	5	20	55	10	15	105
	Environmental	2	5	4	25	5	41
	Industrial	10	7	4	2	70	93
	Totals at the end of the year	68	77	76	47	113	

Example 13: How many students who chose to major in civil engineering at the beginning of the sophomore year changed their major to electrical engineering at the end of the sophomore year?

(A) 2   (B) 5   (C) 6   (D) 7   (E) 8

Solution: 5 students chose to major in civil engineering at the beginning of the sophomore year changed their major to electrical engineering at the end of the sophomore year; correct answer is (B).

Example 14: By the end of the sophomore year the greatest drop out in enrollment was in

(A) Civil engineering   (B) Electrical engineering   (C) Computer engineering
(D) Environmental engineering   (E) Industrial engineering

Solution: At the beginning of the sophomore year 105 students chose to major in computer engineering; at the end of the sophomore year 76 students remained in computer engineering; resulting in a dropout of 105 − 76 = 29.

Example 15: How did the enrollment to all engineering branches change at the end of the sophomore year compared to the beginning of the sophomore year?

(A) Decreased by 8   (B) Increased by 8   (C) Did not change
(D) Decreased by 6   (E) Increased by 6

Solution: At the beginning of the sophomore year, the total enrollment was 66 + 68 + 105 + 41 + 93 = 373 students. At the end of the sophomore year, the total enrollment became 68 + 77 + 76 + 47 + 113 = 381. Thus the enrollment increased by 8 students.

For examples 16 – 17 please refer to the data given in the following graph.

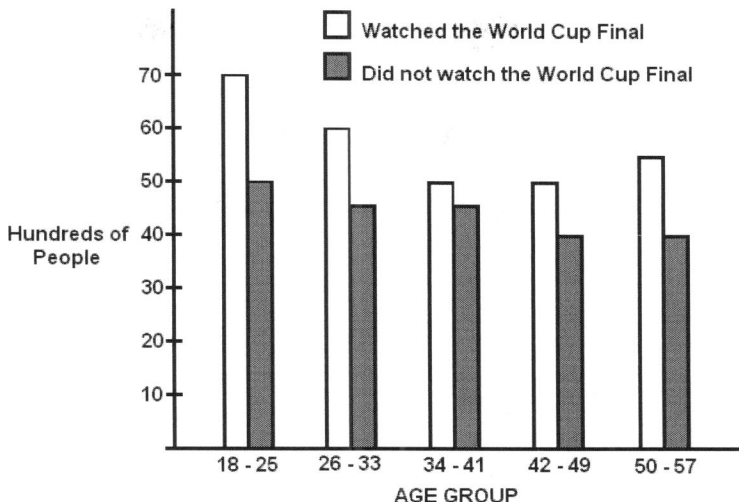

Figure 6

The bar chart given in figure 6 illustrates part of the population in town Soccerville depending on whether or not they watched the 2006 World Cup Final. For example, among the 12000 people in the 18 – 25 age group, 7000 people watched the World Cup Final whereas 5000 people did not.

Example 16: In which age group approximately 53% of the people actually watched the World Cup Final?

(A) 18 – 25　　　　(B) 26 – 33　　　　(C) 34 – 41　　　　(D) 42 – 49　　　　(E) 50 – 57

Solution: In the age group 34 – 41, 5000 watched the final and 4500 people did not, and this means that 5000/(5000 + 4500)×100 = 52.63% of the people watched the final.

Example 17: If the people not shown in the above graph account for 22 percent of the inhabitants in town Soccerville, then what is the total population in this town rounded to the nearest hundred people?

(A) 57300　　　　(B) 57400　　　　(C) 64700　　　　(D) 67400　　　　(E) 229500

Solution: If the people not shown account for 22%, then the people shown account for 78%. The graph shows the 100×(70 + 50 + 60 + 45 + 50 + 45 + 50 + 40 + 55 + 40) = 50500 people that account for 78% of the total population. So the total population is 50500/0.78 = 64743. Correct answer is (C).

For examples 18 and 19 please refer to the data given by the following pie charts:

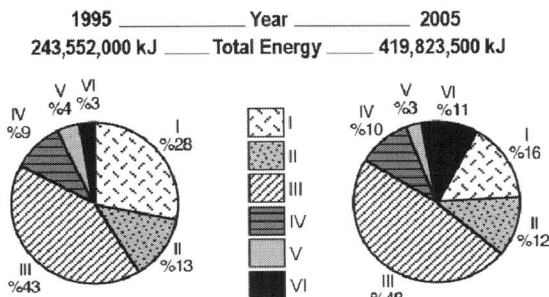

Figure 7

The pie charts given in figure 7 show the energy consumption by the six branches of industry at the city of Energion in the years of 1995 and 2005.

Example 18: How did the energy consumed in industry branch II change from 1995 to 2005?

(A) decreased by approximately 7.7%.

(B) decreased by exactly 1%.

(C) increased by more than 55%.

(D) increased by approximately 18.7%.

(E) stayed almost the same.

Solution: The energy consumed in industry branch II was approximately 244 × 0.13 = 31.72 in 1995 and 420 × 0.12 = 50.4 in 2005. So it increased by 50.4 − 31.72 = 18.68 which is an 18.68/31.72×100 = 58.9% increase. Correct answer is (C).

Example 19: Based on the data given above which of the following cannot be deduced?

(A) From 1995 to 2005, energy consumption increased in all but one branch of the industry.

(B) From 1995 to 2005, energy consumption increased by more than 90% in three branches of the industry.

(C) From 1995 to 2005, the energy consumption in the industry branch VI increased by approximately 270%.

(D) From 1995 to 2005, the energy consumption in one industry branch changed by less than 1%.

(E) From 1995 to 2005, the energy consumption in two branches of the industry almost doubled.

Solution: In order to answer this question we have to calculate the actual amounts of energy used by each industry branch in both years using the graph given:

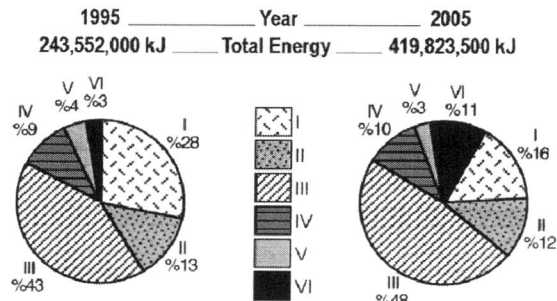

Industry Branch	Energy in 1995	Energy in 2005
I	68.3	67.2
II	31.7	50.4
III	104.9	201.6
IV	22	42
V	9.8	12.6
VI	7.3	46.2

The increase in industry branch VI is actually (46.2 − 7.3)/7.3 × 100 = 533%; correct answer is (C).

Example 20: In order to increase efficiency in company X, the information technology manager decided to record and study the time spent on the phone by the workers. The study resulted in the graph given in figure 8 above and also revealed that the maximum time that must be spent on the phone for company work is typically around 500 hours per month. The IT manager allowed 100 hours for personal usage of workers and decided to charge the workers for every number of hours used in excess of 600 hours per month, at the rate of $4.95 per hour. What was the total money charged from the workers of company X in year 2005?

(A) $13,365   (B) $14,850   (C) $15,150

(D) $22,345   (E) $49,005

TIME SPENT ON THE PHONE BY THE WORKERS OF RUSH ENTERPRISES IN YEAR 2006

☐ **100 hours of time spent on the phone**

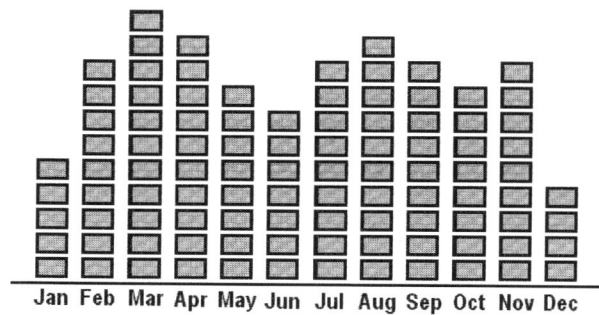

Jan Feb Mar Apr May Jun Jul Aug Sep Oct Nov Dec

Figure 8

Solution:

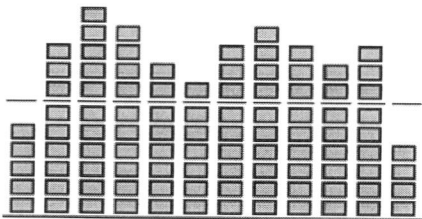

The excess number of hours is 30 × 100 = 3000 hours as shown in the figure to the left. So the money collected is 3000 × 4.95 = $14860. Correct answer is (B).

Let no one enter who does not know geometry.

Inscription on Plato's door at the Academy in Athens.

CHAPTER 3 – Geometry

3.1 BASICS

Points, Lines, Rays, Half Lines, Line Segments, Angles, Planes And Space

Line *l* or AB

Half line]AB

Ray [AB

Line segment]AB[or (AB)

Line segment [AB]

Line segment [AB[or [AB)

Line segment]AB] or (AB]

1. A point has neither width nor thickness, only position.
2. A line is a set of points that straightly continues in both directions, with no thickness.
3. A plane is a set of points that continues infinitely in all directions and has no thickness or depth.

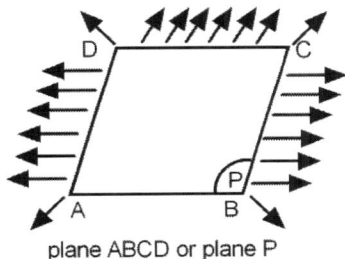

plane ABCD or plane P

4. Two lines are parallel if they lie in the same plane and do not intersect.

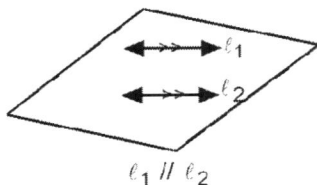

$\ell_1 \parallel \ell_2$

5. The distance between two parallel lines is always constant.

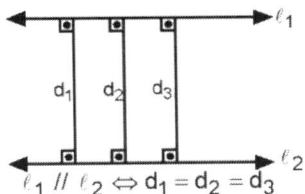

$\ell_1 \parallel \ell_2 \Leftrightarrow d_1 = d_2 = d_3$

6. A line contains at least two points; a plane contains at least three points which are not all in one line; space contains at least four points which are not all in one plane. Two distinct points determine a line; three distinct non collinear points determine a plane and four distinct non coplanar points determine a space.

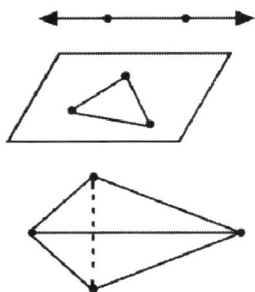

7. Through any two points there is exactly one line.

8. Through any three points there is at least one plane, and through any three points which are not in the same line, there is exactly one plane.

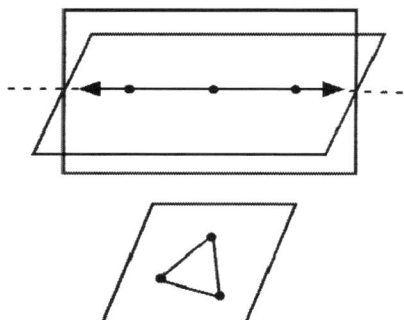

9. If two points are in a plane, then the line that contains those points is in the same plane as well.

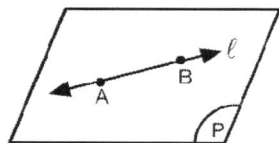

    If $A \in P$ and $B \in P$ then $AB = \ell \in P$

10. The intersection of two distinct non parallel planes is a line.

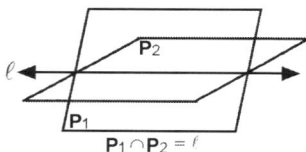

    $P_1 \cap P_2 = \ell$

11.   The intersection of two distinct coplanar lines is a point.

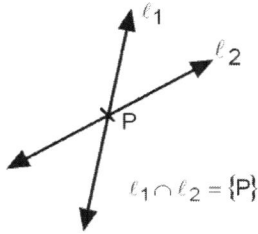

$$\ell_1 \cap \ell_2 = \{P\}$$

12.   Exactly one plane contains both of a line and a point which is not on that line.

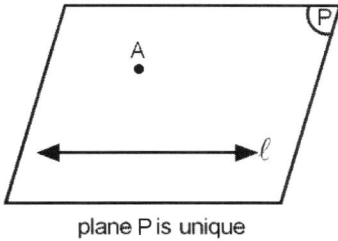

plane P is unique

13.   Exactly one plane contains both of two intersecting lines.

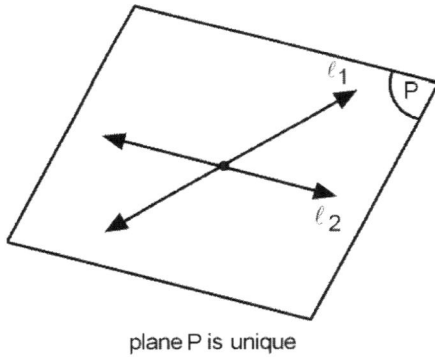

plane P is unique

14.   If two parallel planes are intersected by a third plane, then the resulting lines of intersection are parallel.

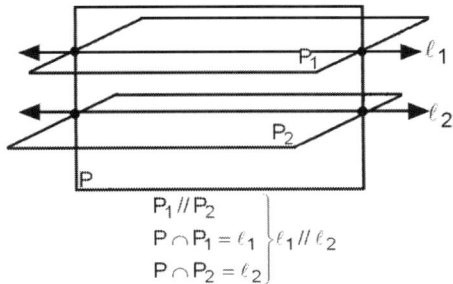

$$P_1 /\!/ P_2$$
$$P \cap P_1 = \ell_1 \ \}\ \ell_1 /\!/ \ell_2$$
$$P \cap P_2 = \ell_2$$

15. If a transversal is perpendicular to a line, then the transversal is perpendicular to any line contained within the same plane and parallel to the given line. In a plane two or more lines perpendicular to the same line are parallel.

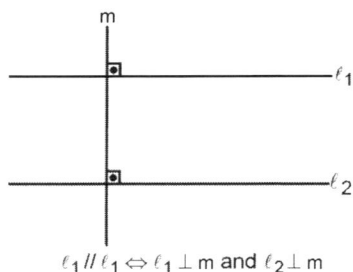

$\ell_1 \,//\, \ell_1 \Leftrightarrow \ell_1 \perp m$ and $\ell_2 \perp m$

16. There is exactly one line parallel to a given line through a point outside the line.

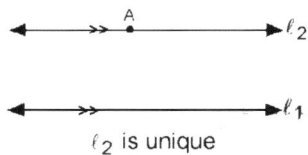

ℓ_2 is unique

17. There is exactly one line perpendicular to a given line through a point outside the line,

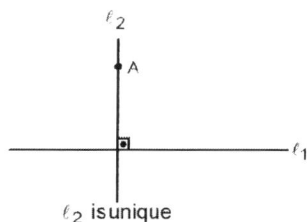

ℓ_2 is unique

18. Two lines parallel to a third line are parallel to each other.

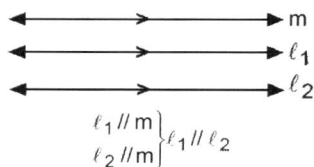

$\left.\begin{array}{l} \ell_1 \,//\, m \\ \ell_2 \,//\, m \end{array}\right\} \ell_1 \,//\, \ell_2$

19. If a point lies on the perpendicular bisector of a line segment, then the distances from the point to the endpoints of the segment are equal. If a point is equidistant from the endpoints of a line segment, then the point lies on the perpendicular bisector of this segment.

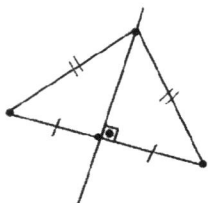

20.   If three parallel lines generate equal segments on one transversal, then they generate equal segments on every transversal.

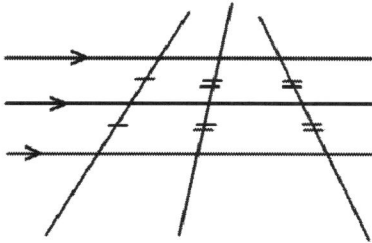

21.   The perpendicular segment from a point to a line is the shortest among all segments from the point to the line.

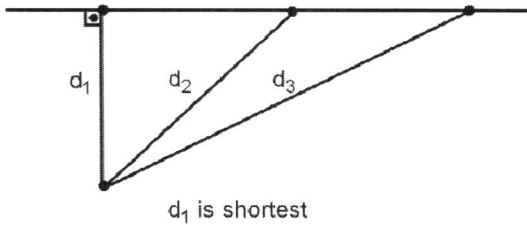

d_1 is shortest

22.   The perpendicular segment from a point to a plane is the shortest among all segments from the point to the plane.

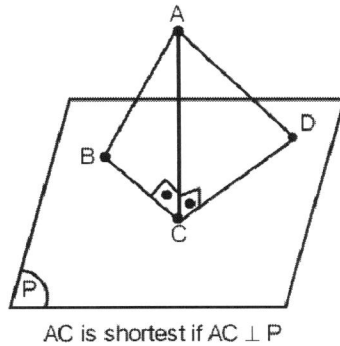

AC is shortest if AC ⊥ P

3.2 LOCUS

Locus is the geometric figure that results when all points that satisfy a certain condition are joined. The phrases of "locus of points" and "set of points" can be used interchangeably (locus: singular, loci: plural).

Two Dimensional Loci

- The locus of points equidistant from a given point in a plane is the circle whose center is the given point.

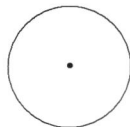

- The locus of points equidistant from a given line in a plane consists of two parallel lines that have the given line in between.

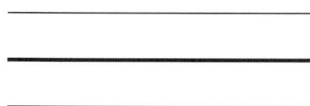

- The locus of points equidistant from two parallel lines in a plane is the line that is equally spaced between these two lines.

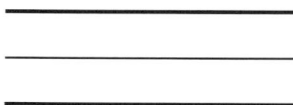

- The locus of points equidistant from two intersecting lines in a plane consists of the bisectors of the vertical angles formed by these lines.

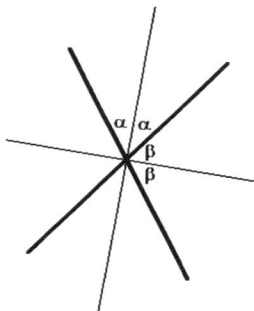

- The locus of points equidistant from two given points in a plane is the perpendicular bisector of the segment that joins these two points.

Conic Sections in Two Dimensions

- The locus of points at a distance r from a given point P in a plane is the **circle** whose center is at P and whose radius is r.

- The locus of points in a plane, whose distances from two fixed points F_1 and F_2 sums up to 2A is the **ellipse** whose foci are at F_1 and F_2 having a major axis of length 2A.

- The locus of points in a plane, whose distances from two fixed points F_1 and F_2 have a constant difference of 2A is the **hyperbola** whose foci are at F_1 and F_2 having a transverse axis of length 2A.

- The locus of points in a plane, equidistant from a given point P and a line d is the **parabola** whose focus is at P and whose directrix is d.

Three Dimensional Loci

- The locus of points equidistant from a given point in space is the sphere whose center is the given point.

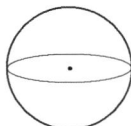

- The locus of points equidistant from a given plane in space consists of two parallel planes that have the given plane in between.

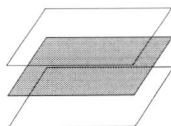

- The locus of points equidistant from two parallel planes in space is the plane that is equally spaced between these two planes.

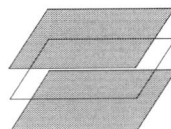

- The locus of points equidistant from two given points in space is the plane that perpendicularly bisects the segment that joins these two points.

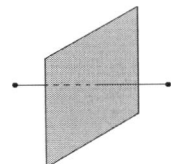

- The locus of points equidistant from a given line in space consists of a hollow cylinedrical surface (a cylindrical tube) whose axis of symmetry is the given line.

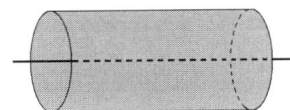

3.3 ANGLES

1. A right angle has the degree measure of 90°.

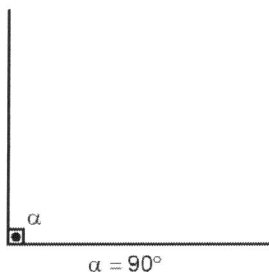

$$\alpha = 90°$$

2. An obtuse angle has a measure that is greater than 90° and less than 90°.

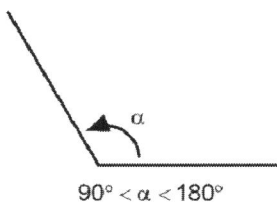

$$90° < \alpha < 180°$$

3. An acute angle has a measure less than 90°.

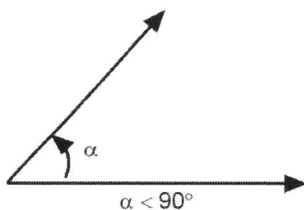

$$\alpha < 90°$$

4. Two angles are complementary if their measures add up to 90°.

5. Two angles are supplementary if their measures add up to 180°.

6. The supplements of congruent angles (or of the same angle) are also congruent.

$$\left.\begin{array}{l}\hat{x}+\hat{y}=180°\\ \hat{x}+\hat{z}=180°\end{array}\right\}\hat{y}=\hat{z}$$

    The complements of congruent angles (or of the same angle) are also congruent.

$$\left.\begin{array}{l}\hat{x}+\hat{y}=90°\\ \hat{x}+z=90°\end{array}\right\}\hat{y}=\hat{z}$$

7. Vertical angles are congruent.

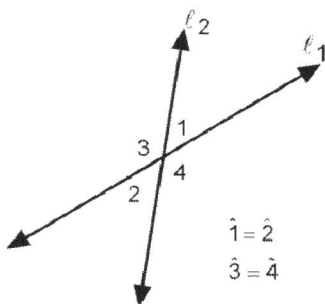

$$\hat{1}=\hat{2}$$
$$\hat{3}=\hat{4}$$

8. If two lines are perpendicular, then they generate congruent adjacent angles. If two lines generate congruent adjacent angles, then the lines are perpendicular.

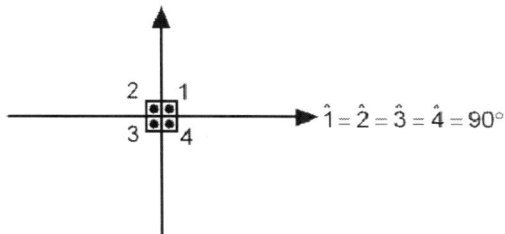

$$\hat{1} = \hat{2} = \hat{3} = \hat{4} = 90°$$

9. If the exterior sides of two adjacent acute angles are perpendicular to each other, then the angles are complementary.

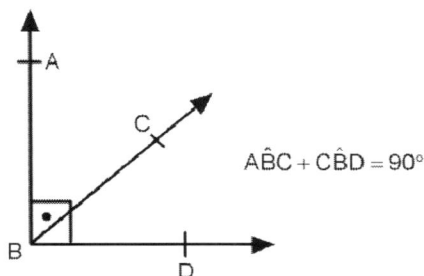

$$A\hat{B}C + C\hat{B}D = 90°$$

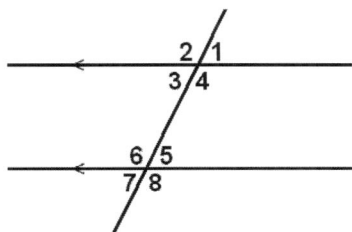

10. If two parallel lines are cut by a transversal, then the corresponding angles are congruent. If two lines are cut by a transversal and the corresponding angles are congruent, then the lines are parallel.

$$\hat{1} = \hat{5}$$
$$\hat{2} = \hat{6}$$
$$\hat{3} = \hat{7}$$
$$\hat{4} = \hat{8}$$

11. If two parallel lines are cut by a transversal, then the alternate interior angles are congruent. If two lines are cut by a transversal and the alternate interior angles are congruent, then the lines are parallel.

$$\hat{3} = \hat{5}$$
$$\hat{4} = \hat{6}$$

12. If two parallel lines are cut by a transversal, then the same side interior angles are supplementary. If two lines are cut by a transversal and the same side interior angles are supplementary, then the lines are parallel.

$$\hat{4} + \hat{5} = 180°$$
$$\hat{3} + \hat{6} = 180°$$

13. If two parallel lines are cut by a transversal, then the alternate exterior angles are congruent. If two lines are cut by a transversal and the alternate exterior angles are congruent, then the lines are parallel.

    $\hat{1} = \hat{7}$

    $\hat{2} = \hat{8}$

14. If two parallel lines are cut by a transversal, then the same side exterior angles are supplementary. If two lines are cut by a transversal and the same side exterior angles are supplementary, then the lines are parallel.

    $\hat{1} + \hat{8} = 180°$

    $\hat{2} + \hat{7} = 180°$

15. If a point lies on the bisector of an angle, then the point is equidistant from the sides of the angle. If a point is equidistant from the sides of an angle, then the point lies on the bisector of the angle.

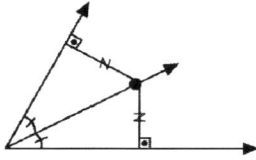

3.4 POLYGONS

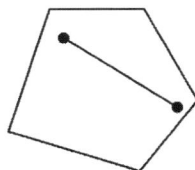 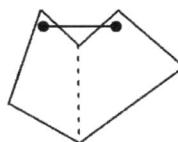

convex   not convex

1.   Sum of the measures of the interior angles of a convex polygon is $(n-2)\cdot 180°$, where n is the number of sides.

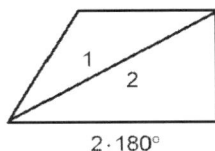 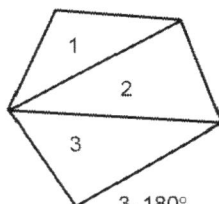 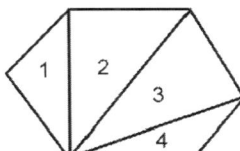

2.   Sum of the measures of the exterior angles of a convex polygon is 360°.

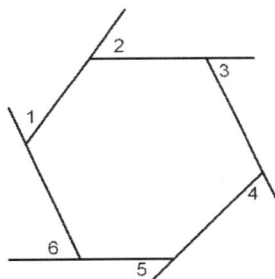 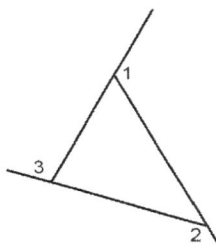

$\hat{1}+\hat{2}+\hat{3}+\hat{4}+\hat{5}+\hat{6}=360°$ $\hat{1}+\hat{2}+\hat{3}=360°$

3.   Area of a regular polygon equals half the product of length of the apothem and the perimeter. ($A = \dfrac{1}{2}aP$; a

is length of the apothem and P is the perimeter of the polygon)

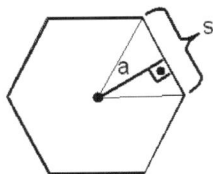

$Area = \dfrac{1}{2}\cdot a\cdot (6s)$

Where $6s = perimeter$

4.   Number of diagonals of a regular polygon having n sides is $\dbinom{n}{2}-n = \dfrac{n\cdot (n-3)}{2}$.

3.5 TRIANGLES

1. Sum of the measures of the angles of a triangle is 180°.

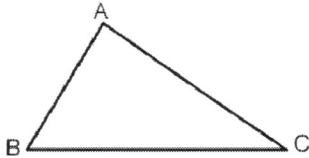

$$\hat{A} + \hat{B} + \hat{C} = 180°$$

2. Measure of an exterior angle of a triangle is equal to the sum of the measures of its remote interior angles.

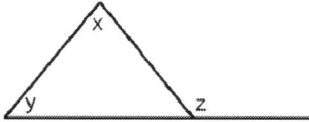

$$\hat{x} + \hat{y} = \hat{z}$$

3. The area A of any triangle is related to the length, a, of any base and the altitude, h_a, to that base by A = $\frac{1}{2}$ a h_a.

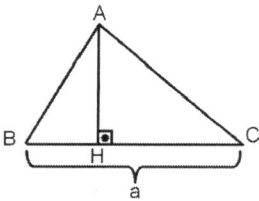

$h_a = AH$

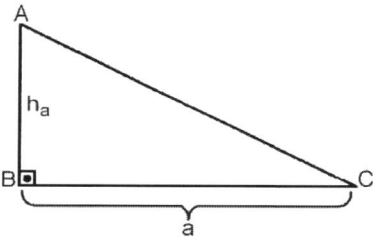

$h_a = AB$

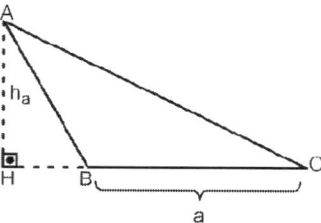

$h_a = AH$

4. If A and B are the midpoints of the sides of a triangle, then AB = $\frac{1}{2}$ CD and AB || CD. AB is also called the midbase.

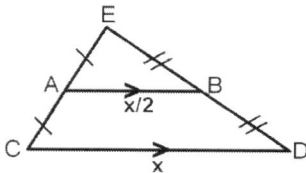

If A & B are midpoints of EC and ED respectively then

AB || CD and

$|CD| = x$

$|AB| = \dfrac{x}{2}$

5. A line containing the midpoint of one side of a triangle being parallel to another side passes through the midpoint of the third side.

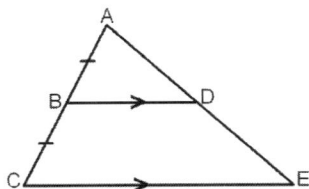

$AB = BC$ and $BD \mathbin{/\!/} CE \Rightarrow AD = DE$

6. If two sides of a triangle are congruent, then the angles opposite those sides are congruent or if two angles of a triangle are congruent, then the sides opposite those angles are congruent.

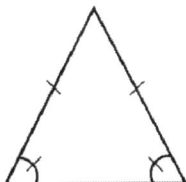

7. The bisector of the vertex angle of an isosceles triangle is perpendicular to the base at its midpoint.

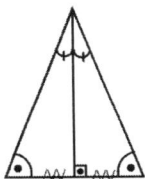

8. If the bisector of the vertex angle of a triangle is perpendicular to the base, the triangle is isosceles. If the bisector of the vertex angle of a triangle intersects the base at its midpoint, the triangle is isosceles. If the altitude to the base intersects the base at its midpoint, the triangle is isosceles.

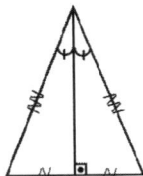

9. In an isosceles triangle ABC, C is the vertex and P is an arbitrarily selected point on the base. If segments PQ and PR are each parallel to one of the congruent sides, then their lengths sum up to the length of a congruent side.

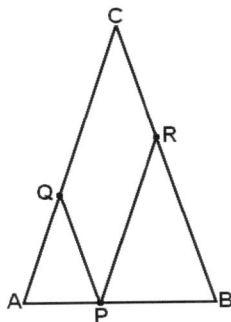

$PQ + PR = CA = CB$

10. In an isosceles triangle ABC, C is the vertex and P is an arbitrarily selected point on the base. If segments PQ and PR are each perpendicular to one of the congruent sides, then their lengths sum up to the length of an altitude to a congruent side.

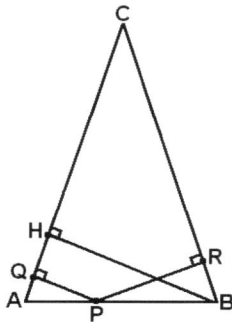

$$PQ + PR = h_a = h_b$$

11. An equiangular triangle is equilateral and an equilateral triangle is equiangular. Each angle of an equiangular triangle has measures 60°. Each angle of an equilateral triangle measures 60°.

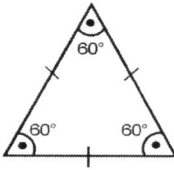

12. If s is the length of one side of an equilateral triangle and h is the length of the length of each side then the following equalities hold:

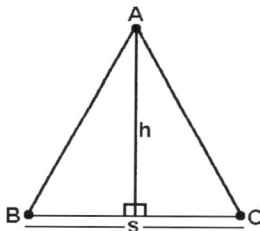

$$\text{Area of } \overset{\triangle}{ABC} = \frac{s^2 \sqrt{3}}{4}$$

$$h = \frac{s\sqrt{3}}{2}$$

13. In an equilateral triangle ABC, P is an arbitrarily selected point inside the triangle. If segments PD, PE and PF are each parallel to one side of the triangle, then their lengths sum up to the length one of the sides.

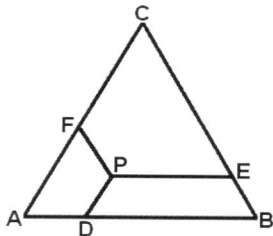

$$PD + PE + PF = a = b = c$$

14. In an equilateral triangle ABC, P is an arbitrarily selected point inside the triangle. If segments PD, PE and PF are each perpendicular to one side of the triangle, then their lengths sum up to the length an altitude.

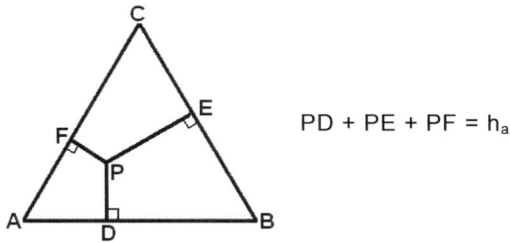

$$PD + PE + PF = h_a$$

15. If two angles of one triangle are congruent to two angles of another triangle, then the third angles are congruent.

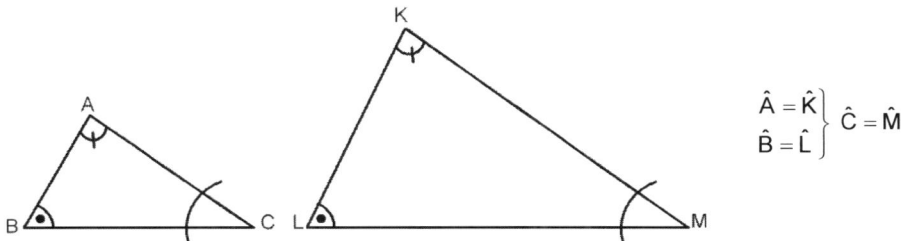

$$\left.\begin{array}{l}\hat{A}=\hat{K}\\\hat{B}=\hat{L}\end{array}\right\} \hat{C}=\hat{M}$$

16. In a triangle, there can be at most one right angle or obtuse angle.

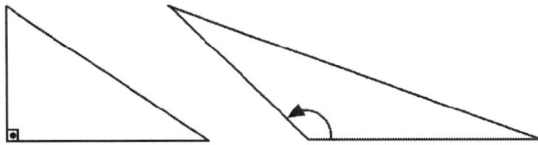

17. Measure of an exterior angle of a triangle is greater than each of the measures of the remote interior angles.

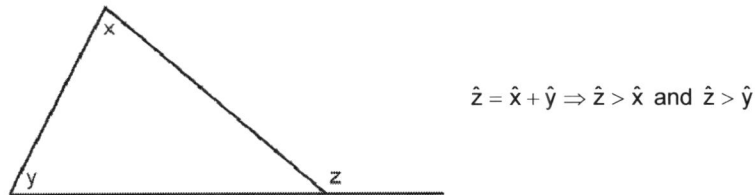

$$\hat{z}=\hat{x}+\hat{y} \Rightarrow \hat{z}>\hat{x} \text{ and } \hat{z}>\hat{y}$$

18. If one side of a triangle is longer than a second side, then the angle opposite the first side is greater than the angle opposite the second side; if one angle of a triangle is greater than a second angle, then the side opposite the first angle is longer than the side opposite the second angle.

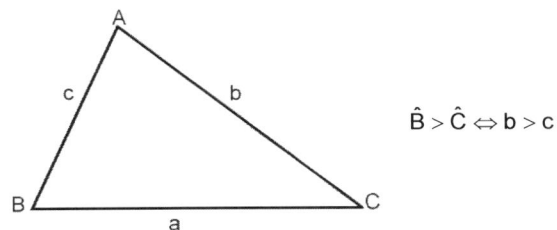

$$\hat{B}>\hat{C} \Leftrightarrow b>c$$

19. The same relation exists between the sides and the angles of a triangle.

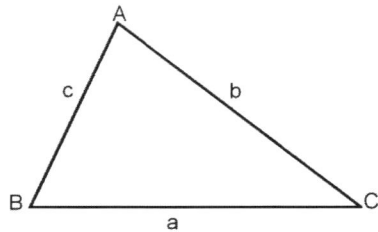

$$\hat{B} < \hat{C} = \hat{A} \Leftrightarrow b < c = a$$

20. Sum of the lengths of any two sides of a triangle is greater than the length of the third side. Difference of the lengths of any two sides of a triangle is less than the lengths of the third side. Sum of the lengths of the two shortest sides of a triangle must exceed the longest side for the triangle to be realized.

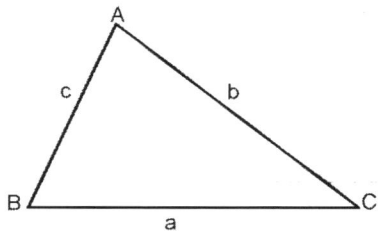

$$|a - b| < c < a + b$$

21. If two sides of one triangle are congruent to two sides of another triangle, but the included angle in the first triangle is larger than the included angle in the second one, then the third side of the first triangle is longer than the third side of the second triangle. If two sides of one triangle are congruent to two sides of another triangle, but the third side of the first triangle is longer than the third side of the second; then the included angle in the first triangle is larger than the included angle in the second.

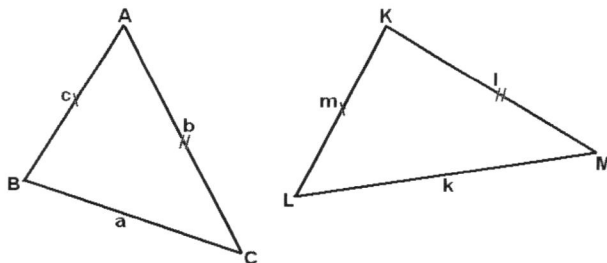

$$c = m$$
$$b = l$$
$$\hat{A} < \hat{K} \Leftrightarrow a < k$$

22. Bisectors of the angles of a triangle intersect at a point equidistant from the three sides of the triangle. This point is the center of the inscribed circle, the unique circle that is tangent to all sides of this triangle.

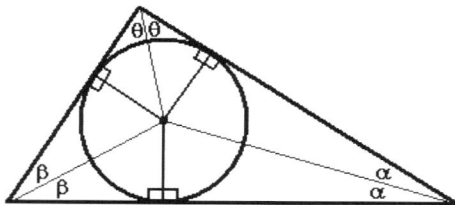

23.   Perpendicular bisectors of the sides of a triangle intersect at a point equidistant from the three vertices of the triangle. This point is the center of the circumscribed circle, the unique circle that passes through the vertices of the triangle.

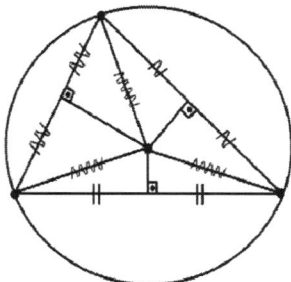

24.   Altitudes of a triangle intersect at a unique point.

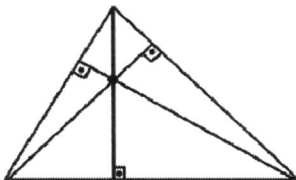

25.   Medians of a triangle intersect at a unique point called the center of gravity or the centroid. The distance from the centroid to a vertex is two thirds of the length of the corresponding median length.

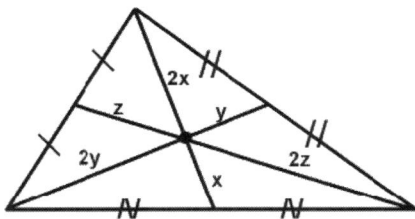

3.6 RIGHT TRIANGLES

1. Midpoint of the hypotenuse of a right triangle is equidistant from all of the three vertices of this triangle (the rule of the "magnificent three"). The median to the hypotenuse of a right triangle has a length that is half the length of the hypotenuse.

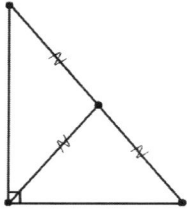

2. A triangle is a right triangle if and only if the square of the length of its longest side (the hypotenuse) is equal to the sum of the squares of the lengths of the remaining two sides (the legs). This is called the Pythagorean theorem.

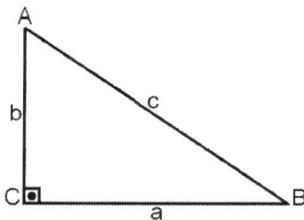

$$\hat{C} = 90° \Leftrightarrow a^2 + b^2 = c^2$$

3. The $45° - 45° - 90°$ triangle.

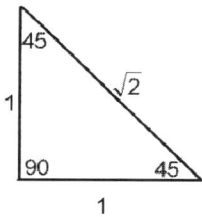

4. The $30° - 60° - 90°$ triangle.

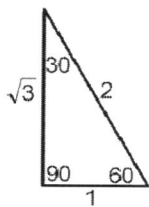

5. Triangles with sides having the lengths of $3 - 4 - 5$, $5 - 12 - 13$, $8 - 15 - 17$ and $7 - 24 - 25$ are right triangles and so are triangles with sides that are enlarged in the same proportion.

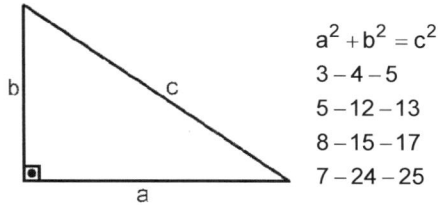

$$a^2 + b^2 = c^2$$
$$3 - 4 - 5$$
$$5 - 12 - 13$$
$$8 - 15 - 17$$
$$7 - 24 - 25$$

6. Euclid's Relations:

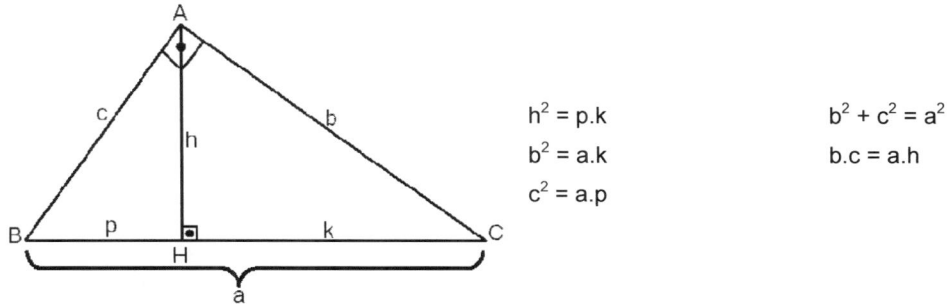

$h^2 = p.k$ $b^2 + c^2 = a^2$

$b^2 = a.k$ $b.c = a.h$

$c^2 = a.p$

7. Acute angles of a right triangle are complementary.

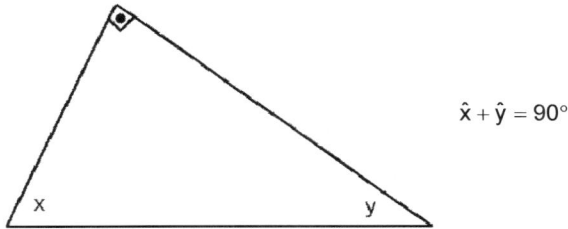

$$\hat{x} + \hat{y} = 90°$$

8. If the altitude is drawn to the hypotenuse of a right triangle, then the two triangles generated are similar to the original triangle and to each other.

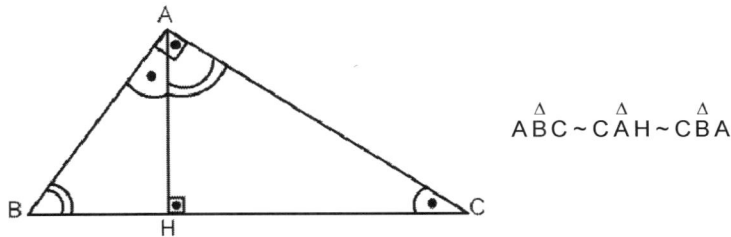

$$\overset{\Delta}{ABC} \sim \overset{\Delta}{CAH} \sim \overset{\Delta}{CBA}$$

9. If the square of the longest side of a triangle is less than the sum of the squares of the other two sides, then the triangle is an acute triangle.

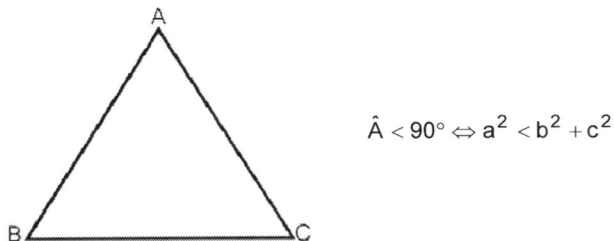

$$\hat{A} < 90° \Leftrightarrow a^2 < b^2 + c^2$$

10. If the square of the longest side of a triangle is greater than the sum of the squares of the other two sides, then the triangle is an obtuse triangle.

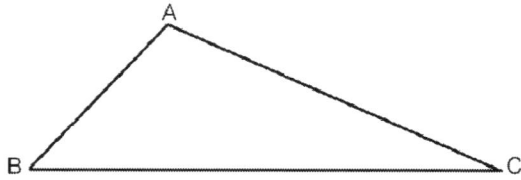

$$\hat{A} > 90° \Leftrightarrow a^2 > b^2 + c^2$$

3.7 CONGRUENCE

1. If two triangles are congruent then all pairs of corresponding parts of the triangles are also congruent. Congruent triangles are identical in every aspect (CPCT: **C**orresponding **P**arts of **C**ongruent **T**riangles).

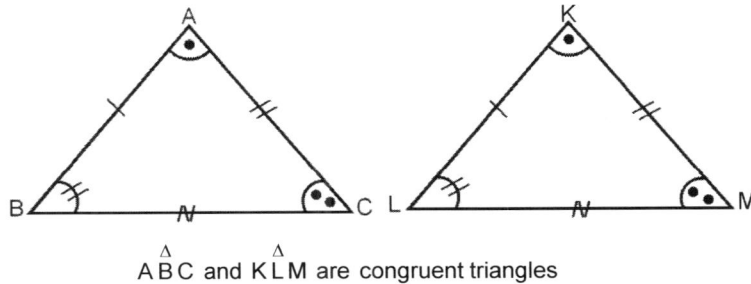

$\overset{\wedge}{ABC}$ and $\overset{\wedge}{KLM}$ are congruent triangles

2. If two sides and the angle included in one triangle are each congruent to the corresponding parts of a second triangle, the triangles are congruent. (SAS: **S**ide **A**ngle **S**ide)

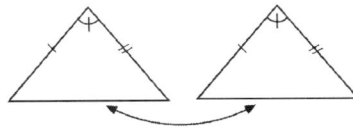

congruent triangles (SAS)

3. If two angles and the included side in one triangle are each congruent to the corresponding parts of a second triangle, the triangles are congruent. (ASA: **A**ngle **S**ide **A**ngle)

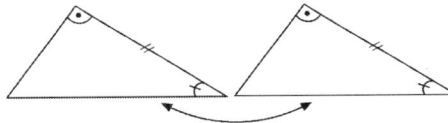

congruent triangles (ASA)

4. If the three sides of one triangle are each congruent to the corresponding sides of a second triangle, then the triangles are congruent. (SSS: **S**ide **S**ide **S**ide)

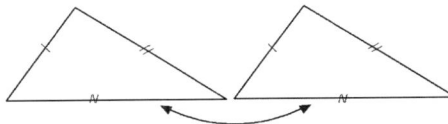

congruent triangles (SSS)

5. If two angles and a side opposite one of the angles are each congruent to the corresponding parts of a second triangle, the triangles are congruent. This is a direct result of the ASA postulate. (SAA: **S**ide **A**ngle **A**ngle)

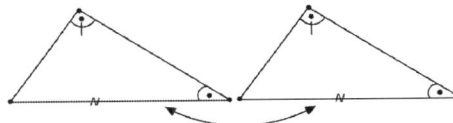

congruent triangles (SAA)

6.   If the hypotenuse and one of the legs of a right triangle are congruent to the corresponding parts of a second right triangle, the two triangles are congruent. This is a direct result of the Pythagorean theorem. (HL: **H**ypotenuse **L**eg)

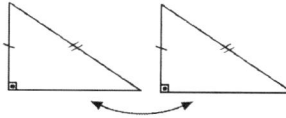

congruent triangles (HL)

7.   If the hypotenuse and one of the acute angles of a right triangle are congruent to the corresponding parts of a second right triangle, the two triangles are congruent. (HA: **H**ypotenuse **A**ngle)

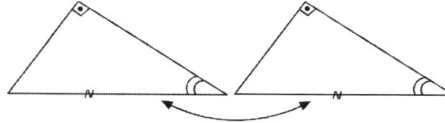

congruent triangles (HA)

8.   If two figures are congruent, they have the same area.

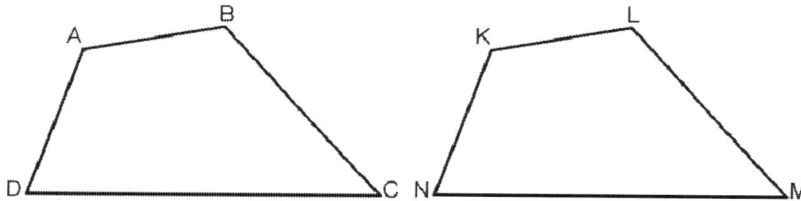

3.8 SIMILARITY

1.   If the lengths of all three pairs of corresponding sides are proportional then the triangles are similar (**SSS**: **S**ide **S**ide **S**ide).

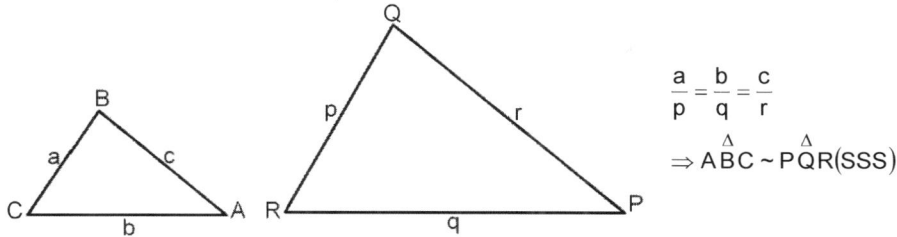

$$\frac{a}{p} = \frac{b}{q} = \frac{c}{r}$$

$$\Rightarrow \overset{\triangle}{ABC} \sim \overset{\triangle}{PQR}(SSS)$$

2.   If any two pairs of corresponding angles are congruent then the triangles are similar (**AA**: **A**ngle **A**ngle or **AAA**: **A**ngle **A**ngle **A**ngle).

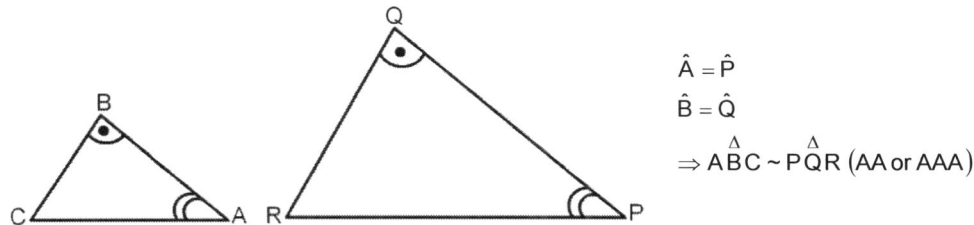

$$\hat{A} = \hat{P}$$
$$\hat{B} = \hat{Q}$$
$$\Rightarrow \overset{\triangle}{ABC} \sim \overset{\triangle}{PQR} \left(AA \text{ or } AAA \right)$$

3.   If two pairs of corresponding sides are proportional and their included angles are congruent then the triangles are similar (**SAS**: **S**ide **A**ngle **S**ide).

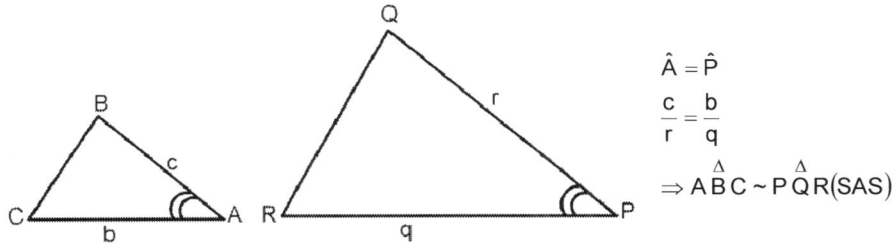

$$\hat{A} = \hat{P}$$
$$\frac{c}{r} = \frac{b}{q}$$
$$\Rightarrow \overset{\triangle}{ABC} \sim \overset{\triangle}{PQR}(SAS)$$

4.   If two triangles are similar, then the pairs of corresponding sides, altitudes, medians, angle bisectors, radii of inscribed circles, radii of circumscribed circles, and the sine of the corresponding angles are proportional with the same scale factor.

5.   A line parallel to one side of a triangle intersecting the other two sides divides those sides proportionally (**Thales** theorem).

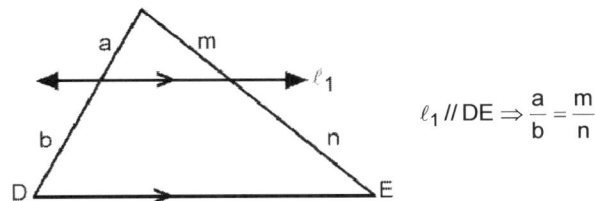

$$\ell_1 \text{ // } DE \Rightarrow \frac{a}{b} = \frac{m}{n}$$

6.   Three parallel lines that intersect two transversals divide the transversals proportionally.

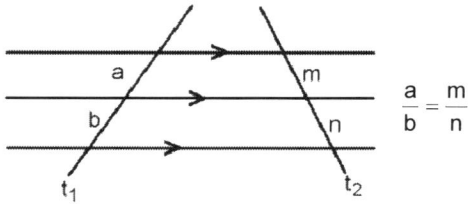

$$\frac{a}{b}=\frac{m}{n}$$

7.   A ray that bisects an angle of a triangle divides the opposite side into segments proportional to the length of the other two sides (**Angle Bisector** Theorem).

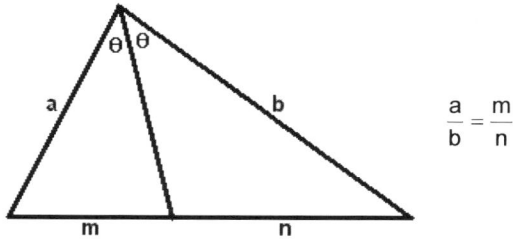

$$\frac{a}{b}=\frac{m}{n}$$

8.   If two figures are similar with a scale factor of k, then the ratio of their perimeters is k and the ratio of their areas is k^2.

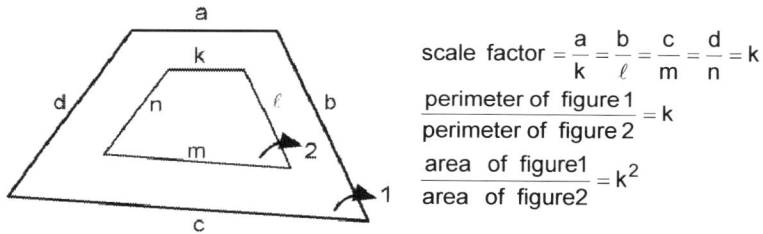

$$\text{scale factor}=\frac{a}{k}=\frac{b}{\ell}=\frac{c}{m}=\frac{d}{n}=k$$

$$\frac{\text{perimeter of figure 1}}{\text{perimeter of figure 2}}=k$$

$$\frac{\text{area of figure1}}{\text{area of figure2}}=k^2$$

3.9 QUADRILATERALS

1.   If both pairs of opposite sides or opposite angles of a quadrilateral are congruent, then the quadrilateral is a parallelogram.

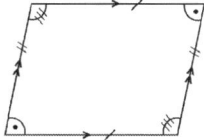

2.   If diagonals of a quadrilateral bisect each other, then the quadrilateral is a parallelogram.

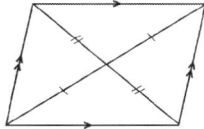

3.   If a pair of opposite sides of a quadrilateral are both parallel and congruent, then the quadrilateral is a parallelogram.

4.   If both pairs of opposite angles of a quadrilateral are congruent, then the quadrilateral is a parallelogram.

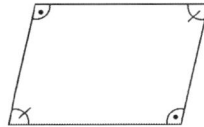

5.   If two lines are parallel, then the perpendicular distance between the lines is always the same.

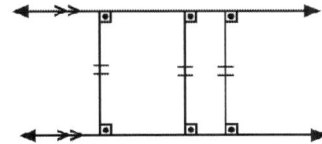

6.   Diagonals of a rectangle are equal in length.

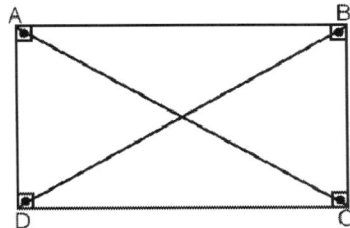

7. Diagonals of a rhombus are perpendicular.

8. Each diagonal of a rhombus bisects two opposite angles of the rhombus.

9. If one angle of a parallelogram measures 90 degrees, then the parallelogram is a rectangle.

10. If two consecutive sides of a parallelogram are congruent; then it is a rhombus.

11. Base angles of an isosceles trapezoid are congruent.

12. Mid – base of a trapezoid is parallel to the bases and has a length is equal to the average of the base lengths. Area of a trapezoid equals half the product of the altitude and the sum of the bases.

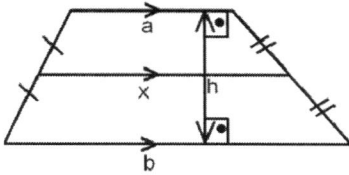

$$x = \frac{a+b}{2}$$

$$\text{Area} = \frac{a+b}{2}h$$

13. If A is the area of a square and s is the length of one side, then $A = s^2$. The perimeter, P, is 4s.

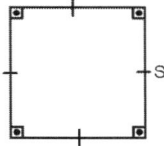

14. If A is the area of a rectangle, l is its length and w its width, then $A = lw$. Perimeter, P, equals $2l + 2w$.

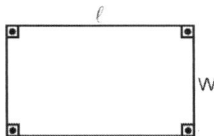

15. Area of a parallelogram equals the product of one of the bases and the altitude to that base. ($A = b.h_b = a.h_a$)

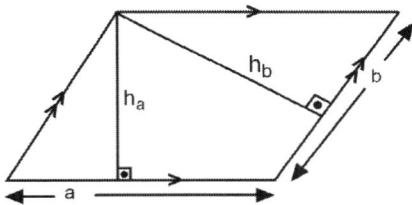

16. Area of a rhombus equals half the product of length of its diagonals ($A = \frac{d_1.d_2}{2}$). In a quadrilateral, if diagonals d_1 and d_2 are perpendicular to each other, area of the quadrilateral (deltoid for instance) equals half the product of its diagonals ($A = \frac{d_1.d_2}{2}$). If diagonals are not perpendicular, area A is given as: $A = \frac{d_1.d_2 \sin(\alpha)}{2}$ where α equals the measure of the angle between the diagonals.

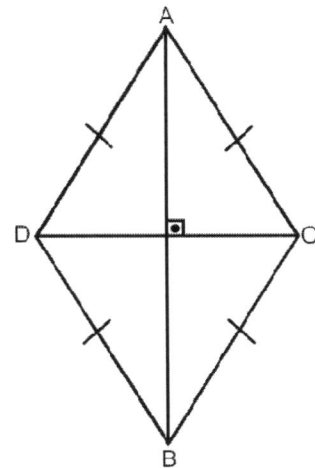

3.10 CIRCLES

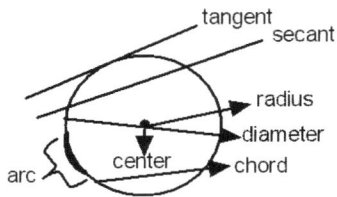

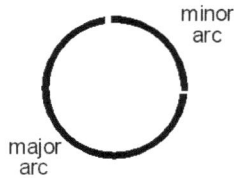

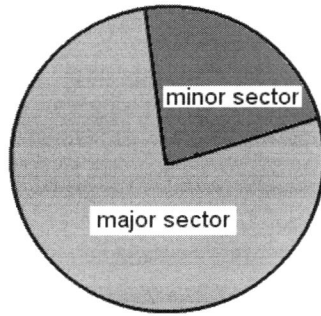

1. Central angle measures as much as its intercepted arc.

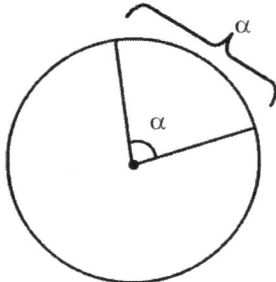

2. Inscribed angle measures half as much as its intercepted arc.

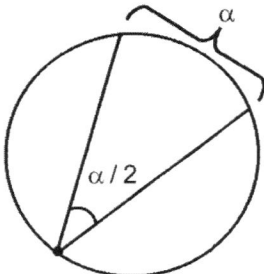

3. Tangent – chord angle measures half as much as its intercepted arc.

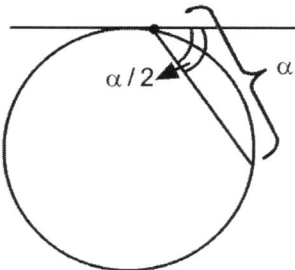

4. An angle inscribed in a semicircle is a right angle and measures 90°.

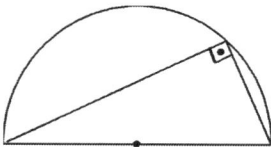

5.   An interior angle in a circle measures half as much as the average of its intercepted arcs.

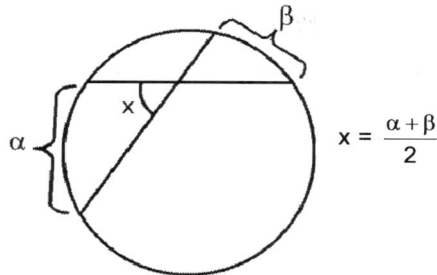

$$x = \frac{\alpha + \beta}{2}$$

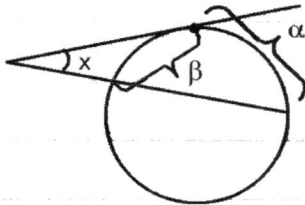

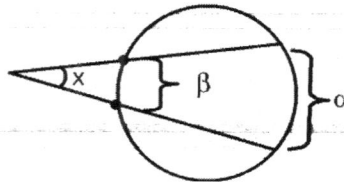

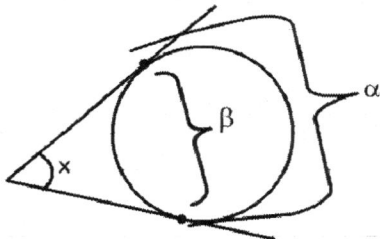

6.   An exterior angle measures half as much as the difference of its intercepted arcs.

$$x = \frac{\alpha - \beta}{2}$$

Special case: $\alpha + \beta = 360° \ x + \beta = 180°$

7.   If a line is tangent to a circle, then the line is perpendicular to the radius at the point of tangency. If a line in the plane of a circle is perpendicular to a radius, then the line is tangent to the circle.

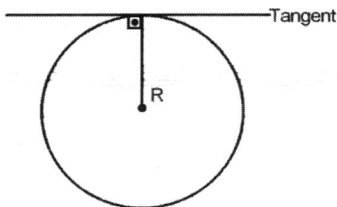

8.   Tangents to a circle from a point outside the circle are congruent.

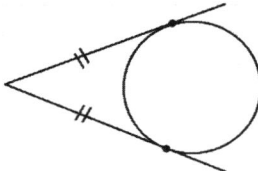

9.	Two minor arcs in a circle are congruent if and only if their central angles have equal measures.

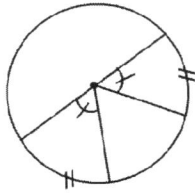

10.	Congruent arcs in a circle contain congruent chords and congruent chords in a circle contain congruent arcs.

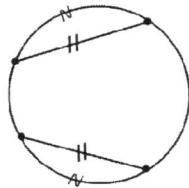

11.	A diameter perpendicular to a chord bisects the chord and its two arcs.

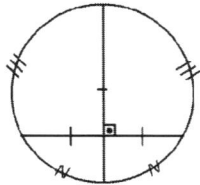

12.	In a circle, congruent chords are equally distant from the center and chords equally distant from the center are congruent.

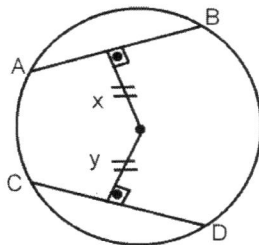

13.	If two inscribed angles intercept the same arc, then their measures are equal.

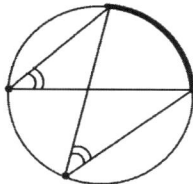

14. If a quadrilateral can be inscribed in a circle, then its opposite angles are supplementary.

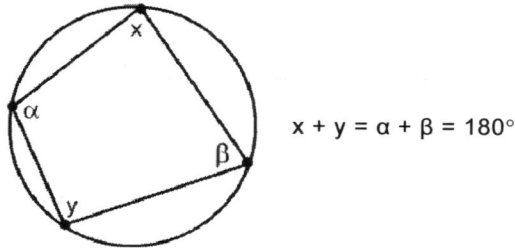

$$x + y = \alpha + \beta = 180°$$

15. If a circle can be inscribed in a quadrilateral, then the following equality holds: x + y = a + b.

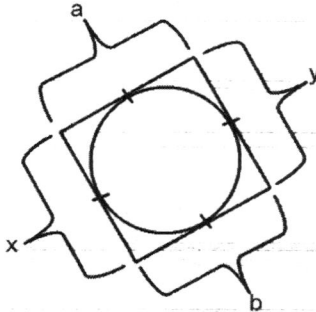

16. The following relations are present concerning the lengths of the tangent and secant lines originating from the same point outside a circle:

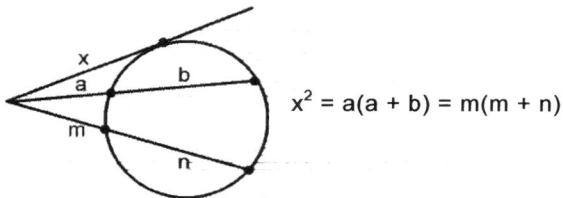

$$x^2 = a(a + b) = m(m + n)$$

17. The following relations are present concerning the lengths of the chords intersecting inside a circle:

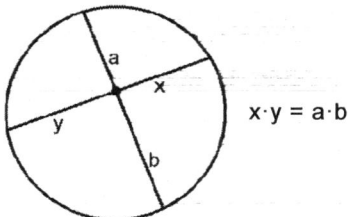

$$x \cdot y = a \cdot b$$

18. Area and perimeter of a circle are given by the following formulas, where r and d represent the radius and the diameter of the circle:

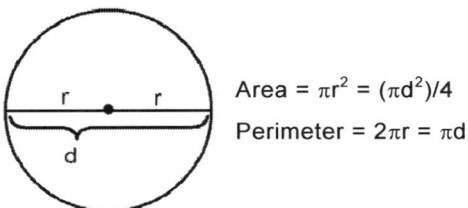

Area = $\pi r^2 = (\pi d^2)/4$

Perimeter = $2\pi r = \pi d$

19.   Area of a circular ring is given as follows:

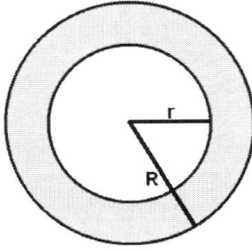

Area = $\pi(R^2 - r^2)$

R and r are the radii of the corresponding circles.

3.11 THREE DIMENSIONAL GEOMETRY

1. If V is the volume of a prism, h is the altitude (the perpendicular distance between the bases), and B is the area of a base, then V = B · h.

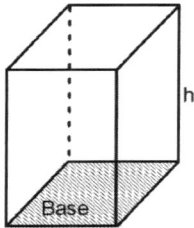

2. If S_L is the lateral surface area of a prism, h is its altitude, and P is the perimeter of a base, then S_L = P·h.

3. If S_T is the total surface area of a prism and B is the area of a base, then

    S_T = h·(perimeter of base) + 2B

4. Every rectangular prism has 8 vertices, 6 faces, 12 sides.

5. Given that number of vertices of a geometric object is V, the number of faces it has is F and the number of sides it has is S then V + F = S + 2.

6. If e is the length of a side of a cube and A is the total surface area of the cube then A = $6e^2$ and if V is the volume of the cube then V = e^3.

    Diagonal of a face of the cube = x = $e\sqrt{2}$

    Diagonal of the cube = y = $e\sqrt{3}$

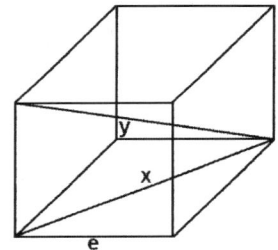

7. If a, b and c are the lengths of sides of a rectangular box then

    V = a·b·c

    S = 2ab + 2ac + 2bc

    x = $\sqrt{a^2 + b^2 + c^2}$

    where V, S and x are volume, surface area and length of the diagonal of the rectangular box respectively.

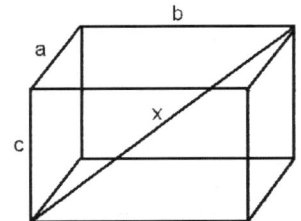

8. If V is the volume of a pyramid or a cone, h its altitude, and B is the area of a base, then V = $\frac{1}{3}$ hB.

    The lateral area of a regular pyramid equals half the perimeter of the base times the slant height. (L.A. = $\frac{1}{2}$ perimeter of base · h_1)

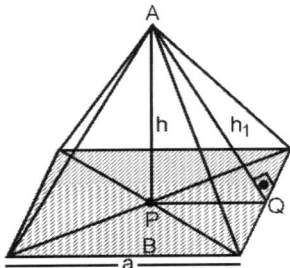

    In order to find h_1, Pythagorean theorem may be used since APQ is a right triangle:

    $$h^2 + \left(\frac{a}{2}\right)^2 = h_1^2$$

9. If V is the volume of a sphere, S is its surface area, and r is its radius, then $V = \dfrac{4}{3}\pi r^3$ and $S = 4\pi r^2$.

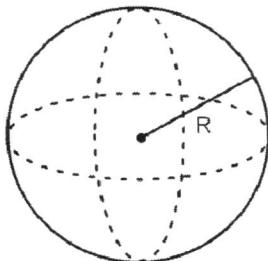

10. Lateral area of a cylinder equals perimeter of the base times the altitude of the cylinder; (L.A. = $2\pi rh$). Volume of a cylinder equals the area of a base times the altitude of the cylinder ($V = \pi r^2 h$).

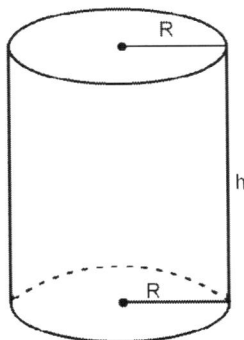

11. Lateral area of a cone equals half the perimeter of the base times the slant height; (L.A. = $\pi R l$). Volume of a cone equals one third the area of the base times the height of the cone ($V = \dfrac{1}{3}\pi R^2 h$).

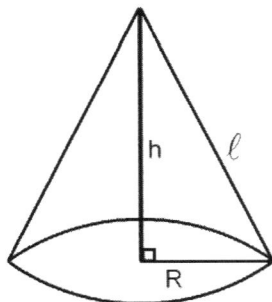

$h^2 + R^2 = l^2$ (l: slant height)

Total surface area = $\pi R^2 + \pi R l$

12. If the scale factor of two similar solids is k, then the ratio of corresponding sides is k and the ratio of corresponding areas is k^2 and the ratio of corresponding volumes is k^3.

3.12 INSCRIBED FIGURES IN TWO DIMENSIONS

Quadrilateral inscribed in a circle

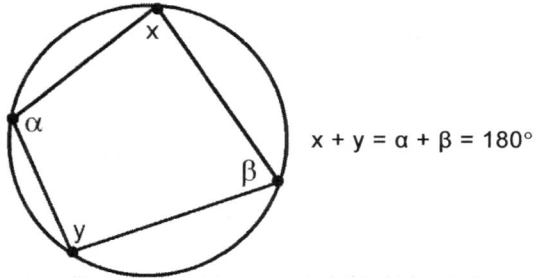

$x + y = \alpha + \beta = 180°$

Circle inscribed in a quadrilateral

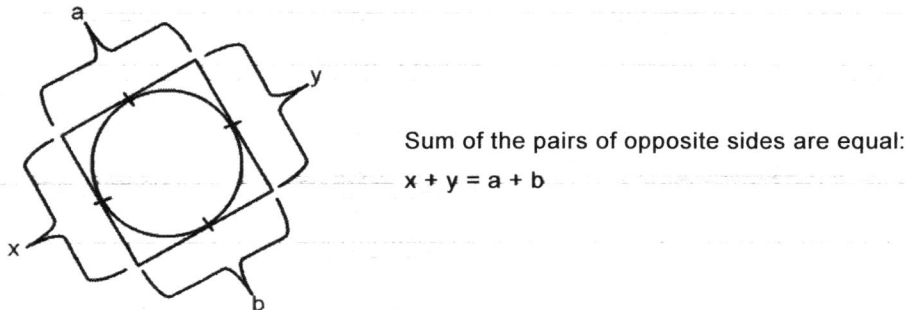

Sum of the pairs of opposite sides are equal:

$x + y = a + b$

Circle inscribed in a square

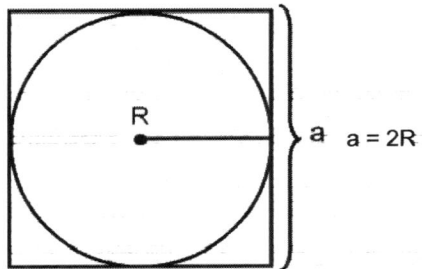

$a = 2R$

Square inscribed in a circle

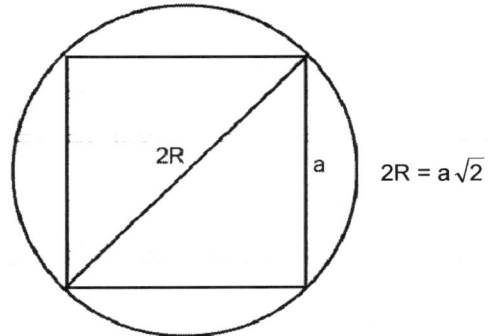

$2R = a\sqrt{2}$

Rectangle inscribed in a circle

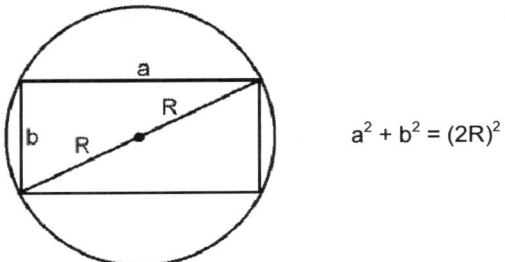

$a^2 + b^2 = (2R)^2$

Circle inscribed in a triangle

The area of the triangle = ur = $\sqrt{u(u-a)(u-b)(u-c)}$ where a, b, and c are the sides and u is the semi – perimeter of the triangle; r is the radius of the inscribed circle.

Triangle inscribed in a circle

The area of the triangle = $\sqrt{u(u-a)(u-b)(u-c)}$ = $\dfrac{abc}{4R}$ where a, b, and c are the sides and u is the semi – perimeter of the triangle; R is the radius of the circumscribed circle.

Equilateral triangle inscribed in a circle

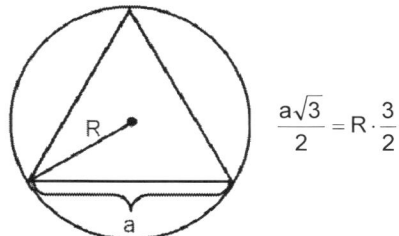

$$\frac{a\sqrt{3}}{2} = R \cdot \frac{3}{2}$$

Circle inscribed in an equilateral triangle

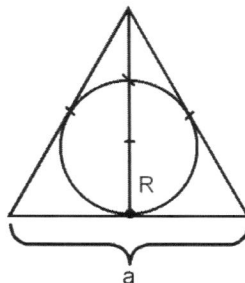

$$\frac{a\sqrt{3}}{2} = 3R$$

Isosceles triangle inscribed in a circle

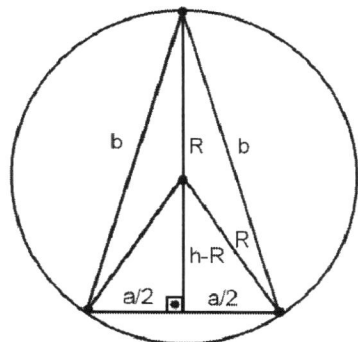

$$(h-R)^2 + (\frac{a}{2})^2 = R^2 \quad \text{and} \quad b^2 = h^2 + (\frac{a}{2})^2$$

Circle inscribed in an isosceles triangle

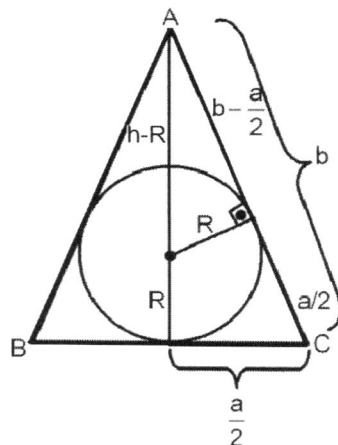

$$(h-R)^2 = R^2 + (b-\frac{a}{2})^2 \quad \text{and} \quad h^2 = b^2 - (\frac{a}{2})^2$$

3.13 INSCRIBED FIGURES IN THREE DIMENSIONS

Sphere inscribed in a cube

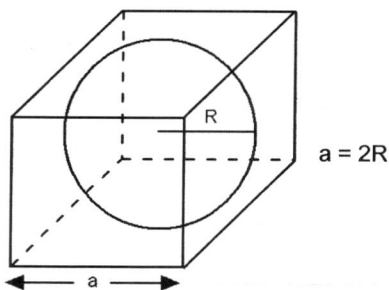

$a = 2R$

Cube inscribed in a sphere

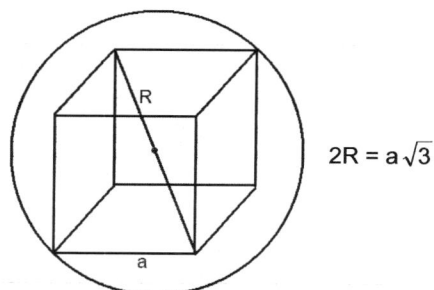

$2R = a\sqrt{3}$

Rectangular box inscribed in a sphere

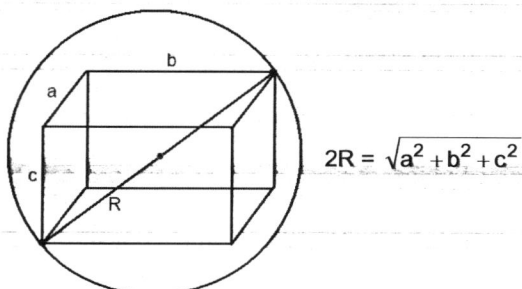

$2R = \sqrt{a^2 + b^2 + c^2}$

Cylinder inscribed in a sphere

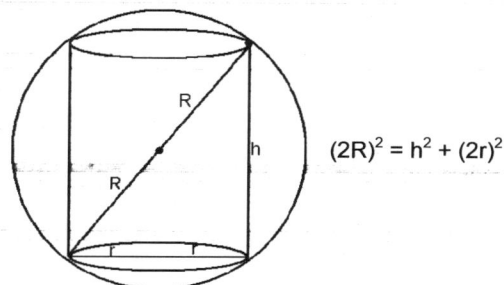

$(2R)^2 = h^2 + (2r)^2$

Cone inscribed in a sphere

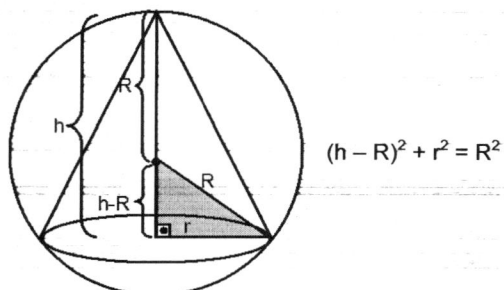

$(h - R)^2 + r^2 = R^2$

Sphere inscribed in a cone

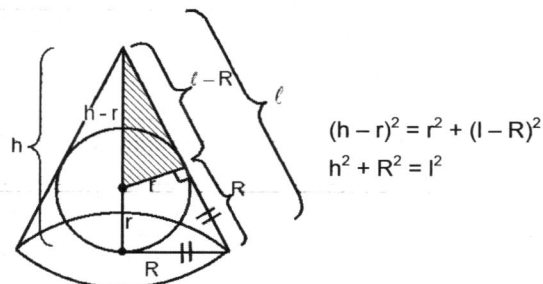

$(h - r)^2 = r^2 + (l - R)^2$

$h^2 + R^2 = l^2$

Cylinder inscribed in a cone

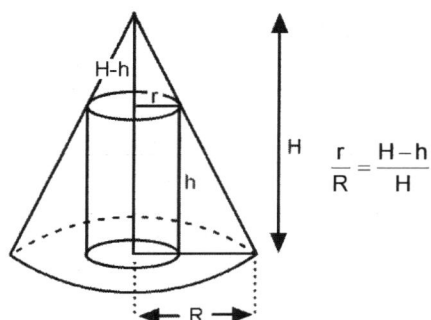

$\dfrac{r}{R} = \dfrac{H - h}{H}$

3.14 COMMON ROTATIONS

Given below is a summary of the common rotations in the context of SAT math subject tests.

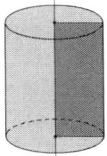

A rectangle rotated about its edge for 360° produces a cylinder.

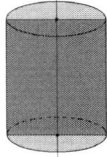

A rectangle rotated about its central axis for 180° produces a cylinder.

A semicircle rotated about its diameter for 360° produces a sphere.

A circle rotated about its diameter for 180° produces a sphere.

A right triangle rotated about one of its legs (for 360°) produces a cone.

An isosceles triangle rotated about its axis of symmetry, (for 180°) produces a cone.

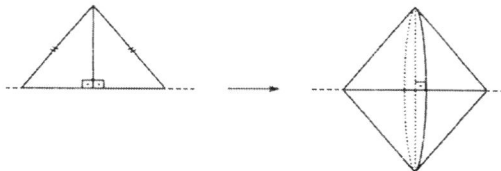

An isosceles triangle rotated (for 360°) about its base produces two cones that have a common base, with their radii each equal to the altitude to the base of the triangle, and, with their altitudes each equal to half of the base length of the triangle.

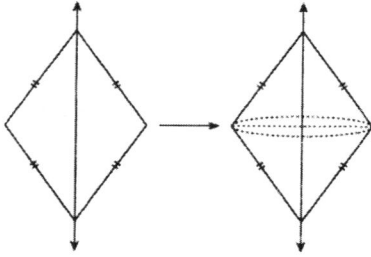

A rhombus rotated (for 180°) about its longer diagonal (one of its axes of symmetry) produces two cones that have a common base with their radii equal half the length of the shorter diagonal of the rhombus and their altitudes equal to the half the length of the longer diagonal.

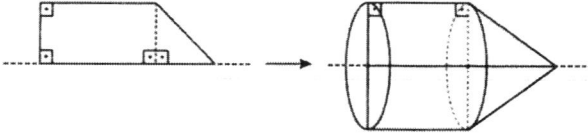

A right triangle and a rectangle with a common side when rotated as given above produces a cylinder and a cone with a common base.

Some men see things as they are and say "Why?"

I see the things that never were and say "Why not!"

Robert F. Kennedy

CHAPTER 4 – Miscellaneous Topics

Complex Numbers, Polar Coordinates and Graphing

Vectors and Three Dimensional Coordinate Geometry

Parametric Equations and Graphing

Conic Sections

Sequences and Series

Variations

Binary Operations

Computer Programs

Logic

Matrices and Determinants

Word Problems

4.1 COMPLEX NUMBERS, POLAR COORDINATES AND GRAPHING

$z = x + yi$ where $i = \sqrt{-1}$ or $i^2 = -1$

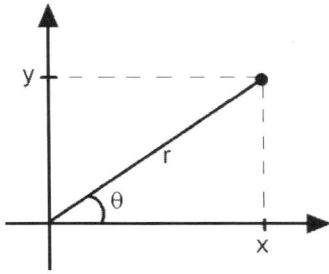

$r \cdot \cos\theta = x$ and $r \cdot \sin\theta = y$

$x + yi = r \cdot \cos\theta + i \cdot r \cdot \sin\theta = r(\cos\theta + i \cdot \sin\theta) = r \cdot cis\theta = r \cdot e^{i\theta}$

$e = 2.71828... = \lim\limits_{n \to \infty} \left(1 + \dfrac{1}{n}\right)^n$

Set of complex numbers $= C = \left\{ x + yi : x, y \in R, i = \sqrt{-1} \right\}$

Rectangular to Polar Conversion

Replace
- x by $r \cdot \cos\theta$
- y by $r \cdot \sin\theta$

Polar to Rectangular Conversion

Replace
- $r \cdot \cos\theta$ by x
- $r \cdot \sin\theta$ by y
- r by $\sqrt{x^2 + y^2}$

Euler's Identity

$e^{i\theta} = \cos\theta + i \cdot \sin\theta = cis\theta$

De Moivre's Identities

$z_1 = r_1 \cdot cis\theta_1 = r_1 . e^{i\theta_1}$;

$z_2 = r_2 \cdot cis\theta_2 = r_2 . e^{i\theta_2}$

Identity 1:

$z_1 \cdot z_2 = r_1 \cdot r_2 . \ e^{i\theta_1} e^{i\theta_2}$

$= r_1 r_2 . e^{i\theta_1 + i\theta_2} = r_1 r_2 . e^{i(\theta_1 + \theta_2)} = r_1 r_2 . cis(\theta_1 + \theta_2)$

$= r_1 r_2 (\cos(\theta_1 + \theta_2) + i\sin(\theta_1 + \theta_2))$

Identity 2:

$\dfrac{z_1}{z_2} = \dfrac{r_1 \, e^{i\theta_2}}{r_2 \, e^{i\theta_2}} = \dfrac{r_1}{r_2} . e^{i(\theta_1 - \theta_2)} = \dfrac{r_1}{r_2} \cdot cis(\theta_1 - \theta_2)$

$= \dfrac{r_1}{r_2} \cdot (\cos(\theta_1 - \theta_2) + i\sin(\theta_1 - \theta_2))$

Identity 3:

$$(z_1)^n = (r_1 \cdot e^{i\theta_1})^n = r_1^n \cdot (e^{i\theta_1})^n = r_1^n \cdot e^{i\theta_1 \cdot n} = r_1^n \cdot cis(n\theta_1)$$

$$= r_1^n \cdot [\cos(n\theta_1) + i\sin(n\theta_1)]$$

Identity 4:

The n'th root of $z = r \cdot cis\theta$

$r = |z| \ ; \ z = r \ cis\theta$

$$z^{1/n} = r^{1/n} cis\left(\frac{\theta + k \cdot 2\pi}{n}\right) \text{ where } k = 0,1,2,.....,n-1$$

TI Usage

$z = x + yi$

$\bar{z} = x - yi = \text{conjugate of } z = conj(z)$

$|z| = \sqrt{x^2 + y^2} = r = abs(z)$

$x = real(z); \ y = image(z)$

Properties of Complex Numbers

1. $i^{4n} \equiv 1; \ i^{4n+1} \equiv i; \ i^{4n+2} \equiv i^2 \equiv -1; \ i^{4n+3} \equiv i^3 = -i$ given that n is a positive integer

2. $a + bi = c + di \Rightarrow a = c \text{ and } b = d.$

3. $z = a + bi \Rightarrow |z| = \sqrt{a^2 + b^2}$

4. $|z_1 \cdot z_2| = |z| \cdot |z_2|$

5. $\left|\dfrac{z_1}{z_2}\right| = \dfrac{|z_1|}{|z_2|}$

6. $|z^n| = |z|^n$

7. $conj(z) = a - bi$

8. $|z| = |-z| = |conj(z)|$

9. $z \cdot \bar{z} = |z|^2 = a^2 + b^2$

Example: What is the reciprocal of 3 + 4i

Solution:

```
1/(3+4i
           .12-.16i
```

Answer: 0.12 − 0.16i

Example: $z = \dfrac{1 + i\sqrt{3}}{-1 + i\sqrt{3}}$, what is the value of z in trigonometric form?

Solution:

```
NORMAL  SCI  ENG        (1+√(3)i)/(-1+√(       .50-.87i
FLOAT 0123456789        3)i              Ans→X
RADIAN DEGREE                  .50-.87i          .50-.87i
FUNC  PAR  POL  SEQ                      abs(X)
CONNECTED  DOT                                      1.00
SEQUENTIAL  SIMUL                        angle(X)
REAL  a+bi  re^θi                                 -60.00
FULL  HORIZ  G-T
CLOCKSET 01/01/01 12:00AM
```

Answer: 1·(cos(−60°) + isin(−60°))

Polar Graphing with TI

Polar graphing allows the user to plot **r** versus **θ** where **r** denotes **radius**, **θ** denotes **angle** and **(r, θ)** represents the **polar coordinates**. Settings must be changed to the **Pol**ar mode so that the Y = Editor will enable that **r** be defined in terms of the parameter **θ**. In the **Pol**ar mode the variable **θ** will appear when the (X,T,θ,*n*) key is pressed.

For example the input and output for the following relation

$r = 1 - 2\cos(\theta)$

will be as follows:

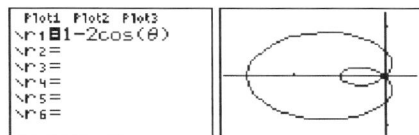

Example: What is the polar representation of the curve given by the relation $x^2 + 3y^2 - 5x + 3y = 0$?

Solution:

$(r \cdot \cos\theta)^2 + 3(r \cdot \sin\theta)^2 - 5r \cdot \cos\theta + 3r \cdot \sin\theta = 0$

$r^2\cos^2\theta + 3r^2\sin^2\theta - 5r\cos\theta + 3r\sin\theta = 0$

$r\cos^2\theta + 3r\sin^2\theta - 5\cos\theta + 3\sin\theta = 0$

$$r = \frac{5\cos\theta - 3\sin\theta}{\cos^2\theta + 3\sin^2\theta}$$

Example: What is the rectangular representation of the curve given by the relation $r = 3\cos\theta + 7\sin\theta$?

Solution:

$r = 3\cos\theta + 7\sin\theta$

$r^2 = 3r\cos\theta + 7r\sin\theta$

$x^2 + y^2 = 3x + 7y$

4.2 VECTORS AND THREE DIMENSIONAL COORDINATE GEOMETRY

A **vector** is a number with magnitude, unit and direction whereas a **scalar** is a number with magnitude, unit and no direction.

- A **position vector** is one whose starting point is the origin. In the following figure the vector $\overrightarrow{OP} = \vec{P}$ is given.

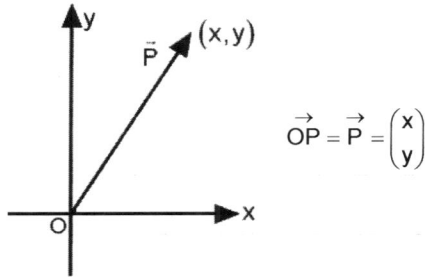

$$\overrightarrow{OP} = \vec{P} = \begin{pmatrix} x \\ y \end{pmatrix}$$

- The **negative** of a vector $\vec{A} = \begin{pmatrix} a_1 \\ a_2 \end{pmatrix}$ is the vector whose direction is exactly the opposite of vector $\vec{A} = \begin{pmatrix} a_1 \\ a_2 \end{pmatrix}$ and it is given by $-\vec{A} = \begin{pmatrix} -a_1 \\ -a_2 \end{pmatrix}$.

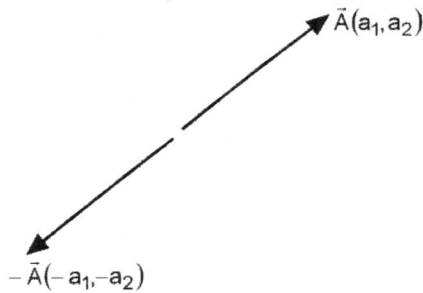

- The **magnitude** of a vector is its length given by $\left| \overrightarrow{OP} \right| = \left| \vec{P} \right| = \sqrt{x^2 + y^2}$

- The **resultant** of two vectors $\vec{A} = \begin{pmatrix} a_1 \\ a_2 \end{pmatrix}$ and $\vec{B} = \begin{pmatrix} b_1 \\ b_2 \end{pmatrix}$ is their vectorial sum and it is given by $\vec{A} + \vec{B} = \begin{pmatrix} a_1 + b_1 \\ a_2 + b_2 \end{pmatrix}$.

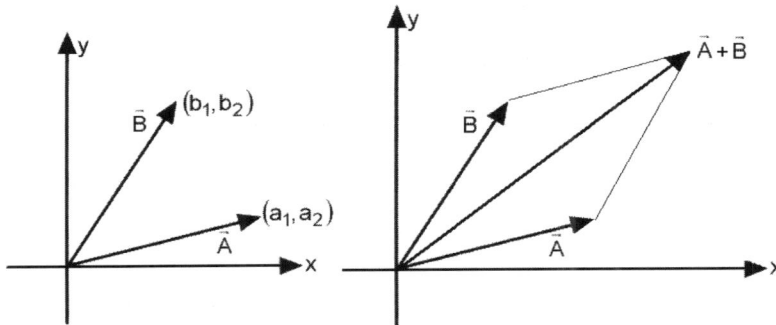

- The magnitude R of the resultant $\vec{A} + \vec{B}$ of two vectors $\vec{A}$ and $\vec{B}$ is given by $R^2 = A^2 + B^2 + 2AB \cdot \cos\alpha$ where A and B are the magnitudes of the vectors $\vec{A}$ and $\vec{B}$ respectively and α is the angle between them. Please also notice that the formula resembles the cosine rule except that the sign of the $2AB \cdot \cos\alpha$ term is negative in the cosine rule, however it is positive the above formula.

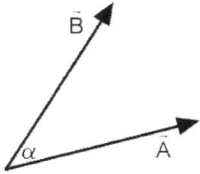

- The vector $\overrightarrow{AB}$ starts at point A and ends at point B and it is given by $\overrightarrow{AB} = \vec{B} - \vec{A}$

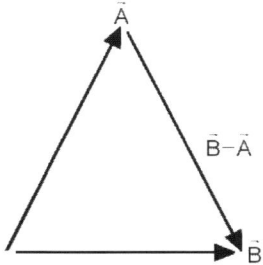

- **Linear combination** of vectors $\vec{A}$ and $\vec{B}$ is the sum given by $m\vec{A} + n\vec{B}$ where m and n are scalars.

- A **unit vector** has a length of 1. If $\hat{a}$ is the unit vector in the direction of $\vec{A}$ then it is given by $\dfrac{\vec{A}}{|\vec{A}|}$.

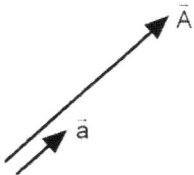

- **Basis vectors** are parallel to the coordinate axes and each of them has a length of 1.

$\vec{A} = \begin{pmatrix} a_1 \\ a_2 \end{pmatrix} = a_1 \vec{i} + a_2 \vec{j}$ where $\vec{i}$ and $\vec{j}$ are the basis vectors.

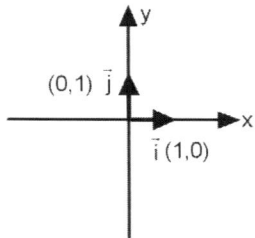

- The **scalar product** (dot product or inner product) of two vectors $\vec{A} \cdot \vec{B} = <\vec{A}, \vec{B}>$ is given by

$\vec{A} \cdot \vec{B} = a_1b_1 + a_2b_2 = |\vec{A}| \cdot |\vec{B}| \cdot \cos\alpha$ where α is the angle between these vectors and $|\vec{A}|$ and $|\vec{B}|$ are the lengths of the corresponding vectors.

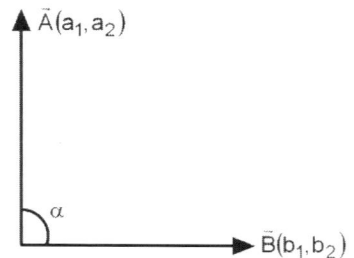

- Given that $\vec{A} = \begin{pmatrix} a_1 \\ a_2 \end{pmatrix}$ and $\vec{B} = \begin{pmatrix} b_1 \\ b_2 \end{pmatrix}$; if the two vectors are **parallel** then $\dfrac{a_2}{a_1} = \dfrac{b_2}{b_1}$.

- Given that $\vec{A} = \begin{pmatrix} a_1 \\ a_2 \end{pmatrix}$ and $\vec{B} = \begin{pmatrix} b_1 \\ b_2 \end{pmatrix}$; if the two vectors are **perpendicular** then: $\alpha = 90°$ which implies that $\cos 90° = 0$

  and $\vec{A} \cdot \vec{B} = |\vec{A}| \cdot |\vec{B}| \cdot \cos 90° = 0$.

  Consequently if the vectors are perpendicular then $a_1 b_1 + a_2 b_2 = 0$

- For the scalar product the following properties also hold:

  a. $(\vec{A})^2 = \vec{A} \cdot \vec{A} = |\vec{A}|^2$

  b. $\vec{A} \cdot \vec{B} = \vec{B} \cdot \vec{A}$

  c. $\vec{A} \cdot (\vec{B} + \vec{C}) = \vec{A}\vec{B} + \vec{A} \cdot \vec{C}$

- For the three dimensional vectors please note the following:

  a. $\vec{OA} = \vec{A} = \begin{pmatrix} a_1 \\ a_2 \\ a_3 \end{pmatrix} \Rightarrow |\vec{A}| = \sqrt{a_1^2 + a_2^2 + a_3^2}$

  b. If $\vec{A} = \begin{pmatrix} a_1 \\ a_2 \\ a_3 \end{pmatrix}$ and $\vec{B} = \begin{pmatrix} b_1 \\ b_2 \\ b_3 \end{pmatrix}$ then $\vec{A} \cdot \vec{B} = a_1 b_1 + a_2 b_2 + a_3 b_3$

    i. $\vec{A} \parallel \vec{B} \Rightarrow \dfrac{a_1}{b_1} = \dfrac{a_2}{b_2} = \dfrac{a_3}{b_3}$

    ii. $\vec{A} \perp \vec{B} \Rightarrow a_1 b_1 + a_2 b_2 + a_3 b_3 = 0$

Example:

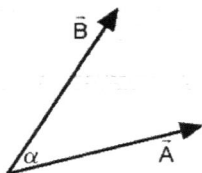

If the magnitudes of vectors $\vec{A}$ and $\vec{B}$ are 10 and 20 respectively and the angle between them is $35°$ then what is the magnitude of $\vec{A} + \vec{B}$?

Solution: $\vec{R} = \vec{A} + \vec{B} \Rightarrow R^2 = 10^2 + 20^2 + 2 \cdot 10 \cdot 20 \cdot \cos 35° \Rightarrow R = 28.77$

Plane Equation

$Ax + By + Cz + D = 0$

Example: $3x - 4y + 5z = 60$ is given.

a)   Find x, y, z intercepts.

b)   Find xy, xz, yz traces.

c)   Find the volume of the pyramid that forms with the coordinate axes and this plane.

Solution:

a) x intercept: y = z = 0 ➜ 3x = 60 (20,0,0)

y intercept : (0, −15,0)

z intercept : (0,0, 12)

b) xy trace : z = 0 ➜ 3x − 4y = 60

yz trace : − 4y + 5z = 60

xz trace : 3x + 4z = 60

c)

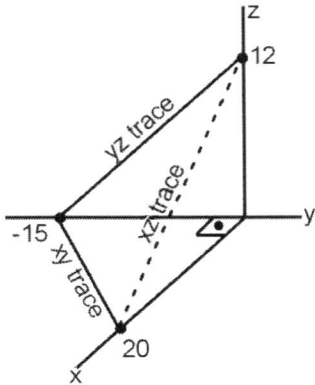

$$V = \frac{BA \cdot h}{3} \text{ (for cones \& pyramids)}$$

$$= \frac{\frac{15 \cdot 20}{2} \cdot 12}{3} = 600$$

3 − D Line Equation

Example:

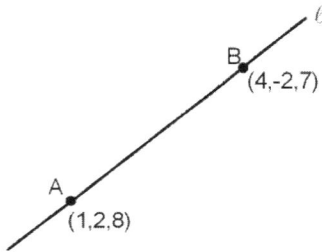

a) Find direction vector of line l

b) Find direction cosines of line l

c) Find cartesian & parametric forms of the line equation for line l.

d) Find distance AB

Solution:

a) **direction vector:** $\vec{AB} = \vec{B} - \vec{A} = (3, -4, -1)$

b) **direction cosines:** $\dfrac{\vec{AB}}{\left|\vec{AB}\right|} = \dfrac{(3,-4,-1)}{\sqrt{9+16+1}} = \left(\dfrac{3}{\sqrt{26}}, \dfrac{-4}{\sqrt{26}}, \dfrac{-1}{\sqrt{26}}\right)$

c) $\vec{AB} = (3,-4,-1)$ and $\vec{AC} = (x - 1, y - 2, z - 8)$

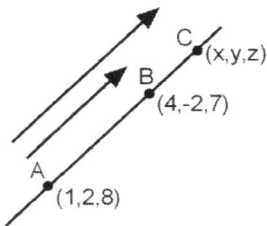

$$\overrightarrow{AB} // \overrightarrow{AC} \Rightarrow \frac{x-1}{3} = \frac{y-2}{-4} = \frac{z-8}{-1} = t$$

Cartesian (rectangular) form: $\frac{x-1}{3} = \frac{y-2}{-4} = \frac{z-8}{-1}$

Parametric form:

x = 3t + 1

y = -4t + 2

z = -t + 8

Vector form:

$$\begin{pmatrix} x \\ y \\ z \end{pmatrix} = \begin{pmatrix} 1 \\ 2 \\ 8 \end{pmatrix} + t \begin{pmatrix} 3 \\ -4 \\ -1 \end{pmatrix}$$

d) $\overrightarrow{AB} = (3,-4,-1) \Rightarrow AB = \sqrt{9 + 16 + 1} = \sqrt{26}$

Distance From a Point to a Plane

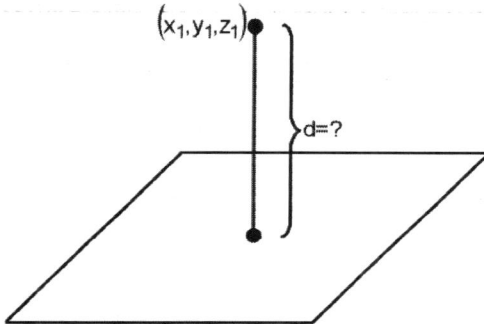

Distance from the point (x_1, y_1, z_2) to the plane Ax + By + Cz + D = 0 is given by:

$$d = \frac{|Ax_1 + By_1 + Cz_1 + D|}{\sqrt{A^2 + B^2 + C^2}}$$

Please note that the above formula resembles the formula used for finding the distance from a point to a line.

Distance Between Two Points

Distance between two points with coordinates (x_1, y_1, z_1) and (x_2, y_2, z_2) is given by:

$$d = \sqrt{(x_1 - x_2)^2 + (y_1 - y_2)^2 + (z_1 - z_2)^2}.$$

Reflections in Three Dimensions

The reflection of a point (x, y, z) across

- the xy plane gives (x, y, -z).
- the xz plane gives (x, -y, z).
- the yz plane gives (-x, y, z).

Sphere equation

$(x - a)^2 + (y - b)^2 + (z - c)^2 = R^2$ where center (a, b, c) and radius = R

Example: $x^2 - 6x + y^2 + 8y + z^2 - 2z + 1 = 0$

Find volume of the above sphere.

Solution: $x^2 - 6x + 9 + y^2 + 8y + 16 + z^2 - 2z + 1 = 9 + 16 + 1 - 1 \Rightarrow (x - 3)^3 + (y + 4)^2 + (z - 1)^2 = 25 \Rightarrow$ Center (3, -4, 1)

and Radius = $\sqrt{25} = 5$.

$$V = \frac{4}{3} . \pi . r^3 = \frac{4}{3} . \pi . 5^3 = \frac{500\pi}{3}$$

4.3 PARAMETRIC EQUATIONS AND PARAMETRIC GRAPHING

Parametric graphing in TI allows its user to plot y versus x when the y – and x – variables are defined in terms of a **parameter "T"** which usually denotes the time variable (for example y and x can represent the y – and x – coordinates that define the position of an object at time t). Settings must be changed to the **Par**ametric mode so that the Y = Editor will enable that the relation between y – and x – be both defined in terms of the parameter **T**. In the **Par**ametric mode the variable T will appear when the $\boxed{X,T,\theta,n}$ key is pressed. Please note that in the **Func**tion mode the variable X used to appear when the $\boxed{X,T,\theta,n}$ key was pressed.

For example the relation x = 3cos(t) and y = 2sin(t) must be input as follows (t will be replaced by T):

and the output will be an ellipse:

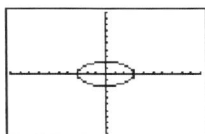

The important issue in the **Par**ametric mode is the fact that the **T** variable in TI is designed to represent the time variable **t** and therefore the default value for **Tmin** in the window settings is 0 (zero) as time is supposed to be always nonnegative.

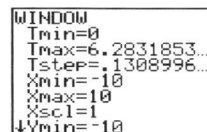

However, **T** does not necessarily have to denote time. For example the parametric equation above could also be given as follows: x = 3cos(θ) and y = 2sin(θ) where **θ** is a parameter that does not represent time. On the other hand although the variable used may be t, it may still not represent time, either. In such cases where the free variable does not denote time, leaving **Tmin** as 0 will result in an incorrect and misleading graph that will represent only a portion of the actual graph. Therefore when **T** is not given to represent time, **Tmin** must be changed to **– Tmax**: The default settings for **Tmax** in **Radian** mode is 2π that appears as 6.28… and **Tmin** must be set to – 2π that will also appear as – 6.28… after enter key is pressed.

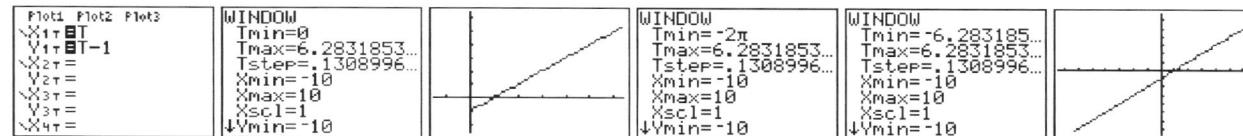

It is also essential to be aware of the fact that the **ZStandard (Zoom Standard)** action will reset **Tmin** back to 0. Therefore after **ZStandard** is performed **Tmin** must be changed to **– Tmax** again when needed.

4.4 CONIC SECTIONS

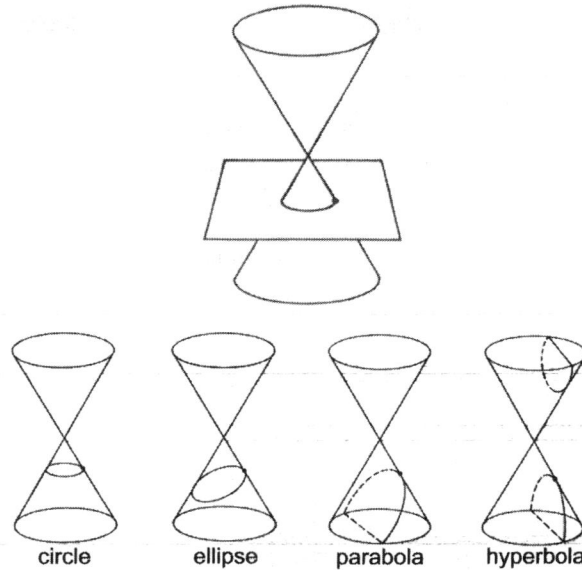

General equation of a conic section is as follows: $Ax^2 + Bxy + Cy^2 + Dx + Ey + F = 0$. One of the following cases hold in general:

i.   If $B^2 - 4AC < 0$ and $A = C$, graph is a circle

ii. If $B^2 - 4AC < 0$ and $A \neq C$, graph is an ellipse.

iii. If $B^2 - 4AC = 0$, graph is a parabola.

iv. If $B^2 - 4AC > 0$, graph is a hyperbola.

However in the SAT II context, B will be zero most of the time, i.e. there will usually be no xy term. The xy term accounts for the cases when the conic section is rotated by an angle which is not an integer multiple of 90 degrees. In such cases you should suspect that the graph is:

i.   a circle if $A = C$;

ii. an ellipse if A and C are unequal but they have the same sign;

iii. a hyperbola if A and C have different signs;

iv. a parabola if either A or C is zero but not both of them are zero, i.e. the case when one of A or C is missing.

Example: By taking cross sections from a right circular cone with a single plane all of the following can be obtained: Point, line segment, circle, ellipse, parabola, triangle and angle.

Circle

Circle is the set of points in a plane at a constant distance from a fixed point in the plane. The **fixed point is the center** of circle; and the **constant distance is the radius**.

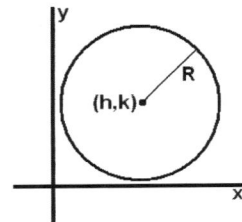

$(x - h)^2 + (y - k)^2 = R^2$ with center at (h, k) and radius = R

The unit circle

It is the circle centered at the origin having the radius of 1. Its equation is $x^2 + y^2 = 1$.

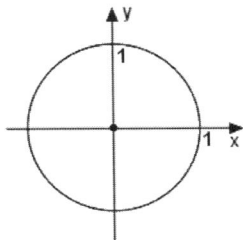

Semicircles centered at the origin:

$$y = \sqrt{R^2 - x^2} \qquad y = -\sqrt{R^2 - x^2} \qquad x = \sqrt{R^2 - y^2} \qquad x = -\sqrt{R^2 - y^2}$$

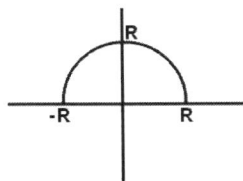 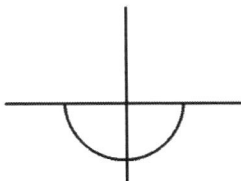 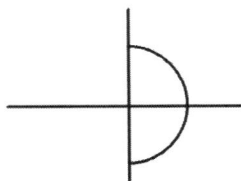 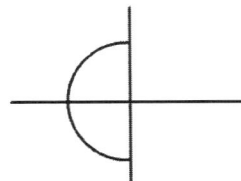

Example: What does each of the following relations represent?

a. $4x^2 + 4y^2 - 8x + 16y + 16 = 0$

b. $4x^2 + 4y^2 - 8x + 16y + 20 = 0$

c. $4x^2 + 4y^2 - 8x + 16y + 24 = 0$

Solution:

a. $4x^2 + 4y^2 - 8x + 16y + 16 = 0 \Rightarrow x^2 + y^2 - 2x + 4y + 4 = 0$

$x^2 - 2x + 1 + y^2 + 4y + 4 = 1 \Rightarrow (x - 1)^2 + (y + 2)^2 = 1$

The relation represents a circle whose center is at (1, −2) and whose radius is 1.

b. $4x^2 + 4y^2 - 8x + 16y + 20 = 0 \Rightarrow x^2 + y^2 - 2x + 4y + 5 = 0$

$x^2 - 2x + 1 + y^2 + 4y + 4 = 0 \Rightarrow (x - 1)^2 + (y + 2)^2 = 0$

The relation represents the point (1, −2).

c. $4x^2 + 4y^2 - 8x + 16y + 24 = 0 \Rightarrow x^2 + y^2 - 2x + 4y + 6 = 0$

$x^2 - 2x + 1 + y^2 + 4y + 4 + 1 = 0 \Rightarrow (x - 1)^2 + (y + 2)^2 = -1$

The relation represents the empty set.

Special Remark:

Let $(x - h)^2 + (y - k)^2 = R^2$ be the equation of the circle with the radius of length R and the center with coordinates (h, k).

- If a point (x_1, y_1) is on the circle then it satisfies the relation $(x_1 - h)^2 + (y_1 - k)^2 = R^2$.
- If a point (x_1, y_1) is inside the circle then it satisfies the relation $(x_1 - h)^2 + (y_1 - k)^2 < R^2$.
- If a point (x_1, y_1) is outside the circle then it satisfies the relation $(x_1 - h)^2 + (y_1 - k)^2 > R^2$.

Example: Circle given by $(x - 1)^2 + (y + 2)^2 = 16$

Point Label	Coordinates	Status
A	(2, 1)	inside the circle
B	(5, −2)	on the circle
C	(0, 4)	outside the circle
D	(1, 2)	on the circle
E	(0,0)	inside the circle
F	(−2, 1)	outside the circle
G	(−3, −2)	on the circle

$(x - h)^2 + (y - k)^2 = R^2$ $(x - h)^2 + (y - k)^2 < R^2$ $(x - h)^2 + (y - k)^2 > R^2$ $(x - h)^2 + (y - k)^2 \leq R^2$ $(x - h)^2 + (y - k)^2 \geq R^2$

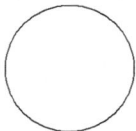

| Points on the circle | Points inside the circle | Points outside the circle | Points on and inside the circle | Points on and outside the circle |

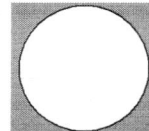

Ellipse

An ellipse is the set of points in a plane whose distances from two fixed points in the plane have a constant sum.

The fixed points are the foci of the ellipse and the constant sum equals 2a.

Ellipses in Standard Position

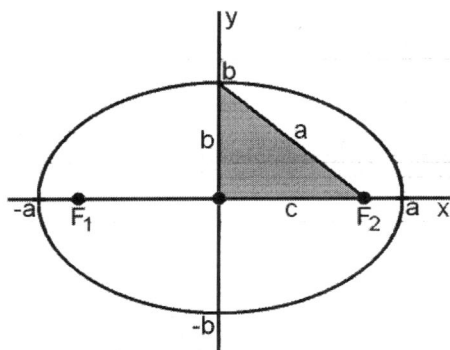

x – ellipse

a = semi – major axis length; b = semi – minor axis length

$$\frac{x^2}{a^2} + \frac{y^2}{b^2} = 1 \quad (a > b > 0)$$

center: (0,0); vertices: (±a,0); co – vertices: (0, ±b)

foci: (±c,0), where $c^2 = a^2 - b^2$

c = center to focus distance

eccentricity: e = c/a and 0 < e < 1

major axis: horizontal; minor axis: vertical

directrices: The lines defined by x = ±a/e

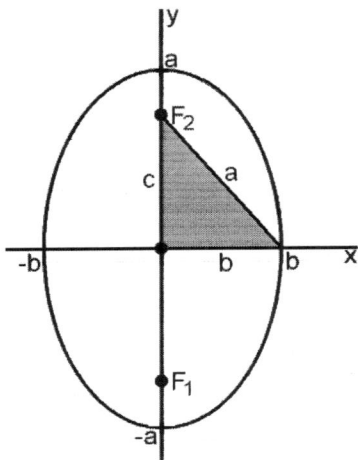

y – ellipse

a = semi – major axis length; b = semi – minor axis length

$$\frac{x^2}{b^2} + \frac{y^2}{a^2} = 1 \quad (a > b > 0)$$

center: (0,0); vertices: (0, ±a); co – vertices: (±b,0)

foci: (0, ±c), where $c^2 = a^2 - b^2$

c = center to focus distance

eccentricity: e = c/a and 0 < e < 1

major axis: vertical; minor axis: horizontal

directrices: The lines defined by y = ±a/e

When coordinates of center is (h, k):

$$\left.\begin{cases} \dfrac{(x-h)^2}{a^2} + \dfrac{(y-k)^2}{b^2} = 1, \text{ major axis horizontal} \\ \dfrac{(x-h)^2}{b^2} + \dfrac{(y-k)^2}{a^2} = 1, \text{ major axis vertical} \end{cases}\right\} \text{ given that } a > b.$$

coordinates of center: (h, k)

foci: ±c units from center along major axis where $c^2 = a^2 - b^2$

vertices: ±a units from center along major axis

length of major axis: 2a

length of minor axis (perpendicular to the major axis at center): 2b

eccentricity = e = $\dfrac{c}{a}$

directrices: The lines perpendicular to the major axis $\pm a/e$ units from center.

Please note that $\dfrac{a}{e} > a$.

length of latus rectum (the chord passing through one of the foci and perpendicular to the major axis) is given by $\dfrac{2b^2}{a}$.

area of an ellipse: πab

Example: Analyze each of the following conic sections:

a. $\dfrac{x^2}{25} + \dfrac{y^2}{9} = 1$

b. $\dfrac{x^2}{25} + \dfrac{y^2}{169} = 1$

c. $\dfrac{(x-2)^2}{100} + \dfrac{(y-1)^2}{36} = 1$

d. $\dfrac{(x+1)^2}{144} + \dfrac{(y-2)^2}{225} = 1$

Solution:

a.

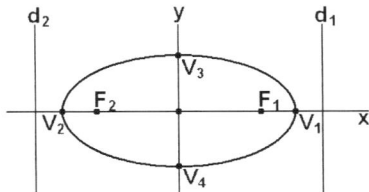

$\dfrac{x^2}{25} + \dfrac{y^2}{9} = 1$

x – ellipse: a = 5 and b = 3; therefore c = 4.

center: (0,0)

foci: $F_1(4,0)$, $F_2(-4,0)$

vertices: $V_1(5,0)$, $V_2(-5,0)$

co – vertices: $V_3(0, 3)$, $V_4(0, -3)$

eccentricity: e = 0.8

directrices: d_1: x = 6.25 and d_2: x = −6.25

major axis: x axis

length of the major axis: 10

minor axis: y axis

length of the minor axis: 6

latus rectum = 3.6

area = 15π

b.

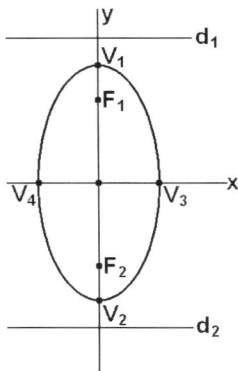

$\dfrac{x^2}{25} + \dfrac{y^2}{169} = 1$

y – ellipse: a = 13 and b = 5; therefore c = 12.

center: (0,0)

foci: $F_1(0, 12)$, $F_2(0, -12)$

vertices: $V_1(0, 13)$, $V_2(0, -13)$

co – vertices: $V_3(5,0)$, $V_4(-5,0)$

eccentricity: e = 12/13

directrices: d_1: y = 169/12 and d_2: x = −169/12

major axis: y axis

length of the major axis: 26

minor axis: x axis

length of the minor axis: 10

latus rectum = 50 /13

area = 65π

c.

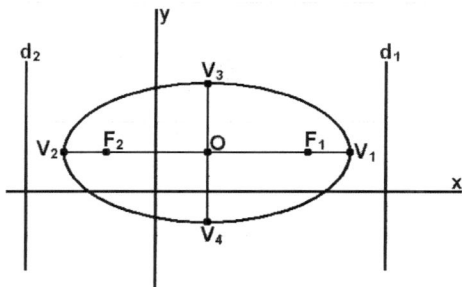

$$\frac{(x-2)^2}{100} + \frac{(y-1)^2}{36} = 1$$

x – ellipse: a = 10 and b = 6 therefore c = 8

center: O(2, 1)

foci: F_1(–6, 1), F_2(10, 1)

vertices: v_1(–8, 1), v_2(12, 1)

co – vertices: v_3(2, 7), v_4(2, –5)

eccentricity: e = 0.8

directrices:

d_1: x = –10.5 and d_2: x = 14.5

major axis: y = 1 line

length of the major axis: 20

minor axis: x = 2 line

length of the minor axis: 12

latus rectum = 7.2

area = 60π

d.

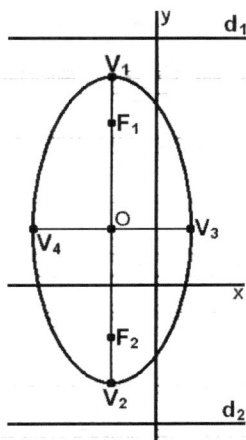

$$\frac{(x+1)^2}{144} + \frac{(y-2)^2}{225} = 1$$

y – ellipse: a = 15 and b = 12 therefore c = 9

center: O(–1, 2)

foci: F_1(–1, 11), F_2(–1, –7)

vertices: V_1(–1, 17), V_2(–1, –13)

co – vertices: V_4(–13, 2), V_3(11, 2)

eccentricity: e = 0.6

directrices:

d_1: y = 27 and d_2: y = –23

major axis: x = –1 line

length of the major axis: 30

minor axis: y = 2 line

length of the minor axis: 24

latus rectum = 19.2

area = 180π

Hyperbola

A hyperbola is the set of points in a plane whose distance from two fixed points in the plane have a constant difference. The fixed points are the foci of the hyperbola.

Hyperbolas in Standard Position

$$\frac{x^2}{a^2} - \frac{y^2}{b^2} = 1$$

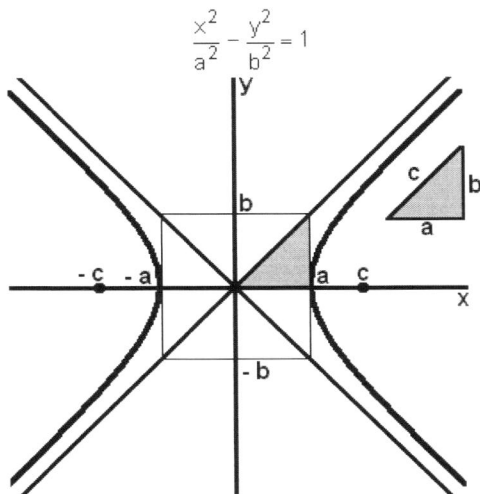

x – hyperbola

a = semi – transversal axis length

b = semi – conjugate axis length

center: (0,0)

vertices: ($\pm a$,0)

foci: ($\pm c$,0), where $c^2 = a^2 + b^2$

c = center to focus distance

asymptotes: $y = \pm \frac{b}{a}x$

eccentricity: e = c/a and e > 1

transverse axis: horizontal

conjugate axis: vertical

directrices: The lines defined by x = $\pm$a/e

$$\frac{y^2}{a^2} - \frac{x^2}{b^2} = 1$$

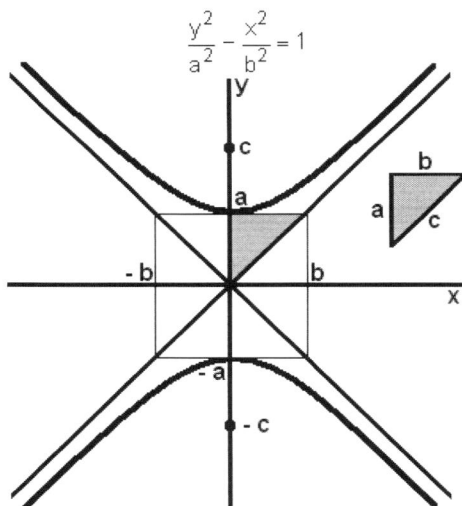

y – hyperbola

a = semi – transversal axis length

b = semi – conjugate axis length

center: (0,0)

vertices: (0, $\pm a$)

foci: (0, $\pm c$), where $c^2 = a^2 + b^2$

c = center to focus distance

asymptotes: $y = \pm \frac{a}{b}x$

eccentricity: e = c/a and e > 1

transverse axis: vertical

conjugate axis: horizontal

directrices: The lines defined by y = $\pm$a/e

When coordinates of center is (h, k):

$$\frac{(x-h)^2}{a^2} - \frac{(y-k)^2}{b^2} = 1,\ \text{transverse axis horizontal}$$

$$\frac{(y-k)^2}{a^2} - \frac{(x-h)^2}{b^2} = 1,\ \text{transverse axis vertical}$$

where $c^2 = a^2 + b^2$.

coordinates of center: (h, k)

vertices: $\pm$a units along the transverse axis from center

foci: $\pm$c units along the transverse from center

conjugate axis: perpendicular to transverse axis at center

eccentricity = e = c/a and e > 1

directrices: The lines perpendicular to the transverse axis ±a/e units from center, please note that $\dfrac{a}{e}$ < a.

length of latus rectum (the chord passing through one of the foci and perpendicular to the transverse axis) is given by $\dfrac{2b^2}{a}$.

asymptotes slopes = $\pm\dfrac{b}{a}$ if transverse axis is horizontal or $\pm\dfrac{a}{b}$ if transverse axis is vertical

Example: Analyze each of the following conic sections:

a. $\dfrac{x^2}{9} - \dfrac{y^2}{16} = 1$

b. $\dfrac{y^2}{144} - \dfrac{x^2}{25} = 1$

c. $\dfrac{(x+4)^2}{9} - \dfrac{(y-7)^2}{16} = 1$

d. $\dfrac{(y-6)^2}{9} - \dfrac{(x-5)^2}{16} = 1$

e. $16y^2 - 9x^2 + 64y + 18x + 55 = 0$

Solution:

a.

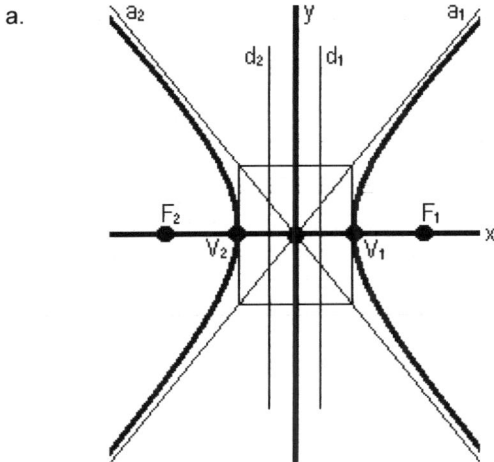

center: (0,0)

vertices: $V_1(3,0)$ and $V_2(-3,0)$

foci: $F_1(5,0)$ and $F_2(-5,0)$

asymptotes: a_1: $y = \dfrac{4}{3}x$ and a_2: $y = -\dfrac{4}{3}x$

eccentricity: e = 5/3

a/e = 1.8

directrices: d_1: x = 1.8 and d_2: x = −1.8

transverse axis: x axis

transverse axis length = 6

conjugate axis: y axis

conjugate axis length = 8

latus rectum = 32 / 3

$$\dfrac{x^2}{9} - \dfrac{y^2}{16} = 1$$

x − hyperbola: a = 3 and b = 4 therefore c = 5

b.

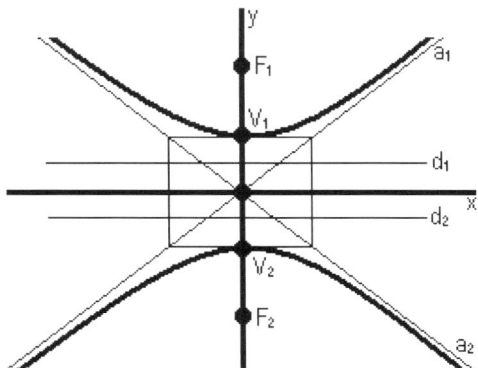

$$\frac{y^2}{144} - \frac{x^2}{25} = 1$$

y – hyperbola: a = 12 and b = 5 therefore c = 13

center: (0,0)

vertices: $V_1(0, 12)$ and $V_2(0, -12)$

foci: $F_1(0, 13)$ and $F_2(0, -13)$

asymptotes: a_1: $y = \frac{12}{5}x$ and a_2: $y = -\frac{12}{5}x$

eccentricity: e = 13/12

a/e = 144/13

directrices: d_1: y = 144/13 and d_2: y = −144/13

transverse axis: y axis

transverse axis length = 24

conjugate axis: x axis

conjugate axis length = 10

latus rectum = 50 /12

c.

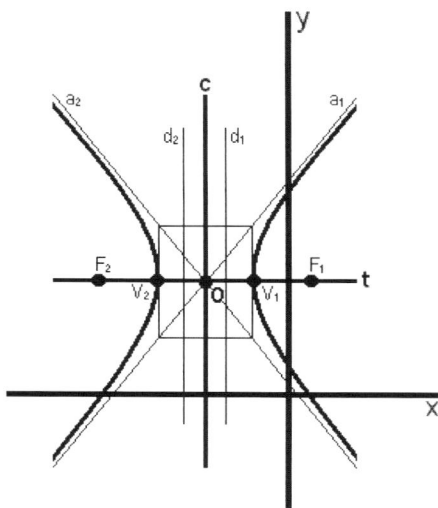

$$\frac{(x+4)^2}{9} - \frac{(y-7)^2}{16} = 1$$

x – hyperbola: a = 3 and b = 4 therefore c = 5

center: O(-4, 7)

vertices: $V_1(-7, 7)$ and $V_2(-1, 7)$

foci: $F_1(1, 7)$ and $F_2(-9, 7)$

asymptotes:

a_1: $y - 7 = \frac{4}{3}(x+4)$ and a_2: $y - 7 = -\frac{4}{3}(x+4)$

eccentricity: e = 5/3

a/e = 1.8

directrices: d_1: x = -4 + 1.8 and d_2: x = -4 − 1.8

transverse axis: y = 7 line

transverse axis length = 6

conjugate axis: x = -4 line

conjugate axis length = 8

latus rectum = 32 / 3

d.

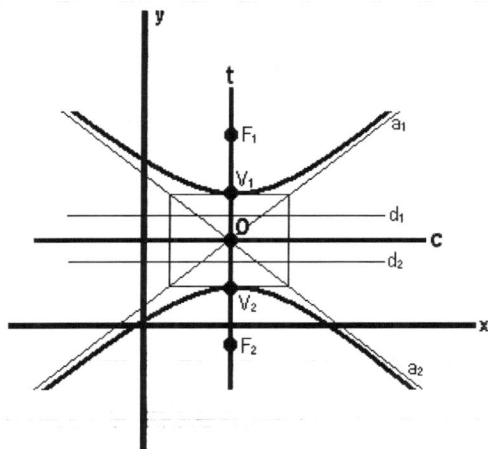

$$\frac{(y-6)^2}{9} - \frac{(x-5)^2}{16} = 1$$

y – hyperbola

a = 3 and b = 4 therefore c = 5

center: O(5, 6)

vertices: $V_1(5, 9)$ and $V_2(5, 3)$

foci: $F_1(5, 11)$ and $F_2(5, 1)$

asymptotes:

a_1: $y - 6 = \frac{3}{4}(x-5)$ and a_2: $y - 6 = -\frac{3}{4}(x-5)$

eccentricity: e = 5/3

a/e = 1.8

directrices: d_1: y = 6 + 1.8 and d_2: y = 6 − 1.8

transverse axis: x = 5 line

transverse axis length = 6

conjugate axis: y = 6 line

conjugate axis length = 8

latus rectum = 32 / 3

e. $16y^2 - 9x^2 + 64y + 18x + 55 = 0$

$16(y^2 + 4y) - 9(x^2 - 2x) = -55$

$16(y^2 + 4y + 4) - 9(x^2 - 2x + 1) = -55 + 64 - 9$

$16(y^2 + 4y + 4) - 9(x^2 - 2x + 1) = 0$

$16(y + 2)^2 - 9(x - 1)^2 = 0$

$16(y + 2)^2 = 9(x - 1)^2$

therefore

$4(y + 2) = \pm 3(x - 1)$

$(y + 2) = \pm\frac{3}{4}(x-1)$

The conic section represents two intersecting lines with slopes of 3/4 and − 3/4 passing through the point (1, −2).

Hyperbolas in the form: xy = k

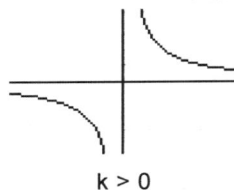

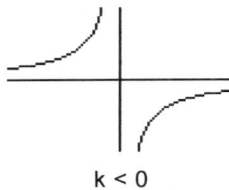

k > 0

k < 0

Example: Analyze the hyperbola xy = 4

Solution: Center: (0, 0); Vertices (2, 2) and (−2, −2)

Transverse axis: the line defined by y = x; Conjugate axis: the line defined by y = −x

Transverse axis length = $4\sqrt{2}$; Conjugate axis length = $4\sqrt{2}$

Asymptotes: y = 0 (the x – axis) and x = 0 (the y – axis)

Hyperbolic Rational Functions

$f(x) = \dfrac{ax+b}{cx+d}$; Domain = $R - \left\{\dfrac{-d}{c}\right\}$; Range = $R - \left\{\dfrac{a}{c}\right\}$

Horizontal asymptote: y = a/c

Vertical asymptote: x = –d/c

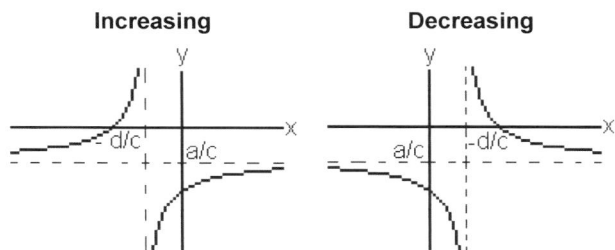

Increasing   **Decreasing**

Parabola

A parabola is the set of points in a plane equidistant from a given fixed point and a given fixed line in the plane. The fixed point is the *focus* of the parabola; the line is the *directrix*.

Parabolas in Standard Position

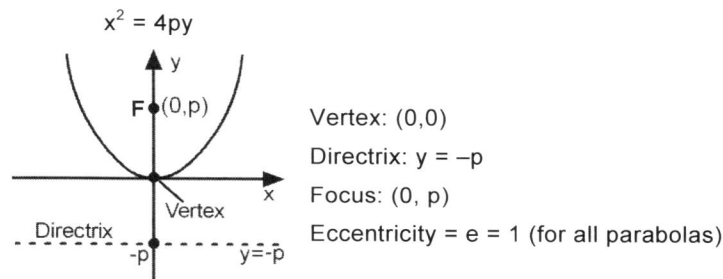

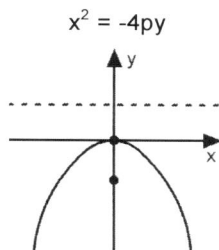

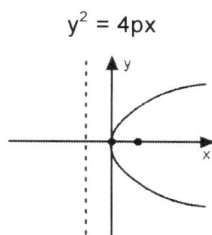

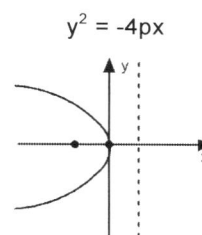

$x^2 = 4py$

Vertex: (0,0)

Directrix: y = –p

Focus: (0, p)

Eccentricity = e = 1 (for all parabolas)

$x^2 = -4py$ $y^2 = 4px$ $y^2 = -4px$

When coordinates of vertex is (h, k):

$(x - h)^2 = \pm 4p(y - k)$ opens up or down – axis of symmetry is vertical

$(y - k)^2 = \pm 4p(x - h)$, opens to the side axis of symmetry is horizontal

Coordinates of vertex: (h, k)

Equation of axis of symmetry: x = h if vertical, y = k if horizontal

Focus: p units along the axis of symmetry from vertex

Equation of directrix: y = –p if axis of symmetry is vertical, x = –p if axis of symmetry is horizontal

Eccentricity = e = 1

Length of latus rectum = 4p

Example: Analyze each of the following conic sections:

a. $y^2 = 8x$

b. $(x + 2)^2 = -4(y - 3)$

a.

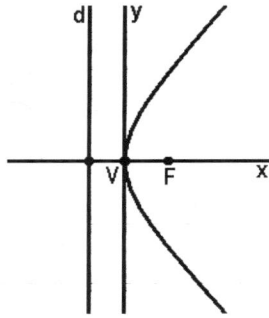

$y^2 = 8x$

Vertex (0,0)

p = 2

Vertex: V(0,0)

Directrix: d: x = −2

Focus: F(2,0)

Eccentricity: e = 1

Latus rectum = 8

b.

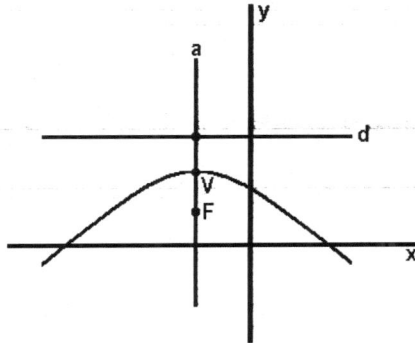

$(x + 2)^2 = -4(y - 3)$

Vertex (−2, 3)

p = 1

Vertex: V(−2, 3)

Directrix: d: y = 4

Focus: F(−2, 2)

Eccentricity: e = 1

Latus rectum = 4

Example: Convert each of the following conic sections to its standard form and state what it represents.

a. $25x^2 + 16y^2 + 150x - 32y + 241 = 0$

b. $16y^2 - 9x^2 + 64y + 18x - 89 = 0$

c. $y^2 + 4y + 2 - 2x = 0$

d. $xy = 0$

Solution:

a. $25x^2 + 16y^2 + 150x - 32y + 241 = 0$

$25(x^2 + 6x + 9) + 16(y^2 - 2y + 1) = -241 + 225 + 16$

$25(x + 3)^2 + 16(y - 1)^2 = 0$

The conic represents the point whose coordinates are (−3, 1)

b. $16y^2 - 9x^2 + 64y + 18x - 89 = 0$

$16y^2 + 64y - 9x^2 + 18x = 89$

$16(y^2 + 4y + 4) - 9(x^2 - 2x + 1) = 89 + 64 - 9$

$16(y + 2)^2 - 9(x - 1)^2 = 144$

$\dfrac{(y+2)^2}{9} - \dfrac{(x-1)^2}{16} = 1$

The conic represents a hyperbola centered at (1, −2); a = 3 and b = 4.

c. $y^2 + 4y + 2 - 2x = 0$

$y^2 + 4y = 2x - 2$

$y^2 + 4y + 4 = 2x - 2 + 4$

$y^2 + 4y + 4 = 2x + 2$

$(y + 2)^2 = 2(x + 1)$

The conic represents a parabola whose vertex is at (−1, −2) and p = 1/2

d. $xy = 0$ means x = 0 or y = 0; representing the x and y axes.

4.5 SEQUENCES AND SERIES

In general, **sequence**s are functions that map positive integers to real numbers. For example for the following sequence

then **n'th term** is given by $a_n = f(n) = \dfrac{1}{n+5}$ where n is a positive integer: $\dfrac{1}{6}, \dfrac{1}{7}, \dfrac{1}{8}, \dots, t_n, \dots$ The term **series** corresponds to

the sum of the terms of a sequence.

Infinite Sequence: $\left\{ \dfrac{1}{6}, \dfrac{1}{7}, \dfrac{1}{8}, \dfrac{1}{9}, \dots\dots\dots\dots \right\}$

Infinite Series: $\dfrac{1}{6} + \dfrac{1}{7} + \dfrac{1}{8} + \dots\dots\dots$

Finite Sequence: $\left\{ \dfrac{1}{6}, \dfrac{1}{7}, \dfrac{1}{8}, \dots\dots\dots\dots, \dfrac{1}{50} \right\}$

Finite Series: $\dfrac{1}{6} + \dfrac{1}{7} + \dfrac{1}{8} + \dots\dots\dots + \dfrac{1}{50}$

Arithmetic Sequences (Sequence ≡ Progression) and Series

Example: 20, 24, 28, 32, 36, 40, …

1. Explicit definition of an arithmetic sequence:

    $a_n = a + (n-1)d$ $a_n = 20 + (n-1) \cdot 4 = 4n + 16$

    a: first term $a = 20$

    d: common difference $d = 4$

2. Recursive definition of an arithmetic sequence:

    $a_{n+1} = a_n + d$ $a_{n+1} = a_n + 4$

    $a_1 = a$ $a_1 = 20$

3. $a_n = a_p + (n-p)d$

    $a_{16} = a_{12} + 4d$

    $a_{12} = a_{16} - 4d$

4. $a_n = \dfrac{a_{n+1} + a_{n-1}}{2} = \dfrac{a_{n+p} + a_{n-p}}{2}$

5. S_n: Sum of the first n terms of an arithmetic series.

    1. If S_n is a quadratic function of n (of the form $p \cdot n^2 + q \cdot n$) then S_n represents an arithmetic series.

    2. $S_n - S_{n-1} = a_n$

    3. $S_n = n\left(\dfrac{a_1 + a_n}{2} \right)$ or $S_n = \dfrac{n}{2}[2a_1 + (n-1)d]$

Geometric Sequences and Series

Example: 20, 40, 80, 160, 320, 640, …

1. Explicit definition of a geometric sequence:

    $a_n = a \cdot r^{n-1}$ $a_n = 20 \cdot 2^{n-1}$

    a: first term $a = 20$

    r: common ratio $r = 2$

2. Recursive definition of a geometric sequence:

    $a_{n+1} = a_n \cdot r$ $a_{n+1} = a_n \cdot 2$

    $a_1 = a$ $a_1 = 20$

3. $a_n = a_p \cdot r^{n-p}$

    $a_{16} = a_{12} \cdot r^4$

    $a_{12} = a_{16}/r^4$

4. $a_n^2 = a_{n+1} \cdot a_{n-1} = a_{n+p} \cdot a_{n-p}$

5. S_n: Sum of the first n terms of a geometric series; $S_n = a\dfrac{1-r^n}{1-r}$

6. If S_n is an exponential function of n (of the form $p + q \cdot r^n$) then S_n represents a geometric series.

7. $S_n - S_{n-1} = a_n$

8. **Infinite geometric series**: $a + ar + ar^2 + ar^3 + \ldots = S = \dfrac{a}{1-r}$ if ($|r| < 1$)

Example: The 1st term of an arithmetic sequence is 3 and the 5th term is 17.

a. What is the 55th term of the sequence?

b. What is the sum of the first 55 terms of this sequence?

Solution:

a. $a_1 = a = 3$ and $a_5 = a + 4d = 3 + 4d = 17 \Rightarrow d = 3.5$

$a_{55} = 3 + 54 \cdot 3.5 = 192$

b. $S_{55} = \dfrac{55}{2}(a_1 + a_{55}) = \dfrac{55}{2}(3 + 192) = 5362.5$

Example: Sum of the first n terms of a sequence is given by $3n^2 - 5n$. What is the nth term of the sequence?

Solution: $a_n = S_n - S_{n-1} = 3n^2 - 5n - (3(n-1)^2 - 5(n-1)) = 6n - 8$

Example: The 2nd term of a geometric sequence is 2 and the 6th term is 162.

- What is the 16th term of the sequence?

- What is the sum of the first 16 terms of this sequence?

Solution: $a_2 = ar = 2$ and $a_6 = ar^5 = 162 \Rightarrow r^4 = 81 \Rightarrow r = \pm 3$ and $a = \pm 2/3$

Therefore $a_{16} = a_2 \cdot r^{14} = 2 \cdot (\pm 3)^{14} = 2 \cdot 3^{14}$

$\text{Sum} = a \cdot \left(\dfrac{1-r^{16}}{1-r}\right) = \pm \dfrac{2}{3} \cdot \left(\dfrac{1-(\pm 3)^{16}}{1-(\pm 3)}\right) = 14348907 \text{ or } -7174454$

Example: The decimal given by 0.1232323... is expressed as a common fraction. What is the simplest form of this fraction?

Solution: $0.1232323\ldots = 0.1 + 0.023 + 0.00023 + 0.0000023 + \ldots = 0.1 + 0.023 (1 + 0.01 + 0.01^2 + \ldots)$

$= 0.1 + 0.023 \cdot \dfrac{1}{1 - 0.01} = \dfrac{61}{495}$

Example:

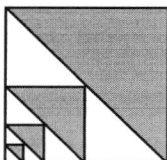

If one side of the outermost square is 4 then what is the total perimeter and the total area of all shaded triangles?

Solution:

Total area = 16 / 2 + 4 / 2 + 1 / 2 + ... = $\dfrac{8}{1-\dfrac{2}{8}} = \dfrac{32}{3}$

Total Perimeter = $8 + 4\sqrt{2} + \dfrac{1}{2}(8 + 4\sqrt{2}) + \dfrac{1}{4}(8 + 4\sqrt{2}) + ... = \dfrac{8 + 4\sqrt{2}}{1-\dfrac{1}{2}} = 16 + 8\sqrt{2}$

Example: Insert 4 arithmetic means between 1 and 10.

Solution: 1 + 5d = 10; therefore d = 1.8; the numbers are 2.8, 4.6, 6.4 and 8.2

Example: Insert 4 geometric means between 1 and 10.

Solution: $1 \cdot r^5 = 10 \Rightarrow r = \sqrt[5]{10} \Rightarrow$ The numbers are $\sqrt[5]{10}$, $\sqrt[5]{100}$, $\sqrt[5]{1000}$, $\sqrt[5]{10000}$

Sigma Notation

Examples:

a. 2 + 4 + 6 + ... + 20 = $\displaystyle\sum_{i=1}^{10}(2i)$

b. 90 + 94 + 98 + ... + 490 = $\displaystyle\sum_{i=1}^{101}(4i + 86)$

c. ln(1) + ln(2) + ln(3) + ln(4) + ln(5) = $\displaystyle\sum_{i=1}^{5} \ln(i)$

Commonly Used Formulas

$$\sum_{i=1}^{n} i = 1 + 2 + 3 + ... + n = \dfrac{n(n+1)}{2}$$

$$\sum_{i=1}^{n} i^2 = 1^2 + 2^2 + 3^2 + ... + n^2 = \dfrac{n(n+1)(2n+1)}{6}$$

$$\sum_{i=1}^{n} i^3 = 1^3 + 2^3 + 3^3 + ... + n^3 = \left[\dfrac{n(n+1)}{2}\right]^2$$

$$\sum_{i=1}^{n} r^{i-1} = 1 + r + r^2 + ... + r^{n-1} = \dfrac{1-r^n}{1-r}$$

4.6 VARIATION

y varies directly as x: $y = k.x \Rightarrow \dfrac{y}{x} = k \Rightarrow$ the ratio of y to x is a constant

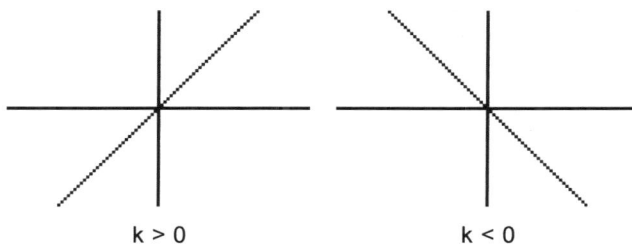

$$k > 0 \qquad\qquad k < 0$$

y varies inversely as x: $y = k.\dfrac{1}{x} \Rightarrow x.y = k \Rightarrow$ the product of y and x is constant

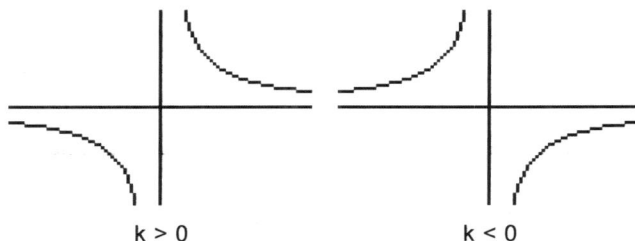

$$k > 0 \qquad\qquad k < 0$$

y varies directly as a and inversely as b: $y = k \cdot \dfrac{a \rightarrow \text{Direct}}{b \rightarrow \text{Inverse}}$; k: constant of variation

When a quantity is related with more than one quantity via direct and/or inverse variation, this is also known as **joint variation**.

Example: It is given that y varies directly as the square of x and inversely as the square root of z.

a. If y = 3 when x = 2 and z = 9 then what will be x when y = 1 and z = 4?

b. What will happen to y when z is quadrupled and x is halved?

Solution:

a. $y = k \cdot \dfrac{x^2}{\sqrt{z}}$

$3 = k \cdot \dfrac{2^2}{\sqrt{9}}$; and k = $\dfrac{9}{4}$; therefore $y = \dfrac{9}{4} \cdot \dfrac{x^2}{\sqrt{z}}$.

$1 = \dfrac{9}{4} \cdot \dfrac{x^2}{\sqrt{4}}$ implies that $x^2 = \dfrac{8}{9}$ and $x = \pm\dfrac{2\sqrt{2}}{3}$

b. $y = \dfrac{\left(\dfrac{1}{2}\right)^2}{\sqrt{4}} = \dfrac{1}{8}$ meaning that y is reduced to one eight.

4.7 BINARY OPERATIONS

A binary operation Δ is a function f(x, y) whose domain is a subset of R^2 i.e. the points in the Cartesian plane. Usually a binary operation is defined as $x \Delta y = f(x, y)$ by a rule given by f.

Closure property: If x and y are both elements of a set A and $x \Delta y$ is also an element of set A for all x, y; then the operation given by Δ is said to be closed over set A. For example positive real numbers are closed under addition but not subtraction.

Associative property: $(x \Delta y) \Delta z = x \Delta (y \Delta z)$ implies that Δ is associative. Addition and multiplication possess the associative property.

Identity element: If there is an element e in set A such that $x \Delta e = e \Delta x = x$ then e is the identity element for the operation Δ. The identity element for addition is 0 whereas the identity element for multiplication is 1.

Inverse element: If for each x in set A there exists an element $x - 1$ such that $x \Delta x - 1 = x - 1 \Delta x = e$ then $x - 1$ is the inverse of x with respect to the operation Δ. The additive inverse of x is $- x$ and the multiplicative inverse of x is $\dfrac{1}{x}$; 0 does not have a multiplicative inverse.

Commutative property: $x \Delta y = y \Delta x$ implies that Δ is commutative. Addition and multiplication possess the commutative property.

Example: For m > 0 and n > 0 it is given that $m^2 \Delta n^2 = \dfrac{1}{m} + \dfrac{1}{n}$. $9 \Delta 4 = ?$

Solution: $9 \Delta 4 = 1/3 + 1/2 = 5/6$

Example: If (a, b) # (c, d) = (a + c, b – d) and (4, 3) # (x, y) = (1, –2) then x + y = ?
Solution:
(4, 3) # (x, y) = (1, –2)
(4 + x, 3 – y) = (1, –2)
4 + x = 1 and 3 – y = –2
x = –3 and y = 5. Therefore x + y = 2.

4.8 COMPUTER PROGRAMS

A computer program is a sequence of instructions performed by the following rules:

1. The last value stored in a variable must be used in a computation.

2. When a certain instruction on a program line is performed, the instruction in the next program line will be performed unless specified by an instruction.

Example: The following instructions are carried out as specified.

1. S = 0 and N = 1

2. If N ≤ 5 go to step 3 otherwise go to step 6

3. Increase S by N

4. Increase N by 1

5. Go to step 2

6. Write the final value of S.

What is the final value of S?

Solution:

$S = 0;\ N = 1$

$N = 1 \le 5 \Rightarrow S = 0 + 1 = 1;\ N = 1 + 1 = 2$

$N = 2 \le 5 \Rightarrow S = 1 + 2 = 3;\ N = 2 + 1 = 3$

$N = 3 \le 5 \Rightarrow S = 3 + 3 = 6;\ N = 3 + 1 = 4$

$N = 4 \le 5 \Rightarrow S = 6 + 4 = 10;\ N = 4 + 1 = 5$

$N = 5 \le 5 \Rightarrow S = 10 + 5 = 15\ N = 5 + 1 = 6$

$S = 15$ is written

4.9 LOGIC

Conjunction: $A \wedge B$, A and B, $A \cap B$

Disjunction: $A \vee B$, A or B, $A \cup B$

Negation of Conjunction: $(A \wedge B)' \equiv A' \vee B'$

Negation of Disjunction: $(A \vee B)' \equiv A' \wedge B'$

Implication: $A \Rightarrow B$; if A, then B; A implies B; A only if B; B, if A;

$(A \Rightarrow B) \equiv (A' \vee B)$

In an implication **A** is the **sufficient** condition and **B** is the **necessary** condition.

Double implication: $A \Leftrightarrow B$; A if and only if B; A iff B

$A \Leftrightarrow B \equiv (A \Rightarrow B) \wedge (B \Rightarrow A)$

1. **Statement**   : $A \Rightarrow B$
2. **Equivalent statement** : $A' \vee B$
3. **Negation**   : $(A' \vee B)' \cong A \wedge B'$
4. **Converse**   : $B \Rightarrow A$
5. **Inverse**   : $A' \Rightarrow B'$
6. **Contrapositive**   : $B' \Rightarrow A'$

Please note that 1, 2 and 6 are all equivalent.

A statement which is **always correct** is a **TAUTOLOGY.**

A statement which is **always false** is a **CONTRADICTION.**

Indirect proof: Proving a statement (A⇒B) is equivalent to proving its contrapositive (B'⇒A') since A⇒B and B'⇒A' are equivalent statements. Proving the contrapositive of a statement instead of the statement itself is called indirect proof. The initial assumption to be made while making an indirect proof is B'.

Negations

(All $\equiv \forall$; Some $\equiv$ At least one $\equiv \exists$; T≡True; F≡False)

(All)' $\equiv$ Some	$(\forall)' \equiv \exists$	(and)' $\equiv$ or	$(\wedge)' \equiv \vee$	(A)' $\equiv$ not A
(Some)' $\equiv$ All	$(\exists)' \equiv \forall$	(or)' $\equiv$ and	$(\vee)' \equiv \wedge$	(A')' $\equiv$ A

$(>)' \equiv \leq$	$(\geq)' \equiv <$	$(1)' \equiv 0$	(True)' $\equiv$ False	$(=)' \equiv \neq$
$(<)' \equiv \geq$	$(\leq)' \equiv >$	$(0)' \equiv 1$	(False)' $\equiv$ True	$(\neq)' \equiv =$

Examples:

(all men are pedestrians)' $\equiv$ some men are not pedestrians

(for some x, x = p)' $\equiv$ for all x, x $\neq$ p

(some boys play rugby)' $\equiv$ all boys don't play rugby.

(all cats are not fish)' $\equiv$ some cats are fish

<u>**Truth Tables**</u>

OR

A	B	$A \vee B$
T	T	T
T	F	T
F	T	T
F	F	F

Think of a safe with 1 lock that has 2 keys. 1 key is sufficient to open the lock.

AND

A	B	$A \wedge B$
T	T	T
T	F	F
F	T	F
F	F	F

Think of a safe with 2 locks and 2 keys. Both keys are needed to open the safe.

IMPLICATION

A	B	A'	$A' \vee B$	$A \Rightarrow B$
T	T	F	T	T
T	F	F	F	F
F	T	T	T	T
F	F	T	T	T

Please note that $A \Rightarrow B$ is false only if A is true and B is false.

Example: Find the equivalent, negation, converse, inverse and contrapositive of the statement "If x = 3, then x^2 = 9".

Solution:

Equivalent: $x \neq 3$ or $x^2 = 9$

Negation: x = 3 and $x^2 \neq 9$

Converse: if $x^2 = 9$, then x = 3 (not correct because x can be –3 as well)

Inverse: If $x \neq 3$, then $x^2 \neq 9$ (not correct because if x = –3 then $x^2 = 9$ still holds)

Contrapositive: If $x^2 \neq 9$, then $x \neq 3$; definitely correct.

4.10 MATRICES AND DETERMINANTS

Matrices are blocks of numbers used to store information (singular – matrix; plural – matrices). Following is a 3 by 5 matrix.

$$\begin{bmatrix} 2 & 0 & 2 & -4 & 7 \\ 5 & 6 & 8 & 0 & -9 \\ 2 & 0 & 7 & 10 & 0 \end{bmatrix}_{3\times5}$$

Matrix Arithmetic

Addition, subtraction and other linear combinations are carried out similarly. It should be noticed that matrices of different orders cannot be linearly combined.

Example: Three matrices are defined as follows:

$$A = \begin{bmatrix} 2 & -5 & 4 \\ 1 & 4 & -2 \end{bmatrix}; B = \begin{bmatrix} 1 & 2 \\ -2 & 5 \end{bmatrix}; C = \begin{bmatrix} -1 & 3 & 0 \\ -3 & -2 & 6 \end{bmatrix}$$

Evaluate

(i) 2B (ii) – 3C (iii) A + C (iv) A + B (v) 2A – 3C

Solution:

(i) $2B = 2 \times \begin{bmatrix} 1 & 2 \\ -2 & 5 \end{bmatrix} = \begin{bmatrix} 2 & 4 \\ -4 & 10 \end{bmatrix}$

(ii) $-3C = -3 \times \begin{bmatrix} -1 & 3 & 0 \\ -3 & -2 & 6 \end{bmatrix} = \begin{bmatrix} 3 & -9 & 0 \\ 9 & 6 & -18 \end{bmatrix}$

(iii) $A + C = \begin{bmatrix} 2 & -5 & 4 \\ 1 & 4 & -2 \end{bmatrix} + \begin{bmatrix} -1 & 3 & 0 \\ -3 & -2 & 6 \end{bmatrix} = \begin{bmatrix} 1 & -2 & 4 \\ -2 & 2 & 4 \end{bmatrix}$

(iv) A + B cannot be calculated as the matrices do not match in dimensions.

(v) $2A - 3C = 2 \begin{bmatrix} 2 & -5 & 4 \\ 1 & 4 & -2 \end{bmatrix} - 3 \begin{bmatrix} -1 & 3 & 0 \\ -3 & -2 & 6 \end{bmatrix} = \begin{bmatrix} 7 & -19 & 8 \\ 11 & 14 & -22 \end{bmatrix}$

Matrix Multiplication

$$A = \begin{bmatrix} 2 & 4 & 7 \\ 5 & 0 & -3 \\ 1 & -3 & 4 \end{bmatrix}; B = \begin{bmatrix} 1 & 3 & -1 \\ 0 & 4 & 6 \\ 2 & -3 & 2 \end{bmatrix}; A \times B = ?$$

The definition involves taking the rows of the left hand matrix and pairing these with the columns of the second matrix.

$$\begin{bmatrix} 2 & 4 & 7 \\ 5 & 0 & -3 \\ 1 & -3 & 4 \end{bmatrix} \times \begin{bmatrix} 1 & 3 & -1 \\ 0 & 4 & 6 \\ 2 & -3 & 2 \end{bmatrix}$$

If the problem is to find the product, the first step is to take the first row of the left hand matrix [2 4 7] and pair it up with the

first column $\begin{bmatrix} 1 \\ 0 \\ 2 \end{bmatrix}$. The pairs are then multiplied and results are added to give a single number: 2 x 1 + 4 x 0 + 7 x 2 = 16.

This number is the result of combining the first row and the first column. It becomes the number in the first row and first column of the resulting matrix. A similar calculation must be carried out for each row and column combination. The

resulting matrix is: $\begin{bmatrix} 16 & 1 & 36 \\ -1 & 24 & -11 \\ 9 & -21 & -11 \end{bmatrix}$.

It should be noted that matrix multiplication is not commutative. This means that the order in which the matrices are multiplied does matter. This is different from ordinary multiplication which is commutative. In the above case B x A =

$\begin{bmatrix} 16 & 7 & -6 \\ 26 & -18 & 12 \\ -9 & 2 & 31 \end{bmatrix}$ which is different from A x B.

Not only square matrices can be multiplied. The necessary condition is that the number of columns of the first matrix must equal the number of rows of the second matrix: $A_{m \times n} \times B_{n \times p} = C_{m \times p}$

Example: For the following matrices: A = $\begin{bmatrix} 1 & 0 \\ 3 & -6 \end{bmatrix}$; B = $\begin{bmatrix} 2 & -4 & -1 \\ 1 & 0 & -3 \end{bmatrix}$; C = $\begin{bmatrix} -2 & -1 \\ -3 & 4 \\ 1 & -4 \end{bmatrix}$; Calculate where possible:

(i) AB

(ii) AC

(iii) BC

(iv) CB

(v) A²

Solution:

(i) AB = $\begin{bmatrix} 1 & 0 \\ 3 & -6 \end{bmatrix} \begin{bmatrix} 2 & -4 & -1 \\ 1 & 0 & -3 \end{bmatrix} = \begin{bmatrix} 2 & -4 & -1 \\ 0 & -12 & 15 \end{bmatrix}$

(ii) AC cannot be calculated.

(iii) BC = $\begin{bmatrix} 2 & -4 & -1 \\ 1 & 0 & -3 \end{bmatrix} \begin{bmatrix} -2 & -1 \\ -3 & 4 \\ 1 & -4 \end{bmatrix} = \begin{bmatrix} 7 & -14 \\ -5 & 11 \end{bmatrix}$

(iv) CB = $\begin{bmatrix} -2 & -1 \\ -3 & 4 \\ 1 & -4 \end{bmatrix} \begin{bmatrix} 2 & -4 & -1 \\ 1 & 0 & -3 \end{bmatrix} = \begin{bmatrix} -5 & 8 & 5 \\ -2 & 12 & -9 \\ -2 & -4 & 11 \end{bmatrix}$

(v) A² = $\begin{bmatrix} 1 & 0 \\ 3 & -6 \end{bmatrix} \begin{bmatrix} 1 & 0 \\ 3 & -6 \end{bmatrix} = \begin{bmatrix} 1 & 0 \\ -15 & 36 \end{bmatrix}$

2 by 2 Matrices

These are the matrices having two rows and two columns.

Identity Matrix

The identity matrix is defined as the matrix such that $AI = IA = A$ for all square matrices A. For 2 by 2 matrices, $I_2 =$

$\begin{bmatrix} 1 & 0 \\ 0 & 1 \end{bmatrix}$. For 3 by 3 matrices, $I_3 = \begin{bmatrix} 1 & 0 & 0 \\ 0 & 1 & 0 \\ 0 & 0 & 1 \end{bmatrix}$. The identity matrix is the identity element for matrix multiplication.

Zero Matrix

All elements of a zero matrix are zeros.

Diagonal Matrix

All elements other than the diagonal elements of a diagonal matrix are zeros. Following are examples of diagonal matrices:

$$\begin{bmatrix} 4 & 0 & 0 \\ 0 & -5 & 0 \\ 0 & 0 & 7 \end{bmatrix} ; \begin{bmatrix} 0 & 0 & 4 \\ 0 & -5 & 0 \\ -9 & 0 & 0 \end{bmatrix}$$

Triangular Matrices

All elements other than the triangular elements are zeros. Following are examples of triangular matrices.

Upper triangular: $\begin{bmatrix} 4 & -2 & 3 \\ 0 & -5 & 0 \\ 0 & 0 & 7 \end{bmatrix}$; Lower triangular: $\begin{bmatrix} 4 & 0 & 0 \\ 9 & -5 & 0 \\ 1 & -2 & 7 \end{bmatrix}$

Inverse of a Matrix

The inverse of a square matrix A is written as A^{-1}. The product of a matrix and its inverse is the identity matrix, I, $A A^{-1} = A^{-1}A = I$. For 2 by 2 matrices, the inverse can be found as follows:

If $A = \begin{bmatrix} a & b \\ c & d \end{bmatrix}$, then, $A^{-1} = \dfrac{1}{\det A}\begin{bmatrix} d & -b \\ -c & a \end{bmatrix} = \dfrac{1}{ad-bc}\begin{bmatrix} d & -b \\ -c & a \end{bmatrix}$ where detA is the determinant of matrix A given by ad − bc.

Matrix Transposition

When a matrix is transposed, its rows and columns are interchanged. Therefore an m by n matrix when transposed gives an n by m matrix. Transpose of a matrix A is denoted as A^{T}.

For example if $A = \begin{bmatrix} 2 & -1 \\ -3 & 2 \\ 1 & 4 \end{bmatrix}$ then $A^{T} = \begin{bmatrix} 2 & -3 & 1 \\ -1 & 2 & 4 \end{bmatrix}$

Two by Two Determinant

$$\begin{vmatrix} a & b \\ c & d \end{vmatrix} = ad - bc$$

Three by Three Determinant

$$\begin{vmatrix} a & b & c \\ d & e & f \\ g & h & k \end{vmatrix} = (aek + dhc + gbf) - (gec + fha + dbk)$$

Properties of Determinants

1. If a row or a column is multiplied by k, determinant is multiplied by k.
2. If all elements are multiplied by k in an n x n determinant, the determinant is multiplied by k^{n}.
3. If two rows are the same or two column are the same then determinant is 0.
4. If two rows are multiples of each other or if two columns are multiples of each other in a determinant then determinant is 0.

Example: $\begin{vmatrix} 19999 & 19998 \\ 20000 & 19999 \end{vmatrix} = ?$

Solution:

$$\begin{vmatrix} x & x-1 \\ x+1 & x \end{vmatrix} = x^2 - (x+1)(x-1)$$

$$= x^2 - (x^2 - 1)$$

$$= x^2 - x^2 + 1 = 1$$

Example: $\begin{vmatrix} 1 & 2 & 3 \\ 0 & 2 & 4 \\ 8 & -1 & 0 \end{vmatrix} = ?$

Solution: Determinant $= 0 + 0 + 64 - 48 + 4 - 0 = 68 - 48 = 20$

Cramer's Rule for 2 Unknowns

$a_1 x + b_1 y = c_1$

$a_2 x + b_2 y = c_2$

$x = ?, y = ?$

$$\Delta = \begin{vmatrix} a_1 & b_1 \\ a_2 & b_2 \end{vmatrix} \qquad \Delta_1 = \begin{vmatrix} c_1 & b_1 \\ c_2 & b_2 \end{vmatrix} \qquad \Delta_2 = \begin{vmatrix} a_1 & c_1 \\ a_2 & c_2 \end{vmatrix}$$

$$x = \frac{\Delta_1}{\Delta} \qquad y = \frac{\Delta_2}{\Delta}$$

Example:

$x + 2y = 3$

$x + 4y = 5$

$x = ?$ and $y = ?$

Solution:

$$\Delta = \begin{vmatrix} 1 & 2 \\ 1 & 4 \end{vmatrix} = 2$$

$$\Delta_1 = \begin{vmatrix} 3 & 2 \\ 5 & 4 \end{vmatrix} = 2 \qquad x = \frac{\Delta_1}{\Delta} = \frac{\begin{vmatrix} 3 & 2 \\ 5 & 4 \end{vmatrix}}{\begin{vmatrix} 1 & 2 \\ 1 & 4 \end{vmatrix}} = \frac{2}{2} = 1 \text{ and } y = \frac{\Delta_2}{\Delta} = \frac{\begin{vmatrix} 1 & 3 \\ 1 & 5 \end{vmatrix}}{\begin{vmatrix} 1 & 2 \\ 1 & 4 \end{vmatrix}} = \frac{2}{2} = 1$$

$$\Delta_2 = \begin{vmatrix} 1 & 3 \\ 1 & 5 \end{vmatrix} = 2$$

Cramer's Rule for 3 Unknowns

$a_1 x + b_1 y + c_1 z = d_1$

$a_2 x + b_2 y + c_2 z = d_2$

$a_3 x + b_3 y + c_3 z = d_3$

$$\Delta = \begin{vmatrix} a_1 & b_1 & c_1 \\ a_2 & b_2 & c_2 \\ a_3 & b_3 & c_3 \end{vmatrix} \quad \Delta_1 = \begin{vmatrix} d_1 & b_1 & c_1 \\ d_2 & b_2 & c_2 \\ d_3 & b_3 & c_3 \end{vmatrix} \quad \Delta_2 = \begin{vmatrix} a_1 & d_1 & c_1 \\ a_2 & d_2 & c_2 \\ a_3 & d_3 & c_3 \end{vmatrix} \quad \Delta_3 = \begin{vmatrix} a_1 & b_1 & d_1 \\ a_2 & b_2 & d_2 \\ a_3 & b_3 & d_3 \end{vmatrix}$$

$$x = \frac{\Delta_1}{\Delta} \quad y = \frac{\Delta_2}{\Delta} \quad z = \frac{\Delta_3}{\Delta}$$

4.11 WORD PROBLEMS

Example: A man goes to the woods with the speed of 30 mph and returns the same route with the speed of 40 mph. If the total time it takes for the round trip is 3.5 hours, what is the total distance he has covered?

Solution: If d is the distance to the woods then the time forward is $\dfrac{d}{30}$ and the time backward is $\dfrac{d}{40}$. Total time is 3.5 therefore $3.5 = \dfrac{d}{30} + \dfrac{d}{40}$. Solving for d we get d = 60 and the total distance covered is 120 miles.

Example: A bus leaves Istanbul for Ankara averaging 56 miles per hour. Half an hour later a second bus leaves from the same station for Ankara averaging 60 miles per hour. How long will it take the second bus to overtake the first?

Solution: If t is the time for the second bus, the time for the first one is (t + 0.5). At the instant when the second bus overtakes the first one, the distances covered by each of them are the same. Ü

Therefore 56(t + 0.5) = 60t and solving for t we get t = 7 hours.

Example: A speed boat goes 100 miles downstream in 2.5 hours. Going upstream it traveled the same distance in 4 hours. What is the rate of the boat in still water, and what is the rate of the stream?

Solution: If b is the rate of the boat and r is the rate of the stream then:

b + r = 100 / 2.5 = 40 and b − r = 100 / 4 = 25.

Solving for b and r we get b = 32.5 and r = 7.5

Example: How many quarts of pure water must be added to 60 quarts of a 15% acid solution in order to obtain a 12% acid solution?

Solution: The quarts of pure acid remains the same for both solutions therefore if q is the quarts of pure acid then $60 \cdot \dfrac{15}{100} = (60 + q) \cdot \dfrac{12}{100}$. Solving for q we get q = 15 quarts.

Example: If the sum of the consecutive integers from − 28 to x, inclusive, is 90, what is the value of x?

Solution: The integers are −28, −27, −26, ..., −1, 0, 1, 2, ..., 28, 29, 30, 31. Therefore x is 31. Please note that the sum of the integers from − 28 to 28 is zero and 29 + 30 + 31 = 90.

Example: An expert can do a job on the computer in 8 hours. His secretary can do the same job in 10 hours. After the expert works on the job for 4 hours, his secretary takes over and completes the job. How many hours did it take the secretary to complete the job?

Solution: The expert does 1/8 of the job in an hour and his secretary can do 1/10 of the job in an hour. If h is the number of hours that the secretary works then $\dfrac{1}{8} \cdot 4 + \dfrac{1}{10} \cdot h = 1$ and solving for h we get h = 5 hours.

Example: Ali and Berna can do a job in 4 days. Berna and Cem can do the job in 5 days. Ali and Cem can do the job in 6 days. In how many days will the job finish if Berna does half of the job; Cem does one third; and Ali does the rest?

Solution:

$\dfrac{1}{a} + \dfrac{1}{b} = \dfrac{1}{4}$; $\dfrac{1}{b} + \dfrac{1}{c} = \dfrac{1}{5}$; $\dfrac{1}{a} + \dfrac{1}{c} = \dfrac{1}{6}$ ⟹ Solving for a, b, and c we get $a = \dfrac{120}{13}$, $b = \dfrac{120}{17}$, and $c = \dfrac{120}{7}$

Berna has worked for $\dfrac{120}{17} \cdot \dfrac{1}{2} = \dfrac{60}{17}$ days; Cem has worked for $\dfrac{120}{7} \cdot \dfrac{1}{3} = \dfrac{40}{7}$ days and Ali has worked for

$\dfrac{120}{13} \cdot \left(1 - \dfrac{1}{2} - \dfrac{1}{3}\right) = \dfrac{20}{13}$ days. The job will be completed in 60/17 + 40/7 + 20/13 = 10.78 days approximately.

Example: If 5 men working 8 hours a day can complete 3 jobs in 10 days, 8 men working 6 hours a day can complete 2 jobs in how many days?

Solution: Number of men and number of days are inversely proportional; number of hours per day and number of days are inversely proportional; number of jobs and number of days are directly proportional.

Therefore:

and $x = \dfrac{5 \cdot 8 \cdot 2 \cdot 10}{8 \cdot 6 \cdot 3} = \dfrac{50}{9}$ days.

Example: Cana is 4 years older than Senem. When Cana was at Senem's age, Senem's age was one third of Cana's age at that time. What is the sum of their ages now?

Solution: If at present Cana = x + 4 and Senem = x $\Rightarrow$ In the past: Cana = x and Senem = x / 3. The age difference between Cana and Senem remains the same therefore: $x - \dfrac{x}{3} = 4$ and x = 6. Sum of their ages is 10 + 6 = 16

Example: In a group of 2,000 students, 900 are studying Spanish, 700 are studying French, and 500 are studying German. What is the greatest possible number of these students that might NOT be studying any of these languages?

Solution: All of the students studying French or German may be a subset of the students studying Spanish, therefore 2000 − 900 = 1100 students is the maximum.

Example: One number is 14 less than another number and the product of the two numbers is 72, what are the numbers?

Solution: If one of the numbers is x, then the other one is $x - 14 \Rightarrow x(x - 14) = 72 \Rightarrow x^2 - 14x - 72 = 0 \Rightarrow (x - 18)(x + 4) = 0$ x = 18 or x = -4; one is 18 and the other one is 4 or one is − 4 and the other one is − 18.

Example: Mr. Acuner invested part of his $80,000 investment in bonds paying 10% and the remaining in stocks paying 7%. If his annual income from both investments is $6, 500.00, how much did he invest in the bonds and in the stocks?

Solution: Money invested in bonds: x and money invested in stocks: 80000 − x

$$x \cdot \dfrac{10}{100} + (80000 - x) \cdot \dfrac{7}{100} = 6500$$

Solving for x we get x = 30000. Mr. Acuner invested $30,000 in bonds and $50,000 in stocks.

Example: The wholesale price of a certain item is $130. A retailer decides to sell this item at a %40 profit. When he sees that the sales are low, he makes a discount of 15% based on the selling price. If the tax rate that he has to apply is 5% what is the dollar amount of money that a customer will have to pay in order to buy this item?

Solution: The customer will have to pay $130 \cdot \left(1 + \dfrac{40}{100}\right) \cdot \left(1 - \dfrac{15}{100}\right) \cdot \left(1 + \dfrac{5}{100}\right) = \$162.44$.

Test Duration: 60 Minutes

Directions: For each of the following problems, decide which is the best of the choices given. If the exact numerical value is not one of the choices, select the choice that best approximates this value. Then fill in the corresponding oval on the answer sheet.

Notes:

- A calculator will be necessary for answering some (but not all) of the questions in this test. For each question you will have to decide whether or not you should use a calculator. The calculator you use must be at least a scientific calculator; programmable calculators and calculators that can display graphs are permitted.
- The only angle measure used on this test is degree measure. Make sure your calculator is in the degree mode.
- Figures that accompany problems in this test are intended to provide information useful in solving the problems. They are drawn as accurately as possible except when it is stated in a specific problem that its figure is not drawn to scale.
- All figures lie in a plane unless otherwise indicated.
- Unless otherwise specified, the domain of any function f is assumed to be the set of all real numbers x for which f(x) is a real number.

Reference Information: The following information is for your reference in answering some of the questions in this test.

- Volume of a right circular cone with radius r and height h: $V=\frac{1}{3}\pi r^2 h$

- Lateral area of a right circular cone with circumference of the base c and slant height l: $S=\frac{1}{2}cl$

- Volume of a sphere with radius r: $V=\frac{4}{3}\pi r^3$

- Surface area of sphere with radius r: $S=4\pi r^2$

- Volume of a pyramid with base area B and height h: $V=\frac{1}{3}Bh$

1. The expression $(x-1)^2(x+2)(3-x)$ is negative if and only if
(A) $1 < x < 3$ (B) $-2 < x < 3$ (C) $x < -2$ or $x > 3$ (D) $-2 < x < 3$ and $x \neq 1$ (E) $-2 < x < 1$

2. For two integers a and b, If 2a and b are consecutive integers; which one of the following is always odd number?
(A) a + b   (B) a − b   (C) a + 2b   (D) a − 2b   (E) 2a − b

3. A computer is programmed to divide a given number N by two if it is even, otherwise multiply by 3 and add 1. Which number must be chosen for N initially so that starting with the 5th number 4 − 2 − 1 will be obtained in a sequence?
(A) 2   (B) 3   (C) 5   (D) 6   (E) 10

4. For every real x, the following equality holds: $2x^2 - 3x + c = (x - 2)(ax + b)$; $a + b - c = ?$

(A) 1   (B) 2   (C) 3   (D) 4   (E) 5

5. If x > 2, then $|2 - x| + |2 + x| =$

(A) 0   (B) 2x   (C) 4   (D) -2x   (E) 2

6. B, D, F, and, H are the midpoints of the sides of the rectangle ACEG given in figure 1. Segments BF and HD intersect at point O (not shown). If a line m divides rectangle ACEG into two congruent parts, then m may pass through

I. Point O

II. Points A and E

III. Points F and C

(A) I only   (B) II only

(C) III only   (D) I and II only

(E) I, II and III

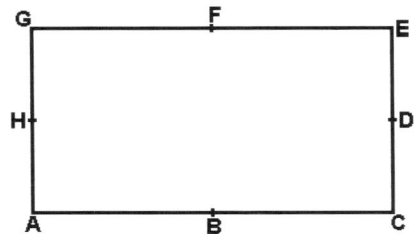

Figure 1

7. If $\sin 20° = A$ and $\sin x° = -A$, then x can equal

I. 20°   II. 160°   III. 200°   IV. 340°

(A) II only   (B) III only   (C) I and II only

(D) II and IV only   (E) III and IV only

8. In the formula $A = BC^2$, if B is halved and C is doubled then

(A) A will be quadrupled.   (B) A will be doubled.   (C) A will stay the same.

(D) A will be halved.   (E) A will be divided by 4.

9. If it is known in figure 2 that WX || ZY then which of the following contains a pair of angles that are always equal in measure?

(A) b and f

(B) a and d

(C) b and h

(D) e and g

(E) f and d

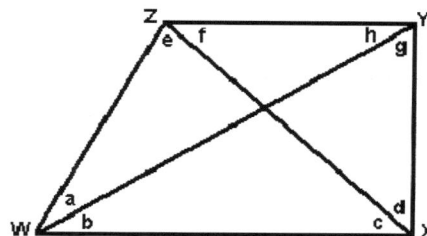

Figure 2

10. The average of 10 numbers is 80, where the greatest and the least numbers are 100 and 20 respectively. What is the average of the numbers other than the greatest and the least?

(A) 60   (B) 68   (C) 80   (D) 85   (E) 100

11. If $a^b < 1$, where $a, b \in R$; then which of the following statements can be true?

   I. $a > 1$ and $b < 0$

   II. $0 < a < 1$ and $b = 0$

   III. $0 < a < 1$ and $b > 0$

(A) I only   (B) II only   (C) III only

(D) I and II only   (E) I and III only

$$x^2 - k \cdot x + 1 = k - 2$$

12. The equation given above has two complex conjugate roots. Which of the following gives all possible values of k?

(A) $-2 < k < 6$ (B) $-6 \le k \le 2$ (C) $k < -2$ or $k > 6$

(D) $k \le 2$ or $k \ge 6$ (E) $-6 < k < 2$

13. First two terms a_1 and a_2 of an arithmetic sequence are 15 and 17 respectively. What is the 30th term in this sequence?

(A) 71   (B) 73   (C) 75   (D) 77   (E) 79

14. What is the magnitude of the complex number given by 12-5i where i^2=-1?

(A) $i\sqrt{13}$ (B) 6.5   (C) 13   (D) 13i   (E) 169

15. In a certain state the tax rate is 4% of the retail price of an item and the rate of profit in the Watch'n Sing Music and Video store is 22%. What will a customer pay for an item that has a wholesale price of $33.50?

(A) 34.84   (B) 38.93   (C) 40.87   (D) 41.45   (E) 42.50

16. When simplified in its greatest domain, the expression $\dfrac{x^2+3x-10}{3x-6} \div \dfrac{x^2+9x+20}{2x+8}$ equals

(A) 1/6   (B) 2/3   (C) $\dfrac{2}{x-2}$ (D) $\dfrac{x+2}{x+5}$ (E) $\dfrac{10x+40}{27x+60}$

17. The sum of two integers a and b varies inversely as their positive difference. If b = 6 when a = 9, what can be a when b is 2?

(A) 7   (B) -3   (C) 3   (D) 5   (E) 6

18. If $x^3+3x^2+kx-12$ is divisible by x + 3, then x^2+k is divisible by

(A) x − 3   (B) x − 2   (C) x − 1   (D) x   (E) x + 1

19. If the graph of the equation $y+2x-12-2p=0$ does not pass through the point (2, 6), the value of p cannot be

(A) − 6   (B) − 1   (C) 0   (D) 1   (E) 4

20. Which of the following common fractions equals the infinite decimal given by 0.424242…?

(A) 21/50   (B) 7/15   (C) 14/33   (D) 5/11   (E) 8/33

21. When simplified in its greatest domain, the expression $\dfrac{\cos^2 x}{1-\sin x}$ equals

(A) $1-\cos x$ (B) $1-\sin x$ (C) $1+\cos x$ (D) $1+\sin x$

(E) None of the above

22. The outer surface of a white cube with edge of length 6 inches is painted to gray and then cut into identical smaller cubes each with an edge of length 1 inch as shown in figure 3. How many smaller cubes have 2 gray faces only?

(A) 16   (B) 64   (C) 48   (D) 216

(E) None of the above

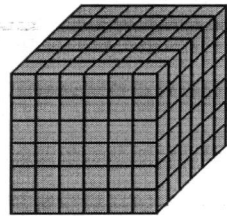

Figure 3

23. If $\log b^3 - \log b = \log 16$, then b is

(A) -4 (B) -2 (C) 2   (D) 2.7   (E) 4

24. If the reciprocal of $x^2 + \sqrt{15}$ is $x^2 - \sqrt{15}$, x equals

I. -2   II. 2   III. 4

(A) I only   (B) II only   (C) III only   (D) I and II only   (E) II and III only

25. The factors of $x^2 + 4$ are

(A) $(x+2)(x-2)$ (B) $(x+2)(x+2)$ (C) $(x-2)(x-2)$ (D) $(x+2i)(x-2i)$ (E) $(x+2i)(x+2i)$

26. A plant grows at the rate of 0.03 cm/hour during daytime and 0.01 cm/hour at nights. If sunrise is at 5 AM and sunset is at 7 PM, what is the amount of growth in cm between 7 AM to 9 PM on the same day?

(A) 0.14   (B) 0.36   (C) 0.38   (D) 0.42   (E) 0.44

27. A student draws simple closed margin lines of uniform width c bordered inside a rectangular paper with dimensions a and b The area outside the margin lines are

(A) $(a - 2c)(b - 2c)$ (B) $(a + 2c)(b + 2c) - ab$ (C) $(a - 2c)(b - 2c) - ab$

(D) $ab - (a - 2c)(b - 2c)$ (E) $ab - (a + 2c)(b + 2c)$

28. Given in figure 4 is a regular pentagon. What is the sum of the measures of the angles given by t, u, x, y, and z?

(A) 360°   (B) 450°

(C) 640°   (D) 720°

(E) 860°

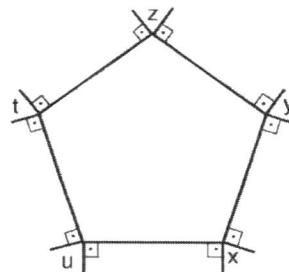

Figure 4

29. In figure 5, AE = 3·EB and the area of the right triangle △AEF is 21. What is the area of the rectangle ABCD?

(A) 28   (B) 42   (C) 56   (D) 63

(E) Given information is not enough.

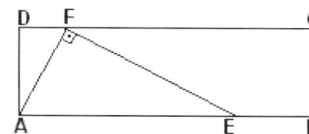

Figure 5

Figure not drawn to scale

30. Tuba drove from her home to the laboratory at an average speed of 35 mph and returned home along the same route at an average speed of 40 mph. If her total driving time for the trip was 2 hours, how many hours did it take Tuba to drive from the laboratory to her home?

(A) 2/3   (B) 3/4   (C) 14/15   (D) 1   (E) 7/6

31. What is the domain of the function given by $f(x) = \dfrac{\sqrt{x^2 - 9}}{3x}$?

(A) -3 ≤ x ≤ 3 and x ≠ 0   (B) x ≤ -3 or x ≥ 3

(C) -3 < x < 3 and x ≠ 0   (D) x < -3 or x > 3

(E) None of the above

32. If f(x) satisfies the relation given by f(a) · f(b) = f(a + b), then f(x) can be

(A) e^x (B) logx   (C) sinx   (D) tanx   (E) x

33. Given in figure 6 is circle M that is tangent to the coordinate axes and the quarter circle O. What is the radius of circle M?

(A) $\dfrac{1}{\sqrt{2}+1}$ (B) $1+\sqrt{2}$ (C) $2+\sqrt{2}$

(D) $\sqrt{2}$ (E) 2

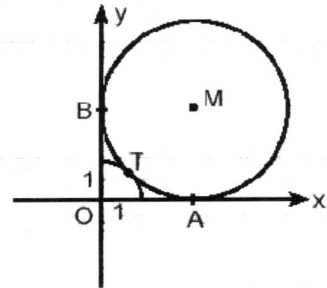

Figure 6

34. The number of workers in a factory are decreased by 20% while the daily number of working hours per worker is increased by 20%. The amount of work done

(A) increases by 20%   (B) increases by 4%

(C) decreases by 4%   (D) decreases by 20%

(E) does not change

35. A telephone call between Istanbul and Ankara costs 30 cents for the first minute and 20 cents for each additional minute. Sena made a 10-minute call from Istanbul to Ankara. Her brother Mehmet also made a call from Istanbul to Ankara, but his call cost three times as much as Sena's. How long was Mehmet's call, in minutes?

(A) 20   (B) 21   (C) 30   (D) 31   (E) 63

36. If the minimum value of $x^2 - x + k$ is greater than the maximum value of $-x^2$, what is the value of k?

(A) k < - 1   (B) k < 0   (C) k > 0   (D) k > $\dfrac{1}{4}$ (E) k > 1

37. The money that Atakan has is neither less than $45 nor greater than $75. If the minimum and maximum prices of a certain item are $1.50 and $2.25 respectively then what is the difference between the minimum and the maximum number of items that Atakan can purchase?

(A) 20   (B) 25   (C) 30   (D) 45   (E) 50

38. Given in figure 7 is a regular hexagon partially shaded and the area of the shaded triangle ADE is $32\sqrt{3}$ square inches. What is the length of a side of the hexagon?

(A) $2\sqrt{3}$ (B) $4\sqrt{3}$ (C) $8\sqrt{3}$

(D) 4   (E) 8

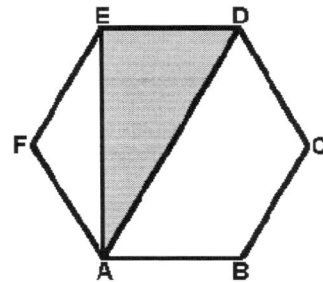

Figure 7

39. If the quadratic function given by $f(x) = ax^2 + bx + c$ intersects the x axis at two distinct points, then which of the following quantities must be nonzero?

     I. a

     II. b

     III. $b^2 - 4ac$

(A) I only   (B) II only   (C) III only

(D) I and III only   (E) I, II and III

40. Shown in figure 8 are, a trapezoid ABCD whose perimeter is 47π inches, and four identical circular pulleys each of which is centered at a vertex of the trapezoid having a radius of length 3 inches. What is the length of the rope that tightly passes over the pulleys?

(A) 50π (B) 51π (C) 53π

(D) 56π (E) 60π

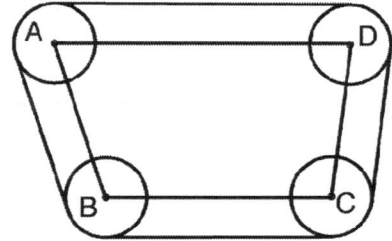

Figure 8

41. Which of the following is the simplified version of $\dfrac{\cos^2\theta - \sin^2\theta}{\cos^4\theta - \sin^4\theta}$ in the largest domain of θ?

(A) -1   (B) 0   (C) 1

(D) $\dfrac{1}{\cos^2\theta - \sin^2\theta}$ (E) $\dfrac{1}{\sin^2\theta - \cos^2\theta}$

42. It is given that $f(x) = a^x$. If both of the points (2, 9) and (3, b) are on the graph of f(x) then b can be

(A) -27   (B) -3   (C) 3   (D) 6   (E) 9

43. A certain brand of wedding ring is made of 80% gold and 20% silver. The price of gold increases by 12% every year, however the price of silver stays the same. To the nearest dollar, what will be the price of the ring 3 years later if it costs $300 at present?

(A) $300   (B) $324   (C) $397   (D) $421

(E) The given information is not enough to solve this question.

44. Among the 100 flight attendants working in Lingua Airways, everyone speaks English, 12 people speak English only and the rest of the people speak French, Spanish or both. If the number of flight attendants who can speak both French and Spanish are 48 and 72 respectively, then how many people can speak exactly two languages?

(A) 12   (B) 16   (C) 32   (D) 40   (E) 56

45. What is the greatest negative x intercept of $f(x) = x^3 - 4x - 1$?

(A) -0.254   (B) -1.861   (C) -2.115   (D) 2.115   (E) 0.254

46. As given in figure 9, circles P and Q are tangent to the line m at points A and B respectively. If the radii of the circles are 2 and 4 inches respectively, and the centers of the circles are 10 inches apart, what is the length of the segment AB in inches?

(A) 9   (B) $7\sqrt{2}$ (C) $4\sqrt{6}$ (D) $2\sqrt{26}$

(E) None of the above

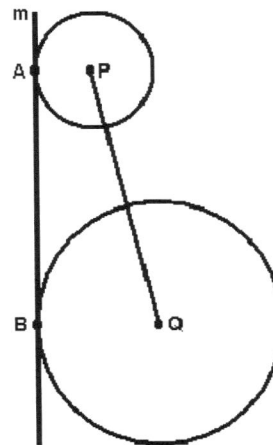

Figure 9
Figure not drawn to scale

47. If $\log_4 15$ and $\log_2 k$ are between the same pair of consecutive integers, which of the following can be the value of k?

(A) 3   (B) 4   (C) 5   (D) 8   (E) 10

48. What is the sum of the zeros of $f(x) = (x - 2)(x^2 - 4)$?

(A) – 8   (B) – 2   (C) 0   (D) 2   (E) 8

For questions 49 – 50 please refer to the following graph.

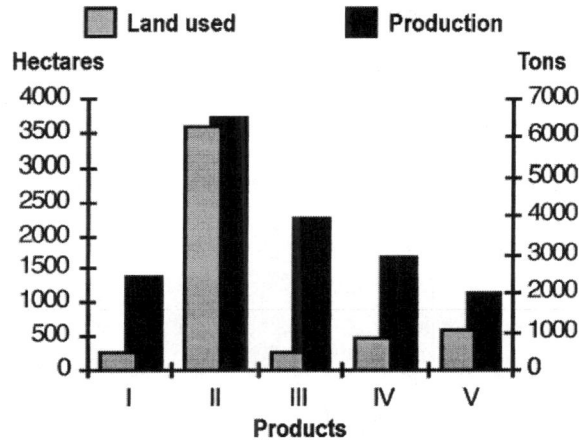

Based on the data given in the graph above AEI, agricultural efficiency index, is defined as the ratio of the tons of production to the hectares of land used in that production.

49. The AEI of a certain product is approximately 5.89. This product is most nearly

(A) I   (B) II   (C) III   (D) IV   (E) V

50. Approximately how many hectares of land must be used in order to obtain 52,879 tons of product I?

(A) 10,600   (B) 10.600   (C) 5,300   (D) 5.300   (E) 7,900

S T O P

END OF TEST

Test Duration: 60 Minutes

Directions: For each of the following problems, decide which is the best of the choices given. If the exact numerical value is not one of the choices, select the choice that best approximates this value. Then fill in the corresponding oval on the answer sheet.

Notes:

- A calculator will be necessary for answering some (but not all) of the questions in this test. For each question you will have to decide whether or not you should use a calculator. The calculator you use must be at least a scientific calculator; programmable calculators and calculators that can display graphs are permitted.
- The only angle measure used on this test is degree measure. Make sure your calculator is in the degree mode.
- Figures that accompany problems in this test are intended to provide information useful in solving the problems. They are drawn as accurately as possible except when it is stated in a specific problem that its figure is not drawn to scale.
- All figures lie in a plane unless otherwise indicated.
- Unless otherwise specified, the domain of any function f is assumed to be the set of all real numbers x for which f(x) is a real number.

Reference Information: The following information is for your reference in answering some of the questions in this test.

- Volume of a right circular cone with radius r and height h: $V=\frac{1}{3}\pi r^2 h$
- Lateral area of a right circular cone with circumference of the base c and slant height l: $S=\frac{1}{2}cl$
- Volume of a sphere with radius r: $V=\frac{4}{3}\pi r^3$
- Surface area of sphere with radius r: $S=4\pi r^2$
- Volume of a pyramid with base area B and height h: $V=\frac{1}{3}Bh$

1. If x = 2.005 · 10 · 200.5 · 1000 then x = ?
(A) $(20.05)^2$ (B) $(200.5)^2$ (C) $(2,005)^2$
(D) $2\cdot(200.5)^2$ (E) $2\cdot(2,005)^2$

2. If $\frac{1}{x}<3$ then x could be

I. $\frac{-1}{3}$ II. 3   III. $\frac{1}{3}$

(A) I only   (B) II only   (C) III only   (D) I and II   (E) I and III

$$x^2 + mx + 4 = 0$$

3. In the equation above m represents a negative integer. Which of the following could be the value of x?

(A) -3   (B) -2   (C) -1   (D) 1   (E) 0

4. What are all values of x for which $x^3 < x^2 < x$?

(A) $x > 1$ (B) $x \geq 1$ (C) $0 < x < 1$ (D) $-1 < x < 1$ (E) $-1 < x < 0$

5. Of the following, which has the least value?

(A) $77777 \cdot 15^{307}$ (B) $7777 \cdot 16^{306}$ (C) $777 \cdot 17^{305}$ (D) $77 \cdot 18^{304}$ (E) $7 \cdot 19^{303}$

6. At what point does the graph $\dfrac{2}{3}x - \dfrac{3}{4}y = \dfrac{4}{5}$ intersect the y - axis?

(A) -4/3   (B) -3/4   (C) -16/15   (D) 16/15   (E) 6/5

7. In figure 10, $\triangle ABC$ is an equilateral triangle. If each side of $\triangle ABC$ is 6 inches long, then what is the area of the shaded region?

(A) $6\sqrt{3}$

(B) $9\sqrt{3}$

(C) 12

(D) 18

(E) 36

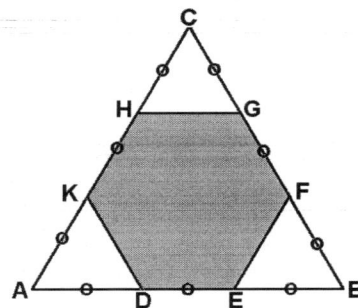

Figure 10

"If x=3, then $x^2 = 9$"

8. Which of the following is the contrapositive of the statement given above?

(A) $x \neq 3$ or $x^2 = 9$.　　　　(B) If $x^2 = 9$, then x=3.　　　(C) If $x \neq 3$, then $x^2 \neq 9$.　　　(D) If $x^2 \neq 9$, then $x \neq 3$.

(E) None of the above

9. Line m has a positive slope and a positive y-intercept. Line n is perpendicular to m and intersects line m at the first quadrant. The x-intercept of n must be

(A) Zero.

(B) Less than the x – intercept of m, therefore negative.

(C) Negative and greater than the x – intercept of m.

(D) Positive and greater than the x – intercept of m.

(E) Greater than the x – intercept of m but it can be negative, zero or positive.

10. Which of the following is the approximate slope of a line perpendicular to the line given by $\dfrac{20x}{3} = \dfrac{25y}{6} - 3$?

(A) -1.60　　　　　(B) -0.63　　　　　(C) 2.14　　　　　(D) 1.60　　　　　(E) 0.63

11. If $x + \dfrac{1}{x} = 4$ then $x^2 + \dfrac{1}{x^2} = ?$

(A) 10　　　　　(B) 12　　　　　(C) 14　　　　　(D) 16　　　　　(E) 18

12. A palindrome is a number that reads the same forward as it does backward. How many distinct five digit palindromes are there?

(A) 900　　　　　(B) 1000　　　　　(C) 90000　　　　　(D) 100000

(E) None of the above.

$$x^2 + y^2 - 6x + 8y + 24 = 0$$

13. What does the equation above represent?

(A) A point   (B) An ellipse   (C) A circle   (D) A hyperbola   (E) A parabola

14. The average of 10 numbers is 80. If the greatest number which is 170 is excluded, what will be the average of the remaining numbers?

(A) 63   (B) 70   (C) 80   (D) 90

(E) Cannot be determined from the information given.

15. It is known in figure 11 that WX || ZY and WY is the bisector of $\angle$ XWZ, then which of the following contains a pair of line segments that are always equal in length?

(A) XY and ZY   (B) XZ and XW   (C) WV and WZ

(D) YZ and WZ   (E) XV and XY

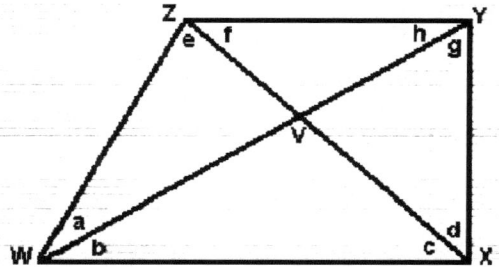

Figure 11

Figure not drawn to scale

16. If $a = \sqrt[3]{5} - 1,$ then $a^3 + 3a^2 + 3a + 2$ equals

(A) 4   (B) 6   (C) $\sqrt[3]{5} - 1$ (D) $\sqrt[3]{5}$ (E) $\sqrt[3]{5} + 1$

17. How many positive integers are in the solution set of $|3x-2|>8$?

(A) None　　(B) 2　　(C) 4　　(D) 6　　(E) Infinitely many

18. What is the x-intercept of the line given by the vector equation $\begin{pmatrix} x \\ y \end{pmatrix} = \begin{pmatrix} 3 \\ 1 \end{pmatrix} + t \begin{pmatrix} 4 \\ 2 \end{pmatrix}$?

(A) 1　　　　(B) 2　　　　(C) 3　　　　(D) 4

(E) None of the above

19. The points on the curve $y = \dfrac{x-1}{x+1}$ represent

(A) a circle　　(B) an ellipse　　(C) a hyperbola　　(D) a parabola　　(E) a straight line

20. If $y = \sqrt{11}x^2 - \sqrt{3}x - \sqrt{2}$, what is the approximate sum of the zeros?

(A) 0.52　　　　(B) -0.43　　　　(C) -2.35　　　　(D) -1.91　　　　(E) -0.82

21. A circle is circumscribed about a triangle with sides of length 5, 12, and 13. The radius of the circle is

(A) 2.5　　(B) 4.5　　(C) 5.5　　(D) 6　　(E) 6.5

22. What is the area of a triangle with sides of length 26, 26, and 20?

(A) 72　　　　(B) 120　　　　(C) 144　　　　(D) 240　　　　(E) 480

23. Which of the following represents the exterior of a circle with the radius of 10 and center at (3,-1)?

(A) $(x+3)^2+(y-1)^2 \geq 100$ (B) $(x+3)^2+(y-1)^2 > 100$ (C) $(x+3)^2+(y-1)^2 < 100$

(D) $(x-3)^2+(y+1)^2 \geq 100$ (E) $(x-3)^2+(y+1)^2 > 100$

24. For the right triangle $\triangle ABC$ given in figure 12, BC is 15 inches long and it is also given that AB + AC = 25 inches. What is the area of $\triangle ABC$ in square inches?

(A) 20   (B) 30   (C) 40

(D) 60   (E) 120

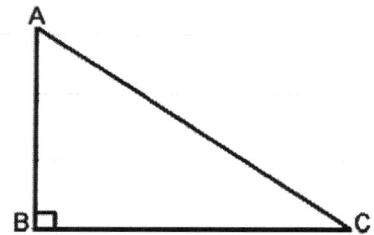

Figure 12

25. Given in figure 13, BE and BR are tangents to the circle whose center is at U. If the length of segment ER is 8 feet then which of the following is false?

(A) Quadrilateral EBRU is a rhombus.

(B) $\triangle EBR$ is an isosceles right triangle.

(C) Segment BU (not shown) is perpendicular to the segment ER.

(D) Area of the quadrilateral EBRU is 32 square inches.

(E) Length of segment BU is equal to the length of segment ER since quadrilateral EBRU is a square.

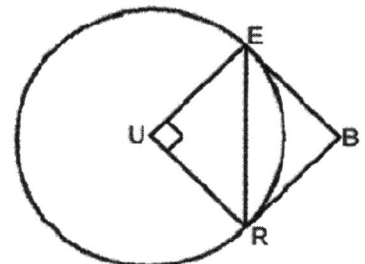

Figure 13

26. If one root of $x^2+mx+12=0$ is 6 then the other root is

(A) -6   (B) -4   (C) -2   (D) 2   (E) 4

$$x^2 - k \cdot x + 1 = k - 2$$

27. The equation given above has two real roots. Which of the following gives all possible values of k?

(A) $-2 < x < 6$ (B) $-6 \leq x \leq 2$ (C) $x < -6$ or $x > 2$

(D) $x \leq -6$ or $x \geq 2$ (E) $-6 < x < 2$

x	1	2	3	4		x	1	2	3	4
g(x)	3	6	11	18		h(x)	7	7	7	7

28. For the functions g(x) and h(x) given above, which of the following cannot be correct?

(A) $h(g(3)) = 7$ (B) $g(x) = x^2 + 2$ (C) $g(4) = 2 \cdot h(x) + 4$ (D) $h(x) = 2 \cdot g(3) - 15$

(E) If $h^{-1}(x)$ denotes the inverse of the function h(x), then $h^{-1}(h(x)) = x$ for all x.

29. Which of the following is a real number for all x?

(A) $\dfrac{x^2}{x^2 - 1}$ (B) $\dfrac{x^3}{x^3 + 1}$ (C) $\dfrac{x^2}{x^2 + 1}$ (D) $\dfrac{1}{x - 1}$ (E) $\dfrac{x}{x + 1}$

30. If the cost of a 2400 ft by 3600 ft rectangular field is $115,200 then what is the cost of this field in dollars per square yards?

(A) 75   (B) 25/3   (C) 3/25   (D) 1/75

(E) None of the above

31. ABC is a right triangle where sin(A)=3/5 and the right angle is at B. Which of the following is false?

(A) $\dfrac{1}{\sin^2 A + \sin^2 C} = 1$

(B) $1+\tan^2 C = \dfrac{1}{\sin^2 A}$

(C) $\dfrac{\cos C}{\sin C} = \tan A$

(D) sinC < cosC < tanC

(E) sinA < tanA < cosA

32. How many 6 letter words do not contain adjacent letters that are the same?

(A) 26^6 (B) P(26, 6)   (C) $25 \cdot 26^5$ (D) C(26, 6)   (E) $26 \cdot 25^5$

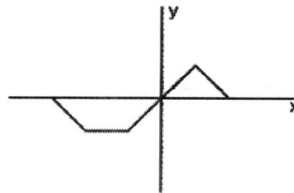

33. Graph of the relation given above is reflected about the y-axis. What will be the resulting graph?

(A)

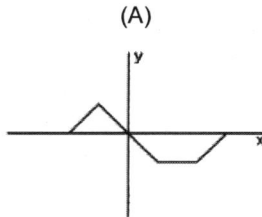

(B)

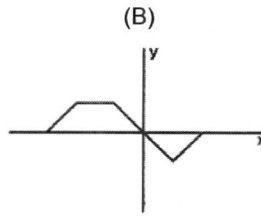

(C)

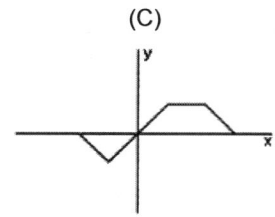

(D)

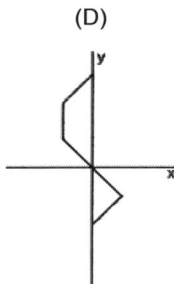

(E)

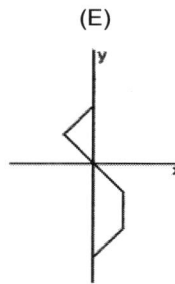

34. A group of students organize a tour so that the cost per person is $12.50 when a minimum of 20 people join the tour. However, the tour operator decides to decrease the cost per person by ¢25 for every 3 additional people joining the tour. If 3n more people join the group what will be the total amount of money collected by the tour operator?

(A) (20+n)·(12.50-0.25n)　　(B) (20+n)·(12.50-n)　　　　(C) (20+3n)·(12.50-0.25n)　　(D) (20+3n)·(12.50-n)

(E) None of the above.

35. Given In figure 14, circles P and Q are tangent to each other and to the line m at points A and B respectively. If the radii of the circles are 2 and 4 inches respectively, what is the length of the segment AB in inches?

(A) 6　　　　(B) $\sqrt{34}$　　　(C) $4\sqrt{2}$　　　(D) $16\sqrt{2}$　　　(E) $2\sqrt{10}$

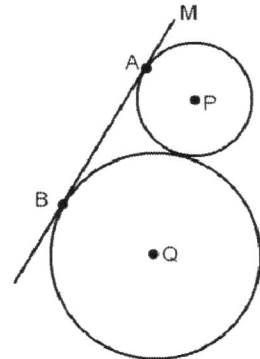

Figure 14
Figure not drawn to scale

36. If the volume of a cube is tripled, then its surface area will be multiplied by which of the following numbers?

(A) 1.40　　　　　(B) 1.42　　　　　(C) 1.96　　　　　(D) 2.08　　　　　(E) 3

37. A piece of wire 100 inches long is bent to form a circular loop and the diameter of this loop is measured to be 31.5 inches. If this data is used to approximate the value of π, then what will be the error percentage made in this calculation?

(A) 0.033%　　　　(B) 0.317%　　　　(C) 1.05%　　　　(D) 3.17%　　　　(E) 3.3%

38. Two points A and B are 10 feet apart in a plane. How many points in this plane are 6 feet away from A and 8 feet away from B?

(A) 2　　　　(B) 4　　　　(C) 6　　　　(D) 8　　　　(E) More than 8

39. The outer surface of a white cube with an edge of length 6 inches is painted to gray as in figure 15 and then cut into identical smaller cubes each with an edge of length 1 inch. How many smaller cubes have no gray faces?

(A) 16   (B) 64   (C) 96   (D) 216

(E) None of the above

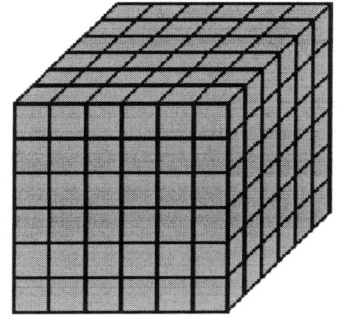

Figure 15

40. What is the area of a square whose diagonal has the endpoints of (-3, -8) and (1, -2)?

(A) 13   (B) 26   (C) 40   (D) 52

(E) None of the above

41. What is the value of $\dfrac{\log_3 27 \cdot \log_8 16}{\log_4 56 - \log_4 7}$?

(A) $\dfrac{8}{3}$ (B) $\dfrac{3}{8}$ (C) 0.37   (D) 2.40   (E) 2.66

42. Given that $A^2+B^2=64$ and B=10, which of the following is a possible value of AB?

(A) 60   (B) -60   (C) 60i   (D) $20\sqrt{41}$ (E) $-20\sqrt{41}$

43. How many digits is the number $(27)^{1977}$?

(A) 1978   (B) 2829   (C) 2830   (D) 5337   (E) 5338

     Page 207

44. The three dimensional object given in figure 7 consists of 4 rectangular faces and 2 right trapezoidal faces as is given in figure 16. AB and BD each measure 30 inches whereas BH, CJ and DE measure 10, 12 and 15 inches respectively. What is the shaded area rounded to the nearest 10 square inches?

(A) 350   (B) 360   (C) 370

(D) 380   (E) 390

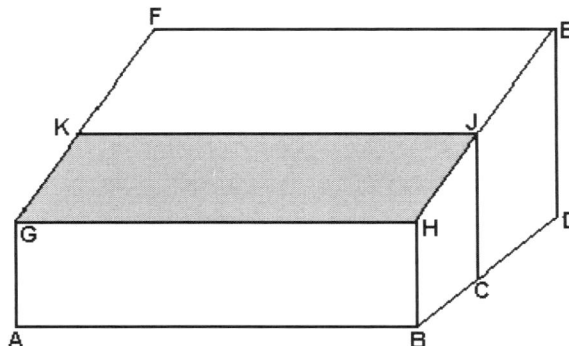

Figure 16
Figure not drawn to scale

45. What is the locus of points in space that are at a distance of 15 feet from two points that are 25 feet apart?

(A) 2 points

(B) 4 points

(C) A circle

(D) Two intersecting spheres

(E) Two cones having the same base

46. All distinct 5 digit numbers are written on separate cards and one card is picked at random. What is the probability that the number written on this card contains distinct digits?

(A) $\dfrac{1}{9 \cdot 10^4}$ (B) $\dfrac{1}{9^5}$ (C) $\left(\dfrac{9}{10}\right)^4$ (D) $\dfrac{9 \cdot 8 \cdot 7 \cdot 6}{10^4}$

(E) None of the above

47. It is given that $f(x) = x^4 + 2x^3 - 4$ and $g(x) = -x^4 - 2x^2 + 4$. If m is the minimum value of $f(x)$ and n is the maximum value of $g(x)$, then what is the value of $m - n$?

(A) -9.7   (B) -9.6   (C) 9.7   (D) 9.6   (E) -1.7

48. Given in figure 17, AB = CD = 6 inches and AE = ED. What is the area of the shaded region in square inches?

(A) 9   (B) 18   (C) 27   (D) 36

(E) Cannot be determined from the information given.

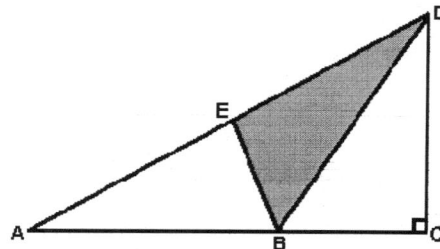

Figure 17

49. When simplified in the greatest domain of x, the expression given by $\dfrac{1+\sin x}{\cos^2 x}$ equals

(A) $\dfrac{1}{1-\sin x}$ (B) $\dfrac{1}{1-\cos x}$ (C) $1-\sin x$ (D) $1-\cos x$

(E) None of the above

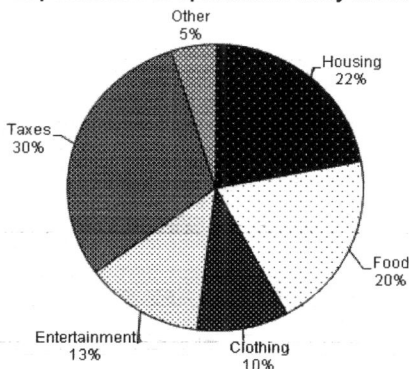

Expenditures of Spendalot Family in 2003

Other 5%
Housing 22%
Taxes 30%
Food 20%
Entertainment 13%
Clothing 10%

Figure 18

50. The pie chart given in figure 18 above shows the classification of the expenditures of Spendalot family whose total household income in 2003 was $240,000. In 2004, the household income increased to $300,000 and the dollar amounts spent on Housing, Food, Clothing and Other stayed the same. However in 2004, taxes increased to %35 of the total household income and the family members decided to decrease their expenditures on entertainment by 25% over the previous year and deposit the remaining money in a savings account. Approximately what percent of the household income went into savings in 2004?

(A) 3.4%   (B) 3.5%   (C) 11.6%   (D) 14.5%

(E) None of the above

S T O P

END OF TEST

Test Duration: 60 Minutes

Directions: For each of the following problems, decide which is the best of the choices given. If the exact numerical value is not one of the choices, select the choice that best approximates this value. Then fill in the corresponding oval on the answer sheet.

Notes:

- A calculator will be necessary for answering some (but not all) of the questions in this test. For each question you will have to decide whether or not you should use a calculator. The calculator you use must be at least a scientific calculator; programmable calculators and calculators that can display graphs are permitted.
- The only angle measure used on this test is degree measure. Make sure your calculator is in the degree mode.
- Figures that accompany problems in this test are intended to provide information useful in solving the problems. They are drawn as accurately as possible except when it is stated in a specific problem that its figure is not drawn to scale.
- All figures lie in a plane unless otherwise indicated.
- Unless otherwise specified, the domain of any function f is assumed to be the set of all real numbers x for which f(x) is a real number.

Reference Information: The following information is for your reference in answering some of the questions in this test.

- Volume of a right circular cone with radius r and height h: $V = \dfrac{1}{3}\pi r^2 h$

- Lateral area of a right circular cone with circumference of the base c and slant height l: $S = \dfrac{1}{2}cl$

- Volume of a sphere with radius r: $V = \dfrac{4}{3}\pi r^3$

- Surface area of sphere with radius r: $S = 4\pi r^2$

- Volume of a pyramid with base area B and height h: $V = \dfrac{1}{3}Bh$

1. If x + 4y − 6z = 5 and 2x − 2y + 3z = − 10, find the value of x?

(A) − 3   (B) − 1   (C) 0   (D) 1   (E) 3

2. What is the value of $\left(\dfrac{\left(\dfrac{1}{2}\right)^{-1} : \left(\dfrac{1}{2}\right)^{2}}{\left(\dfrac{1}{2}\right)^{3}} \right)^{\frac{1}{2}}$?

(A) $\dfrac{1}{8}$ (B) $\dfrac{1}{4}$ (C) 1   (D) 4   (E) 8

3. For a set of 11 consecutive positive integers, which of the following must be correct?

I. Median is a positive integer.

II. Median equals mean.

III. There is no mode in this set.

(A) I only   (B) II only   (C) III only   (D) I and II only   (E) I, II, and III.

4. When $64.8 \cdot 10^{-6}$ is written in the decimal form, what is the number of zeros between the decimal point and the first nonzero digit counted from left?

(A) 8   (B) 6   (C) 5   (D) 4   (E) 3

5. What is the sum of the integers that satisfy the inequality given by $(x-2)^2(x+3)(5-x)>0$?

(A) 3   (B) 4   (C) 5   (D) 6   (E) 7

6. It is given in figure 19 that $\dfrac{\text{Area(OPR)}}{\text{Area(OST)}} = \dfrac{1}{4}$. Which of the following are correct?

I. b > c

II. 2b + c = 0

III. OT > OR

(A) I only   (B) II only   (C) III only

(D) I and II only   (E) I, II and III

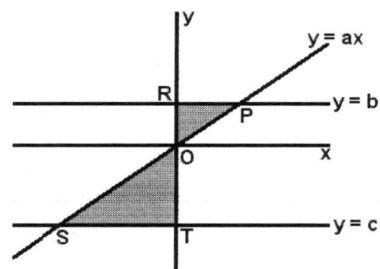

Figure 19

Figure not drawn to scale

7. Which of the following is not in the solution set of 5x − 2y < 21?

(A) (3, 4)   (B) (6, 6)   (C) (-3,1)   (D) (4, -2)   (E) (2, 3)

8. A certain brand of wedding ring is made in such a way that 20% of its price is because of the gold and the rest is because of the silver used in producing the ring. The price of gold increases by 12% every year, however the price of silver stays the same. To the nearest dollar, what will be the price of the ring 3 years later if it costs $100 at present?

(A) $100 (B) $108 (C) $132 (D) $140

(E) None of the above

9. What is the maximum value of the function $-x^2 + 2x - 2$?

(A) -2 (B) -1 (C) 1 (B) 2

(E) None of the above

10. If b and $-4a$ are consecutive integers, which of the following is always odd?

(A) a + b (B) a - b (C) a + 2b (D) a – 2b (E) 2a + b

11. In the formula $E = mc^2$, the effect of doubling the value of c is to

(A) Multiply the value of E by 4 (B) Double the value of E

(C) Multiply the value of E by 0.5 (D) Multiply the value of E by 0.25

(E) None of the above

12. If in figure 20, the tangent of angle ACB is 2 then what is the length of BC?

(A) 3 (B) 6 (C) 9 (D) 12

(E) none of the above

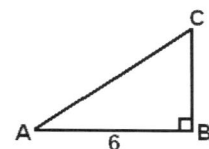

Figure 20

Figure not drawn to scale

13. The solution set of the inequality $9 - x^2 \geq x - 3$ is

(A) $-4 \leq x \leq -3$ (B) $-3 < x < 4$ (C) $-3 \leq x \leq 4$ (D) $-4 < x < 3$ (E) $-4 \leq x \leq 3$

14. If the point (5, -2) is on the graph of y=f(x), then which of the following points must be on the graph of $y = f(|x|)$?

(A) (-2, -5)   (B) (-5, 2)   (C) (5, -2)   (D) (-2, 5)   (E) (-5, -2)

15. Which of the following describes the interior region of the circle with center (4,3) and radius 2?

(A) $(x+4)^2 + (y+3)^2 \leq 4$ (B) $(x-4)^2 + (y-3)^2 \leq 4$ (C) $(x-4)^2 + (y-3)^2 < 4$

(D) $(x+4)^2 + (y+3)^2 < 4$ (E) $(x-4)^2 + (y-3)^2 > 4$

16. It is given in figure 21 that OABC is a square, In order to calculate the shaded area which of the following must be known?

(A) Coordinates of B and G   (B) Coordinates of F and G

(C) Coordinates of C and F   (D) Coordinates of B and E

(E) Coordinates of D and G

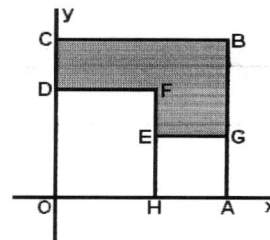

Figure 21

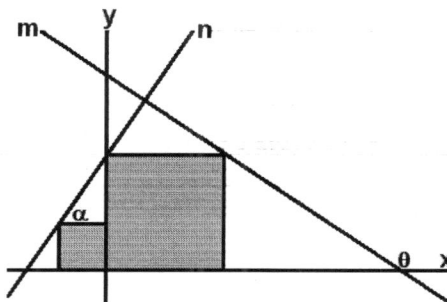

Figure 22

Figure not drawn to scale

17. In figure 22, each shaded region represents a square and lines m and n are perpendicular. What is the relation between the angles indicated by α and θ?

(A) $\theta = 2\alpha$ (B) $\theta - \alpha = 90°$ (C) $\theta + \alpha = 90°$ (D) $\theta + \alpha = 180°$

(E) Cannot be determined from the information given

18. If $\sin^2x + \cos^2x - 3\sin x = 0$, then $\sin x =$

(A) $\dfrac{1}{27}$
(B) $\dfrac{1}{9}$
(C) $\dfrac{1}{3}$
(D) 1
(E) $-\dfrac{1}{3}$

19. If the length of the longest chord of that can be drawn within a circle C_1 equals the radius of another circle C_2, what is the ratio of the area of C_1 to the area of C_2?

(A) 4
(B) 2
(C) 1
(D) 1 / 2
(E) 1 / 4

20. Eren remembers only the first five digits of his seven-digit e-mail password, but he is sure that neither of the last two digits is zero. In order to find out what his password is he has to try out at least how many attempts?

(A) 100
(B) 99
(C) 90
(D) 81
(E) 80

21. In figure 23 given, circles P and Q are tangent to the line m at points A and B respectively. If the radii of the circles are 2 and 4 inches respectively, and the centers of the circles are 10 inches apart, what is the length of the segment AB in inches?

(A) 5
(B) 6
(C) 7
(D) 8
(E) None of the above

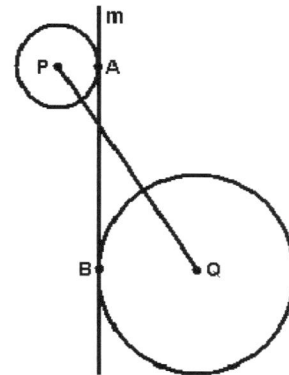

Figure 23
Figure not drawn to scale

22. If $-3 < x^2 < 15$ then x cannot be

(A) $-\pi$
(B) $\sqrt{7}$
(C) $\sqrt[3]{15}$
(D) $-\sqrt{7} - \sqrt{5}$
(E) $\sqrt{12} - 1$

23. In figure 24, a circle with radius r is given. If the parallel chords AB and CD are equal in length, then, the length of segment AC

(A) equals 2r.

(B) is less than r.

(C) greater than 2r.

(D) greater than r but less than 2r.

(E) cannot be determined from the information given.

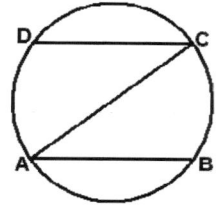

Figure 24

24. It is given that two complementary angles have a ratio of 5:13. What is the measure of the smaller angle?

(A) 5°   (B) 25°   (C) 35°   (D) 55°   (E) 65°

25. What is the greatest domain of the function given by $f(x) = \dfrac{3x}{\sqrt{9 - x^2}}$?

(A) $-3 \le x \le 3$ (B) $x \le -3$ or $x \le 3$ (C) $-3 < x < 3$ and $x \ne 0$ (D) $-3 < x < 3$ (E) $x < -3$ or $x > 3$

26. Mualla, who is on the corner of a rectangular garden as in figure 25, wishes to walk from A to C. She may choose to walk through the edges; from A to B then from B to C; or she may walk directly through the diagonal from A to C. If she chooses to walk through the diagonal then she saves x% of the way. x cannot be

(A) 11   (B) 17   (C) 22   (D) 26   (E) 31

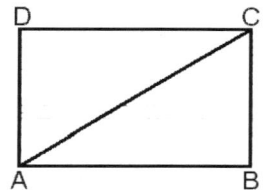

Figure 25

27. For $\triangle ABC$ given in figure 26, m($\hat{A}$) = 70°, BD bisects $\hat{B}$ and CD bisects $A\hat{C}E$. m($\hat{D}$) = ?

(A) 70°   (B) 60°   (C) 55°   (D) 45°   (E) 35°

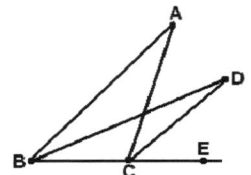

Figure 26

Figure not drawn to scale

28. In figure 27, which pair of points can be joined to give a line with negative slope?

(A) A and E

(B) A and D

(C) B and D

(D) B and C

(E) C and D

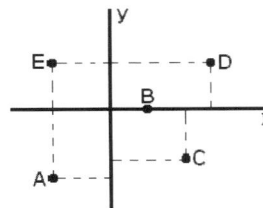

Figure 27

29. If $f(x) = x(x-1)(x+2)$ then for what values of x is $f(x) < |f(x)|$?

(A) $x < -2$ and $0 < x < 1$ 　　　　(B) $-2 < x < 0$ and $x > 1$ 　　　　(C) for all values of x

(D) $x < -2$ or $0 < x < 1$ 　　　　(E) $-2 < x < 0$ or $x > 1$

30. For every real value of x, the equation given by $4x^2 - 6x + 2c = (2x - 4)(ax + b)$ is satisfied; $a + b - c = ?$

(A) 3 　　　　　(B) 4 　　　　　(C) 5 　　　　　(D) 6 　　　　　(E) 7

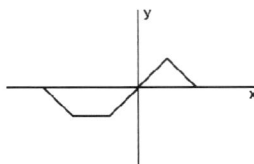

31. Graph of the relation given above is reflected about the origin. What will be the resulting graph?

(A)

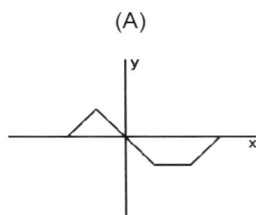

(B)

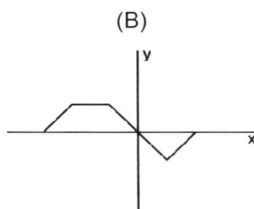

(C)

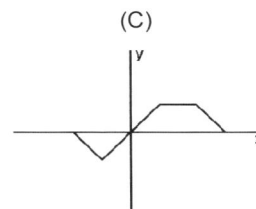

(D)

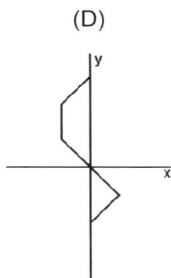

(E)

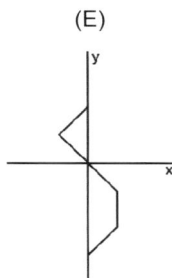

32. A rectangle ABCD and its diagonal AC are given in figure 28. Which of the following equals sin CAD?

(A) tan DCA

(B) cos BCA

(C) $\sqrt{1 - \cos CAD}$

(D) cos BAC

(E) sin CAB

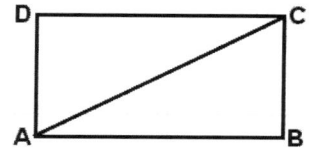

Figure 28

33. What is the equation of the line m given in figure 29?

(A) y = – 0.75x

(B) y = – 0.75x – 2

(C) y = 0.75x

(D) y = 0.75x – 2

(E) y = 0.93x

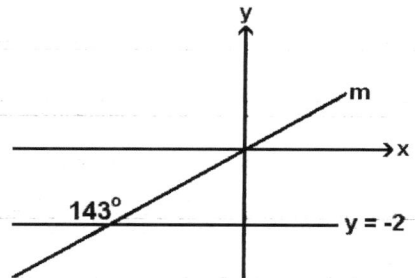

Figure 29

Figure not drawn to scale

34. If the only solution of the equation $a^{4x} = a^{2x+1}$ is x = 0.5, then a can be

(A) any nonzero real number.

(B) any positive real number.

(C) any negative real number.

(D) any real number other than -1 and 1.

(E) any nonzero real number other than -1 and 1.

35. What is the area of the shaded region given in figure 30?

(A) $\frac{1}{3}$

(B) $\frac{2}{3}$

(C) $\frac{3}{2}$

(D) $\frac{4}{5}$

(E) $\frac{5}{6}$

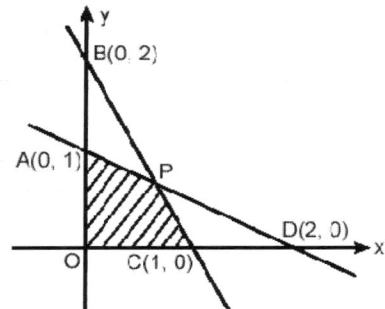

Figure 30

Figure not drawn to scale

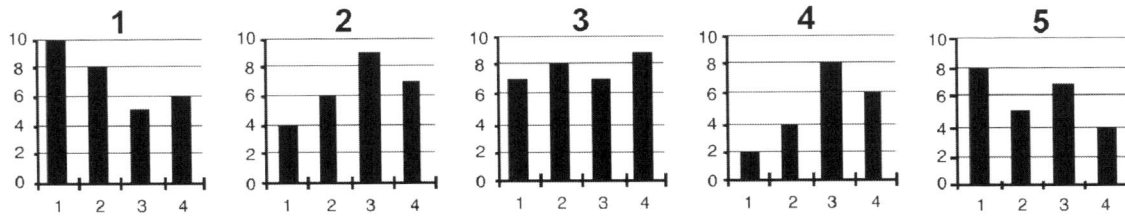

36. Five different groups of data are represented by the graphs given above. In each group there are 4 numbers each of which is between 0 and 10 inclusive. For which of the above graphs is the median the greatest?

(A) 1   (B) 2   (C) 3   (D) 4   (E) 5

37. The rectangle in figure 31 consists of eight unit squares. What is the length of x?

(A) $\dfrac{2}{3}$ (B) $\dfrac{17}{10}$ (C) $\dfrac{7}{4}$

(D) $\dfrac{4}{\sqrt{5}}$ (E) $\dfrac{4}{\sqrt{6}}$

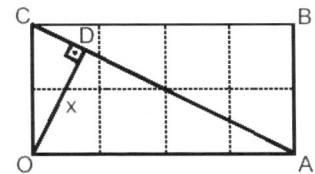

Figure 31

38. If $|a| \le 6$ and $a - 2b + 2 = 0$, then how many integer values of b are there?

(A) 3   (B) 4   (C) 5   (D) 6   (E) 7

39. If x = -2, y = -1 and z = 1, the expression given by $\dfrac{a^2 + xbc + xac + yb^2}{a \cdot z + b}$ simplifies to

(A) a – b – 2c   (D) a – b – c   (B) a – b + 2c   (E) a + b + c   (C) a + b + 2c

40. A bacteria population that has 128 inhabitants initially doubles every hour. How many inhabitants will there be after 12 hours?

(A) 2^{12} (B) 2^{15} (C) 2^{18} (D) 2^{19} (E) 2^{20}

41. If $a^4 < b^4$, which of the following must be true?

    I. $a < b$ II. $a^2 < b^2$ III. $|a| < |b|$

(A) I only   (B) II only   (C) III only   (D) II and III only   (E) I, II, and III

42. A $\otimes$ operation is defined by $a \otimes b = \begin{cases} a+b & \text{if} & a > b \\ a-b & \text{if} & a \le b \end{cases}$. What is the result of $(1 \otimes 1) \otimes (2 \otimes 1)$?

(A) -6 (B) -4 (C) -3 (D) -1 (E) 0

For questions 43 and 44 please refer to the data given by the following pie charts:

1995 _____ **Year** _____ **2005**
243,552,000 kJ _____ **Total Energy** _____ **419,823,500 kJ**

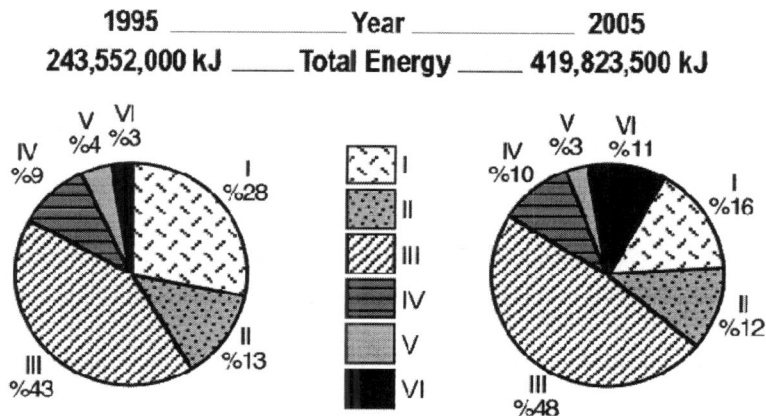

The pie charts above show the energy consumption by the six branches of industry at the city of Energion in the years of 1995 and 2005.

43. How did the energy consumed in industry branch II change from 1995 to 2005?

(A) decreased by approximately 7.7%.   (B) decreased by exactly 1%.

(C) increased by more than 55%.   (D) increased by approximately 18.7%.

(E) stayed almost the same.

44. Based on the data given above which of the following cannot be deduced?

(A) From 1995 to 2005, energy consumption increased in all but one branch of the industry.

(B) From 1995 to 2005, energy consumption increased by more than 90% in three branches of the industry.

(C) From 1995 to 2005, the energy consumption in the industry branch VI increased by approximately 270%.

(D) From 1995 to 2005, the energy consumption in one industry branch changed by less than 1%.

(E) From 1995 to 2005, the energy consumption in two branches of the industry almost doubled.

45. Circle C is given by the equation $(x + 3)^2 + (y - 4)^2 = R^2$. If $(0, 2)$ is one endpoint of a diameter of this circle, then the other endpoint is

(A) (-6, 6) (B) (6, -6) (C) (6, -10) (D) (3, 0) (E) (-3, 8)

46. If $\sin \theta = 0.82$, then $\sin (180° - \theta) = ?$

(A) -0.57 (B) -0.82 (C) 0.82 (D) 0.57

(E) None of the above

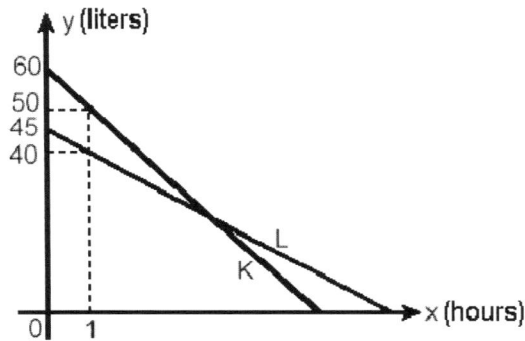

Figure 32
Figure not drawn to scale

47. The graph given in figure 32 above shows the liters of gasoline that remains in the fuel depot of two cars K and L that each uses a constant amount of gasoline an hour. If both of the cars have started their engines at the same time but use up gasoline at different rates, how many hours later will they have the same amount of gasoline remaining?

(A) 2 (B) 3 (E) 3.5 (C) 5 (D) 15

48. In the figure 33, two lines intersected on the circle with an acute angle of 45°. If the radius of the circle is 4, what is the length of segment AB (not shown)?

(A) 3.14   (B) 3.46   (C) 5.66   (D) 6.28

(E) Given information is not enough to find the length of AB.

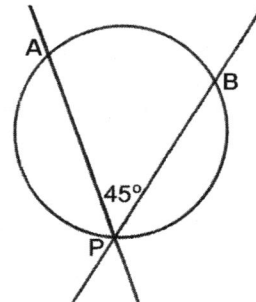

Figure 33

Figure not drawn to scale

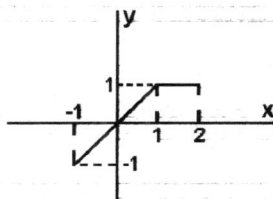

Figure 34

49. Graph of f(x-1) is given in figure 34 above. What is the graph of f(x)+1?

(A)

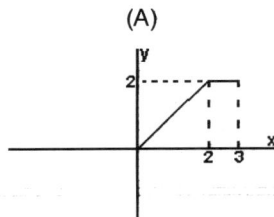

(B)

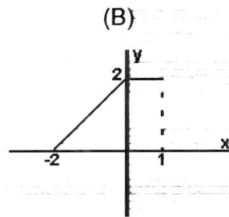

(C)

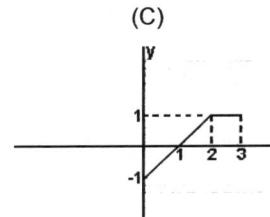

(D)

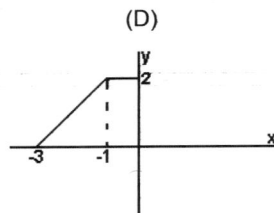

(E)

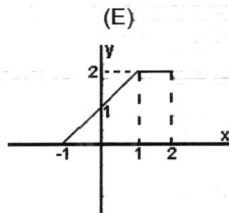

50. Which of the following gives all possible values of f(x) for the function defined by $f(x) = \sqrt{16 - x^2}$?

(A) $-16 \leq f(x) \leq 16$ (B) $-4 \leq f(x) < 4$ (C) $0 < f(x) \leq 4$ (D) $0 \leq f(x) \leq 4$ (E) $f(x) \geq 0$

S T O P

END OF TEST

Test Duration: 60 Minutes

Directions: For each of the following problems, decide which is the best of the choices given. If the exact numerical value is not one of the choices, select the choice that best approximates this value. Then fill in the corresponding oval on the answer sheet.

Notes:

- A calculator will be necessary for answering some (but not all) of the questions in this test. For each question you will have to decide whether or not you should use a calculator. The calculator you use must be at least a scientific calculator; programmable calculators and calculators that can display graphs are permitted.

- For some questions in this test you may have to decide whether your calculator should be in the radian mode or the degree mode.

- Figures that accompany problems in this test are intended to provide information useful in solving the problems. They are drawn as accurately as possible except when it is stated in a specific problem that its figure is not drawn to scale.

- All figures lie in a plane unless otherwise indicated.

- Unless otherwise specified, the domain of any function f is assumed to be the set of all real numbers x for which f(x) is a real number.

Reference Information: The following information is for your reference in answering some of the questions in this test.

- Volume of a right circular cone with radius r and height h: $V = \frac{1}{3}\pi r^2 h$

- Lateral area of a right circular cone with circumference of the base c and slant height l: $S = \frac{1}{2}cl$

- Volume of a sphere with radius r: $V = \frac{4}{3}\pi r^3$

- Surface area of sphere with radius r: $S = 4\pi r^2$

- Volume of a pyramid with base area B and height h: $V = \frac{1}{3}Bh$

1. If $\frac{6}{x} + \frac{3}{y} = 4$ and $\frac{3}{x} + \frac{6}{y} = \frac{7}{2}$ what is the value of xy?

(A) 1/6   (B) 2/3   (C) 3/2   (D) 6

(E) None of the above

2. If $f(x) = x^2 + 4x - 5$, then f(-2) =

(A) -17   (B) -9   (C) 7   (D) 9   (E) 17

3. If the magnitudes of vectors a and b are 15 and 8, respectively, then the magnitude of vector a + b could not be

(A) 6   (B) 8   (C) 10   (D) 12   (E) 14

4. If $\dfrac{\cos x}{\sin x} = -1$ and $0 \le x \le \pi$, then x =

(A) 0   (B) $\dfrac{\pi}{4}$ (C) $\dfrac{\pi}{2}$ (D) $\dfrac{3\pi}{4}$ (E) π

5. The tenth term in an arithmetic sequence is 6, and the sixteenth term is 12. What is the 117th term of this sequence?

(A) 113   (B) 114   (C) 115   (D) 116   (E) 117

6. f(−3) = 0 for all of the following functions except

(A) $f(x) = x^3 - 4x + 15$ (B) $f(x) = |x + 3|$ (C) $f(x) = x^2 - 9$

(D) $f(x) = x^2 + 3x - 3$ (E) $f(x) = x + 3$

7. If the graph of $y = x^2 + ax + b$ crosses the x-axis at x = − 9 and x = 1, then what is the value of a?

(A) − 9   (B) − 8   (C) − 1   (D) 8   (E) 9

8. Which of the following graphs is symmetric with respect to the origin?

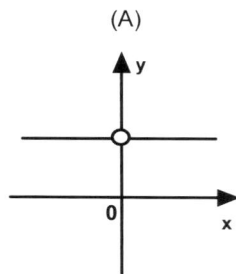

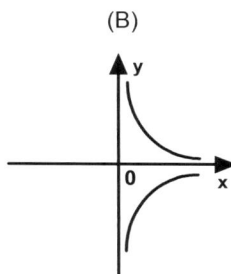

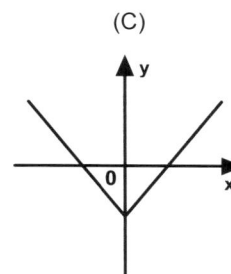

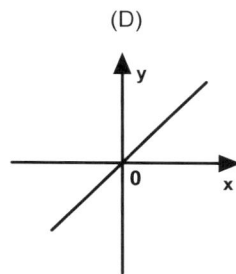

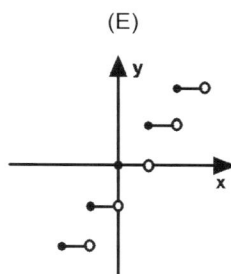

9. If $a^5 < b^5$, which of the following must be true?

    I. $a < b$

    II. $a^4 < b^4$

    III. $|a| < |b|$

(A) I only   (B) II only   (C) III only   (D) II and III only   (E) I, II, and III

10. Line m is tangent to circle O at the point (12, -9). If the center of O is at the origin, what is the y – intercept of line m?

(A) -25   (B) -20   (C) -15   (D) 15   (E) 25

11. For which of the following could y be a function of x?

	I.		II.		III.
x	y	x	y	x	y
0	-1	4	- 1	0	10
1	0	3	- 1	1	1
2	1	2	- 1	2	0
1	2	1	- 1	3	0.1
4	3	0	- 1	4	0.01

(A) II only   (B) III only   (C) I and II only   (D) II and III only   (E) I, II, and III

12. $\dfrac{8!}{9!-8!} =$

(A) 1/8!   (B) 1/9   (C) 1/8   (D) 8!   (E) 8!/9

13. As the value of k approaches 4, to what value does $\dfrac{k^2-16}{k-4}$ approach?

(A) – 16   (B) - 4   (C) 4   (D) 8

(E) It does not approach to any real value.

14. In figure 1, what is the slope of the line d?

(A) $-\sin\theta$

(B) $-\cos\theta$

(C) $-\tan\theta$

(D) $-\cot\theta$

(E) $-\csc\theta$

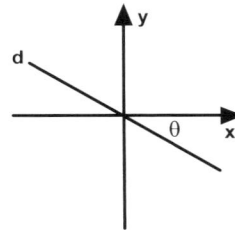

Figure 1

15. If $\ln x = 3$, then x =

(A) 1.098   (B) 1.099   (C) 1.986   (D) 20.08   (E) 20.09

16. Which one(s) of the following are correct?

   I. Even functions are never invertible.

   II. Odd functions are always invertible.

   III. A function is invertible if and only if it is one to one and onto.

(A) I only   (B) II only   (C) III only   (D) I and III only   (E) I, II and III

17. Turgay drove from his home to the club at an average speed of 80 miles per hour and returned home along the same road at an average speed of 70 miles per hour. If his total driving time for the round trip was 2 hours, how many minutes did it take Turgay to drive from the club to his home?

(A) $\dfrac{225}{4}$ (B) $\dfrac{224}{3}$ (C) $\dfrac{16}{15}$ (D) 64

(E) None of the above

18. If $\sin\theta = \cos\theta$, which of the following could be the radian value of θ?

(A) 45°   (B) 0.78   (C) 1.57   (D) 3.92   (E) 3.93

19. If $e^{2x} = 2+x$, then x can be

(A) -1.99   (B) -0.448   (C) 0.447   (D) 0.45   (E) 1.98

20. Which of the following lines is the reflection of the line y = -4 with respect to the line y = -x?

(A) y = - 4   (B) x = - 4   (C) y = 4   (D) x = 4   (E) x = 4 + y

21. There are totally 24 marbles in a bag of which 7 are blue, 8 are red and 9 are green. If two marbles are selected at random from the bag without replacement, what is the probability that they will be of different colors?

(A) $\dfrac{7 \cdot 8 + 7 \cdot 9 + 8 \cdot 9}{48^2}$

(B) $\dfrac{7 \cdot 8 + 7 \cdot 9 + 8 \cdot 9}{48 \cdot 47}$

(C) $\dfrac{7 \cdot 8 + 7 \cdot 9 + 8 \cdot 9}{24^2}$

(D) $\dfrac{7 \cdot 8 + 7 \cdot 9 + 8 \cdot 9}{24 \cdot 23}$

(E) $1 - \dfrac{9 \cdot 8 + 8 \cdot 7 + 7 \cdot 6}{24 \cdot 23}$

22. Which of the following is the polar coordinate equation described by the graph in figure 2?

(A) r = 3   (B) 3sin θ = r   (C) 3cos θ = r

(D) rsin θ = 3   (E) rcos θ = 3

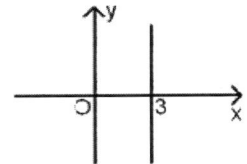

Figure 2

23. Which of the following functions satisfies the relation |f(x)| = f(x)?

(A)   (B)   (C)   (D)   (E)

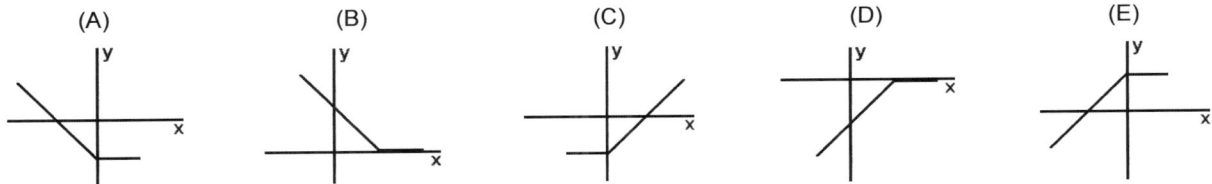

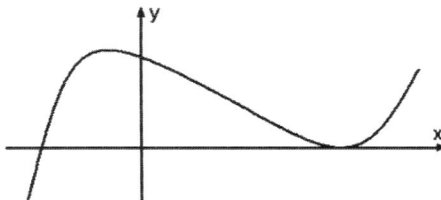

Figure 3

24. Given in figure 3 above is the graph of a polynomial function f(x). If a, b and c are all distinct positive real numbers then f(x) can be

(A) $f(x) = -(x + a)(x - b)^2$

(B) $f(x) = (x - a)(x - b)(x - c)$

(C) $f(x) = (x + a)(x - b)^2$

(D) $f(x) = -(x - a)(x - b)(x + c)$

(E) $f(x) = (x - a)(x + b)^2$

25. A function h(x) is said to be one to one if it satisfies the following condition: If x and y are in the domain of h given that $x \neq y$; then for all x and y, $h(x) \neq h(y)$. Which of the following functions is one to one?

(A) $h(x) = x^3 - 4x$
(B) $h(x) = x^4$
(C) $h(x) = \sin x$
(D) $h(x) = \tan x$
(E) $h(x) = 2^{3x}$

26. A point P is midway between the points A(2, -2, 8) and B(6, -5, - 4). What is the length of segment AP?

(A) 4
(B) 5
(C) 6.5
(D) 12
(E) 13

27. "No rooms have five windows."

If the statement given above is false, then which of the following must be correct?

(A) All rooms have five windows.
(B) Some rooms have five windows.
(C) Exactly one room has five windows.
(D) Some rooms do not have five windows.
(E) Some rooms have more than five windows.

28. If $f(x) = \ln(5x)$, then $f^{-1}(x) =$

(A) $\dfrac{\ln x}{5}$

(B) $\dfrac{e^x}{5}$

(C) $e^{\frac{x}{5}}$

(D) $\ln(x^5)$

(E) e^{5x}

29. If $\sin x = \dfrac{\sqrt{3}}{2}$, then $\dfrac{1}{4}\cos 3x =$

(A) -1 (B) $-\dfrac{1}{4}$ (C) $\pm\dfrac{1}{4}$ (D) $\dfrac{1}{2}$ (E) 1

30. If $f(x, y) = \dfrac{|x| - |y|}{|2x + 2y|}$, then $f(x, -y) =$

(A) $\dfrac{|y| - |x|}{|2x - 2y|}$ (B) $\dfrac{|x| - |y|}{|2x + 2y|}$ (C) $\dfrac{|y| - |x|}{|2x + 2y|}$ (D) $\dfrac{|x| + |y|}{|2x - 2y|}$ (E) $\dfrac{|x| - |y|}{|2y - 2x|}$

31. The diameter of the base of a right circular cone is 16 and the slant height of the cone is 10. What is the volume of this cone?

(A) 402   (B) 670   (C) 1206   (D) 1609   (E) 2011

32. $(x + 1)^2 - 5(x + 1) + 4 = (x - 1)^2 + a(x - 1) + b$ for all values of x, then b =

(A) -4 (B) -2 (C) 2   (D) 4

(E) None of the above

33. Line m is given by the parametric equations $x(t) = 4t - 2$ and $y(t) = 2 - 4t$. For what value of t does line m intersect the line y=2x?

(A) -2 (B) -0.5 (C) 0   (D) 2   (E) 0.5

34. At Payalot Bank, a savings account earns 5% interest per year. If Hikmet Can opens a savings account with a $10,000 deposit and makes no other deposits, how much will be contained in his account after ten years?

(A) $15,000.00   (B) $15,513.28   (C) $16,288.95   (D) $17,103.39   (E) $19,288.95

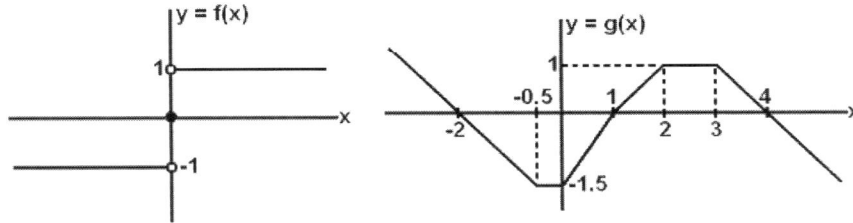

Figure 4

35. Given in figure 4 above are the graphs of the functions f(x) and g(x). Which of the following is the solution set of f(g(x)) = 1?

(A) -2 < x < 1 or x > 4   (B) x > 0   (C) $2 \le x \le 3$

(D) x < -2 or 1 < x < 4   (E) x = 1

36. Which of the following cannot be the function represented by the graph shown in figure 5 if the coordinates of points A and B are $(\pi, 2)$ and $(3\pi, -2)$ respectively?

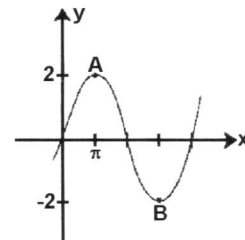

Figure 5

Figure not drawn to scale

(A) $f(x) = 2\sin\left(\dfrac{x}{2}\right)$

(B) $f(x) = -2\sin\left(\dfrac{x}{2} + \pi\right)$

(C) $f(x) = 2\cos\left(\dfrac{x}{2} + \pi\right)$

(D) $f(x) = 2\cos\left(\dfrac{x}{2} - \dfrac{\pi}{2}\right)$

(E) $f(x) = -2\cos\left(\dfrac{x}{2} + \dfrac{\pi}{2}\right)$

37. If a triangle has sides of lengths 82, 82, and 41, what is the measure of the smallest angle in this triangle rounded to the nearest degree?

(A) 14°   (B) 15°   (C) 29°   (D) 76°   (E) 151°

Event	Mehmet Can's Score	Mean Score	Standard Deviation
A	82	76	2
B	87	71	4
C	94	86	4
D	95	80	5
E	96	78	6

38. The chart above shows data for five events that Mehmet Can took place. On which of the five events did he score highest relative to the rest of the people who took part?

(A) Event A   (B) Event B   (C) Event C   (D) Event D   (E) Event E

39. In figure 6 given, x = ?

(A) 270

(B) 303

(C) 360

(D) 442

(E) 962

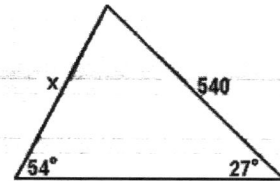

Figure 6

Figure not drawn to scale

40. A rectangular solid as shown in figure 7 is inscribed in a sphere. What is the radius of this sphere?

(A) 5.70   (B) 6.22   (C) 8.60

(D) 10.30   (E) 12.45

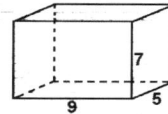

Figure 7

Figure not drawn to scale

41. If the radius of a sphere is increased by 14 percent, its volume is increased by approximately

(A) 10%   (B) 14%   (C) 29%   (D) 30%   (E) 48%

42. If $f(x)$ satisfies the relation given by $f(a^n) = n \cdot f(a)$, then $f(x)$ can be

(A) 2^x (B) lnx   (C) sinx   (D) tanx   (E) x

43. If, in figure 8, the magnitude of vector $\vec{a}$ is 10 and the magnitude of vector $\vec{b}$ is 15, what is the magnitude of the vector given by $\vec{a} + \vec{b}$?

(A) 8.90   (B) 15.35   (C) 22.45   (D) 23.89   (E) 25.00

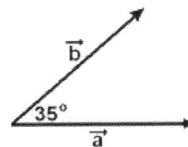

Figure 8

Figure not drawn to scale

44. If the points A(-5, 7) and B(0, -5) are the endpoints of a diameter of circle O, what is the radius of circle O?

(A) 2.5   (B) 6.0   (C) 6.5   (D) 12.0   (E) 13.0

45. Six people will be photographed in such a way that Ali, Berk and Cem will sit in the front while Deniz, Emre and Fatih will stand up at the back. In how many ways can these six people be photographed?

(A) 6!   (B) $(3!)^2$ (C) 2(3+2+1)   (D) 6+5+4+3+2+1

(E) None of the above.

46. The graph of a polynomial function P(x) is given in figure 9. Which of the following is not always correct about P(x)?

(A) P(0) > 0

(B) P(x) = P(-x)

(C) P(x) has exactly four real zeros.

(D) P(x) contains nonnegative even powers of x only.

(E) The degree of P(x) can be any integer greater than 3.

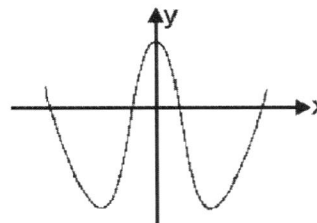

Figure 9

47. Each of the numbers A through E given in figure 10 can be expressed as x + yi where $i = \sqrt{-1}$ and both of x and y being real numbers. $16 - 30i$ can be the square of

(A) A only.

(B) C only.

(C) E only.

(D) A or C.

(E) B or E.

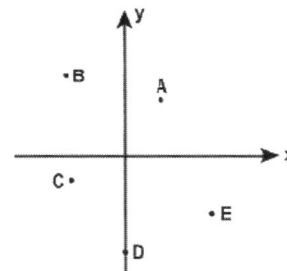

Figure 10

48. If it is given that $y = 1 - \dfrac{2}{x}$ and x is a negative real number, how does y change as x decreases

to $-\infty$?

(A) It decreases to $-\infty$.   (B) It increases to ∞.   (C) It decreases to zero.

(D) It increases to zero.   (E) It decreases to a nonzero value.

49. Timur is looking up at the top of a building at a 20° angle of elevation. He walks x meters closer to the building until he can look up at the top of the building at a 40° angle of elevation. If the top of the building is 100 meters above the height of Timur's eye level then x=?

(A) 100·(tan40° + tan20°)

(B) $\dfrac{100}{\tan 20°} + \dfrac{100}{\tan 40°}$

(C) 100·(tan40° − tan20°)

(D) $\dfrac{100}{\tan 20°} - \dfrac{100}{\tan 40°}$

(E) None of the above

50. $f(x) = \begin{cases} 1 & \text{if } 3x \text{ is an integer} \\ 0 & \text{otherwise} \end{cases}$

What is the period of the function f(x) defined above?

(A) -1/3   (B) 1/3   (C) 2/3   (D) 1   (E) f(x) is not a periodic function.

S T O P

END OF TEST

Test Duration: 60 Minutes

Directions: For each of the following problems, decide which is the best of the choices given. If the exact numerical value is not one of the choices, select the choice that best approximates this value. Then fill in the corresponding oval on the answer sheet.

Notes:

- A calculator will be necessary for answering some (but not all) of the questions in this test. For each question you will have to decide whether or not you should use a calculator. The calculator you use must be at least a scientific calculator; programmable calculators and calculators that can display graphs are permitted.

- For some questions in this test you may have to decide whether your calculator should be in the radian mode or the degree mode.

- Figures that accompany problems in this test are intended to provide information useful in solving the problems. They are drawn as accurately as possible except when it is stated in a specific problem that its figure is not drawn to scale.

- All figures lie in a plane unless otherwise indicated.

- Unless otherwise specified, the domain of any function f is assumed to be the set of all real numbers x for which f(x) is a real number.

Reference Information: The following information is for your reference in answering some of the questions in this test.

- Volume of a right circular cone with radius r and height h: $V = \dfrac{1}{3}\pi r^2 h$

- Lateral area of a right circular cone with circumference of the base c and slant height l: $S = \dfrac{1}{2}cl$

- Volume of a sphere with radius r: $V = \dfrac{4}{3}\pi r^3$

- Surface area of sphere with radius r: $S = 4\pi r^2$

- Volume of a pyramid with base area B and height h: $V = \dfrac{1}{3}Bh$

1. If $1 - \left(\dfrac{x}{16}\right)^2 = \dfrac{3}{4}$, then x could be

(A) – 2   (B) – 4   (C) – 6   (D) – 8   (E) – 10

2. If m + n = mp where m, n and p are all nonzero real numbers, then which of the following statements are always correct?

     I. If m and n are integers so is p.

     II. If m and p are integers so is n.

     III. If m and p are positive so is n.

(A) II only   (B) I and II only   (C) I and III only   (D) II and III only   (E) I, II and III

3. If $a^5 = 55$ then $\log_a 555 = ?$

(A) 7.5   (B) 7.6   (C) 7.7   (D) 7.8   (E) 7.9

4. What is the number of digits in the product of the numbers 3,737,373,737 and 3,579?

(A) 11   (B) 12   (C) 13   (D) 14   (E) 15

5. If 2.5% of y is 25.25 then what is 6.5% of 2y?

(A) 6.565   (B) 13.13   (C) 65.65   (D) 131.3

(E) None of the above

6. An operation is defined by $(a, b) \Uparrow (c, d) = (a - c, b - d)$. If $[(1, 2) \Uparrow (-1, -2)] \Uparrow (m, n) = (5, 6)$ then $(m, n) = ?$

(A) (3, 2)   (B) (3, -2)   (C) (-3, 2)   (D) (-3, -2)   (E) (-2, 3)

7. The quadratic equation given by $ax^2 + bx + c = 0$ has two zeros of the form $p + \sqrt{q}$ and $p - \sqrt{q}$ where p and q are nonzero rational numbers. Which of the following must be correct?

     I. a is nonzero

     II. a, b and c are all rational numbers

     III. $4ac - b^2 < 0$

(A) I only   (B) II only   (C) I and II only   (D) II and III only   (E) I, II and III

8. The function f is given by $f(x) = x + [2x]$, where [x] is the greatest integer less than or equal to x. If $1 \le x < 1.5$, then f can also be given by which of the following?

(A) x   (B) x + 1   (C) x + 1.5   (D) x + 2   (E) x + 3

9. If $f(m) = e^{-2m}$, what is the least integer m such that f(m) is less than 0.00002?

(A) 5   (B) 6   (C) 7   (D) 8   (E) 9

10. If x is a nonzero integer, what is greatest possible value of $15 - \dfrac{3}{x}$?

(A) 13.5   (B) 14   (C) 15   (D) 18

(E) It cannot be determined from the information given.

11. If the unit circle is translated 1 unit up and 2 units toward left, the resulting circle will be given by which of the following?

(A) $(x - 1)^2 + (y - 2)^2 = 1$ (B) $(x + 1)^2 + (y + 2)^2 = 1$ (C) $(x + 2)^2 + (y + 1)^2 = 1$

(D) $(x + 2)^2 + (y - 1)^2 = 1$ (E) $(x - 1)^2 + (y + 2)^2 = 1$

12. Ege has a midterm average of 80 in physics, which makes up 60 percent of her overall grade. If the final exam makes up the remaining 40 percent, what must be her score on the final exam to give her an overall grade of exactly 84?

(A) 88   (B) 90   (C) 92   (D) 94   (E) 96

13. If the point with coordinates (5, 7) is on the graph of f(x, y) = 0 which is symmetric with respect to the y − axis, which of the following points is also on the same graph?

(A) (7, -5)   (B) (7, 5)   (C) (-5, -7)   (D) (-5, 7)   (E) (5, -7)

14. The cosine of an acute angle is one third of the sine of the same angle. What is the tangent of this angle?

(A) 0   (B) $\dfrac{1}{3}$ (C) 1   (D) 3

(E) It cannot be determined from the information given.

15. Which of the following gives all values of k for which $x^3 - 3x^2 - 9x = k$ has 2 or more real roots?

(A) k > 27 or k < -5   (B) $-5 \le k \le 27$ (C) $-27 \le k \le 5$

(D) k = 5 or k = -27   (E) $-27 < k < 5$

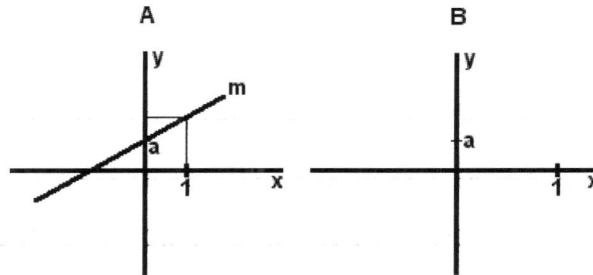

Figure 11

16. The line m given in figure 11.A will be sketched on the coordinate axes in figure 11.B where x axis is enlarged and y axis stays the same. Which of the following is correct regarding line m?

(A) It will be steeper.

(B) It will be less steep.

(C) It will stay the same.

(D) It will be reflected in the x axis.

(E) It will be reflected in the y axis.

17. If $3^{x^2} \cdot 3^{2x} = 27$ and x < 0, then x can be

(A) -3   (B) -2   (C) -1   (D) 1   (E) 3

18. Given in figure 12, the lengths of AB, BD and AD are 9, 10, and 17 inches respectively. What is the measure of angle α, rounded to the nearest degree?

(A) 35°   (B) 37°   (C) 47°

(D) 53°   (E) 73°

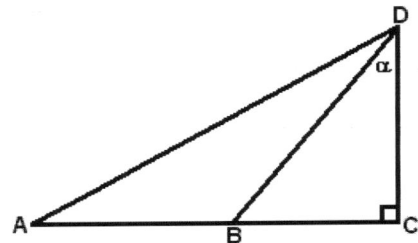

Figure 12

Figure not drawn to scale

19. What is the fundamental period of the function given by $f(x) = -3 \cdot \sin(\pi x) + 4 \cdot \cos(\pi x) + 1$?

(A) 1   (B) 2   (C) 2π (D) π (E) 5

20. If $2x + 1$ is a factor of $6x^3 - 5x^2 - 14x - k$ then $k = $?

(A) -5   (B) -3   (C) -1   (D) 3   (E) 5

21. What is the range of the function given by $f(x) = \dfrac{2}{\sqrt{x+1}}$?

(A) All real numbers greater than or equal to -1   (B) All real numbers greater than -1

(C) All numbers other than -1   (D) All positive real numbers

(E) All nonnegative real numbers

22. If $\dfrac{3}{x+yi} + \dfrac{2}{1+2i} = 1$ then $x - yi = $?

(A) $0.4 - 0.8i$ (B) $0.6 - 0.8i$ (C) $1.8 - 2.4i$ (D) $0.6 + 0.8i$ (E) $1.8 + 2.4i$

23. The money in a bank account grows according to the rule $10,000 \cdot 1.0948^{\frac{t}{2}}$ where the initial investment is $10,000 and t is the number of years that has passed since the account was opened. What is the annual rate of interest?

(A) 4.5%   (B) 4.6%   (C) 4.7%   (D) 9.4%   (E) 9.5%

24. If $\cos x = 0.40$, what is the value of $\cos(2x)$?

(A) 0.32   (B) 0.68   (C) 0.80   (D) -0.32   (E) -0.68

25. If $x = \ln(y^4 - 1)$ for $|x| > 1$, then what is y in terms of x?

(A) $\pm \sqrt[4]{e^x + 1}$ (B) $\sqrt[4]{e^x + 1}$ (C) $\sqrt{e^{4x} + 1}$ (D) $\pm \sqrt[4]{e^x - 1}$ (E) $\sqrt{e^x - 1}$

26. Which of the following contains all possible values of $y = \dfrac{x-5}{2x}$ when x takes on positive integer values starting with 1?

(A) $-2 \le y < \dfrac{1}{2}$ (B) $-2 \le y < 0$ (C) $y \ge -2$ (D) $-\dfrac{1}{2} \le y < 2$

(E) All real numbers

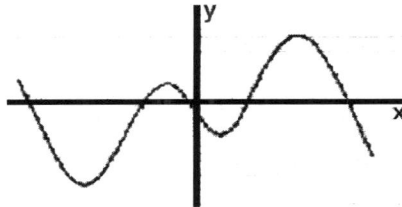

Figure 13

27. The graph in figure 13 could be a portion of the graph of which of the following functions?

     I. $f(x) = ax^3 + bx^2 + cx + d$

     II. $g(x) = ax^5 + bx^4 + cx^3 + dx^2 + ex + f$

     III. $h(x) = ax^7 + bx^6 + cx^5 + dx^4 + ex^3 + fx^2 + gx + h$

(A) I only   (B) II only   (C) I and II only   (D) II and III only   (E) I, II and III

Figure 14

28. AB is a line segment given in figure 14 and P is a variable point in space so that P is always the vertex of the isosceles triangle PAB. The locus of all such points P is

(A) the plane of segment AB.

(B) half of the plane of segment AB.

(C) part of the plane of segment AB.

(D) the perpendicular bisector line of segment AB.

(E) the perpendicular bisector plane of segment AB.

29. The length of the hypotenuse of a right triangle is given by h(x,y) where x and y are the length of the legs of this triangle. What is the domain of h(x,y) when h(x,y) = 1?

(A) the unit circle.

(B) portion of the unit circle that lies in the first quadrant

(C) portion of the unit circle that lies in the first and second quadrants

(D) portion of the unit circle that lies in the first and fourth quadrants

(E) portion of the unit circle that lies in the first, second and fourth quadrants

30. A single player game is played in such a way that the player tosses a coin until it comes up heads. What is the probability that the game will be over at an odd numbered trial; that is at the 1st, 3rd, 5th trial, etc?

(A) 1/2   (B) 1/3   (C) 1/4   (D) 2/3   (E) 3/4

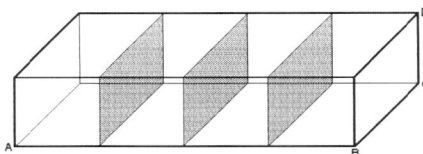

Figure 15
Figure not drawn to scale

31. A piece of marble in the shape of the rectangular block given in figure 15 has the dimensions AB = 12, BC = 8 and CD = 6 inches. The box will be given three equally spaced cuts at the shaded rectangular surfaces. By what percent does the total surface area of the resulting 4 pieces change with respect to that of the original block?

(A) It decreases by %67.   (B) It increases by %67.   (C) It stays the same.

(D) It decreases by %33.   (E) It increases by %40.

32. In figure 16, rectangle OABC is rotated in the counterclockwise direction for θ degrees about point O, to get rectangle OA'B'C'. If the coordinates of B are (x, y) then what are the coordinates of point B'?

(A) (x·cosθ, x·sinθ)

(B) (− y ·sinθ, y·cosθ)

(C) (x·sinθ − y·cosθ, x·cosθ + y·sinθ)

(D) (x·cosθ − y·sinθ, x·sinθ + y·cosθ)

(E) (x·cosθ + y·sinθ, x·sinθ − y·cosθ)

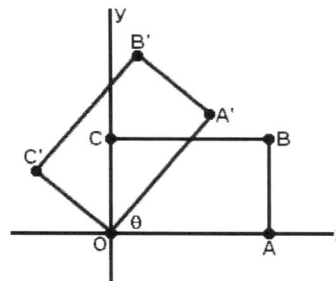

Figure 16

33. Which of the following does not result in a 4 by 5 matrix?

(A) $I_4 \cdot B_{4X5}$

(B) $A_{4X2} \cdot B_{2X5}$

(C) transposition of A_{5X4}

(D) $A_{4X5} - B_{4X5}$

(E) $A_{5X5} \cdot B_{5X4}$

34. If $(x - y)^2 + (x + y)^2 + 2(x - y) - 3(x - y) = 0$ then the set of points (x,y) represents

A) a circle

B) an ellipse

C) a parabola

D) a hyperbola

E) none of the above

35. A factory concentrates on the production of four products, each having a different price. In this factory, production is planned on a monthly basis when one, two, three, or four products may be produced in various quantities. For which of the following production plans is standard deviation the least?

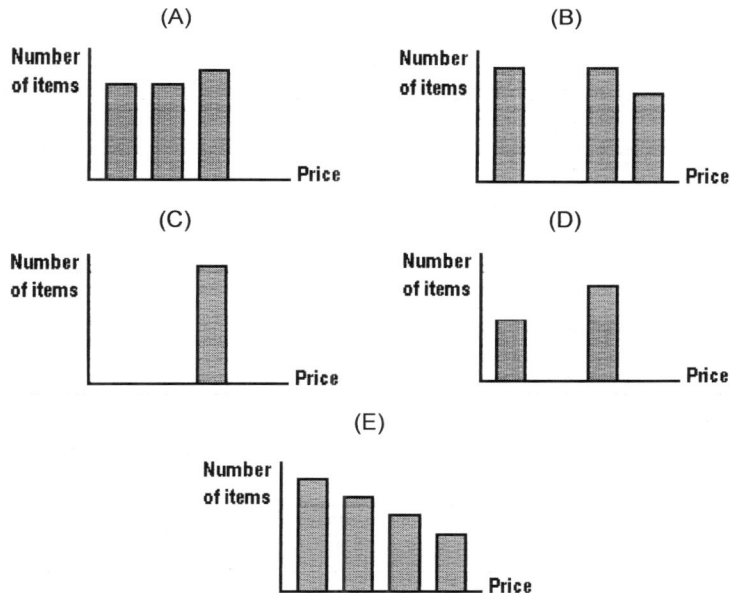

(A)

Number of items | Price

(B)

Number of items | Price

(C)

Number of items | Price

(D)

Number of items | Price

(E)

Number of items | Price

36. Two planes start from the same point P and travel along separate straight routes that originate at P, forming an angle of 50°, how many miles apart are the two planes after each has traveled 2200 miles?

(A) 1859   (B) 1860   (C) 2344   (D) 2345   (E) 3111

37. Which of the following figures best describes the region that represents the set of all points (x,y) for which $|x| + |y| \leq$ 1?

(A)   (B)   (C)   (D)   (E)

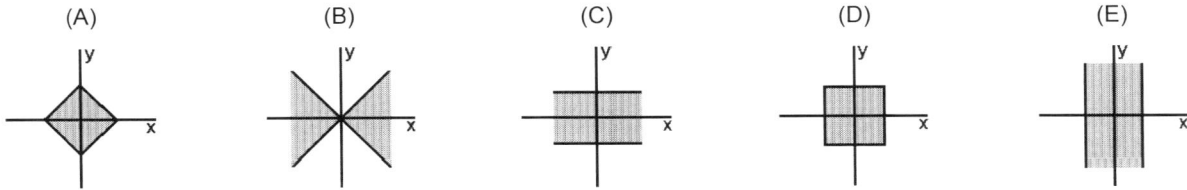

38. If $f(x) = \sqrt{x-1}$ and $g(x) = x^2$, which of the following is the graph of y = g(f(x))?

(A)   (B)   (C)

(D)   (E)

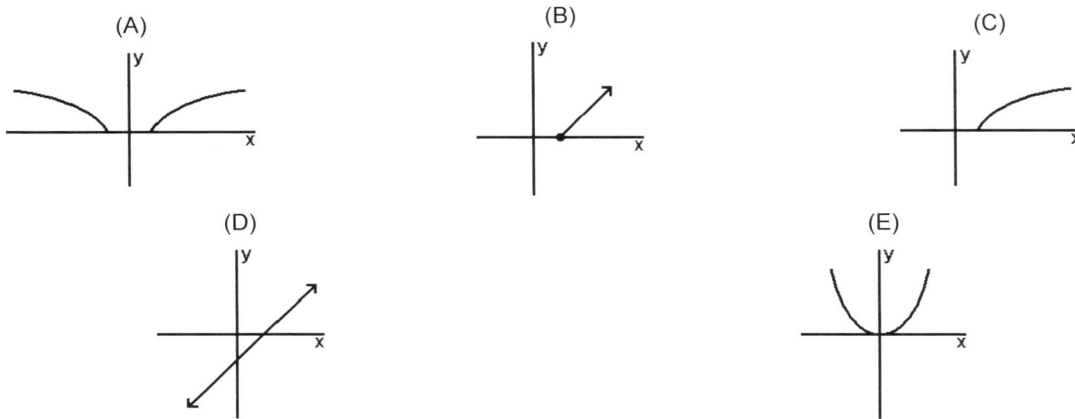

39. How many diagonals can be drawn on the faces of a cube so that no two of them have a common point?

(A) Two   (B) Three   (C) Four   (D) Five   (E) Six

40. Which of the following is a counterexample of the statement "$\sqrt{n}$ is irrational if n is a rational number"?

(A) $\log_2 8$ (B) e^2 (C) 4   (D) 2   (E) π

41. A function $f(x)$ has the property that $f(x_2) \geq f(x_1)$ when $x_2 > x_1$; which of the following can be the graph of f?

(A)   (B)   (C)   (D)   (E)

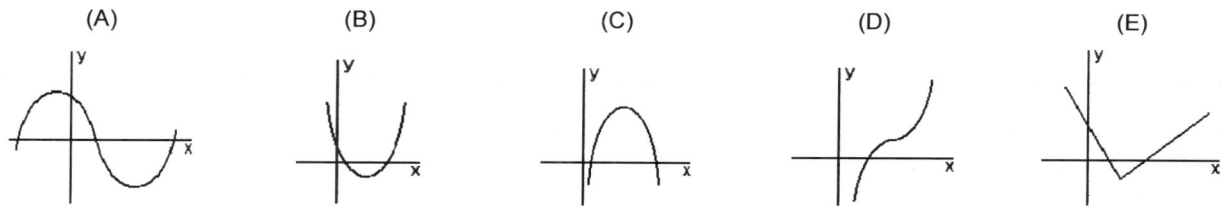

42. In the city of Mathmania, the inverse of a function $f(x)$ is defined incorrectly as the reflection of $f(x)$ with respect to the line $y = -x$ instead of the line $y = x$. If a Mathmanian student has calculated the inverse of a function as $\dfrac{2x - 3}{4}$ then what is the inverse of $f(x)$ when calculated correctly?

(A) $f^{-1}(x) = \dfrac{4x + 3}{2}$ (B) $f^{-1}(x) = \dfrac{3x + 4}{2}$ (C) $f^{-1}(x) = \dfrac{2x + 3}{4}$

(D) $f^{-1}(x) = \dfrac{3x - 2}{2}$ (E) $f^{-1}(x) = \dfrac{4x - 3}{2}$

43. Which of the following is equivalent to $\{x: x \geq 8 \text{ or } x \leq 0\}$?

(A) $\{x: |x + 2| \geq 6\}$ (B) $\{x: |x - 4| \geq 4\}$ (C) $\{x: 4 \leq x + 4 \leq 12\}$

(D) $\{x: |x - 4| \leq 4\}$ (D) $\{x: |x + 4| \leq 4\}$

44. If the first four terms of a sequence are 1, 5, 17 and 53, which of the following can be the nth term of this sequence?

(A) $n + 5n^2 + 17n^3 + 53n^4$ (B) $4n^2 - 8n + 5$ (C) $2 \cdot 3^{n-1} - 1$ (D) $4n - 3$

(E) None of the above

45. A board of 4 mathematics and 5 physics professors is to be selected from a group of 20 mathematics professors and 16 physics professors, respectively. How many different boards can be formed?

(A) 9,213   (B) 17,324   (C) 21,162,960   (D) 28,217,280   (E) $1.678 \cdot 10^{11}$

46. Which of the following cannot be correct for a quadratic function $f(x) = ax^2 + bx + c$ where $a \neq 0$?

(A) The functions $f(x)$ and $f(2x)$ intersect at a single point.

(B) The functions $f(x)$ and $2 \cdot f(x)$ intersect at a single point.

(C) The functions $f(x)$ and $f(x + 2)$ have exactly one point in common.

(D) $f(x) = f(x + 2)$ results in a quadratic equation whose discriminant is zero.

(E) $f(x) = f(x + 2)$ results in a linear equation whose solution set is not empty.

47. For every positive number z, a function f_z is defined by $f_z(x) = \begin{cases} x - 1 & x \leq 0 \\ 1 - \dfrac{x}{z} & 0 < x \leq z \\ x + zx^2 & x > z \end{cases}$. What is the value of

$f_2(-3) + f_2(3) - f_3(1)$?

(A) -4 (B) -0.5 (C) $\dfrac{2}{3}$ (D) 16.33   (E) 21

48. The shaded portion in figure 17 is the graph of the inequality given by

(A) $(y - 3x)(y + x) \leq 0$ (B) $\left(y - \dfrac{x}{3}\right)(y + x) < 0$

(C) $\left(y - \dfrac{x}{3}\right)(y + x) \geq 0$ (D) $(y + 3x)(y - x) \leq 0$

(E) $\left(y - \dfrac{x}{3}\right)(y + x) \leq 0$

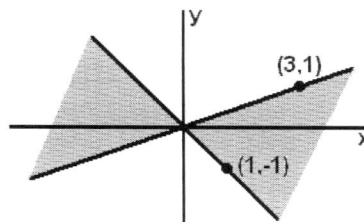

Figure 17

Figure not drawn to scale

49. The number of vertices and edges of a three dimensional object are 7 and 12 respectively. If each face of this object is a convex polygon then how many faces does this object have?

(A) 5   (B) 6   (C) 7   (D) 8

(E) It cannot be determined from the information given.

50. It is given that $y = \sqrt{4t^2 + 1}$; $x = \sqrt[3]{2t^2 + 3}$; and $x = 4z^2 - 3$. If $z = 5t$ then y is

(A) 0.211   (B) 1.085   (C) 1.086   (D) 1.1783   (E) 1.805

S T O P

END OF TEST

Test Duration: 60 Minutes

Directions: For each of the following problems, decide which is the best of the choices given. If the exact numerical value is not one of the choices, select the choice that best approximates this value. Then fill in the corresponding oval on the answer sheet.

Notes:

- A calculator will be necessary for answering some (but not all) of the questions in this test. For each question you will have to decide whether or not you should use a calculator. The calculator you use must be at least a scientific calculator; programmable calculators and calculators that can display graphs are permitted.
- For some questions in this test you may have to decide whether your calculator should be in the radian mode or the degree mode.
- Figures that accompany problems in this test are intended to provide information useful in solving the problems. They are drawn as accurately as possible except when it is stated in a specific problem that its figure is not drawn to scale.
- All figures lie in a plane unless otherwise indicated.
- Unless otherwise specified, the domain of any function f is assumed to be the set of all real numbers x for which f(x) is a real number.

Reference Information: The following information is for your reference in answering some of the questions in this test.

- Volume of a right circular cone with radius r and height h: $V = \frac{1}{3}\pi r^2 h$

- Lateral area of a right circular cone with circumference of the base c and slant height l: $S = \frac{1}{2}cl$

- Volume of a sphere with radius r: $V = \frac{4}{3}\pi r^3$

- Surface area of sphere with radius r: $S = 4\pi r^2$

- Volume of a pyramid with base area B and height h: $V = \frac{1}{3}Bh$

1. If x is positive and y is negative then x + y can be

I. positive   II. negative   III. zero

(A) I only   (B) II only   (C) I and III only   (D) II and III only   (E) I, II and III

2. It is given that a, b, and c are three numbers defined in terms of positive integers x and y that are both greater than 10 and x is less than y. If a, b, and c are defined as:

$$a = \frac{x}{y}, \ b = \frac{10x}{10y+1}, \text{ and } c = \frac{100x}{100y+11};$$

which of the following is correct?

(A) c < b < a   (B) c < a < b   (C) a < b < c   (D) a < c < b   (E) b < c < a

3. If $4^x < x + 4$ then which of the following cannot be the value of x?

(A) -3.5   (B) -2.5   (C) -1.5   (D) 0.5   (E) 1.5

4. What is the distance between the x and y intercepts of the line given by $\dfrac{x}{0.4} - 1.7y - 5.1 = 0$?

(A) 2.19   (B) 2.20   (C) 3   (D) 3.62   (E) 3.63

5. The function $f(x) = x^2$ is given for all x such that $x \geq 0$. $f^{-1}(x) = $?

(A) $\pm\sqrt{x}$ (B) $\sqrt{x}$ (C) $-\sqrt{x}$ (D) 2x   (E) x/2

6. If $x^{51} - 3x^{50} = k^2$ where k is an integer, then x can be

(A) 22   (B) 24   (C) 26   (D) 28   (E) 30

7. If f(x) satisfies the relation given by $\dfrac{f(a)}{f(b)} = f(a-b)$, then f(x) can be

(A) 10^x (B) logx   (C) sinx   (D) tanx   (E) x

$$\left(\sqrt{x^2 + y^2} - 1\right)(x + y - 1) \geq 0$$

8. The set of points (x, y) in the coordinate plane that satisfy the relation given above are correctly described by which of the following?

(A)   (B)   (C)   (D)   (E)

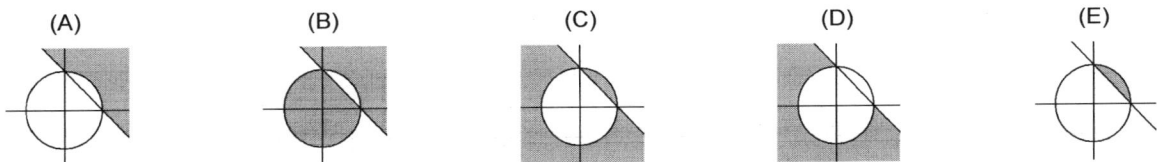

9. The points on the line y=3x+1 are reflected across the line y=2x-3, then which point stays fixed?

(A) (0,1)   (B) $(-\frac{1}{3}, 0)$ (C) (0, -3)   (D) $(\frac{3}{2}, 0)$ (E) (- 4, -11)

10. If f(x) is defined by $f(x) = \begin{cases} 3 & x \geq 1 \\ x-1 & x \leq -3 \end{cases}$ then f(–5) – f(2)·f(–3)=?

(A) – 18   (B) – 6   (C) – 4   (D) 3   (E) 6

11. Rectangle ABCD has its vertices located at (-1, -1), (5, -1), (5, 3), and (-1, 3). A line m divides rectangle ABCD into two congruent parts. The equation of line m cannot be

(A) y = –2x + 5   (B) y = –2x + 3   (C) y = – x + 3   (D) y = x – 1   (E) y = 3x – 5

12. f(2x+1)=x, f(x)=?

(A) $\frac{x-1}{2}$ (B) $\frac{1-x}{2}$ (C) $\frac{x+1}{2}$ (D) $\frac{2}{x-1}$ (E) $\frac{1}{2x+1}$

13. For a set of 12 consecutive positive odd integers, which of the following must be correct?

I. Median is a positive even integer.

II. Median equals mean.

III. There is no mode in this set.

(A) I only   (B) II only   (C) III only   (D) I and II only   (E) I, II, and III.

14. The equation given by $x^2 - k \cdot x + 1 = k - 2$ has two real roots. k can be

(A) any real number between -6 and 2 inclusive.   (B) any real number between -2 and 6 inclusive.

(C) any real number less than -6 or greater than 2.   (D) any real number less than -2 or greater than 6.

(E) any real number less than or equal to -6 or greater than or equal to 2.

15. The cone given in figure 18 is cut into two parts with equal volumes by a slice made parallel to the base. $\frac{AB}{AC} = ?$

(A) $\frac{1}{\sqrt[3]{2}}$
(B) $\frac{1}{\sqrt{2}}$
(C) $\sqrt{2}$
(D) $\sqrt[3]{2}$

(E) None of the above

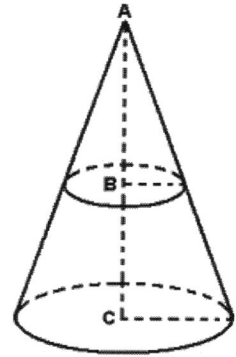

Figure 18
Figure not drawn to scale

16. First two terms a_1 and a_2 of an arithmetic sequence are 5 and 7 respectively. What is the sum of the first 30 terms in this sequence?

(A) 61   (B) 63   (C) 957   (D) 1020   (E) 1085

17. What is the domain of the function given by $f(x) = \frac{\sqrt{9-x^2}}{3x}$?

(A) -3 < x < 3 and x ≠ 0   (B) -3 < x < 3   (C) x ≤ -3 or x ≤ 3
(D) -3 ≤ x ≤ 3 and x ≠ 0   (E) -3 ≤ x ≤ 3

18. f(x) is defined by the recursive relation given by f(x) = (x−1)·f(x+1). If f(1.3) = 2.1 then what is f(-0.7)?
(A) -1.47   (B) 1.47   (C) -2.50   (D) 2.50
(E) Cannot be determined from the information given

19. If P(x) is a polynomial function defined by $P(x) = (x+1)^2 \cdot (x-4)$ then which of the following is false?
(A) P(x) intersects the x − axis twice.
(B) P(x) has two distinct zeros.
(C) Sum of the zeros of P(x) is 2.
(D) Product of the zeros of P(x) is − 4.
(E) The leading coefficient of P(x) is 1.

20. Which one(s) of the following functions satisfy the relation f(-x) = f(x)?

   I. $f(x) = x^4 - x$

   II. $f(x) = \cos(x) + 2x^2 + 3$

   III. $f(x) = x \cdot \sin(x)$

(A) I only   (B) II only   (C) III only   (D) II and III only   (E) I, II, and III.

21. Slopes of two intersecting lines are 3/7 and 15/7 respectively. Which of the following is the obtuse angle between these two lines rounded to the nearest degree?

(A) 42°   (B) 60°   (C) 120°   (D) 138°

(E) None of the above

22. Which of the following is the graph of the relation given by (x+3)(y-1)=xy?

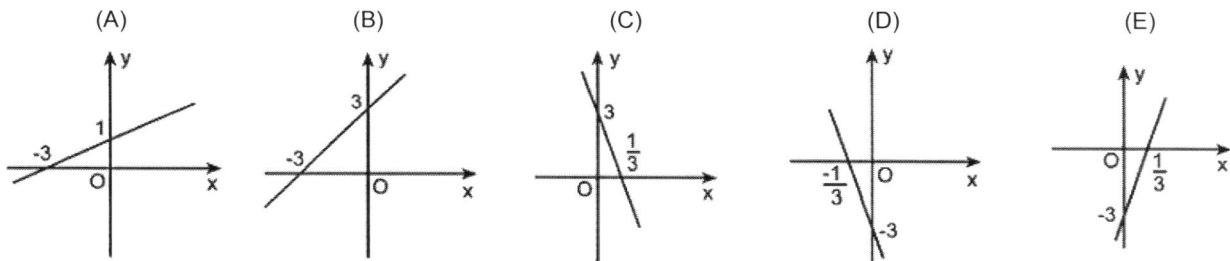

(A)   (B)   (C)   (D)   (E)

23. Given in figure 19, AB = x and CD = y. What is y in terns of x?

(A) $\dfrac{x\left(\sqrt{3}+1\right)}{\sqrt{3}}$ (B) $\dfrac{x\left(\sqrt{3}+1\right)}{\sqrt{3}-1}$ (C) $\dfrac{x\sqrt{3}}{\sqrt{3}-1}$

(D) $\dfrac{x}{\sqrt{3}-1}$ (E) $\dfrac{x}{\sqrt{3}+1}$

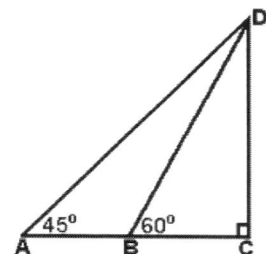

Figure 19

Figure not drawn to scale

24. Which of the following describes the exterior region of the circle with center (4,3) and radius 2?

(A) $(x+4)^2 + (y+3)^2 \leq 4$ (B) $(x-4)^2 + (y-3)^2 \leq 4$ (C) $(x-4)^2 + (y-3)^2 < 4$

(D) $(x+4)^2 + (y+3)^2 < 4$ (E) $(x-4)^2 + (y-3)^2 > 4$

25. What is the measure of the smallest angle of triangle ABC given in figure 20?

(A) 33.5°   (B) 33.6°   (C) 62.1°   (D) 84.2°   (E) 84.3°

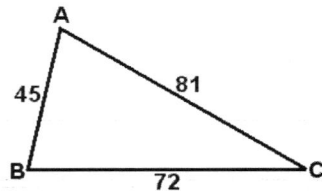

Figure 20

x	1	2	3	4
g(x)	- 4	-1	4	11

x	1	2	3	4
h(x)	9	7	5	3

26. For the continuous functions g(x) and h(x) given above, how many of the following statements are possible?

    I.   h(x) can be defined as bx + c.

    II. g(x) can be defined as $x^2 + d$.

    III. g(x) has a zero between 2 and 3.

    IV. g(x) and h(x) are both invertible in the interval 1 < x < 4.

    V. The equation g(x) = h(x) has a root between 1 and 4.

(A) 1   (B) 2   (C) 3   (D) 4   (E) 5

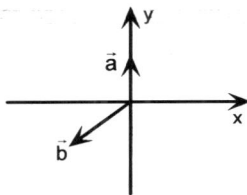

Figure 21

27. Vectors $\vec{a}$ and $\vec{b}$ are as given in the figure 21 above. Which of the following can be the graph of $\vec{a} - \vec{b}$?

    (A)   (B)   (C)   (D)   (E)

$$2x - y = 4$$
$$x + 2y - 3z = 3$$
$$-x + y + z = -3$$

28. A·X = B represents the system of equations given above where A is the matrix of coefficients, X is the matrix of variables and B is the matrix of results. What is the determinant of matrix A?

(A) – 8   (B) – 4   (C) 0   (D) 4   (E) 8

29. Which of the following is a real number for all x?

(A) $\log_{0.5}(x+1)$ (B) $\log_3(x-1)$ (C) $\log_{(x-1)}(x+1)$ (D) $\log_x(x^2+1)$ (E) $\log_4(x^2+1)$

30. How many 5 digit integers contain distinct digits?

(A) 10^5 (B) 9^5 (C) $9 \cdot 10^4$ (D) $9^2 \cdot 8 \cdot 7 \cdot 6$ (E) $9 \cdot 8 \cdot 7 \cdot 6 \cdot 5$

31. As indicated in figure 22, the outer surface of a white cube with and edge of length 6 inches is painted to gray and then cut into identical smaller cubes each with an edge of length 1 inch. How many smaller cubes have 1 gray face only?

(A) 16   (B) 64   (C) 96   (D) 216

(E) None of the above

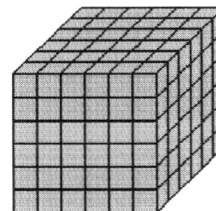

Figure 22

32. What is the amplitude of the function given by f(x) = 5·sin(x) – 12·cos(x) – 2?

(A) 5   (B) 12   (C) 13   (D) -13

(E) None of the above

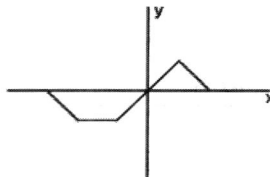

Figure 23

33. Graph of f(x) is given in figure 23 above. What will be the graph of -|f(x)|?

(A)

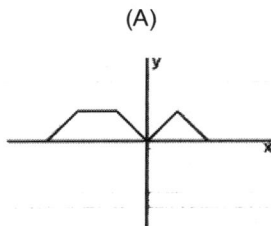

(B)

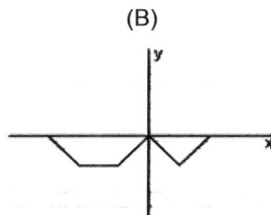

(C)

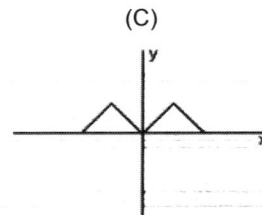

(D)

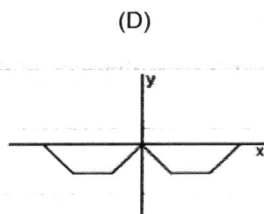

(E)

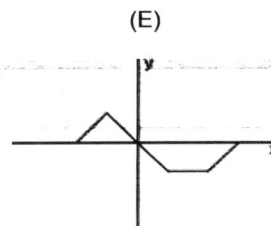

34. If both of the points $(2, e^4)$ and $(-2, b)$ are on the graph of $f(x) = a^x$ then $b = ?$

(A) $-e^2$ (B) e^2 (C) e^{-4} (D) $-e^4$ (E) e^4

35. There are totally 24 marbles in a bag of which 7 are blue, 8 are red and 9 are green. If two marbles are selected at random from the bag without replacement, what is the probability that they will be both green?

(A) $\left(\dfrac{9}{48}\right)^2$ (B) $\left(\dfrac{9}{24}\right)^2$ (C) $\dfrac{9}{24} \cdot \dfrac{8}{23}$ (D) $\dfrac{9}{48} \cdot \dfrac{8}{47}$

(E) None of the above.

36. The intersection of two spheres with distinct radii can be

    I. A point

    II. A circle

    III. A sphere

(A) I only   (B) II only   (C) IIII only   (D) I or II only   (E) I, II, or III

37. What is the equation of the line that passes through the point $\left(3, -\dfrac{1}{2}\right)$ and is perpendicular to the line

$2 = 3x - 2y$?

(A) $2y - 3x = -2$ (B) $2y + 10 = 3x$ (C) $6y = -4x + 9$

(D) $6y - 4x = +9$ (E) $3y - 2x = 10$

38. What is the primary period of the function given by $f(x) = 3 \cdot \sin^2(2x) + 1$?

(A) 2π (B) π (C) $\dfrac{\pi}{2}$ (D) $\dfrac{\pi}{4}$

(E) None of the above

                     A: $x + y + z = 2$

                     B: $-x - y - z = 4$

                     C: $x = y = z$

39. In the three dimensional space which one(s) of the following is correct regarding the equations given above?

(A) Planes A and B are both parallel to line C.

(B) Lines A and B are both parallel to plane C.

(C) Planes A and B are both perpendicular to line C.

(D) Lines A and B are both perpendicular to plane C.

(E) Planes A and B are neither parallel nor perpendicular to line C.

40. Given in figure 24, is a rectangular box whose dimensions are given in inches. What is measure of angle $\angle$ DHB rounded to the nearest degree?

(A) 33°　　　　(B) 34°　　　　(C) 45°　　　　(D) 46°　　　　(E) 56°

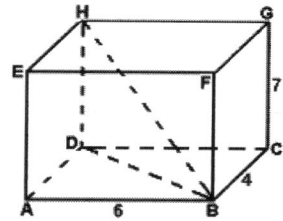

Figure 24

Figure not drawn to scale

41. If the equation given by $ax^2 + bx + c = 0$ has two real and distinct solutions, then which of the following quantities must be nonzero?

I. a　　II. b　　III. $b^2 - 4ac$

(A) I only　　　　(B) II only　　　　(C) III only　　　　(D) I and III only　　　　(E) I, II and III

42. First two terms a_1 and a_2 of a geometric sequence are 5 and 7 respectively. What is the first term in this sequence that exceeds 2000?

(A) a_{17}　　　　(B) a_{18}　　　　(C) a_{19}　　　　(D) a_{20}　　　　(E) a_{21}

43. In figure 25, there is 1 triangle in the first row, 3 triangles in the second row, 5 triangles in the third row and so on. What is the number of triangles in the 2005th row?

(A) 2003　　　　(B) 2005　　　　(C) 4007

(D) 4009　　　　(E) 4011

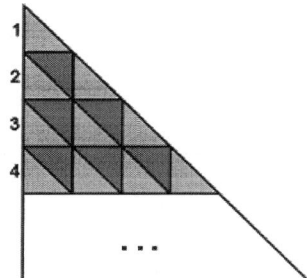

Figure 25

44. A point (x, y, z) in the three dimensional coordinate space satisfies the relations given by x·y = 12, y·z = 24 and x·z = 18. How many such points are there?

(A) No points   (B) One point   (C) Two points   (D) Three points   (E) Six points

45. Which of the following is not a correct representation of the shaded region in figure 26?

(A) $y^2 \le x^2$

(B) $y^4 \le x^4$

(C) $|x| \ge |y|$

(D) $(1 - x)(1 + x) \le (1 - y)(1 + y)$

(E) x > y or x > -y or -x > y or -x > -y

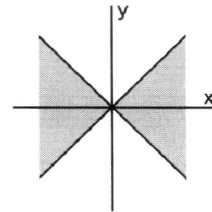

Figure 26

46. $\lim\limits_{x \to 1} \dfrac{x^2 - 1}{x + 1} = ?$

(A) -2   (B) -1   (C) 0   (D) 1   (E) Undefined

47. A right circular cone whose base radius is 6 cm is inscribed in a sphere as is given in figure 27. If the volume of the cone is 216π cm^3 then what is the radius of the sphere?

(A) 9   (B) 10   (C) 12   (D) 13   (E) 15

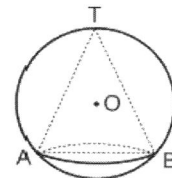

Figure 27

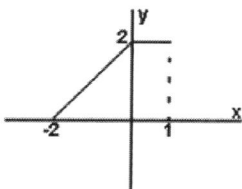
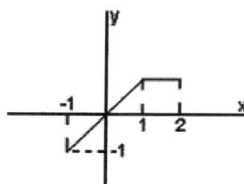

Graph of f(x)   Graph of g(x)

48. Graphs of f(x) and g(x) are given above. What is the relation between f(x) and g(x)?

(A) g(x)=f(x-1)+1   (B) f(x)+1=g(x+1)   (C) g(x)=f(x+1)+1   (D) f(x)=g(x-1)+1   (E) g(x)+1=f(x-1)

49. In figure 28, OABC is a square and coordinates of points E and D are (0,2) and (1,0) respectively. Which of the following pairs of lines give the coordinates of point B when intersected?

(A) $x + \dfrac{y}{2} = 1$ and $y - x = 0$ (B) $\dfrac{x}{2} - y = 1$ and $y + x = 0$

(C) $\dfrac{x}{2} + 2y = 1$ and $y - x = 0$ (D) $x - \dfrac{y}{2} = 1$ and $y + x = 0$

(E) x + y = 1 and y + x = 0

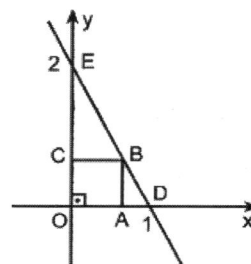

Figure 28
Figure not drawn to scale

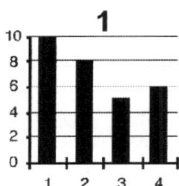
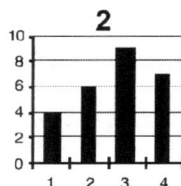
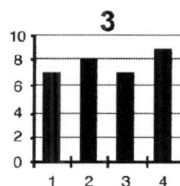
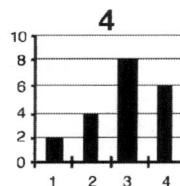
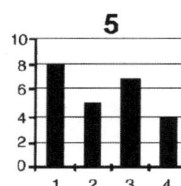

50. Five different sets of data are represented by the graphs given above. Standard deviation is the least for the data set given by which of the above graphs?

(A) 1   (B) 2   (C) 3   (D) 4   (E) 5

S T O P

END OF TEST

Answers to Level 1 – Model Tests

Model Test 1		Model Test 2		Model Test 3	
1.	C	1.	C	1.	A
2.	E	2.	D	2.	E
3.	E	3.	D	3.	E
4.	E	4.	C	4.	D
5.	B	5.	A	5.	C
6.	D	6.	C	6.	E
7.	E	7.	A	7.	D
8.	B	8.	D	8.	B
9.	C	9.	D	9.	B
10.	D	10.	B	10.	E
11.	E	11.	C	11.	A
12.	E	12.	A	12.	A
13.	B	13.	C	13.	E
14.	C	14.	B	14.	E
15.	E	15.	D	15.	C
16.	B	16.	B	16.	B
17.	A	17.	E	17.	B
18.	B	18.	A	18.	C
19.	B	19.	C	19.	E
20.	C	20.	A	20.	E
21.	D	21.	E	21.	D
22.	C	22.	D	22.	D
23.	E	23.	E	23.	A
24.	D	24.	D	24.	B
25.	D	25.	D	25.	D
26.	C	26.	D	26.	E
27.	D	27.	D	27.	E
28.	A	28.	E	28.	D
29.	C	29.	C	29.	D
30.	C	30.	C	30.	C
31.	B	31.	D	31.	C
32.	A	32.	E	32.	D
33.	B	33.	A	33.	C
34.	C	34.	C	34.	E
35.	D	35.	C	35.	B
36.	D	36.	D	36.	C
37.	C	37.	C	37.	D
38.	E	38.	A	38.	E
39.	D	39.	B	39.	A
40.	C	40.	B	40.	D
41.	C	41.	A	41.	D
42.	A	42.	C	42.	C
43.	E	43.	C	43.	C
44.	E	44.	B	44.	C
45.	A	45.	C	45.	A
46.	C	46.	D	46.	C
47.	A	47.	A	47.	B
48.	D	48.	A	48.	C
49.	D	49.	A	49.	B
50.	C	50.	C	50.	D

Answers to Level 2 – Model Tests

Model Test 1		Model Test 2		Model Test 3	
1.	D	1.	D	1.	E
2.	B	2.	A	2.	A
3.	A	3.	E	3.	E
4.	D	4.	D	4.	E
5.	A	5.	D	5.	B
6.	D	6.	D	6.	D
7.	D	7.	E	7.	A
8.	D	8.	D	8.	B
9.	A	9.	B	9.	E
10.	A	10.	D	10.	E
11.	D	11.	D	11.	B
12.	C	12.	B	12.	A
13.	D	13.	D	13.	E
14.	C	14.	D	14.	E
15.	E	15.	C	15.	A
16.	D	16.	B	16.	D
17.	D	17.	A	17.	D
18.	E	18.	B	18.	D
19.	D	19.	B	19.	D
20.	D	20.	E	20.	D
21.	E	21.	D	21.	D
22.	E	22.	E	22.	A
23.	B	23.	B	23.	C
24.	C	24.	E	24.	E
25.	E	25.	A	25.	B
26.	C	26.	A	26.	E
27.	B	27.	D	27.	C
28.	B	28.	E	28.	E
29.	C	29.	B	29.	E
30.	E	30.	D	30.	D
31.	A	31.	B	31.	C
32.	B	32.	D	32.	C
33.	E	33.	E	33.	B
34.	C	34.	A	34.	C
35.	D	35.	C	35.	C
36.	C	36.	B	36.	D
37.	C	37.	A	37.	C
38.	B	38.	B	38.	C
39.	B	39.	C	39.	C
40.	B	40.	C	40.	D
41.	E	41.	D	41.	D
42.	B	42.	C	42.	C
43.	D	43.	B	43.	D
44.	C	44.	C	44.	C
45.	B	45.	C	45.	E
46.	E	46.	D	46.	C
47.	C	47.	D	47.	B
48.	E	48.	E	48.	E
49.	D	49.	C	49.	A
50.	B	50.	B	50.	C

Scaled Score Conversion Table
Mathematics Level 1 Test

Raw Score	Scaled Score	Raw Score	Scaled Score	Raw Score	Scaled Score
50	800	28	590	6	390
49	790	27	580	5	380
48	780	26	570	4	380
47	780	25	560	3	370
46	770	24	550	2	360
45	750	23	540	1	350
44	740	22	530	0	340
43	740	21	520	-1	340
42	730	20	510	-2	330
41	720	19	500	-3	320
40	710	18	490	-4	310
39	710	17	480	-5	300
38	700	16	470	-6	280
37	690	15	460	-7	270
36	680	14	460	-8	260
35	670	13	450	-9	260
34	660	12	440	-10	250
33	650	11	430	-11	240
32	640	10	420		
31	630	9	420		
30	620	8	410		
29	600	7	400		

Scaled Score Conversion Table Mathematics Level 2 Test					
Raw Score	Scaled Score	Raw Score	Scaled Score	Raw Score	Scaled Score
50	800	28	650	6	480
49	800	27	640	5	470
48	800	26	630	4	460
47	800	25	630	3	450
46	800	24	620	2	440
45	800	23	610	1	430
44	800	22	600	0	410
43	800	21	590	-1	390
42	790	20	580	-2	370
41	780	19	570	-3	360
40	770	18	560	-4	340
39	760	17	560	-5	340
38	750	16	550	-6	330
37	740	15	540	-7	320
36	730	14	530	-8	320
35	720	13	530	-9	320
34	710	12	520	-10	320
33	700	11	510	-11	310
32	690	10	500	-12	310
31	680	9	500		
30	670	8	490		
29	660	7	480		

Solutions to Level 1 – Model Test 1

1. (C)

$$\begin{array}{ccccc} & -2 & & 1 & & 3 \\ \hline - & | & + & \| & + & | & - \end{array}$$

x<-2 or x >3

2. (E)
2a is even therefore b is odd and 2a-b is always odd.

3. (E)
(A) 2,1,4,2,1
(B) 3,10,5,16,8
(C) 5,16,8,4,2
(D) 6,3,10,5,16
(E) 10,5,16,8,**4,2,1**

4. (E)
$2x^2 - 3x + c = ax^2 + xb - 2ax - 2b$
$2x^2 - 3x + c = ax^2 + x(b - 2a) - 2b$
$a = 2$
$-3 = b - 2a$
$-3 = b - 4$
$c = 26$
$c = -2$
$2 + 1 - (-2) = 5$

5. (B)
$x > 2$
$|2 - x| = -2 + x$
$|2 - x|^2 = 2 + x$
$-2 + x + 2 + x = 2x$

6. (D)
If line m divides rectangle into two congruent regions then it must pass through the center of the rectangle which is valid for only I and II.

7. (E)
sin20°=A
sin160°=sin(180°-20°)=sin20°=A
sin200°=-sin20°=A
sin340°=-sin20°=-A

8. (B)
$\dfrac{B}{2} \cdot (2C)^2 = \dfrac{B}{2} \cdot 4C^2 = 2 \cdot BC^2 = 2A$

9. (C)
b and h are alternate interior angles therefore they are equal in measure.

10. (D)
$\dfrac{sum}{10} = 80 \Rightarrow sum = 800$

average of the remaining numbers $= \dfrac{800 - 120}{8} = 85$

11. (E)
Case II is false because in case II $a^b = 1$.

12. (E)
$b^2 - 4ac < 0$
$k^2 - 4 \cdot 1 \cdot (3 - k) < 0$
$k^2 - 12 + 4k < 0 \Rightarrow -6 < k < 2$

13. (B)
$a_2 = a_1 + b$
$17 = 15 + d$
$d = 2$

$a_1 = 15$
$a_2 = 17$
$a_{30} = a_1 + 29d$
$a_{30} = 15 + 29 \cdot 2$
$a_{30} = 15 + 58 = 73$

14. (C)
$|12-5i| = \sqrt{12^2 + (-5)^2} = 13$

15. (E)
$3.55 \cdot 1.22 \cdot 1.04 = 42.5$

16. (B)
$\dfrac{(x + 5)(x - 2)}{3 \cdot (x - 2)} \cdot \dfrac{2 \cdot (x + 4)}{(x + 4)(x + 5)} = \dfrac{2}{3}$

17. (A)
$(a + b) \cdot (a - b) = k$
$(9 + 6) \cdot (9 - 6) = (a + 2) \cdot (a - 2) = k$
$45 = a^2 - 4$
$a^2 = 49$
$a = \pm 7$

18. (B)
$P(x) = x^3 + 3x^2 + kx - 12$
$P(-3) = 0$
$(-3)^3 + 3 \cdot (-3)^2 + k \cdot (-3) - 12 = 0$
$-3k = 12$
$k = -4$
$Q(x) = x^2 - 4 = (x - 2) \cdot (x + 2)$

19. (B)
$6 + 2 \cdot 2 - 12 - 2p \neq 0$
$10 - 12 - 2p \neq 0$
$-2 \neq 2p$
$p \neq -1$

20. (C)
$0.424242... = \dfrac{42}{99} = \dfrac{14}{33}$

21. (D)
$\cos^2 x = 1 - \sin^2 x$
$\Rightarrow \dfrac{(1 - \sin x)(1 + \sin x)}{(1 - \sin x)} = 1 + \sin x$

22. (C)
There are 4 of such cubes on each side therefore there are totally 4·12=48 of them.

23. (E)
$3\log b - \log b = \log 16$
$2\log b = \log 16$
$\log b^2 = \log 16$
$b^2 = 16$
$b = 4$

24. (D)
$\dfrac{1}{x^2 + \sqrt{15}} = x^2 - \sqrt{15}$
$1 = \left(x^2 + \sqrt{15}\right)\left(x^2 - \sqrt{15}\right)$
$1 = x^4 - 15$
$x^4 = 16$
$x = \pm 2$

25. (D)
$x^2 + 4 = 0 \Rightarrow x^2 = -4 \Rightarrow x = \mp 2i$
So $(x + 2i)$ and $(x - 2i)$ are factors of $x^2 + 4$

26. (C)
Total amount of growth is
12·0.03+2·0.01=0.38

27. (D)

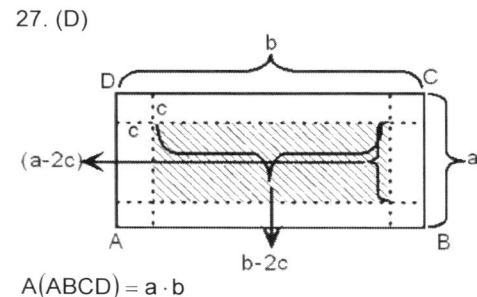

$A(ABCD) = a \cdot b$

Shaded area =(a-2c)(b-2c)
The area outside the margin lines is equals
ab-(a-2c)(b-2c)

28. (A)

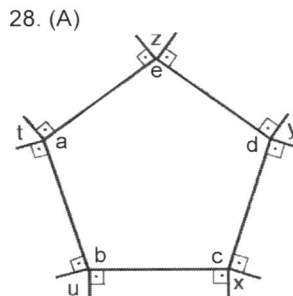

$z + t + u + x + y =$
$(180 - e) + (180 - a) + (180 - b) + (180 - c) + (180 - d)$
$= 180 \cdot 5 - 540 = 360°$

29. (C)
$A\left(A\overset{\Delta}{F}B\right) = \dfrac{21}{3} \cdot 4 = 28$
$A(ABCD) = 2 \cdot 28 = 56$

30. (C)
The distance that she covers in each direction is the same, therefore 35(2-t)=40t and t=14/15 hours.

31. (B)
$x^2 - 9 \geq 0$ and $x \neq 0$
thus $x \leq -3$ or $x \geq 3$

32. (A)
$f(x) = e^x$
$f(a) \cdot f(b) = e^a \cdot e^b = e^{a+b}$
$f(a + b) = e^{a+b}$
$f(a) \cdot f(b) = f(a + b)$

33. (B)
$x\sqrt{2} = 1 + x \Rightarrow x\sqrt{2} - x = 1 \Rightarrow x\left(\sqrt{2} - 1\right) = 1$
$x = \dfrac{1}{\sqrt{2} - 1} = \sqrt{2} + 1$

34. (C)
$100 \cdot \dfrac{80}{100} \cdot \dfrac{120}{100} = 96$ which implies a 4% decrease.

35. (D)
Sena : $30 + 2 \cdot 9 = 30 + 180 = 210$
Mehmet : 360 cents
$630 = 30 + 20 \cdot h$
$600 = 20 \cdot h \Rightarrow h = 30$
$30 + 1 = 31$

36. (D)

Maximum value of $-x^2$ is 0 and the minimum value of

$x^2 - x + k$ is obtained when x = h then

$h = \dfrac{-b}{2a} = \dfrac{1}{2}$. Minimum value of $x^2 - x + k$ is

$f\left(\dfrac{1}{2}\right) = \dfrac{1}{4} - \dfrac{1}{2} + k = \dfrac{-1}{4} + k > 0$

$k - \dfrac{1}{4} > 0 \Rightarrow k > \dfrac{1}{4}$

37. (C)

Atakan's money = x

$45 \le x \le 75$

Price of the item = p

$1.50 \le p \le 2.25$

Maximum number of items he can purchase is 75/1.5=50.

Minimum number of items he can purchase is 45/2.25=20.

50-20=30.

38. (E)

$\dfrac{(6-2) \cdot 180}{6} = 120°$

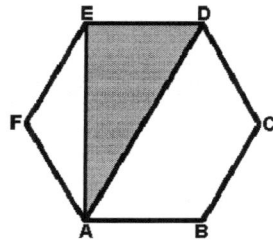

$|EA| = a\sqrt{3}$

$|ED| = a$

$Area = \dfrac{a \cdot a\sqrt{3}}{2} = 32\sqrt{3}$

$a^2 = 64 \Rightarrow a = 8$

39. (D)

$b^2 - 4ac > 0 \Rightarrow b^2 - 4ac \neq 0$

$a \neq 0$

40. (C)

$47\pi + 2\pi r = 47\pi + 2 \cdot 3 \cdot \pi = 53\pi$

41. (C)

$\dfrac{\left(\cos^2\theta - \sin^2\theta\right)}{\left(\cos^2\theta - \sin^2\theta\right)\left(\cos^2\theta + \sin^2\theta\right)} = \dfrac{1}{1} = 1$

42. (A)

$a^2 = 9$ and $a = \pm 3$

therefore $b = 3^3 = 27$ or $(-3)^3 = -27$

43. (E)

The price per weight of gold and of silver are not known therefore answer cannot be determined.

44. (E)

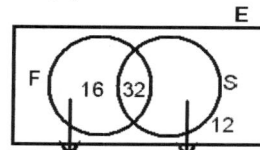

48-32   72-32=40

$S(F \cup S) = 100 - 12 = 88$

$88 = S(F) + S(S) - S(S \cap F)$

$88 = 48 + 72 - S(S \cap F)$

$S(S \cap F) = 38$

$40 + 16 = 56$

45. (A)

$y = x^3 - 4x - 1$ is graphed and its greatest negative x intercept is found to be -.254.

46. (C)

$x^2 + 2^2 = 10^2 \Rightarrow x^2 = 96$

$x = 4\sqrt{6}$

47. (A)

$\log_4 15 = 1.03$

$\Rightarrow 1 < \log_2 k < 2$

$\log_2 k < 2 \Rightarrow 0 < k < 4$

Therefore k can be 3.

48. (D)

Sum of the zeros is $2 + 2 - 2 = 0$

49. (D)

$IV : \dfrac{3000}{500} = 6$; therefore the product is most nearly IV as 5.89 is close to 6.

50. (C)

AEI of I is 2500/250 = 10 therefore 52,879/10=5,279 which is close to 5,300.

Solutions to Level 1 – Model Test 2

1. (C)

$2.005 \cdot 1000 = 2005$

$200.5 \cdot 10 = 2005$

$x = 2005 \cdot 2005 = (2005)^2$

2. (D)

I) $x = -\dfrac{1}{3}$ $\dfrac{\frac{1}{3}}{-\frac{1}{3}} = -3 < 3$ true

II) $\dfrac{1}{3} < 3$ true

III) $\dfrac{1}{\frac{1}{3}} = 3 < 3$ false

3. (D)

$m = -\dfrac{x^2 + 4}{x}$

If x is 1 then m is -5.

4. (C)

$x^3 < x^2 < x$ implies that x is positive and less than 1.

5. (A)

If a number is greater so is its logarithm:

$\log\left(77777 \cdot 15^{307}\right) = 307\log 15 + \log 77777$
$= 365.95$

$\log\left(7777 \cdot 17^{305}\right) = 305\log 17 + \log 7777$
$= 379.177$

$\log\left(777 \cdot 17^{305}\right) = 305\log 17 + \log 777$
$= 378.177$

$\log\left(77 \cdot 18^{304}\right) = 304\log 18 + \log 77$
$= 383.489$

$\log\left(7 \cdot 19^{305}\right) = 305\log 19 + \log 7$
$= 390.87$

6. (C)

$x = 0$

$\dfrac{-3}{4}y = \dfrac{4}{5} \Rightarrow y = \dfrac{-16}{15}$

7. (A)

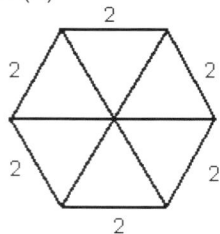

$\dfrac{6}{3} = 2 \Rightarrow A = 6 \cdot \dfrac{2^2\sqrt{3}}{4} = \dfrac{6 \cdot 4\sqrt{3}}{6\sqrt{3}}$

8. (D)

The contrapositive of the statement "if p then q" is "if not q then not p".

Therefore answer is: If $x^2 \neq 9$ then $x \neq 3$

9. (D)

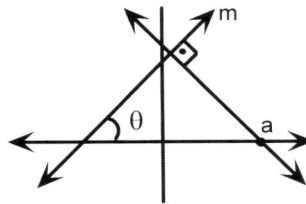

$\theta < 90°$ positive slope
a is positive and greater than the x intercept of m.

10. (B)

$\dfrac{25y}{6} = \dfrac{20x}{3} + 3$

$y = \dfrac{6}{25} \cdot \left(\dfrac{20x}{3} + 3\right)$

slope $= \dfrac{6}{25} \cdot \dfrac{20}{3} = \dfrac{8}{5}$

If the slope of the line perpendicular to the given line is m

then: $\dfrac{8}{5} \cdot m = -1$ and $m = \dfrac{-5}{8} = -0.63$

11. (C)

$\left(x + \dfrac{1}{x}\right)^2 = x^2 + 2 + \dfrac{1}{x^2} = 16$

$x^2 + \dfrac{1}{x^2} = 16 - 2 = 14$

12. (A)

The number has the form of abcba where a is nonzero and a, b, c are not necessarily distinct. Therefore there are 9·10·10·1·1=900 such numbers.

13. (C)

$(x - 3)^2 - 9 + (y + 4)^2 - 16 + 24 = 0$

$(x - 3)^2 + (y + 4)^2 = 1$

Center$(3, -4)$ $r = 1$ circle

14. (B)

$\dfrac{\text{sum}}{10} = 80$

$\text{sum} = 800$

$\text{new sum} = 800 - 170 = 630$

$\text{new average} = \dfrac{630}{9} = 70$

15. (D)

$a = b$ $b = h$ $a = h$

$WZ = ZY$

16. (B)

$\sqrt[3]{5} - 1 \to a$

$a^3 + 3a^2 + 3a + 2 = 6$

17. (E)
$3x - 2 > 8$ or $3x - 2 < -8$

$x < -2$ or $x > \dfrac{10}{3}$

18. (A)
$x = 3 + 4t$

$y = 1 + 2t$

$\dfrac{x - 3}{4} = \dfrac{y - 1}{2}$

$y = 0 \Rightarrow \dfrac{x - 3}{4} = \dfrac{-1}{2}$

$\Rightarrow x = 1$

19. (C)
$y = \dfrac{x - 1}{x + 1}$ represents a hyperbola whose asymptotes are the coordinate axes.

20. (A)
$ax^2 + bx + c = 0$

$x_1 + x_2 = \dfrac{-b}{a} = \dfrac{\sqrt{3}}{\sqrt{11}} = 0.52$

21. (E)
Since $5^2 + 12^2 = 13^2$, the triangle is right angled and the diameter of its circumscribed circle is its hypotenuse therefore radius equals 13/2=6.5.

22. (D)

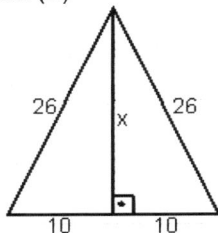

$26^2 - 10^2 = x^2 \Rightarrow x = 24$

$Area = \dfrac{20 \cdot 24}{2} = 240$

23. (E)
$(x - 3)^2 + (x + 1)^2 > 10^2$

$(x - 3)^2 + (x + 1)^2 > 100$

24. (D)
$AC = y$

$AB = x$

$x + y = 25$

$y^2 - x^2 = 15^2$

$(y - x)(y + x) = 225$

$y - x = 9$ and $y + x = 25$

$y = 17$ and $x = 8$

$Area = \dfrac{8 \cdot 15}{2} = 4 \cdot 15 = 60$

25. (D)
Area of quadrilateral EBRU is 8·8/2=32 square feet (not 32 square inches).

26. (D)
$6^2 + 6m + 12 = 0$

$36 + 12 + 6m = 0$

$48 = -6m$

$m = -8$

$x^2 - 8x + 12 = 0$

$(x - 6)(x - 2) = 0$

$x = 2$

27. (D)
$x^2 + kx + 1 + 2 - k = 0$

$x^2 - kx + 3 - k = 0$

$k^2 - 4 \cdot 1 \cdot (3 - k) \geq 0$

$k^2 + 4k - 12 \geq 0$

therefore

$k \leq -6$ or $k \geq 2$

28. (E)
h is a constant function therefore it is not invertible.

29. (C)
The function given in C is defined for all real numbers.

30. (C)
1 square yards is 9 square feet therefore the cost in dollars per square yards is given by

$\dfrac{115200}{2400 \cdot 3600} = \dfrac{115200}{9 \cdot 2400 \cdot 3600} = \dfrac{3}{25}$

31. (D)

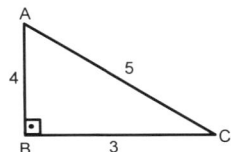

$\sin C = \dfrac{4}{5} = 0.8$

$\tan C = \dfrac{4}{3} = 1.33$

$\cos C = \dfrac{3}{5} = 0.6$

$\tan C > \sin C > \cos C$

D is false

32. (E)
Correct answer is given in E since leftmost letter can be one of the 26 letters of the alphabet and each successive letter is one of the remaining 25 letters.

33. (A)
Correct answer is given in A.

34. (C)
Total amount of money equals number of people times price per person and it equals
$(20 + 3n) \times (12.5 - 0.25n)$

35. (C)
$AB^2 + 4 = 36 \Rightarrow AB^2 = 32 \Rightarrow AB = 4\sqrt{2}$

36. (D)
Let volume = V = 1 which implies that a side of the cube is given by a = 1 and its surface area is given by $6 \cdot 1^2$=6. If volume is tripled then the length of one side becomes a=$\sqrt[3]{3} = 1.44$ since a^3=3. The new surface area is $6 \cdot 1.44^2$=12.48 and $\dfrac{12.48}{6} = 2.08$.

37. (C)
$\dfrac{31.5}{2} = 15.75$

$2\pi r = 2 \cdot \pi \cdot 15.75 = 98.960177$

$100 - 98.96017 = 1.03983$

$1.03983 \div 98.96017 \cdot 100 = 1.05\%$

38. (A)

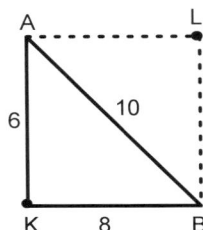

K, L two points

39. (B)
Inner cubes have no gray faces and there are 4·4·4=64 of them.

40. (B)
$d = \sqrt{(1+3)^2 + (-2+8)^2}$

$d = \sqrt{16 + 36} = \sqrt{52} = \sqrt{2} \cdot \sqrt{26}$

$d = a\sqrt{2} = \sqrt{2} \cdot \sqrt{26}$

$a = \sqrt{26}$

$\text{Area} = a^2 = \left(\sqrt{26}\right)^2 = 26$

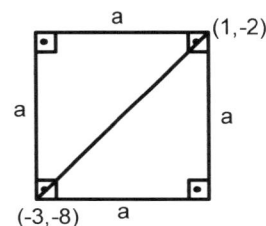

41. (A)
$\log_a b$ can be calculated as $\dfrac{\log b}{\log a}$ using the graphing calculator. A simple calculation will yield the result 2.67 which implies that the answer is A.

42. (C)
$A^2 + 100 = 64$

$A^2 = -36 \Rightarrow A = \pm 6i$

$AB = \mp 6i \cdot 10 = \pm 60i$

43. (C)
$\log 27^{1977} = 1977 \cdot \log 27 = 2829,8 \cong 2830$

44. (B)

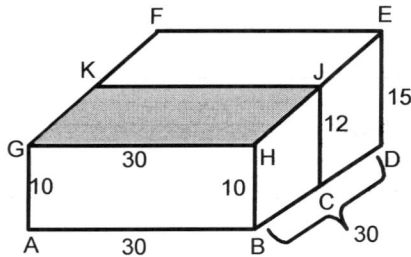

Let HJ = y.

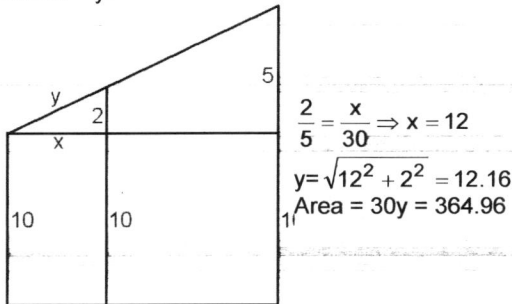

$$\frac{2}{5} = \frac{x}{30} \Rightarrow x = 12$$

$$y = \sqrt{12^2 + 2^2} = 12.16$$

Area = 30y = 364.96

45. (C)
The locus is the intersection of two spheres each having a radius of 15 feet whose centers are 25 feet apart. Therefore it is a circle.

46. (D)

$$\frac{\underset{\text{except 0}}{9} \quad \underset{}{9 \ 8 \ 7 \ 6}}{\underset{\text{except 0}}{9} \quad \underset{}{10 \ 10 \ 10 \ 10}} = \frac{9 \cdot 8 \cdot 7 \cdot 6}{10^4}$$

47. (A)
Graph $x^4 + 2x^3 - 4$ find min $\Rightarrow m = -5 \cdot 69$
Graph $x^4 - 2x^2 + 4$ find max $\Rightarrow n = 4$
$-5.69 - 4 = -9.69 = -9.7$

48. (A)
$$A\left(\overset{\Delta}{ABC}\right) = \frac{6 \cdot 6}{2} = 3 \cdot 6 = 18$$

$$AE = ED$$

$$A\left(\overset{\Delta}{AEB}\right) = A\left(\overset{\Delta}{EBD}\right) =$$

Shaded region $= \frac{18}{2} = 9$

49. (A)
$$\frac{1 + \sin x}{1 - \sin^2 x} = \frac{(1 + \sin x)}{(1 + \sin x)(1 - \sin x)} = \frac{1}{1 - \sin x}$$

50. (C)
Housing+Food+Clothing+Other=57%
240,000·0.57=136,800

Amount spent for entertainment in 2003 was 240,000·0,13=31,200$
In 2004 this amount is decreased by 25% then 31,200·0.75=23,400$
In 2004 savings is
300,000·0.65 − 136,800 − 23,400 = 34,800 and this amount corresponds to $\frac{34,800}{300,000} \cdot 100 = 11.6\%$.

Solutions to Level 1 – Model Test 3

1. (A)
$$\begin{aligned} x + 4y - 6z &= 5 \\ + \ 4x - 4y + 6z &= -20 \\ \hline 5x &= -15 \end{aligned}$$
$2 \cdot (2x - 2y + 3z) = 4x - 4y + 6z = -20$
$x = -3$

2. (E)
$$\left[2 \div \frac{\frac{1}{4}}{\frac{1}{8}}\right]^{\frac{1}{2}} = \left[\frac{2 \cdot 4}{\frac{1}{8}}\right]^{\frac{1}{2}} = (64)^{\frac{1}{2}} = 8$$

3. (E)
I) Median is the 6th number so it is a positive integer.
II) In any arithmetic sequence median = mean.
III) There is no mode in this set because no element repeats more than once.

4. (D)
$64.8 \cdot 10^{-6} = 0.0000648$

5. (C)

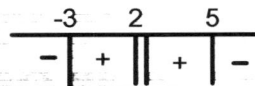

-2,-1,0,1,3,4
-2+(-1)+0+1+3+4=5

6. (E)
OPR ~ OST
$$\Rightarrow \frac{OP}{OS} = \frac{OR}{OT} = \frac{PR}{ST} = \frac{1}{2}$$
b>0 and c<0 so b>c
2b+c=0
OT=2OR so OT>OR

7. (D)
$4 \cdot 5 - 2 \cdot (-2) = 20 + 4 = 24$ is not less than 21 so (4,-2) is not in the solution set of 5x-2y<21

8. (B)
$100 \begin{array}{l} \rightarrow \$80\text{silver} \\ \rightarrow \$20\text{gold} \end{array}$ $20(1 + 0,12)^3 \cong 28$
Total Price=80+28=108

9. (B)
Graph $y = -x^2+2x-2$ to find that the max value of the function is $y= -1$.

10. (E)
b must be odd since -4a is even, therefore 2a+b is always odd.

11. (A)
$m(2c)^2 = 4mc^2$
Multiply the value of E by 4.

12. (A)
Let BC = x.
$\tan A\hat{C}B = 2$
$\dfrac{6}{x} = 2 \Rightarrow x = 3$

13. (E)
$9 - x^2 \geq x - 3$
$x^2 + x -12 \leq 0$
$(x+4)(x-3) \leq 0$
$-4 \leq x \leq 3$

14. (E)
f(|x|) is symmetric with respect to the y axis so (-5,-2) is also on this graph.

15. (C)
$(x - 4)^2 + (y - 3)^2 < 4$

16. (B)
F,G must be known. For example F(3,4) G(5,1)
$A(OABC) = 5^2 = 25$
$A(OHFD) = 12$
$A(HAGE) = 2$
Shaded area $= 25 - 14 = 11$

17. (B)
$\theta = \alpha + 90° \Rightarrow \theta - \alpha = 90°$

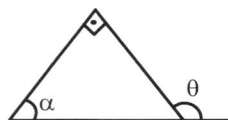

18. (C)
$\sin^2 x + \cos^2 x = 1$
$1 - 3\sin x = 0 \Rightarrow \sin x = \dfrac{1}{3}$

19. (E)
The longest chord of C_1 is the diameter of C_1.
$\text{Area of } C_1 = \pi\left(\dfrac{d}{2}\right)^2 = \dfrac{\pi d^2}{4}$
$\text{Area of } C_2 = \pi d^2$
$\dfrac{\frac{\pi d^2}{4}}{\pi d^2} = \dfrac{1}{4}$

20. (E)
None of the last two digits can be 0; therefore there are 9 possibilities for each of the last two digits. Totally there are $9 \cdot 9 = 81$ possibilities. However when 80 of the possibilities are tried and each of them fails, the remaining possibility turns out to be the correct one. So 80 try outs will be enough.

21. (D)

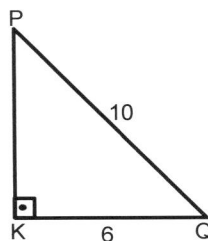

$|PK| = |AB| = \sqrt{100 - 36} = 8$

22. (D)
$\left(-\sqrt{7} - \sqrt{5}\right)^2 = 23.83 \Rightarrow x \neq -\sqrt{7} - \sqrt{5}$

23. (A)
ABCD is a rectangle, therefore AC equals the diameter.

24. (B)
$\dfrac{a}{b} = \dfrac{5}{13} \Rightarrow a = 5k \text{ and } b = 13k$
$18k = 90 \Rightarrow k = 5$
$a = 5 \cdot 5 = 25°$

25. (D)
$9 - x^2 > 0 \Rightarrow -3 < x < 3$

26. (E)
When ABCD is a square, AB+BC=2a and AC=$a\sqrt{2}$ = 1.41a. Therefore the greatest saving corresponds to (2a-1.41a)/(2a)·100 = 29.3%. The amound of road that she saves cannot exceed this number.

27. (E)
$\hat{D} = \dfrac{\hat{A}}{2} \Rightarrow \hat{D} = \dfrac{70°}{2} = 35°$

28. (D)
Line BC has a negative slope.

29. (D)
What the question means to ask is the part of f(x) that lies below the x axis, which corresponds to answer choice (D).

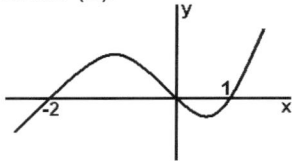

30. (C)
$4x^2 - 6x + 2c = (2x - 4)(ax + b)$
$= 2ax^2 + 2xb - 4ax - 4b$
$= 2ax^2 + (2b - 4a)x - 4b$
$4 = 2a \Rightarrow a = 2$
$-6 = 2b - 4a$
$-6 = 2b - 8 \Rightarrow b = 1$
$2c = -4b \Rightarrow c = -2$
$2 + 1 + 2 = 5$

31. (C)
Correct answer is given in C. Please note that the two figures must be symmetric about the origin.

32. (D)
$C\hat{A}D = \theta$
$\sin\theta = \cos(90° - \theta)$
$\sin C\hat{A}D = \cos B\hat{A}C$

33. (C)
$\tan 37° = \text{slope} = 0.75$
$\Rightarrow y = 0.75x$

34. (E)
$a^{4x} = a^{2x+1}$
x = 0.5 being the only solution implies that a must be other than 0, 1 and -1.

35. (B)
Lines DA and BC are the medians of the triangle OBD and their intersection P is the centroid of the triangle. Shaded region corresponds to 2/6 of the area of OBD and it equals $\frac{2}{6} \cdot \frac{2 \cdot 2}{2} = \frac{2}{3}$.

36. (C)
$1: 5,6,8,10 \Rightarrow \text{Median} = \frac{6+8}{2} = 7$
$2: 4,6,7,9 \Rightarrow \text{Median} = \frac{6+7}{2} = 6.5$
$3: 7,7,8,9 \Rightarrow \text{Median} = \frac{7+8}{2} = 7.5$
$4: 2,4,6,8 \Rightarrow \text{Median} = \frac{4+6}{2} = 5$
$5: 4,5,7,8 \Rightarrow \text{Median} = \frac{5+7}{2} = 6$

37. (D)
$\frac{1}{x^2} = \frac{1}{2^2} + \frac{1}{4^2}$
$\frac{1}{x^2} = \frac{1}{4} + \frac{1}{16} \Rightarrow x = \frac{4}{\sqrt{5}}$

38. (E)
$-6 \le a \le 6$
$a - 2b + 2 = 0 \Rightarrow a = 2b - 2$
$-6 \le 2b - 2 \le 6 \Rightarrow -2 \le b \le 4$
$b \in \{-2,-1,0,1,2,3,4\}$

39. (A)
$\frac{a^2 - 2bc - 2ac - b^2}{a+b} = \frac{a^2 - b^2 - 2c(b+a)}{a+b}$
$= \frac{(a-b)(a+b) - 2c \cdot (a+b)}{a+b} = \frac{(a+b)[a-b-2c]}{(a+b)}$
$= a - b - 2c$

40. (D)
$128 \cdot \underbrace{2 \cdot 2 \cdot 2 \dots 2}_{12\ times}$
$= 128 \cdot 2^{12}$
$= 2^7 \cdot 12^{12}$
$= 2^{19}$

41. (D)
I is not valid for some cases for example when a is positive and b is negative.

42. (C)
$(1 \otimes 1) \otimes (2 \otimes 1) = 0 \otimes 3 = -3$.

43. (C)
$1995: \text{Branch II} = 243,552,000 \cdot 0.13 = 31.7\ \text{millions}$
$2005: \text{Branch II} = 419,823,500 \cdot 0.12 = 50.4\ \text{millions}$
$31.7 \rightarrow 50.4 = 18.7 / 31.7 \cdot 100 = 59\%\ \text{increase}$

44. (C)
1995 : Branch VI $= 244 \cdot 0.03 = 7.32$
2005 : Branch VI $= 420 \cdot 0.11 = 46.2$
$\dfrac{46.2 - 7.32}{7.32} = 572\%$ increase
C is false.

45. (A)

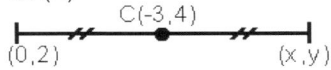

$\dfrac{x+0}{2} = -3 \Rightarrow x = -6$
$\dfrac{y+2}{2} = 4 \Rightarrow y = 6$
$(x,y) = (-6,6)$

46. (C)
$\sin^{-1} 0.82 = \theta = 55{,}1°$
$\sin(180° - 55{,}1°) = 0.82$

47. (B)
$60 - 10t = 45 - 5t$
$5t = 15$
$t = 3$

48. (C)

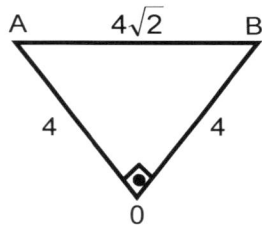

$|AB| = 4\sqrt{2} \cong 5.66$

49. (B)
f(x)+1 shifs f(x) 1 unit up.

50. (D)
Graph $\sqrt{16 - x^2}$
$0 \le f(x) \le 4$

Solutions to Level 2 – Model Test 1

1. (D)
$\dfrac{2}{x} + \dfrac{1}{y} = \dfrac{4}{3}$

$\dfrac{1}{x} + \dfrac{2}{y} = \dfrac{7}{6}$

$\Rightarrow y = 3$ and $x = 2$

$xy = 6$.

2. (B)
$f(-2) = (-2)^2 + 4(-2) - 5 = 4 - 8 - 5 = -9$

3. (A)
$|15 - 8| < |\vec{a} + \vec{b}| < 15 + 8$

$\Rightarrow 7 < |\vec{a} + \vec{b}| < 23$

Magnitude cannot be 6.

4. (D)
$\dfrac{\cos x}{\sin x} = \cot x = -1 \Rightarrow x = \operatorname{arc}\cot(-1) = \dfrac{3\pi}{4}$

5. (A)
$a_{10} = 6 = a + 9d$ and $a_{16} = 12 = a + 15d$
Therefore $d = 1$ and $a = -3$.
$a_{117} = -3 + (117 - 1)\cdot 1 = 113$

6. (D)
for $f(x) = x^2 + 3x - 3$
$f(-3) = (-3)^2 + 3\cdot(-3) - 3 = -3 \neq 0$

7. (D)
$\left.\begin{array}{l} f(-9) = 81 - 9a + b = 0 \Rightarrow b = 9a - 81 \\ f(1) = 1 + a + b = 0 \Rightarrow b = -a - 1 \end{array}\right\}$
$9a - 81 = -a - 1 \Rightarrow a = 80$

8. (D)
Graph in D is symmetric with respect to the origin.

9. (A)
If $a = -5$ and $b = 2$ then I is correct only.

10. (A)

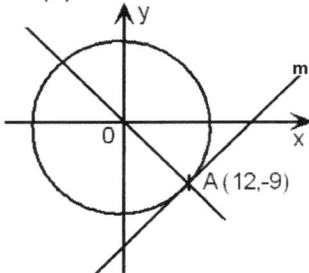

Slope line $OA = \dfrac{-9}{12} = \dfrac{-3}{4}$

Slope of line $m = \dfrac{-1}{\dfrac{-3}{4}} = \dfrac{4}{3}$

equation of line m: $y - 9 = \dfrac{4}{3}(x - 12)$

y-intercept of line m:

$y + 9 = \dfrac{4}{3}(0 - 12) \Rightarrow y = -25$

11. (D)
i is not a function, since 1 has two images, namely 0 and 2; ii and iii are functions.

12. (C)
$\dfrac{8!}{8!(9-1)} = \dfrac{1}{8}$

13. (D)
$\lim_{k \to 4} \dfrac{k^2 - 16}{k - 4} = \lim_{k \to 4} \dfrac{(k - 4)(k + 4)}{k - 4} = 8$

14. (C)
$\tan(180° - \theta) = -\tan\theta$

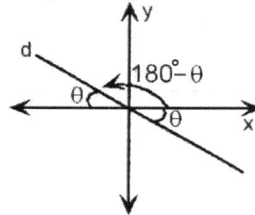

15. (E)
$\ln x = 3 \Rightarrow x = e^3 \cong 20.085$

16. (D)
I is correct since even functions are not one-to-one. In II odd functions may be one-to-one or not, so they are not always invertible. III is also correct.

17. (D)
$80 \cdot (2 - t) = 70 \cdot t \Rightarrow t = \dfrac{16}{15}$ hours or 64 minutes.

18. (E)
$\sin\theta = \cos\theta \Rightarrow$
$\dfrac{\sin\theta}{\cos\theta} = 1 \Rightarrow \tan\theta = 1$
$\Rightarrow \theta = \arctan(1)$
$\Rightarrow \theta_1 = 45°, \theta_2 = 225°$
$\theta_1 = \pi/4 = 0.785$ radians
$\theta_2 = \dfrac{5\pi}{4} = 3.926$ radians

19. (D)

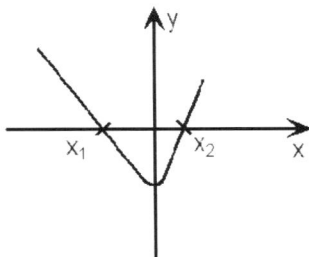

i) plot the graph of $y = e^{2x} - x - 2$

ii) find the zeros:

$x_1 = -1.980$

$x_2 = .4475$

20. (D)

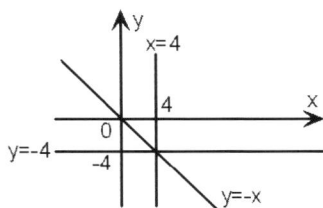

21. (E)

$$1 - \left(\frac{\binom{7}{2}}{\binom{24}{2}} + \frac{\binom{8}{2}}{\binom{24}{2}} + \frac{\binom{9}{2}}{\binom{24}{2}} \right) = 1 - \frac{\frac{7 \cdot 6}{2} + \frac{8 \cdot 7}{2} + \frac{9 \cdot 8}{2}}{\frac{24 \cdot 23}{2}}$$

$$= 1 - \frac{7 \cdot 6 + 8 \cdot 7 + 9 \cdot 8}{24 \cdot 23}$$

22. (E)

x=3 is the given line; therefore $r\cos\theta = 3$.

23. (B)

The function that satisfies this condition must be entirely nonnegative; that is the one that is never below the x axis. This corresponds to choice (B).

24. (C)

The function has a positive double root and a negative single root and the coefficient of the leading term is positive; therefore answer is C.

25. (E)

A function being one to one implies that no two x values are mapped to the same y value, $h(x) = 2^{3x}$ is a one to one function.

26. (C)

$AP = \frac{1}{2}AB$

$AB = \sqrt{(2-2)^2 + (-2+5)^2 + (8+4)^2} = 13$

$\Rightarrow AP = \frac{13}{2} = 6.5$

27. (B)

No rooms has five windows is false so at least one room must have five windows or some rooms must have five windows.

28. (B)

$f(x) = \ln(5x)$

$y = \ln(5x)$

$x = \ln(5y)$

$5y = e^x \Rightarrow y = \frac{e^x}{5}$

$f^{-1}(x) = \frac{e^x}{5}$

29. (C)

$Sinx = \frac{\sqrt{3}}{2} \Rightarrow x = 60° \text{ or } 120°$

$\Rightarrow \frac{1}{4}Cosx = \frac{1}{4}Cos180° \text{ or } \frac{1}{4}Cos360°$

$\Rightarrow \frac{1}{4}Cosx = \mp\frac{1}{4}$

30. (E)

$$f(x,-y) = \frac{|x| - |-y|}{|2x + 2(-y)|} = \frac{|x| - |y|}{|2x - 2y|} = \frac{|x| - |y|}{|2y - 2x|}$$

31. (A)

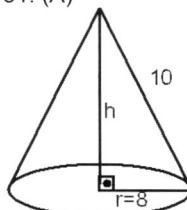

$d = 16 \Rightarrow r = 8$

$h^2 + r^2 = 10^2 \Rightarrow h = \sqrt{10^2 - 8^{20}} = 6$

$V = \frac{1}{3}\pi \cdot 8^2 \cdot 6 = 402.12$

32. (B)

Let $x = 1$

$(1+1)^2 - 5 \cdot (1+1) + 4 = (1-1)^2 + a(1-1) + b$

$4 - 10 + 4 = 0 + b \Rightarrow b = -2$

33. (E)

$y = -4t + 2$

$x = 2 - 4t$

$\Rightarrow y = -x$

Solve y = -x and y = 2x simultaneously and you get x = y = 0 which implies that 2 - 4t = 0 and t = 0.5.

34. (C)

Money accumulated in the account =

$10,000 \cdot (1.05)^{10} = 16,288.946$

35. (D)

f(g(x))=1 implies that g(x) is positive; so x < -2 or 1 < x < 4.

36. (C)

For $f(x) = 2\cos\left(\dfrac{x}{2} + \pi\right)$

$x = 0 \Rightarrow y = 0$

$x = \pi \Rightarrow y = 2$

$x = 2\pi \Rightarrow y = 0$

$x = 3\pi \Rightarrow y = -2$

$x = 4\pi \Rightarrow y = 0$

37. (C)

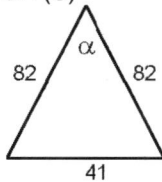

By the cosine rule:

$41^2 = 82^2 + 82^2 - 2 \cdot 82 \cdot 82 \cdot \cos\alpha$

$\Rightarrow \cos\alpha = 0.875 \Rightarrow \alpha = 28.955°$

38. (B)

Mehmet Can's score is 4 standard deviations greater than the mean in event B. Therefore answer is B.

39. (B)

By the sine rule:

$\dfrac{540}{\sin 54°} = \dfrac{x}{\sin 27°} \Rightarrow x = \dfrac{540 \cdot \sin 27°}{\sin 54°} = 303.02$

40. (B)

Diameter of the sphere equals the diagonal of the rectangular prism.

So, $d = \sqrt{9^2 + 7^2 + 5^2} = 12.449$ and r = 6.22.

41. (E)

$\left(\dfrac{\dfrac{4}{3}\pi \cdot (1.14r)^3 \cdot 100}{\dfrac{4}{3}\pi \cdot r^3} - 100\right)\% = 48\%$

42. (B)

$f(x) = \ln x \Rightarrow f\left(a^n\right) = \ln a^n = n \cdot \ln a = n \cdot f(a)$

$\Rightarrow f\left(a^n\right) = n \cdot f(a)$

43. (D)

$\left|\vec{a} + \vec{b}\right|^2 = \left|\vec{a}\right|^2 + \left|\vec{b}\right|^2 + 2 \cdot \left|\vec{a}\right| \cdot \left|\vec{b}\right| \cdot \cos 35°$

$\left|\vec{a} + \vec{b}\right| = 100 + 225 + 2 \cdot 10 \cdot 15 \cdot \cos 35°$

$\Rightarrow \left|\vec{a} + \vec{b}\right| = \sqrt{570.74} = 23.89$

44. (C)

$d = \sqrt{(-5 - 0)^2 + (7 - (-5))^2} = \sqrt{25 + 144} = 13$

$\Rightarrow r = 6.5$

45. (B)

$\left.\begin{array}{l} D,E,F \rightarrow 3! \\ A,B,C \rightarrow 3! \end{array}\right\} 3! \cdot 3! = (3!)^2$

46. (E)

E is false because the degree of P(x) must be an EVEN integer greater than 3 and not ANY integer greater than 3.

47. (C)

It can easily be verified through TI that the square of a number in the 4th quadrant, i.e. a number of the form c − di, is a − bi where a and b, c, and d are positive real numbers.

48. (E)

As x decreases to $-\infty$, $y = 1 - \dfrac{2}{x}$ decreases to 1 since 2/x decreases to 0.

49. (D)

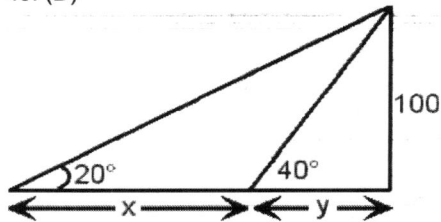

$\tan 40° = \dfrac{100}{y} \Rightarrow y = \dfrac{100}{\tan 40°}$

$\tan 20° = \dfrac{100}{x + y} = \dfrac{100}{x + \dfrac{100}{\tan 40°}}$

$\Rightarrow x = \dfrac{100}{\tan 20°} - \dfrac{100}{\tan 40°}$

50. (B)

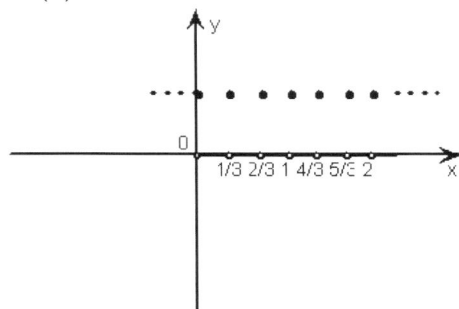

The function given above is periodic with period 1/3.

Solutions to Level 2 – Model Test 2

1. (D)
$$1 - \frac{3}{4} = \left(\frac{x}{16}\right)^2 \Rightarrow \frac{1}{4} = \left(\frac{x}{16}\right)^2$$
$$\Rightarrow \frac{x}{16} = \mp\frac{1}{2} \Rightarrow x = \mp 8$$

2. (A)
I. m = 10 and n = 8 implies that p = 1.8 so this statement is not always correct.
II. This statement is always correct since
n = mp – m and n is an integer if m and p are both integers.
III. If m = 10 and p = 0.1 then n = -9 so this statement is not always correct.

3. (E)
a = 55^(1/5) = 2.23 and
$$\log_a 555 = \frac{\log 555}{\log 2.23} = 7.88$$

4. (D)
When the product is carried out with the TI the result is $1.33 \cdot 10^{13}$ which implies that the product has 14 digits.

5. (D)
$$\left. \begin{array}{l} y \cdot \dfrac{25}{100} = 25.25 \\ y = \dfrac{2525}{2.5} \end{array} \right\} 2y \cdot \dfrac{6.5}{100} = 2 \cdot \dfrac{2525}{2.5} \cdot \dfrac{6.5}{100} = 131.3$$

6. (D)
$$\underbrace{\left[(1,2) \Uparrow (-1,-2)\right]}_{(1-(-1),2-(-2))} \Uparrow (m,n) = (5,6) \Rightarrow (2,4) \Uparrow (m,n) = (5,6)$$
$$\Rightarrow (2-m, 4-n) = (5,6)$$
$$\Rightarrow 2-m = 5 \text{ and } 4-n = 6$$
$$\Rightarrow m = -3 \text{ and } n = -2$$

7. (E)
Since $ax^2 + bx + c = 0$ is a quadratic equation having two roots, a must be nonzero so I is correct.
$$\left. \begin{array}{l} x_1 = p + \sqrt{q} \\ x_2 = p - \sqrt{q} \end{array} \right\} \begin{array}{l} x_1 + x_2 = 2p \\ x_1 \cdot x_2 = p^2 - q \end{array}$$
$$ax^2 + bx + c = 0$$
$$\Rightarrow x^2 - \left(-\frac{b}{a}\right)x + \frac{c}{a} = 0$$
$$\Rightarrow 2p = \frac{-b}{a} \text{ and } \frac{c}{a} = p^2 - q$$
Since p and q are rational, so are a,b, and c; therefore II is also correct. q is nonzero therefore $b^2 - 4ac > 0$ is also correct and this implies that $4ac - b^2 < 0$.

8. (D)
$$1 \le x < 1.5 \Rightarrow 2 \le 2x < 3 \Rightarrow [2x] = 2$$
$$f(x) = x + [2x] = x + 2$$

9. (B)
$f(m) = e^{-2m} < 0.0002 \Rightarrow m > 5.4099$ So, the least integer value of m that satisfies the above inequality is 6.

10. (D)
The divisors of 3 are 1, 3, -1, and -3. So, for
x = -1, $15 - \frac{3}{-1} = 18$ is the greatest value of the given expression.

11. (D)
The unit circle has the equation: $x^2 + y^2 = 1$ After the translation the length of the radius will not change. The new center will be (-2,1).
So, the new equation will be
$$(x - (-2))^2 + (y - 1)^2 = 1^2 \Rightarrow (x + 2)^2 + (y - 1)^2 = 1$$

12. (B)
$$80 \cdot \frac{60}{100} + F \cdot \frac{40}{100} = 84 \Rightarrow F \cdot \frac{4}{10} = 84 - 48$$
$$\Rightarrow F = 90$$
Where F represent the final score.

13. (D)
The function must satisfy the relation $f(x,y) = f(-x,y)$. So, if (5,7) is a point on the graph of f(x,y) then (-5,7) must also be a point on the same graph.

14. (D)
$$\cos\theta = \frac{1}{3} \cdot \sin\theta \text{ therefore } \frac{\sin\theta}{\cos\theta} = \tan\theta = 3.$$

15. (C)

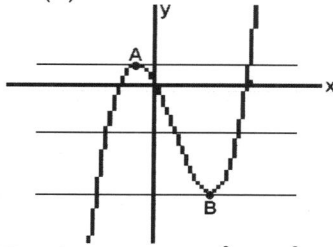

The function $y = x^3 - 3x^2 - 9x$ is graphed and the coordinates of points A and B are found to be (-1,5) and (3,-27). Therefore k must satisfy $-27 \le k \le 5$.

16. (B)
The line will be less steep since the graph will be stretched horizontally.

17. (A)
$3^{x^2} \cdot 3^{2x} = 27 \Rightarrow 3^{x^2+2x} = 3^3$
$\Rightarrow x^2 + 2x = 3 \Rightarrow x^2 + 2x - 3 = 0$
$\Rightarrow (x+3)(x-1) = 0 \Rightarrow x_1 = -3 \; x_2 = 1$

18. (B)

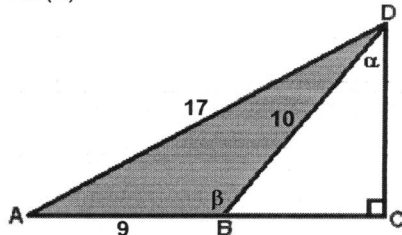

In the shaded triangle ABC, cosine rule is applied:
$17^2 = 9^2 + 10^2 - 2 \cdot 9 \cdot 10 \cdot \cos\beta$
$\Rightarrow \cos\beta = -0.6$ and $\beta = 127°$ which implies that $\alpha = 37°$.

19. (B)
The function given by f(x) will be plotted and the horizontal distance between two adjacent maxima will be calculated as 2 which is the fundamental period.

20. (E)
$2x + 1 = 0$
$x = \frac{1}{2} \Rightarrow 6 \cdot \left(-\frac{1}{2}\right)^3 - 5 \cdot \left(-\frac{1}{2}\right)^2 - 14 \cdot \left(-\frac{1}{2}\right) - k = 0$
$\Rightarrow 6 \cdot \left(-\frac{1}{8}\right) - 5 \cdot \frac{1}{4} + 7 - k = 0 \Rightarrow k = 0$

21. (D)
If the function given by f(x) is plotted then the range will easily be recognized as y > 0.

22. (E)
$\frac{3}{x+yi} = 1 - \frac{2}{1+2i} \Rightarrow \frac{3}{x+yi} = 0.6 + 0.8i$
$\Rightarrow x + yi = \frac{3}{0.6 + 0.8i}$
$\Rightarrow x + yi = 1.8 - 2.4i$
$\Rightarrow x - yi = 1.8 + 2.4i$

23. (B)
$10{,}000 \cdot (1.0948)^{t/2} = 10{,}000 \cdot \left(\sqrt{1.0948}\right)^t$
$= 10{,}000 \cdot (1.04633)^t = 10{,}000 \cdot (1+0.04633)^t$.
So, $0.04633 = \frac{4.633}{100} \rightarrow 4.6\%$

24. (E)
$\cos(2x) = 2\cos^2 x - 1 = 2 \cdot (0{,}4)^2 - 1 = -0.68$

25. (A)
$x = \log_e(y^4 - 1) \Rightarrow e^x = y^4 - 1 \Rightarrow y^4 = e^x + 1$
$\Rightarrow \sqrt[4]{y^4} = \sqrt[4]{e^{x+1}}$
$\Rightarrow |y| = \sqrt[4]{e^{x+1}} \Rightarrow y = \mp\sqrt[4]{e^{x+1}}$

26. (A)
$y = \frac{x-5}{2x}$ will be sketched and TABLE facility of TI will be used as well.

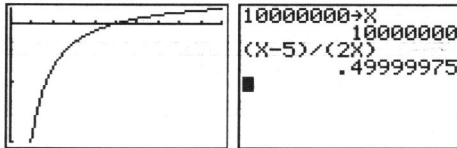

The function starts with -2 and reaches a maximum of ½ when x becomes infinitely large. Therefore answer is A.

27. (D)
The graph has 5 real zeros and an odd degree therefore it can be II or III.

28. (E)
Let R be the perpendicular bisector plane of segment AB in space. Any point $P \in R$ satisfies the relation PA = PB. Therefore PAB is an isosceles triangle.

29. (B)
The equation of the unit circle is. $x^2 + y^2 = 1$. Since x and y must be positive we can only take the portion of the unit circle that lies in the first quadrant.

30. (D)
The requested probability is given by:
$1/2 + 1/8 + 1/32 + \ldots = (1/2) / (1-1/4) = 2/3$.

31. (B)
Surface Area of the bigger rectangular box:
$2 \cdot (12 \cdot 8 + 12 \cdot 6 + 8 \cdot 6) = 432$
Total Surface Area of the resulting places:
$2 \cdot (3 \cdot 8 + 3 \cdot 6 + 8 \cdot 6) \cdot 4 = 720$
The percent change is: $\dfrac{720 - 432}{432} \cdot 100 = 67\%$

32. (D)
$\begin{bmatrix} \cos\theta & -\sin\theta \\ \sin\theta & -\cos\theta \end{bmatrix}$ is the standard matrix to rotate any point

for θ degrees about the origin. Thus:
$\begin{bmatrix} \cos\theta & -\sin\theta \\ \sin\theta & -\cos\theta \end{bmatrix} \cdot \begin{bmatrix} x \\ y \end{bmatrix} = \begin{bmatrix} x \cdot \cos\theta - y \cdot \sin\theta \\ x \cdot \sin\theta + y \cdot \cos\theta \end{bmatrix}$
which means B has the coordinates of $(x \cdot \cos\theta - y \cdot \sin\theta, x \cdot \sin\theta + y \cdot \cos\theta)$. The same result can be achieved by right angle trigonometry.

33. (E)
$A_{5x5} \cdot B_{5x4}$ results in a 5x4 matrix.

34. (A)
$x^2 - 2xy + y^2 + x^2 + 2xy + y^2 + 2x - 2y - 3x + 3y = 0$
$2x^2 + 2y^2 - x + y = 0 \Rightarrow x^2 - \dfrac{x}{2} + y^2 + \dfrac{4}{2} = 0$ It's a
$\Rightarrow \left(x - \dfrac{1}{4} \right)^2 + \left(y + \dfrac{1}{4} \right)^2 = \left(\dfrac{1}{2\sqrt{2}} \right)^2$
circle centered at $\left(\dfrac{1}{4}, -\dfrac{1}{4} \right)$ having a radius of $\dfrac{1}{2\sqrt{2}}$.

35. (C)
In C, production consists of the same product; therefore standard deviation is zero and it is the least.

36. (B)
By the cosine rule:
$x^2 = 2200^2 + 2200^2 - 2 \cdot 2200 \cdot 2200 \cdot \cos 50°$
$\Rightarrow x = 1859.52$ miles

37. (A)
|x| + |y| = 1 is a rhombus and |x| + |y| ≤ 1 represents all points on and inside the rhombus.

38. (B)
Sketch $y = \left(\sqrt{x-1} \right)^2$ with the TI and you will see that the graph looks like B.

39. (C)

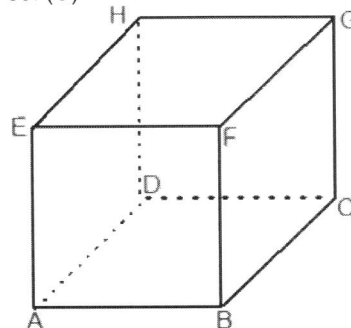

In the cube given above AC, BG, ED and FH are four facial diagonals such that no two of them have a common point.

40. (C)
4 is a rational number but $\sqrt{4} = 2$ is not an irrational number.

41. (D)
$f(x_2) \geq f(x_1)$ when $x_2 > x_1$ means that f(x) is a non decreasing function as in D.

42. (C)
Before reflection, the function was
$-x = \dfrac{2 \cdot (-y) - 3}{4} \Rightarrow -4x + 3 = -2y \Rightarrow y = 2x - \dfrac{3}{2}$
So, it's correct inverse is: $f^{-1}(x) = \dfrac{x + \dfrac{2}{2}}{2} = \dfrac{2x + 3}{4}$

43. (B)
$|x - 4| \geq 4$ is equivalent to the given statement.

44. (C)
Plugging 1, 2, 3, and 4 for n in choice C we get 1, 5, 17 and 53.

45. (C)
$\dbinom{20}{4} \cdot \dbinom{16}{5} = 4{,}845 \cdot 4{,}368 = 21{,}162{,}960$

46. (D)
f(x)=f(x+2) yields a linear equation and not a quadratic equation whose discriminant is zero.

47. (D)
$f_2(-3) + f_2(3) - f_3(1) =$
$(-3 - 1) + (3 + 2 \cdot 3^2) - \left(1 - \dfrac{1}{3} \right) = 16{,}33$

48. (E)
The shaded region corrsponds to choice E.

49. (C)
For any solid having convex faces, the following equality holds: V + F = E + 2 where V, F and E are the number of vertices, faces and edges respectively.
V = 7, E = 12; so F = 7.

50. (B)
$z = 5t$

$\Rightarrow x = 4 \cdot (5t)^2 - 3 = 100t^2 - 3$

$x = \sqrt[3]{2t^2 + 3}$

$100t^2 - 3 = \sqrt[3]{2t^2 + 3}$

$\Rightarrow t^2 = 0.04456 \Rightarrow y = \sqrt{4t^2 + 1} \cong 1.08547$

Solutions to Level 2 – Model Test 3

1. (E)
x = 3 and y = 2 yields 3 + 2 = 5 which is positive.
x = -3 and y = -3 yields − 3 − 3 = − 6 which is negative.
x = 3 and y = - 3 yields 3 − 3 = 0 which is zero.

2. (A)
Let x = 11 and y = 12

$a = \dfrac{11}{12} = 0.92$

$b = \dfrac{110}{121} = 0.909$

$c = \dfrac{1100}{1200 + 11} = 0.908$

$c < b < a$

3. (E)
x = 1.5 does not satisfy the given inequality.

4. (E)
The x and y intercepts are (2.04,0) and (0, -3).
The distance between these points is given by
$\sqrt{(2.04)^2 + (-3)^2} = 3.63$.

5. (B)
y=x² and $x \geq 0$ therefore $f^{-1}(x) = \sqrt{x}$

6. (D)
$x^{50} \cdot (x - 3) = k^2$ implies that x − 3 is a perfect square. Therefore x can be 28.

7. (A)
If f(x)=10ˣ then $\dfrac{10^a}{10^b} = 10^{a-b}$.

8. (B)
Both must be positive or both must be negative. Therefore the points of concern are either inside the circle and below the line or outside the circle and above the line. Therefore answer is B.

9. (E)
The point of intersection stays fixed.
2x − 3 = 3x + 1
x = - 4 and y = -11 ⇒ (-4, -11)

10. (E)
f(-5) = -5 − 1= - 6; f(2) = 3; f(-3) = - 3 − 1= - 4
-6 − 3·(-4) = - 6 + 12 = 6

11. (B)
The center of symmetry is the point of where the diagonals intersect $\left(\dfrac{-1+5}{2}, \dfrac{3-1}{2}\right) = (2,1)$ and line m must pass through this point. Therefore it cannot be B since (2,1) does not satisfy y = -2x + 3.

12. (A)
$f(x) = \dfrac{x-1}{2}$

13. (E)
1,3,5,7,9,11,13,15,17,19,21,23
median $= \dfrac{11+13}{2} = 12$ and it is even; mean=12 and there is no mode in this set since no element repeats more than once.

14. (E)
x²-5x+1-k+2=0
x²-kx+3-k=0
b² - 4ac≥0
k² - 4(3 - k) ≥0
k² - 12 + 4k≥0
k≥2 or k≤-6

15. (A)
If ratio of volumes is k^3 then ratio of sides is k for two similar solids.
$k^3 = \dfrac{1}{2} \Rightarrow k = \dfrac{1}{\sqrt[3]{2}}$; therefore $\dfrac{AB}{AC} = \dfrac{1}{\sqrt[3]{2}}$.

16. (D)
$a_1 = 5$
$a_2 = 5 + d = 7 \Rightarrow d = 2$.
$S_n = \dfrac{(a_1 + a_n)}{2} \cdot n \Rightarrow S_{30} = \dfrac{(a_1 + a_{30})}{2} \cdot 30$
$a_{30} = a_1 + 29d = 5 + 29 \cdot 2 = 63$
$S_{30} = \dfrac{(a_1 + a_{30})}{2} \cdot 30 = \left(\dfrac{5 + 63}{2}\right) \cdot 30 = 1020$

17. (D)
$9 - x^2 \geq 0$ and $x \neq 0$ which implies that $-3 \leq x \leq 3$ and $x \neq 0$.

18. (D)
f(0.3)=(0.3-1) ·f(1.3)
f(0.3)=(-0.7)·2.1=-1.47
f(-0.7)=(-0.7-1)f(0.3)
f(-0.7)=(-1.7) · (-1.47)=2.5

19. (D)
$P(x) = (x+1)^2 \cdot (x-4)$ has three zeros $x_1 = x_2 = -1$ and $x_3 = 4$. Therefore product of the zeros is
$(-1)(-1)(4) = 4$.

20. (D)
$f(-x)=f(x)$ implies that $f(x)$ is symmetric with respect to the y axis. If the given functions are graphed, only II and III are symmetric with respect to the y axis.

21. (D)
If the angle between lines is θ and m_1 and m_2 are the slopes of lines then

$$\tan\theta = \left|\frac{m_1 - m_2}{1 + m_1 \cdot m_2}\right| = \left|\frac{\frac{15}{7} - \frac{3}{7}}{1 + \frac{45}{49}}\right| = 0.893$$

Therefore $\theta = 42°$ is the acute angle between the lines and $180° - 42° = 138°$ is the obtuse angle.

22. (A)
$(x+3)(y-1)=xy$ implies that $xy - x + 3y - 3 = xy$ and $- x + 3y - 3 = 0$ which is the equation of the line given in A.

23. (C)
$$\tan 60° = \frac{y}{y-x} \Rightarrow \sqrt{3} = \frac{y}{y-x}$$
$$y\sqrt{3} - x\sqrt{3} = y$$
$$\sqrt{3}y - y = x\sqrt{3}$$
$$y.\left(\sqrt{3} - 1\right) = x\sqrt{3}$$
$$y = \frac{x\sqrt{3}}{\sqrt{3} - 1}$$

24. (E)
If (a,b) is the center and r is the radius of a circle then $(x-a)^2+(y-b)^2=r^2$ where (x,y) are the points on the circle. The exterior region of the circle is given by $(x-4)^2+(y-3)^2>4$.

25. (B)

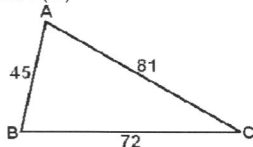

Two similar figures contain the same angles; therefore the figure given above can be simplified to the figure below and the angles will stay the same.

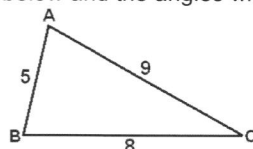

Use cosine rule to find the smallest angle:
$5^2 = 9^2 + 8^2 - 2 \cdot 9 \cdot 8 \cdot \cos C$
Therefore $\cos C = 0.83$ and $C = 33.6°$.

26. (E)
All of the given conditions are possible.

27. (C)

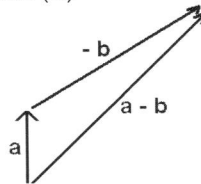

$a - b = a + (-b)$ and correct answer is given in C.

28. (E)
$$\det \begin{vmatrix} 2 & -1 & 0 \\ 1 & 2 & -3 \\ -1 & 1 & 1 \end{vmatrix} = 8 \text{ by the calculator.}$$

29. (E)
$\log_4(x^2+1)$ is defined for all x.

30. (D)

9	9	8	7	6

$9^2.8.7.6$

31. (C)
One face contains 16 such cubes and all 6 faces contain $16 \cdot 6 = 96$ such cubes.

32. (C)
Sketch the graph, find a local maximum and a local minimum point.
$$\text{Amplitude} = \frac{y_{max} - y_{min}}{2} = \frac{11 - (-15)}{2} = 13$$

33. (B)

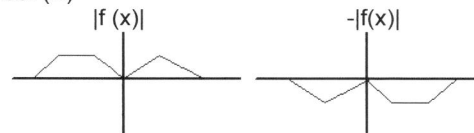

34. (C)
$e^4=a^2 \Rightarrow e^2=a$
$b=a^{-2} \Rightarrow b=(e^2)^{-2} = e^{-4}$

35. (C)
$$\frac{_9C_2}{_{24}C_2} = \frac{9 \cdot 8}{24 \cdot 23}$$

36. (D)
The intersection of two sphres with distinct radii can not be a sphere.

37. (C)
$$\text{Slope} = \frac{3}{2} \Rightarrow \frac{3}{2} \cdot m = -1 \Rightarrow m = \frac{-2}{3}$$
$$y + \frac{1}{2} = \frac{-2}{3}(x - 3) \Rightarrow 6y = -4x + 9$$

38. (C)
If the given function is graphed the horizontal distance between two adjacent maxima will be $\dfrac{\pi}{2}$ which equals the primary period.

39. (C)
A and B are planes whose normal vectors are parallel to $(1,1,1)$. C is a line whose direction vector is $(1,1,1)$. Therefore answer is C.

40. (D)
$|HB| = \sqrt{36+16+49} = \sqrt{101}$

$|DB| = \sqrt{16+36} = \sqrt{52}$

$\sin D\hat{H}B = \dfrac{\sqrt{52}}{\sqrt{101}} = 0.717 \Rightarrow D\hat{H}B = 46°$

41. (D)
$b^2-4ac>0$ therefore $b^2-4ac \neq 0$ and $a \neq 0$.

42. (C)
$a_1=5$ and $a_2=7$ therefore $r = \dfrac{a_2}{a_1} = \dfrac{7}{5}$

$a_{19} = a_1 \cdot r^{18} = 5 \cdot \left(\dfrac{7}{5}\right)^{18} = 2134$ is the first term that exceeds 2000.

43. (D)
The number of triangles in a row is given by $\{1, 3, 5, 7, \ldots\}$ which is an arithmetic sequence whose first term is 1 with a common difference of 2; $a_{2005} = 1+2004 \cdot 2 = 1+4008 = 4009$.

44. (C)
$xy = 12$; $yz = 24$ and $xz = 18$; this system has two solutions $(x, y, z) = (3, 4, 6)$ and $(x, y, z) = (-3, -4, -6)$.

45. (E)
A, B, C and D represent the region given but E does not.

46. (C)
$\lim\limits_{x\to 1} \dfrac{(x-1)(x+1)}{(x+1)} = \lim\limits_{x\to 1}(x-1) = 0$

47. (B)

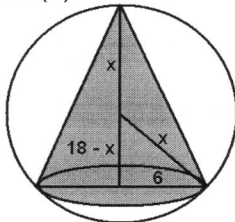

Volume=
$\dfrac{\pi r^2 h}{3} = \dfrac{\pi \cdot 36 \cdot h}{3} = 216\pi \Rightarrow h = 18$

$x^2=(18-x)^2+36 \Rightarrow x=10$

Volume=$\dfrac{\pi r^2 h}{3} = \dfrac{\pi \cdot 36 \cdot h}{3} = 216\pi \Rightarrow h = 18$
$x^2=(18-x)^2+36 \Rightarrow x=10$

48. (E)
$f(x)$ is shifted 1 unit right and 1 unit down to get $g(x)$; therefore $f(x-1)-1=g(x)$ and $f(x-1)=1+g(x)$.

49. (A)
Equation of the given line is $\dfrac{x}{1}+\dfrac{y}{2} = 1$ and (a,a) is on this line therefore $\dfrac{a}{1}+\dfrac{a}{2} = 1$ and

$a = 2/3$. Therefore point B is $\left(\dfrac{2}{3},\dfrac{2}{3}\right)$. In A the lines given

by $x+\dfrac{y}{2} = 1$ and $y = x$ also intersect at $\left(\dfrac{2}{3},\dfrac{2}{3}\right)$.

50. (C)
The data is closest to the mean in set 3; hence standard deviation is the least for this data set.

INDEX

Made in the USA
Middletown, DE
31 May 2015